a boundary 2 boo

Feminism and Postmodernism

Edited by Margaret Ferguson and
Jennifer Wicke

Duke University Press
Durham and London 1994

Printed in the United States of America
on acid-free paper ∞
Except for the article by David Simpson, "Feminisms and Feminizations in the Postmodern," the text of this book was originally published as volume 19, number 2 of *boundary 2: an international journal of literature and culture*.
Library of Congress Cataloging-in-Publication Data
Ferguson, Margaret.
Feminism and Postmodernism / edited by Margaret Ferguson and Jennifer Wicke.
p. cm.
"A boundary 2 book."
Most of the essays were previously published in a special issue of Boundary 2.
Includes bibliographical references and index.
ISBN 0-8223-1460-6 (cloth) : $34.95. —ISBN 0-8223-1488-6 (paper) : $15.95
1. Feminist theory. 2. Postmodernism. I. Ferguson, Margaret W. II. Wicke, Jennifer. III. Boundary 2.
HQ1206.F4533 1994
305.42'01—dc20 93-47925

Contents

Acknowledgments

This volume originated in conversations between its two editors (in New Haven, New York, Boulder, and Santa Fe); it emerged as a special issue of *boundary 2* before assuming its current form. We warmly thank Paul Bové and Meg Sachse, the editor and managing editor of *boundary 2*, for their invaluable help in the process of giving our book intellectual and material shape. We are also grateful to Robyn Dutra, who made our index; and we warmly thank Anne Keyl, our editor at Duke University Press, for helping us with the metamorphosis from journal issue to book. Finally, we thank our contributors for their visions and revisions, and for their patience with the ironies of communicating in an age of mechanical, but not always predictable, postmodernist-feminist reproduction.

Margaret Ferguson and Jennifer Wicke
Boulder and New York City, August 1993

Introduction: Feminism and Postmodernism; or, The Way We Live Now

Jennifer Wicke
Margaret Ferguson

It may seem odd to echo Trollope in the introduction to a collection whose domain appears to be at the farthest remove from the vanished certainties of the world of the nineteenth-century realist novel. Yet, the boldness of Trollope's title can also serve to mark a strong boundary line for our own volume—in a quite simple sense, the awkward pairing formed by linking feminism and postmodernism is a description of our lives. The feminism practiced, theorized, and lived by many women (and men) today is set against, or arises within, the vicissitudes of a transforming postmodernity—as a set of practices, an arena of theory, and a mode of life. This may not be a comfortable dwelling place, but it does make up a world, a form of life (shifting the echoes to those notions of Heidegger or Wittgenstein which are apt here), with which feminism necessarily conjures. The animating idea of this volume is that postmodernism is, indeed, a name for the way we live now, and it needs to be taken account of, put into practice, and even contested within feminist discourses as a way of coming to terms with our lived situations. This is not to say that postmodernity is to be celebrated unquestioningly; if it truly is a rubric covering the conditions of theory and practice in our time, this demands resistance at least as much as an empowering embrace. How feminism will transform postmodernism, as well as how postmodernism alters feminism, are the pressing questions of this moment.

The crossing-over of critical terms implied by the subterfuge of *and*, as in Feminism and Postmodernism, wherein the neutrality of the *and* covers a multitude of critical questions and fierce debates, if not sins, can allow for cross-fertilization, and even for crossing out or mutual cancellation. As theoretical discourses, both feminism and postmodernism are porous, capacious; equally, they are discourses on the move, ready to leap over borders and confound boundaries. Their intersection in this issue is meant both to provide active and passive positions for each discourse vis-à-vis the other and to show that that binary does not begin to exhaust the positionalities it is possible to invent in the name of feminism and postmodernism.

In seeking out and gathering essays for this book, we, as editors, could not rest comfortably with entirely provisional meanings for either term of the title. Tipping our hand to reveal the versions of *postmodernism* and *feminism* we held to in order to make our choices of texts is useful if only to underscore the multiple ironies of such a linkage. For *feminism*, we read materialist feminism, feminist theory and practice—however divergent—premised on material conditions, on the social construction of gender, and on an understanding of the gender hierarchy as relational and multiple and never in itself simply exhaustive. This is not a matter of formulating an arena of female difference or differences; rather than articulating an essential "difference," or a woman's "text" or "voice," we start from the premise that feminist issues never arrive single-handedly. Materialist feminism attempts to move beyond the additive logic of female differences to a grounded, but volatile, understanding of gender in relation to myriad other determinations. Such an understanding includes the possibility that in given instances gender is not the bedrock oppression.

Postmodernism is equally hard to qualify or pin down, but in this collection it does connote a historical shift, not merely an immanent feature of language. We approach postmodernism as a moment that, for theory, might be regarded as the critical historicizing of poststructuralisms, in general, the acknowledgment that shifts in theory also are located historically and systemically. Postmodernism so conceived has a material situation, what David Harvey calls "the condition of postmodernity," a situation, of course, open to debate and reconceptualization but still to be seen in relation to concrete phenomena of material, social, economic, and cultural life.[1] This designation may be one that, retrospectively, is going to look confining or ill-advised, and, indeed, some theorists like Stuart Hall and even David Harvey are hedging their bets and using *post-Fordism* to characterize this feature of our social world; post-Fordism, which refers to what comes after the capitalist economics of *Fordism* (Gramsci's name for the mode of production he found best characterized by Henry Ford's assembly-line techniques of rationalizing labor), is conceptually inadequate—and not catchy enough—to cover phenomena like Madonna's iconic image or the photographic work of Cindy Sherman, since the term is so exclusively economistic a notion. *Postmodernism*, in our view, still has some shelf life left as the best umbrella term for the cultural, social, and theoretical dimensions of our period. The attempt to think through the transformations in "geoculture" (Isaiah Berlin's helpful phrase for our new site)[2] by dint of a historically specific postmodernism will surely remain useful for the immediate future.

Feminist postmodernism once read as an oxymoron, and postmodern feminism still has an uncertain valence. Craig Owens wrote his now-classic article "The Discourse of Others" precisely to complain of the absence of feminist theory per se within postmodernism, while feminist practices, in the form of art, mass culture, and politics, were so evident and prominent within it.[3] Nancy Fraser and Linda Nicholson wrote a memorable essay framing the "encounter between feminism and postmodernism," making it clear that feminism has many reasons to be wary of the encounter but also has many things to gain in a theoretical sense.[4] This present vol-

1. The geographer David Harvey's comprehensive socioeconomic and cultural treatment of postmodernism as a distinct historical phase appears in his 1989 book *The Condition of Postmodernity: An Enquiry into the Origins of Cultural Change* (Oxford: Basil Blackwell Ltd., 1989).

2. Immanuel Wallerstein has an interesting discussion of the linkage of racism/sexism in the global world system in his *Geopolitics and Geoculture: Essays on the Changing World System* (Cambridge: Cambridge University Press, 1991).

3. Craig Owens's article appears in *The Anti-Aesthetic: Essays on Postmodern Culture* (Port Townsend, Wash.: Bay Press, 1983), a now-standard collection on postmodernism, edited by Hal Foster.

4. See "Social Criticism without Philosophy: An Encounter between Feminism and Postmodernism," in *Theory, Culture and Society* 5, nos. 2–3 (1988): 373–94, and also Sabina Lovibond, "Feminism and Postmodernism," *New Left Review* 178 (1989): 5–28. For further important work in this vein, consult Nancy Fraser's book *Unruly Practices* (Minneapolis: University of Minnesota Press, 1989), and the collection edited by Linda Nicholson, *Feminism/Postmodernism* (New York: Routledge, 1990). Teresa Ebert's review of this

ume is impelled by the task of reading each discourse through the lens of the other, putting each term under the pressure of a conjunction across disciplinary and political lines. Feminist theory and practice, in the materialist sense outlined above, now require an understanding of the transformations of postmodernity, while a postmodern politics entails feminism as a cutting edge of its critique. The essays in this collection trace the mutually inflecting politics of feminism and postmodernism into the arenas of cultural production, legal discourse, and philosophical thought. Taking a variety of paths, these essays turn the prism of postmodern feminism onto cultural objects, explore the theoretical dimensions of politics or the politics of theory, and often reflect back on the act of writing itself.

This book includes essays on a wide range of cultural productions originating in and circulating across many different geopolitical sites. From the women's prison in Egypt, which forms the setting of the story by Salwa Bakr, as translated by Barbara Harlow and published here in English for the first time, through the prostitution laws invoked in such countries as Austria, France, England, and South Africa, as analyzed by Anne McClintock in "Screwing the System: Sexwork, Race, and the Law," to a popular U.S. MTV video—Madonna's "Like a Prayer"—which reproduces a highly charged image of Catholic Italian-American womanhood, as examined by Carla Freccero—the phenomena studied in this collection cross, and even confound, boundaries among nations, languages, and media. The writers assess conjunctions and collisions between feminism and postmodernism without presupposing any stable definition of either of these concepts.

Defined, provisionally, in terms of the tasks it attempts, a postmodern feminism can analyze the gendering of representations into canonical and noncanonical divisions exemplifying sexual difference, as Claire Detels incisively shows: Categories of postmodern theory give feminism a foothold in the solidly masculinist terrain of music theory, where postmodernity makes the case for the blurring of canon boundaries further interrogated by feminist questions of value and hierarchy. Marjorie Garber illustrates the implicit hierarchizations of cultural monumentality for a range of Western literary masterpieces in " 'Greatness': Philology and the Politics of Mimesis," even in the instance of the sale of wisdom as a cultural commodity in the Great Books Series. Here, postmodern feminism exhibits itself also as a style of commentary, an aesthetics of analysis capable of using postmodern theory

---

collection, "Postmodernism's Infinite Variety," in *The Women's Review of Books* 8, no. 4 (January 1991): 24–28, is an excellent introduction to the issue in its own right.

as a feminist power tool. Kathryn Bond Stockton's essay provides a surprising postmodern encounter between Victorian theories of the body and an Irigarayan materialist spirituality, wherein materialist feminism is invigorated by taking to the dance floor with postmodern discourses to provide a revivified (sexual, textual) body politics. In all these instances, postmodernism is a strategic form for feminist writing, as well as for analysis.

Postmodernism has entered the feminist legal realm of equality, rights, and political identity in particularly charged ways in recent years, as several essays in this issue propose. Mary Poovey investigates postmodern masculine subjectivities for their ramification on the concrete political issue of abortion rights in "Feminism and Postmodernism—Another View"; she exhibits the postmodern technological basis underpinning our images of masculinity and femininity by investigating the film *Terminator 2* with its real female cyborg. Andrew Ross offers a postmodern spin on the cultural politics of male bonding and its unexpected bridge to the environmental movement's feminist wing, and the polyglot, and surprising nature, of postmodern politics, legalisms, and their strange affinities. As Andrew Ross has argued elsewhere, along with Donna Haraway, Meaghan Morris, and other critics, postmodernism must be specifically confronted as a congeries of technological and informational forms transforming both the objects and the subjects of knowledge. A feminist postmodernism will understand the mediated nature of knowledge and representation, as well as the altered political subject produced by these mediations.

Both postmodern theory and feminist theory are rooted in longstanding cultural debates, with important philosophical and political repercussions. David Simpson's essay analyzes the effects of a long-durational perspective on the place of feminism(s) in the postmodern; by arguing that there was an important relation between the evolution of "feminization" (as a process of cultural categorizing and usually of devaluing) on the one hand, and, on the other, the construction of the category of "literature" within modernity, Simpson questions some of the radical epistemological claims that postmodernism's general turn to the literary has sponsored. Also tracing a complex history across the (disputed) border between modernity and postmodernity, Toril Moi examines the philosophical categories Simone de Beauvoir deployed as vital aspects of her feminist critique of the notion of the feminine in *The Second Sex*. Demonstrating that Beauvoir's narrative is ready for a postmodern rereading, Moi also shows that the feminist turn back to Beauvoir needs to be accomplished with the same political and theoretical finesse evident in some recent returns to figures such as Benjamin,

Adorno, and Freud. In "Feminism and the Politics of Postmodernism," Linda Nicholson looks back at yet another major architect of the modernism/postmodernism debate, Karl Marx, to explore crucial ambiguities in his critique of universal and "universally foundational" philosophical claims. Noting that in many ways Marx anticipates postmodern philosophers' emphases on "local" rather than universal knowledge (and knowledge claims), Nicholson also argues, in concert with other recent feminist thinkers, that Marx's central concept of *production* works to occlude the significance of gender as a constituent of oppression. Nicholson surveys the theoretical and practical tensions that emerge when contemporary U.S. feminists engage the sometimes abstract and gender-blind, but nonetheless philosophically challenging, discourses of postmodernity.

In preparing this collection, we ourselves encountered the increasingly fraught dimensions of feminist and postmodern politics. The primary issue was the perceived urgency of identity politics, the felt need to line up contributors along a spectrum of identities—racial, gender, sexual, and regional—in order to cover what then becomes the "topic" with a multitude of representative voices. Not only was this a politics far removed from our own questioning of identities as the sole basis for political response, but supplying this "correctness" proved to be impossible, in any event, for the ironic reason that so many competing demands are made of those who fill identity slots that the perfect ensemble of identities proved elusive to muster. In this way, people are living out many of the contradictions of an identity politics that invades theoretical and economic realms (book publishing, for example) with increasing fervor. Being forced to think through the consequences of a rainbow coalition of feminism and postmodernism, since it could not be provided, in any case, was salutary. A major aspect of the way we live now is the haunting requirement to match up identities with putative experiences, to click invisible designations into place, to "have one or more of each." While our contributors are widely and even wildly diverse, what has emerged as salient on the political front, too, is how imperative it is to resist identity as the sole criterion of either a feminist or a postmodern politics.

The triumphal displaying of Camille Paglia recently has interesting implications for feminism and postmodernism. Paglia has adopted something like a postmodern antifeminism with strong individualist overtones; her success in gaining access to a huge variety of media and cultural outlets is partially a function of the postmodern condition itself, wherein Paglia can annex herself to star figures like Madonna and extol her postmodernity as an antifeminist stance. What Paglia foregrounds, often archly and outrageously, is sexual difference, wielding it like a cleaver to separate the girls from the boys. Her emphasis on sexuality is perversely useful to the concerns of a feminist postmodernism, since it underscores not only the dangers of a postmodernism sans feminist concerns but also the greater peril of any feminism unable to accept representation, fantasy, and, ultimately, sexuality as a postmodern phenomenon. Carla Freccero, in writing about an ethnic background she shares both with Madonna and with Paglia, is able to show a different trajectory than Paglia does for feminist postmodernism in the intricacies of sex, race, and gender that Madonna flaunts, and even theorizes; Anne McClintock pushes our understanding of sexuality past easy determinations of oppression in her assessment of sex as labor and its international scope. Camille Paglia is an admitted thorn in the side of feminism, but she can be, perhaps, a goad for a feminist postmodernism able to harness the flamboyant, and potentially liberatory, fantasies the imagistic world of the postmodern sets free.

Finally, feminism and postmodernism urgently converge in a need to theorize systemic relations and a global politics. In this light, Laura E. Lyons's interview with Mairead Keane, Irish feminist and National Head of Sinn Fein's Women's Department, tests the parameters of feminist politics in a national and an international context. What feminism means pragmatically in a situation of political organizing and ongoing conflict must affect our notion of feminism and postmodernism as a practice, including the chance that the relations will become complex and even oppositional. The increasing fragmentation of the categories of gender, class, race, sexuality, ethnicity, and religion challenges easy coalitions and the privileging of singular political identities, including that of 'woman' or even 'feminist'.[5] At the same time, such de-centering offers fresh possibilities for political alignments and furthers a reconceptualization of the multiple sites of feminism. This book seeks to map the boundaries between postmodernism and feminism while also envisioning a new terrain for their crossing in a materialist feminist politics.

Feminist materialist thought requires a geocultural reorientation as well, and it is to supply this that our particular admixture of feminism and postmodernism is shaken and bottled as a collection of essays. To point to

5. In their estimable volume *Postmodern Theory: Critical Interrogations* (New York: Guilford Press, 1991), authors Steven Best and Douglas Kellner consign the discussion of feminism to a chapter entitled "Marxism, Feminism and Political Postmodernism." This is acute in many ways—especially for materialist feminism—but it also brings out the tensions in the "practical" notion of feminism as primarily praxis.

a globalism is neither to gesture toward global unity nor to exhort that global differences be given their due—in short, this collection does not advocate a refurbished pluralism or relativism, nor is it calling for a thousand flowers of feminist postmodernism to bloom. Globalism, in this theoretical construct, refers to the location of feminist theory as a lever in the ongoing global discursive relation, whose power dynamics, as we know, are not equal. There are reasons why feminism, as currently construed, emerges at particular times in the histories of Western and European states and why it is attached to particular formations within capitalist societies. Such a realization is not a questioning of the grounds of feminist struggle, and certainly not a disparagement of feminist theory as "Western" or taintedly capitalist. On the contrary. The transcultural scope of women's oppression, however, has been theorized by a feminism that has often thought of itself in universalizing terms without seeing the systematicity of the actual social relations obtaining in the movement from the local to the global plane of analysis, where the real location of (much) feminist theory is thereby effaced. A materialist feminism above all needs to situate itself, while seeing that situations change over time, needs to keep abreast of the dialectic within feminist theory between the local and the global, and needs to note unflinchingly the limits of the discourse in order to make it better. A purely celebratory or identity politics precludes the radical disidentifications that must be made in the global circumstances of feminist politics today and evades the multiple overdeterminations that forge an identity and its resulting politics. Postmodernism has also been a culprit in failing to consider its location. There has been a tendency to embrace its tenets, or at least its alluring cultural shapes, without thought for the placement of postmodernism in a larger system. This larger system entails not only the division of power, wealth, and labor across the globe, where the central features of postmodernity—information, technologization of knowledge, dependence on the image—carry out a fearfully inequitable hierarchy, but also the specific educational and publishing institutions, themselves part of larger socioeconomic systems. It is often postmodernity, in this sense, that exacts an enormous price from those who produce it or who experience its political fallout. Even dystopian postmodernists like Jean Baudrillard can fail to critique the dissymmetries postmodernism, as a social form and as a theory, can create, while theorists as alert as Donna Haraway have at times too readily utopianized the cyborgean potential of the postmodern.[6]

6. This is argued more fully by Jennifer Wicke in "Postmodernism: The Perfume of Information," *Yale Journal of Criticism* 1, no. 2 (1989): 145–60. For Donna Haraway's fascinat-

Ultimately, the task for a feminist postmodernism or a postmodern feminism is to remain self-aware and self-critical—to be theory, in the strongest definition of the term. Theory, however, as we know, is notoriously susceptible to putting on airs, to assuming master status, and, beyond that, to erasing its own tenuous location. Such criticisms could indeed be leveled against this volume for its use of a language—(standard) English—which at the present time marks and enforces hierarchies of power that are both linguistic and political.[7] This volume's multiple but notably partial efforts to reflect on the political implications of writing from specific geographical and institutional locations (chief among them U.S. universities) underscore the fact that a "global" feminist theory is as yet unformed; it may look something like a combination of feminism and postmodernism, or that may be simply a way station. Achieving a global feminist theory without totalizing, without mastery, is the possibility ever at the edge of our horizons. In the meantime, lodged in the productive and conflictual uncertainties of feminism and postmodernism, this is the way we live now.

---

ing and important essay "Manifesto for Cyborgs," and an important critique of it by Joan Scott, see the anthology *Coming to Terms: Feminism, Theory, Politics*, ed. Elizabeth Weed (New York and London: Routledge, 1989). This collection also contains an essay by Margaret Ferguson situating the problems of a feminist rhetoric of identity and difference with great relevance to the assumptions of this collection (see "Commentary: Postponing Politics," 34–44).

7. For an incisive treatment of the problems attending the "globalization" and hegemony of English, see Ngugi wa Thiongo'o, "English: A Language for the World?" in *The Yale Journal of Criticism* 4 (1990): 271–93. See also, on the issue of language hierarchies, Talal Asad, "The Concept of Cultural Translation in British Anthropology," in *Writing Culture*, ed. James Clifford and George E. Marcus (Berkeley and Los Angeles: University of California Press, 1986), 141–66.

Postmodern Identities and the Politics of the (Legal) Subject

Jennifer Wicke

Postmodernism has an alchemical sheen, the ability to conjoin with disparate words and impart a heady gloss to them, a *frisson* of difference, a catalyzing agency, the torque of the new. In just such a manner, the coming together of "postmodernism" and the Legal Subject, with the stern capital *L* of the Law intact, promises to be a dynamic coupling, postmodernism offering to put its delirious spin on the rigor, and fixity, of the body of law. Of course, in this scenario postmodernism carries all the significations of glamour and seduction, the law remaining an unwilling or at least staid partner in the dalliance. Equally galvanizing is the conjuncture of postmodernism with feminism, since feminism has a rather dutiful mien these days in contrast to the potential exhilaration given off by postmodernity, however misleadingly. These intertwinings give off theoretical sparks but also real tensions in praxis, especially when the issue is how to adjudicate the problems of identity in the real world situation of feminist politics. In addressing postmodernism as it carves out the terrain of identity, as a conceptual term, and then following the collision of this logic with the formidable dominance of the (female) subject of and under the law, I will be mapping a tension that may signal a misalliance between postmodernism and the politics of identity, one with political consequences. The two senses of a legal subject—as a subject area under the heading of the law, and as the human subject constituted by legal discourse—both come into play in this tension with the importunities of postmodern identity, that term itself covering both the identity of the postmodern and what we could consider a newly determined postmodern identity politics. The inevitable "postmodernizing" of legal discourse, which may have many local insights to offer, should not come in the guise of depoliticizing the discursive ammunition that the law provides the legal subject within the nets of postmodern hegemonic forms. In short, while embracing the postmodern insofar as it provides a critique of the self-evident field of Law, I will suggest also the ambivalences inherent in this embrace.[1]

One of the most interesting, albeit appalling, features of contemporary life in the United States is the extent to which arguments over the nature of female subjectivity are crystallized in an ongoing series of trials—literal and figurative, spectacular or less so—a series that sets the subject of female identity in the seat of legal testimony. These trials, whether they take place in an actual courthouse or not, are cultural attempts to assess or regulate or demarcate Woman within a legal or political discourse. They are interrogations of the "feminine" enjoined by the spectacular techniques of postmodern media. (While men are put on spectacular trial as well, as the cases of Mike Tyson or William Kennedy Smith or even Jeffrey Dahmer bear out, what is at issue is not their status as men, or masculine beings, but rather the nature of their actions and how those are to be legally defined.) As such, the trials have a much more complex role to play in the formation of the politics of the female subject than their surface transparency would suggest. It is tempting to code them simply as outrageous and insidious demonizations of women, given credence by the legal trappings that surround the event. In a rather spooky way, however, the proliferation of trial images connects to the issue of postmodern identity formation as it intersects with feminism. The results of this intersection are not as clear-cut as might be anticipated—the results, as they say, are surprising.

The primary shibboleth of postmodern theory, without any doubt, is its deprecation of "identity" in any form, whether conceptual or logical

1. This essay is dedicated to the late Mary Jo Frug, for her pioneering efforts toward a postmodern legal feminism.

self-identity, referential identity, or the singular identity of the subject. This is quite appropriate, since postmodern theory owes its inheritance of the questioning of identity to its roots in poststructuralism of the Derridean kind, where it is taken as a given that identities must be dissolved, unbound, or at least thoroughly spliced and diced wherever they appear. Judith Butler gives a virtually classic statement of this project of postmodern philosophical feminist inquiry: "The task is to formulate within this constituted frame a critique of the categories of identity that contemporary juridical structures engender, naturalize, and immobilize."[2] Commenting on the problem of identity, also under the sign of a postmodern political philosophical inquiry, Ernesto Laclau writes that "the 'essential identity' of the entity in question will always be transgressed and redefined. . . . [It] cannot be constituted as an object separate from those conditions since we know that the conditions of existence of any contingent identity are internal to the latter."[3] Both capsule versions presented here illuminate the degree to which a feminist and politically oriented postmodern theory takes identity as its target.

Yet we confront the very evident paradox that identity politics has never reigned more supreme than now, at what postmodernists, including myself, might term "the current conjuncture." Across the board of political and cultural agitation, the emphasis is fully on delimiting a politics predicated on identities, celebrating identities, calling for the representation of identities, marketing identities, and subdividing identities into cunningly strategic political slices. Within feminism, the issue of identity politics folds back into the ongoing debates about essentialism versus social construction of gender identity. It should be clear simply from lived experience that as much as postmodern theory is squarely and utterly in the camp of social construction—for gender identities and any and all identities, as elucidated above—a postmodern identity politics exists and is terrifically influential. Considering only the domain of feminist theory and practice in this essay, I want to analyze how postmodernism paradoxically authorizes a politics of identity simultaneous with its critique of identity. The terrain for this analysis will be that of the trial of the (legal) subject, the woman putatively on trial, and the audience for that inquisition.

Postmodern feminism operates in a contradictory climate, one partially of its own making. While contradictions are inevitable, as philosophers

2. Judith Butler, *Gender Trouble* (New York: Routledge, 1990), 5.

3. Ernesto Laclau, *New Reflections on the Revolution of Our Time* (New York: Verso, 1990), 24.

from Hegel to Marx to Nietzsche to Derrida to de Beauvoir have pointed out, and contradictions are productive and engendering, they can also stymie thought. As an often unwilling, but at times enthusiastic, participant in the discourse of what could be called postmodern feminism or feminist postmodernism, I nonetheless see the need to arraign the problems of a postmodern politics of identity more thoroughly than has been done, by pushing past the feint of identity bashing to the proliferation of postmodern identity *fixations*.

Postmodernism or postmodernity cannot be taken as a given in any cultural discourse, particularly where disciplinary and discursive and even ontological boundaries are being crossed. Such difficulties are rife in any foregrounding of postmodernity, in any context whatever, because the postmodern has a highly equivocal conceptual status, an uncertain provenance, and a variable and often conflictual set of interlocutors. There are more than thirty-one flavors of postmodernism, and sorting out the indicia and differentia of these critical brands entails opening a theoretical Pandora's box, especially apt for feminism.

It is necessary to elide a fragmented history and gloss over problems in formulating a feminist postmodern; I do this not nonchalantly but with concern for the occlusions that will follow in my critical wake. Any serious consideration of postmodernity would have to stem both from a historical periodization where the term *postmodern* described a genuine convergence of historical phenomena at a specific, if loosely chosen, time, and also from a recognition that *postmodernism* refers to a congeries of theoretical suppositions about the nature of language, texts, and human subjects within the lens of the social. Interestingly, the major articulations of the postmodern have arisen in camps that construe these two assumptions as antithetical, and that has implications for the politics inherent in any postmodernizing of feminist discourse, especially in the area of identity formation.

Fredric Jameson's essay "Postmodernism and Consumer Society" is a touchstone here, for regardless of what flavor of postmodernism one is led to choose, one has to consider this essay.[4] Jameson is the first to state succinctly that postmodernism is a historical moment that expresses

4. Fredric Jameson's seminal essay has appeared in several forms, shorter and longer, over time, but one signal version of it appears in *Postmodernism and Its Discontents*, ed. E. Ann Kaplan (London: Verso Press, 1988), 13–29. See also the recently collected essays by Fredric Jameson on postmodern topics in *Postmodernism, or, The Cultural Logic of Late Capitalism* (Durham: Duke University Press, 1991).

"the logic of the culture of late capitalism." Jameson gets at postmodernity initially through the attempt to understand the aesthetic objects postmodernity necessarily produces, since for him all art and culture will stem from the material conditions of the society in which it is produced and received. Postmodernist art will be a bricolage, a collection of scraps and fragments pasted together, hybridizing high art and mass culture, recycling images and narratives, determinedly unoriginal.

After Jameson's informal "laws" of postmodernity are set up, the method and the object of postmodern study are irretrievably altered; the ramifications for legal discourse are also clear, since the assumptions about the legal text shift accordingly. Not that the legal text now is shaped as either parody or pastiche, but rather, the legal text ceases to emanate from an origin point of timeless authority or as a singular transmission. Beyond the consideration of discrete legal texts as altered textual objects, the "postmodern" would invade an account of the Law *tout court*, to put it punningly; postmodern critical attitudes would direct attention to the filtering of legal discourse through electronic media, as in televised courtroom trials and even phenomena like the much-watched congressional querying of Judge Thomas. By the terms *legal* or *the law* here I mean something more attenuated, what Foucault referred to as the juridicopolitical, perhaps—how subjects are formed by the state. This has keen relevance for the molding of female subjects in the spectacular public discourses of law and testimony. The ineluctably hybrid and multiple nature of contemporary discursive objects would invade even the more sacred precincts of legal thought and action; since legal discourse is not by and large self-consciously artistic, what is meant by this is the cultural framing by which and through which legal forms are perceived and acted out. None of these changes can be considered without taking into account the material, historical specificity of a vast societal change undergone in Western countries, at least since World War II, and prescient varieties of postmodern thought articulate the political effects of "late capitalism" and postindustrial society as these inflect all aspects of modern society and its subjects.

Secondly, Jameson discerns a change in the *affect* the work of art evokes or evinces, from the anxiety or alienation of modernism's subject, nicely emblematized for Jameson in Edvard Munch's painting *The Scream*, to what must be called the schizophrenic subject of postmodernism. "Schizophrenia" is the emergent psychic norm of the postmodern, the consumer consciousness disintegrating into a succession of instants, condemned through the ubiquity of mass images and commodified information to live in a timeless now rather than the centering, full time of meaning and history. It is precisely the gendering of this consumer consciousness that Jameson's essay tends to veer away from, however, and that gap leaves us with a continued fissure in our understanding: How is it that the multiplicity and fragmentedness of identity are celebrated by postmodern theory and also denigrated by it as a "female" consciousness?

Jameson's postmodernism tends to homogenize or totalize the concept at times, making postmodernism hold too many contradictory phenomena. What is most salient for a feminist postmodernism tracing some line of descent from Jameson is the absence of any specificity for feminism within this totalization. This is not to make the rather dreary charge that Jameson is insufficiently aware of feminism but, instead, to exhort us to look at the ways that identity politics emerges from within this version of the postmodern. Jameson praises the struggles of feminist groups, along with those of gay activists and people of color, as exemplary of postmodern politics: local, critical, and, yes, entirely identity-based. Jameson's postmodernism is hugely systemic—that is at once its great strength and its weakness, in that it can't quite locate the local, although it knows it must be there. (I admit to much preferring this flaw over its opposite, the far more common problem of seeing only the local, while denigrating systemic analysis and global critiques.) Feminism is present, for Jameson, in the form of identity movements or identity images. That theoretical move has real consequences, because he sees theory (in the form of cultural critique) as sidelined by postmodernism, paralyzed by its insidious grip. The nostalgic and despairing cast of Jamesonian postmodernism has had its effects, since it has become only too easy in light of it to overemphasize the impotence of the subject, or person, caught in its toils, and to fail to recognize the many opportunities for refashioning and redesigning the cultural contours of postmodern forms. Jameson confronts this emptiness and longs for the lost social community that pre-dates such amnesia and exists now only in the glimpse of utopia conjured up within mass culture. Without dredging up such longings, one may agree that postmodernity does resituate the cultural scene in all its parameters and that the notion of the legal subject can be stretched beyond recognition by this new postmodern space.

A fairly recent and spectacular example of the implosion of postmodernity into the legal subject occurred in the Wisconsin trial of a man for rape. The court was told that the raped woman was suffering from a multiple-personality disorder and that only *one* of the personalities was the rape victim. This rich scenario of the postmodernizing of legal subjectivity unfolded with Jamesonian melancholia in the nexus between the media and the courts, as the labile, fissured identity of a sort of folk-postmodernism, or postmodernism via the *National Enquirer* (as sensationalized "multiple-personality disorder"), encountered the legal norms of selfhood and singular self-identity, as well as the legal subject in the mode of truth-telling and self-incrimination. The trial took place with great public attention to the media event of testimony being funneled through a shape-shifting identity on the part of the plaintiff, only one of whose personalities, and thus bodies, had been raped, while the "others" remained unmolested by what would, had they been entirely present during the sex, in their cases have been consensual. Who "she" was, and the apparent impossibility of ascertaining a single, unified victim for the crime of rape, since the offended personality had agreed to sex but was considered to be too immature or troubled to be genuinely consenting, opened a *mise-en-abŷme* in the notion of the legal subject, an abyss all too readily filled by the simulacral aspects of the trial. Played out in the tabloids, on tabloid TV, on "regular" television news, and in a host of media forms including National Public Radio, it produced a simulacral theater in which the public at large was asked to witness the implausible fascinations and conundrums of this postmodern predicament. The defendant had to be tried simultaneously as a more traditional legal subject, in other words as a coherent psychic identity for whom the words *understanding* and *truth* had some fixed relevance. The spectacular display of the multiple personalities, or the literalized (if technically erroneous) "schizophrenia" on display in the media-pervaded courtroom, showed the difficulties inherent in introducing a postmodern identity definition into a courtroom still operating within another paradigm for the legal subject, on the basis of which the defendant was found guilty.

A "postmodern identity" of this sort—kitschy, spurious, and the product of an unholy alliance with a self-promoting form of psychology—is not at all what postmodern theoreticians seek to propose. Instead, a turbulence in the zone of culture, not in feminist postmodernism, preemptively tossed out a female subject in pieces, a fluctuating feminine subjectivity, and forced its apparition onto the cultural screen. Here the trial for rape was as much a trial of this problematic new cultural identity as it was for the assault that may or may not have happened; the discourse of the legal subject was asked, as it were, to confirm the status of an unprecedented legal identity. A boundary line between the setting of the trial and such collective inquisition sites as the "Oprah Winfrey" show was blurred throughout the trial. The guilt of the man in question was found to inhere in realizing that this woman was mentally ill and still proposing sex with her—a violation of the protective law surrounding such dealings with those assumed not to be in a position to defend themselves or their desires. The neutralization of identity into a quiver of self-inventoried alternative personalities leaves the legal subject in pieces as well, on one side of this divide only, the side where an alliance between a performative self and the multiple screening images of radio, television, and print can be effected. On the other side, the legal subject remains in full force, and the issue of "intention" is still rigidly invoked. The imbalance of this encounter leaves lop-sided the engagement of postmodern identity with the legal subject because it is so irresolvably bound up in a cultural staging. Postmodern theorizing can helpfully point out the fluid borders of such a staging and the ways they overlap with legal norms; nonetheless, to efface or erase the legal subject, however much predicated on an illusory unity, singularity, intentionality, would be an enormous political loss. One primary feminist take on the trial was to applaud the guilty verdict as an instance of a woman's voice, however fragmented and representationally obscure, being listened to; the dangers lie in attributing all the polymorphousness to only one side of the gender divide. Multiple identities coalesce around a subsuming "female" identity. The difficulties for a feminist postmodernism in riding these rapids lie in too readily privileging the dissolving of identity, while in this case the woman's "truth" was equally elusive.

At the other remove from Jameson's melancholy in the face of the postmodern is the influential discussion of the postmodern conducted in the work of Jean-François Lyotard, especially in the slim volume *The Postmodern Condition: A Report on Knowledge*, where Lyotard's claims are entirely different. The crux of his book is that in postmodernity, the major narratives governing social experience since the Enlightenment have disappeared, and that the disappearance of these meta-narratives has left instead the liberating potential of local, interlocking language games, which replace the overall structures.[5] The monumental public narratives of evolution, progress, class struggle, or even Enlightenment have all dissolved for Lyotard into the play of atomized, technologically assisted subjects who don't connect with one another in any overarching way, for example, by being members of a proletariat. Constructing political responses by way of

5. Jean-François Lyotard, *La Condition postmoderne* (Paris: Minuit, 1979), subsequently translated as *The Postmodern Condition: A Report on Knowledge* (Minneapolis: University of Minnesota Press, 1984).

reference to the teleological or progressive scenarios of the past is doomed and frivolously wrongheaded; there are no Manichean rents in the social fabric but a closely knit weave of intricate interconnections. Both the utopianism and the teleology inherent in Jameson's historicist postmodernism are avoided by Lyotard in favor of what might be called an avant-garde utopian gesture. The adhesive of the Lyotardian version of the postmodern has had remarkable sticking power, in that a typical summary of postmodernism involves recounting that it has made linear narratives of history obsolete and has transfigured the relationship of individual subjects to social and historical narratives in correspondingly major ways. This is exceptionally tricky for feminist theory of a postmodern stripe, not because there *is* one great narrative of the feminist revolution—a ridiculous notion—but because the ability to narrate the discontinuous and fragmentary stages of feminism within history is still a necessity, not an archaic relic of a despised linearity.

Much of the debate about postmodernism arises because postmodern theory may simply be the attempt to *historicize* the discourses of poststructuralism, which have been very resistant to this process from within, often denying the need for any complex historical consciousness at all, as is Lyotard's preference. For his thought, language games are all that are left, and however agonistic they may be, no larger accretion of collective identities on the historical terrain of struggle is to be expected. This marks a signal failure in the articulation of the postmodern, leaving it with a black hole of analysis, a now-invisible site of the actual, concrete, conflictual struggles against hegemony. Putting it this way risks sounding retrograde, but only within the canons of a rarefied, ahistorical postmodernism we would do better to abjure.

To step back and consider the problems of "postmodern identity" is to confront an immediate contradiction. Following a poststructuralist logic would entail putting the concept of identity under heavy scrutiny, and, indeed, insofar as "identity" can be construed as analogous to a stable, univocal self, an innate or immanent nature, a fixed or self-evident being, postmodern thought has scoured those Augean stables and evacuated any such stability. Postmodern identity comes with such certification of its fragmented, fractured nature, of its fissuring by the myriad social discourses which construct it, its elusive relation to self-presence, its foregone inconclusion, that to work one's way back to the relatively stable plane of an identity per se is perhaps inconceivable and undesirable.

Nonetheless, and at the same time, while postmodernism eschews any essence or origin, any authoritative center or even fixed point of leverage, identity has come to be a more and more pressing concern within formations of the postmodern. While the postmodern itself, as theory, cannot buttress an identity-formation and remain internally consistent, postmodernity or postmodern sociohistorical conditions make a demand for the structures of identity to contest the fragmentation of civil society. *Postmodern identity* is to that extent an oxymoron; it is also a neologism for identity, a new way of saying that there is an identity peculiar to the postmodern, and peculiarly postmodern.

This new composite "postmodern identity" has real repercussions for the intersection of the legal subject and postmodernism, whether in terms of a change in the interpretive matrix of the law, in the confrontation of legal discourse with changed social circumstances, or in the postmodernizing of law itself, and it has ramifications for the collision of postmodernism with feminism as well. The link must initially be teased out through the relation of the two words *identity* and *subject*. *Subject* has two valences for this discussion, one the more general meaning of a locus of subjectivity, the individual human subject, and the other the pinned or fixed object of subjection, a *subjected* identity. Michel Foucault plays on these differences in his essay "The Subject in Power," where he hypothesizes a subject formed out of its very subjections, become a subject by virtue of being made subject (to).[6] *Identity* does not have the neat internal play of ambiguity as a word, but the same doubleness holds good; an identity could be said to be the adopted agency of one who has been identified as the result of some social process—for example, a gay identity presupposing having been socially identified as gay, and then adopting that designation as a place from which to situate one's identity. An "identity" of this sort is connected to the "subject" in that identity is the self-chosen and usually communal expression of a subject-position, making a particular subject-position active as a functioning social identity, with the understanding that both of these states take place in the plural, not the singular. A pendant to this discussion would require pointing out that Foucault perhaps develops this understanding of the subject after repeated critiques of the impossibility of discerning an agent of change within his sociohistorical schema, which proposes the dispersal of power relations to such an attenuated degree that revolution or change or resistance is difficult to hypothesize or explain.

6. Michel Foucault's later essays and interviews turn on these questions; "The Subject in Power" is translated and anthologized in *Art after Modernism*, ed. Brian Wallis and Marcia Tucker (Boston: David R. Godine, 1984).

The Lyotardian version of postmodernism tunnels into this aspect of identity and subjects it to philosophical critique. In the most attenuated sense, the grounds for collective identity are swept away with the meta-narratives, so that class no longer serves as an identity marker of any predictive force, for example, and subjects are instead bundles of activated discursive shards, where there is never to be any one exclusive or overpowering identity. Thus, for Lyotard, there is always room to maneuver on the speech-activated board of culture and never any entirely hegemonic counterforce to confront. The exception to this is what Lyotard has come to see as the circumstances of the "Third World," whose sad job it is simply to survive, while our First World, postmodern task is to multiply creatively the features of our worlds. The forces arrayed against Third World survival are not enumerated or explored in Lyotardian postmodernism, presumably because these might threaten to look remarkably like relics of the disintegrated meta-narratives, and even the split between the First World and the Third World, in Lyotard's fuzzy terminology, would need to be theorized in some interlinking fashion. Barring this connection, the grounds on which identities form are murky at best. The strength of Lyotard's post-Enlightenment discourse has, however, truly set an agenda within postmodernism, which reverberates to the perceived conceptual inadequacy in both political and philosophical categories of the subject. *Local determination* is the arresting catchphrase for a society configured as interlocking, often antagonistic, microidentities. Lyotard does turn attention, in *Le Differend*, to larger situations of injustice, and he postmodernly characterizes these in linguistic terms; proper names act as signifiers for *differends*, circumstances of injustice that fall outside prior genres of discourse and reduce their sufferers to silence or to coded names. Auschwitz is Lyotard's main example of such a *differend*; so enormous is the matter of the Holocaust that it makes the struggles of, say, feminism seem rather paltry in their formulation. Since these struggles are *not* paltry, it becomes difficult to establish the grounds on which recourse could be sought in specifically postmodern terms.

This postmodern political dilemma connects with problems in Critical Legal Studies, where that discourse also seeks to "deconstruct" or dissolve the language of rights, scrutinizing rights as innately unstable and indeterminant, and replacing the rights vocabulary with one of needs. Among the many resulting difficulties is the status of needs, as identity groups come under a protectionist shield of need where they remain victims in need of help.[7] Critical Legal Studies has also implied that a rights discourse

7. Roberto Mangabeira Unger's *The Critical Legal Studies Movement* is the best source

like that of Native American demands for the upholding of treaties predicated on an identity as a tribe succumbs to a self-defeating legitimation of government power in the first place. Along these lines one thinks of the current upheavals in Wisconsin surrounding the spearfishing rights of the Lac du Flambeau–area Indians who are fighting for an enhanced and protected fishing domain on the terms of the government's initial dealings with their tribe, on promises made in original treaties, and on the definition of their cultural identity as land-based. The symbolic gestures of the Mexican-American movement of the 1960s and 1970s, coalescing in New Mexico in the Tierra Amarilla area and dedicated to the return of property traced back to land grants honored by the Treaty of the Mexican-American War, had a similar thrust; the battle in the courts revolved around the honoring of these claims as the treaty promised to uphold them, despite the dubious historical circumstances under which the treaty was signed. To seek to dissolve these rights away under the acid bath of postmodern multiplicity simply erases the grounds for self-determination, which can only be coded as an identity (collective or individual) possessing rights. Self-determination would seem to entail the embrace of legal subject-hood, as the vocabulary of rights may still be the only viable means to securing that selfhood. A postmodernism that ignores or deplores this necessity reveals its supposition that rights are already adequately secured, and that the legal arena cannot be bent to a variety of discursive purposes. A related struggle is ensuing in those localities where gay rights activists are applying pressure for the right to marry. Marriage can be subjected to a withering critique as a transparently ideological institution, but in this case, too, the importance of reserving a vocabulary of rights as a legal subject transcends those objections, since the political objectives of securing gay marriage rights for those who want them outweigh any hesitance about the identities presupposed by marriage. This becomes very vexed politically in other areas, however, as in the abortion rights battle, for example. The nature of the rights claimed can open the door to the refusal of abortion itself, as the ominous bumper sticker to be seen on some Operation Rescue cars spells out: Equal Rights for Unborn Women.

A paradox of the postmodern, then, is the coincident and vociferous rise of an identity-based politics hard on the heels of a postmodernist,

---

text (Cambridge: Harvard University Press, 1983). Essays that tackle the movement on its terms include Nancy Fraser, "Struggle over Needs," in *Unruly Practices* (Minneapolis: University of Minnesota Press, 1989), and Robert A. Williams, Jr., "Taking Rights Aggressively," in *Law and Inequality* 5 (1987).

or at least poststructuralist, consensus that questions identity at large as an essentialist category. Even where there is some circumspection about making the "mistake" of essentialism (and here I'll admit I concur with the assessment that it is a mistake), a separatist identity politics comes to the fore, and with it a kind of "serial identity" politics, along the lines of serial monogamy, is especially rampant. In this mode, identities are seen as additive or cumulative, with smaller and smaller subdivisions to mark more and more specialized identity formations. (Ultimately, this serves as fodder for right-wing jokes about the special claims of, say, disabled Latina lesbian mothers, a reactionary misunderstanding of what needs to be better theorized by feminism. I'll return to the possibilities for this in concluding.) Part of the impetus for this discursive and political phenomenon arises out of cultural and historical roots in the United States, where an individualizing rhetoric permeates all our major social forms. The community identity models itself on individual identity and coheres around shared attributes that are seen as defining, while the extent to which these community identities arise in relation to a social dominant becomes obscured. Onto this atomizing and even sentimentalizing identity politics a postmodernism of local determination gets grafted, with powerful, but often mixed, results. Even the brilliantly helpful theorists Ernesto Laclau and Chantal Mouffe seem to articulate this impasse, in their certifiably postmodern reconstruction of the social sphere, *Hegemony and Socialist Strategy*.[8] Grafting a dizzying postmodern vocabulary to an incisive political armature, the two arrive at a formulation for radical democracy which would mandate that "the epistemological niche from which 'universal' classes and subjects spoke has been eradicated, and it has been replaced by a polyphony of voices, each of which constructs its own irreducible discursive identity." They go on shortly thereafter to conclude that this politics is founded on the "affirmation of the contingency and ambiguity of every 'essence,' and on the constitutive character of social division and antagonism." Irreducible, perhaps essential, identities in a polyphonic harmony of voices? This is a sound that can also be heard as the raucous, antagonistic atonality of the social. The one-note song of an irreducible identity is hard to fuse with the dissolving logic of identity, the insistence on internal differences. The laudable goal of opening up social space to a multiplicity of approaches, a postmodern post-Marxism, ends up depending on the mobilization of *singular* identities. As long as the

8. The following quotations are from pp. 191 and 193 of Ernesto Laclau and Chantal Mouffe, *Hegemony and Socialist Strategy* (London: Verso Press, 1985).

postmodern in practice involves such contradictions, the relation between postmodern identity and the legal subject will be in question, too—these confusions in practice will infect the transfer of postmodern elements to the legal sphere.

Another legally informed narrative may help to highlight this shortcoming, by way of an excursion into another postmodern flavor or type crystallized in the work of Jean Baudrillard, who intersects with both Jameson and Lyotard, despite coming to some remarkably different conclusions. Baudrillard is the coiner of the all-important postmodernist word *simulacrum*, his term for the substitution of the screen for the "real" or even the "spectacle" that comprises modern culture. For Baudrillard, we are now, as a result of the technology of the image, so thoroughly imbricated in the image that even the human body is a kind of prosthetic screen. We now live our lives not as actors in psychic dramas on a stage or in a scene but as sites of the arbitrary coupling of bits of information, images, termini, and so on floating past us in the hyperreal space of the image-filled simulacrum, an "ob-scene" that has no accessible reverse side. There are echoes of Jameson here: Both theorists depend on an idea of the proliferation and takeover of the technologies of postmodern life, and on the schizophrenia that induces; Baudrillard, however, has no nostalgia for the realm of history or of concerted political action as does Jameson; Baudrillard's thought is entirely eschatological and apocalyptic, pushed up to the very edge. There is no arena for action, no public discourse; we are seduced by the image and in fact live within it, like the boy in the bubble, tethered to the simulacral bubbles that surround us. Baudrillard's apocalypticism also has affinities to Lyotard's apolitical postmodernism, because it questions any role for agency, any collectivity, any escape from the clutches of the image.

Into that divide I am inserting feminism, or feminist theory more appropriately, and will be addressing both a cultural artifact, a kind of text put under the lens of critique, and engaging feminism as a cultural activity lodged in an intercultural space. The cultural text I want to take up to allow myself to follow these two paths simultaneously is a recent one, the Clarence Thomas Supreme Court confirmation hearings before the Senate committee in their Anita Hill phase, the most engulfing national cultural event since the CNN-itis of the Gulf War set in. The hearings during those several days amounted to what Alexander Cockburn has called an "electronic Nuremberg rally," in the sense that for the space of Friday to Tuesday a tremendously high proportion of the U.S. population was galvanized in front of the same television spectacle and was entrancedly repeating its script as conversation on the subway, newspaper editorial, family dinner table argument, or the subject of frantic telephone calls. The national consciousness had a laser-like focus, perhaps less in the acuity of its thought than in the pure intensity of its gaze at the unfolding hearings; the television set became our collective skull, our joint screening room, our shared flickering site of Plato's cave. Enmeshed in a cathartic spasm, we, as a suddenly unified Nielsen group, ate, slept, and dreamed Clarence Thomas and Anita Hill; watched Tom Brokaw's sunny midwestern forehead furrow; leafed through dog-eared copies of *The Exorcist*; sent telegrams to Washington with frenzied abandon; pored over the newspaper transcripts and caught the talk shows as if they were unofficial extensions of the Senate chambers. This cultural event was like a spike driven very deep into the body politic, a moment in cultural time pumped full of cultural juice. I want to use this collective text as a way of setting feminist theory in motion against the vectors of postmodern theory and identity politics, partly because one cannot let such a cultural text simply get away, and also because the strange spectacle of cultural immersion in the Anita Hill/Clarence Thomas contretemps can illuminate the politics of the (legal) subject and the postmodern locations of contemporary feminism.

Why is this episode so perfect for such an appraisal? Although it was deplored variously as a spectacle, a circus, a nauseating panorama of pornography, or, in Clarence Thomas's words, "a high-tech lynching," if one subtracts the judgmental perspective, all these definitions insisted on the mediated, the represented, status of the discursive battle. Because that is what it was, a battle of cultural discourses coming from many locations, imbricated in different agendas and histories and vocabularies, on a collision course through the cathode ray tube of television. While the hearings were not a trial, it was so easy to forget that, and essentially the treatment of Anita Hill's testimony became wreathed in the legal trappings of the "trials" of subjectivity that were to follow it—the use of the scenario of a trial setting to uncover some presumably core truth about female subjectivity. The hearings underscore the painfully obvious fact that arguments in culture are filtered through cultural representations, which have their own forms and genres and strategies. This impinges with particular strength on issues of gender and feminism—here the gap between a feminism acknowledging the complex social formations we can call "postmodernity" and a feminism that does not is evident.

Second, the hearings, if they can be so called, hinge on the intersection of cultural discourses and cultural locales. Everything overlaps and crisscrosses here: the sacred trio of race, class, and gender, above all, but also region, occupation, age, and the internationalism of a global audience, the legislative and executive branches of government, mass culture and high culture, education, entertainment, and religion. That hurly-burly of the discourses, that promiscuity of cultural forms and nuances and levels, is grist for the mill of thinking about feminism in a contradictory, multiple, and differential way. One can read in those discourses, as in a glass darkly, some of the energizing and some of the problematic aspects of the feminisms being articulated in our culture today.[9]

There will be no way to go on productively without making it apparent that I consider Anita Hill to have described precisely, if reluctantly, exactly what occurred between herself and Clarence Thomas during their time as colleagues—employee and boss, respectively—on the EEOC. My reading has to depend on that as a kind of bedrock, against which to chart certain distortions and perturbations that ensue. Is this simply the feminist viewpoint of this cultural event, or the feminist bias, as Senator Alan Simpson, for example, might have it? I would argue not, for there are many possible feminist angles on the Hill/Thomas tangle; and some of those feminist angles are quite at variance with the feminist cultural criticism I will try to elucidate. A veritable whirlpool of misogynies, racisms, and reactionary theories emerged in the fetid wash of the hearings—not just a single kind of sexism, or one brand of racism, and so on—and correspondingly, there were many ways of framing the results within terms self-described as feminist. That may seem impossible, or counterintuitive—wasn't the symbolic march of the seven female lawmakers on Capitol Hill indicative of a unitary, coherent, and singular feminist interpretation of the stakes of the hearings and the meaning of Anita Hill's experience of sexual harassment? Without at all discounting the importance of that gesture and the interesting implications it had politically, my answer has to be no.

A way to gauge just how different feminist theorizations of the event can be lies in the omnipresence of Catharine MacKinnon on many broadcasts of the hearings, as a commentator on the proceedings and as a jurist who herself generated the crucial legal terms of the debate itself; Catharine MacKinnon tried the first sexual harassment case and was re-

9. The most salient discussion of the trials I have encountered is, not surprisingly, bell hooks's "The Feminist Challenge: Must Every Woman Be a Sister?" (*Zeta Magazine*, December 1991). My own account here had already been written, but the importance of her essay must be noted. Hooks makes the wonderful, dead-on point that Hill herself is not (or was not then) a feminist and that that changes everything.

sponsible for the legal language invoking sexual harassment as a specific form of discriminatory damage. MacKinnon's place on the networks and in the analysis of the unfolding phenomenon was absolutely earned by her groundbreaking legal work and her pivotal feminist position in the delineation of sexual harassment as a bona fide harm. Nothing in my discussion here is meant to question the tremendous achievement that MacKinnon, and others, it should be added, made by bringing sexual harassment to its embodiment in law. However, as a feminist theorist, what was MacKinnon's vision of what Clarence Thomas had done? As she stated repeatedly, and then elaborated, his sexual harassment of Hill was merely a subset of something else—his use of pornography. Pornography was, for MacKinnon, the root cause, the only cause, of the sexual harassment that was offensive and indeed illegal behavior. Anita Hill was at the receiving end of a pornographic discharge; she was violated, then, by exposure to pure pornography, in this instance pornography in the workplace. How does MacKinnon make the leap from a specific pattern of sexually harassing linguistic encounters to victimization by pornography? Her definition of women, and the resulting definition of feminism, demands it: MacKinnon wishes to describe women as a class, as a single group, and she does this by analogy to class itself, in the Marxist sense, although her use of Marxist thought is stunningly reductive and untouched by the subtler branches of theory. It is fair to say that MacKinnon is indubitably not a practitioner of anything to be remotely called feminist postmodernism or postmodern feminism.[10] If work or labor fixes and articulates class, then, MacKinnon claims, sex fixes gender, and she means sex in the literal sense—work is extracted or taken from you as a worker, and sex is extorted or taken from you if you are a woman. The mere existence of, let's say, a heterosexual pornographic text in an empty locked room is nonetheless a violation of women as a class. In MacKinnon's view, pornography is the name for, and the literal site of, the gender hierarchy obtaining between men and women in society. Clarence Thomas's statements to Anita Hill were an epiphenomenon of pornography and pornographic desire; it became of the utmost importance for MacKinnon to describe Thomas as a pornography addict, Anita

10. I have it on very good authority from an auditor that at a spring 1992 series of lectures given at Princeton University MacKinnon replied to all questions about the possibly more sophisticated approaches to representation that exist with a reference to such cavils as "deconstruction crap." "Real is real," she propounded. The recent championing of MacKinnon by the philosopher Richard Rorty has to be one of the most peculiar chapters in contemporary critical thinking.

Hill thus becoming indistinguishable from a woman depicted in a pornographic film or magazine, victimized by the gaze of pornography outright. Work, power, competition, all vanish from this scenario—what defines Anita Hill as a woman in MacKinnon's feminism is that she is this recipient of a pornographic barrage. Pornography belongs entirely to men, pornography expresses men, pornography is the root cause, the monolithic source, of the lack of equality between men and women. Censor and eradicate pornography and Clarence Thomas's comments become impossible, for MacKinnon; the flip side is also true—until and unless all pornography is snuffed out, gender relations are doomed to take the course of sexual harassment. The only feminist response, on these terms? To espy pornography wherever it lurks and to devote all one's feminist energies to public enemy number one, pornography.

Catharine MacKinnon's commentary on Hill's charges against Thomas emanate from cultural feminism, that feminism which embraces the notion of a univocal woman's culture and innate experience, whose defining characteristic is vulnerability to pornography and violation. For MacKinnon, then, Anita Hill was Everywoman, susceptible to the depredations of pornography. Such a position on her part echoes what happened to a major strand of feminism in the 1980s—its energies were siphoned off into a crusade against pornography that blurred the distinction between feminist politics and reactionary repressive rhetoric. It has been pointed out repeatedly, and most notably by the anti-MacKinnon feminist coalition centering on FACT—Feminists Against Censorship Taskforce—that the one constituency delighted to embrace the antipornography position has been the radical antifeminist right. This amounts to a derailment of cultural feminism into the dead-end endeavors of a pure politics of image. Such a politics involves a deep fear of representation, in the form of imagery or words, and supplants a mediated understanding of human culture. Boiled down to the brass tacks of pornography, this entails assuming that representations are precisely what they represent—there is no intermediate zone of fantasy, cultural play, or even just framing going on. By this token, there is nothing more salient, nothing more urgent, than removing pornography from society's midst. All women are equally affected by pornography, all women are equally alienated from pornography, all women are harmed by pornography at all times—so much for racism, or lack of prenatal health care, differing opportunities for professional advancement, female poverty, etc. All are traceable, it would seem, to pornography.

This analysis is off the mark, but it is remarkably interesting for revealing how much a transmogrified social terrain of postmodernity affects even those responses that try to eschew it. In the cultural spectacle I am detailing, this particular voicing of a feminist challenge to events was loudly heard, but it certainly was not the only feminist response. The prominence of MacKinnon, though, was in direct proportion to the irrelevance of what this ostensibly crucial legal feminist had to say about the hearings. Every other cultural variable in the hearings had to drop away. The crucial element of Anita Hill as a black woman and Clarence Thomas as a black man was not part of the pornography/politics of the image scene, nor was it any problem at all that the attackers of Anita Hill and her testimony all spoke in tones of anguish about pornography—another instance of the radical right finding it perfectly easy to adopt those criteria on their own behalf. One can bracket for now the terrible hypocrisy of this gesture on their part, in order to see what the pornography aspect actually did to the cultural spectacle. Paradoxically, it undercut the feminist politics of the hearings by making it appear both that Anita Hill was readily definable as a woman wronged, if indeed she had been, by pornography, and that women are not outraged by the fact of sexual harassment as a means of making the workplace a disturbing space for them professionally but instead are to be protected from exposure to sexual talk and sexual overtures. The offense, then, lies in jeopardizing women's innocence or sexual vulnerability, not in channeling male discomfort about women in the workplace into a hostile parade of sexual overtures.

That picture of things should not be compatible with a feminist viewpoint, but the picture unfortunately dovetailed with one prominent feminist theorist's construction of the situation. This helped lead to another aspect of the cultural drama then played out. If along one axis of cultural thought Anita Hill had to be seen as a victim in order to qualify as having been sexually harassed, then the corollary to that for many people was the proof that she had been damaged, that she was indeed a victim. And here a new cultural slot opened up which Anita Hill could not, and did not, fill. For her to have been a victim, by these lights, would have to mean that she had lost her job, lost her success, lost her prestige, lost her professional respect, lost her emotional center of gravity: Something along these lines needed to be fulfilled. Frustratingly, Anita Hill refused to fit into the niche where an ages-old narrative of female victimization could be intertwined with a feminist victimization. Victim was simply the wrong category, but a powerful cultural vocabulary on both the feminist and the antifeminist sides of the discussion of women in our culture demands it. The litmus test for victim status was how Anita Hill's story played on the female-dominated talk shows—by female dominated I mean that their audiences are 90 percent female, even if women are not always the "host." Anyone watching any of these shows as an adjunct to the hearings knows that Anita Hill did not win over the female mass audience. The precise reason for this was the failure of her "story"—and it was turned into a narrative with infinite twists and turns—to cohere as a tale of victimage. Anita Hill did not cry, one important sign of victimization in the Kabuki theater of the talk show, where any query must be met with welling tears. Clarence Thomas was lucky in having the background visuals of his wife's tears in looming and vicarious close-up; she was a victim in the liquid garb of TV gender, and clearly her emotion resulted from the pain caused her by the tearless Anita Hill. Tears, or at least visible emotion, are the proof-text of having been hurt in the melodrama of our national life, and Anita Hill disqualified herself in that arena. It might not have mattered, except that the hearings themselves became overridden by a modern-day televisual version of the test for witches—thrown in water, the innocent non-witch would prove it by drowning.

I'm not insinuating for a moment that Anita Hill should have behaved an iota differently than she did; what I am trying to indicate is the complexity of the cultural moment. One immediately visible implication is that there was no single woman's version of this event. While a vociferous reaction to confirming Clarence Thomas in the wake of these accusations was strongly articulated by women, many of them defining themselves as feminists, they were joined by men in this outcry, and both were in the distinct minority if we are to believe all the polls. If I have discarded the efficacy of a cultural feminism based on the politics of the image, then what dimension of feminism accounts for the abandonment of the precepts of sexual harassment by so many—the majority—of women? Class and race have their day here. A large number of women, and probably men, seem to have been disaffected by Anita Hill's testimony because it was offered by someone now identifiable as a middle-class professional, despite having had a background as materially deprived and as subject to racism as Clarence Thomas's. Race figured acutely in this equation. As the African American historian Nell Painter wrote in a *New York Times* op-ed piece after the hearings, when Clarence Thomas himself introduced the history of lynching as a metaphor for the grueling hearings, an implicit scenario floated in the cultural unconscious—lynching suggested the punishment of a black man for the rape of a white woman, and there was no white woman involved. Consequently, the black woman voicing the complaint against Thomas was invisible to most of the white national audience, since her harassment occasioned no indignation in comparison to the rape of a white woman, and for the black audience her accusation resonated uncomfortably with a history of blaming black men and thus further weakening them vis-à-vis white men. The African American journalist Salim Muwakkil analyzed the response of the black community in Chicago, in part through editorials in black-owned newspapers and so on, and found sympathies overwhelmingly with Thomas, on the grounds that Anita Hill was jealous because Thomas had married a white woman and wished to penalize him after the fact for this. These responses are clearly not coming from the same direction that, say, Senator Strom Thurmond's were, although they also lead to the support of Thomas's confirmation. What can be glimpsed here is the way that feminism, or at least gender status, cannot be kept separate from its instantiation in other divisions of culture. In all of these examples another variable has counted for more, has weighed more heavily, in a certain cultural equilibration.

What that evacuation points to is the dead end—at least insofar as politics is concerned—represented by an exclusive politics of identity. The general repudiation of Anita Hill's sexual harassment charges is symptomatic of, on the one hand, the undeniable grip of sexism still prevailing, but also of the weak response a politics of identity will be able to make in the face of that sexism. The politics of image despises the image but also lives and dies for the image, since that comes to be the only grounds of political evaluation: Is that a good image or a bad image? is the question, not How do images work and how diversely? The politics of identity embraces a similar contradiction. A group accepts its singularity as a social category—of race, or sex, or sexual persuasion, for example—as the basis for identifying a common struggle. That identity, though, as Denise Riley asserts in *"Am I That Name?" Feminism and the Category of 'Women' in History*,[11] is comprised as much of what has been shunted off onto the category of that social identity—let's say in this case women—as of what can be imagined as an alternative social identity. The nets of identity politics can become too tight as rigorous tests are administered to determine if a member truly belongs with the special identity of a group. What often happens is that all of the group political energy becomes devoted to policing the identity line, making determinations about when and how and whether it has been crossed over in certain instances, thus invalidating the identity of that individual mem-

11. Denise Riley, *"Am I That Name?" Feminism and the Category of 'Women' in History* (Minneapolis: University of Minnesota Press, 1988), chap. 5, passim.

ber. As an initial starting place, some invocation of identity will inevitably be made, but the danger, as Riley and many other feminists and theorists of other movements have pointed out, is that offering up the identity, honing it, and patrolling it are too likely to come to constitute the sum total of the politics of the group if a freewheeling recognition of the instability of that identity is not built in from the start.

Let me circle back to the Thomas hearings after having passed through this critical interlude. Again and again we heard that in Thomas's indirect rebuttal to Hill's charges, to which he did not listen, the race card had trumped the gender card in our national game of bridge. Thomas's portrayal of himself as subject to the indignities of a stereotyping discourse about black male sexual prowess effectively silenced the Democratic senators, who did not want to risk looking like they believed those stereotypes, and empowered Republican senators, many of them with highly suspect backgrounds of bigotry and race-baiting, to "protect" Thomas by charging racism. Throughout this, it was very hard to have it be admitted that the woman bringing testimony of sexual harassment was herself black. In a *New York Times* op-ed page editorial, Orlando Patterson, a Caribbean-American historian of slavery, swept away this seeming incongruity by his analysis that Anita Hill had succumbed to white feminist puritanism, no doubt through having been educated at Yale Law School in proximity to so many white feminist puritans. Patterson simply asserted that the remarks attributed to Thomas were standard badinage between black southern men and women; the interpretation of them as sexual harassment was a strange form of brainwashing undergone by Hill, who had, Patterson opined, forgotten her roots in black culture. So much for stereotypes, Patterson said; yes, Thomas had said these things, the fault lay in betraying one's racial culture and lining up with female sexual puritans on the other side of the color line.[12] Thomas's white senatorial supporters did not take this line at all; they professed horror at remarks about pubic hair and Long Dong Silver and were very far from attributing these to friendly intercultural interaction; no, by their lights Anita Hill lied, lied because she was in love with Thomas, or psychologically unstable, or a dupe of liberals, or a lesbian. These incongruities and irreconcilable attitudes all cluster around the perceived need to

12. Patterson's essay is reprinted in *Reconstruction* 1, no. 4 (1992): 64–77, and is followed by an extraordinarily thoughtful exchange between Patterson and Rhonda Datcher, an African American graduate student in mathematics. She offers brilliant and telling rejoinders to his ethnographic remarks, as he concedes in his final statement.

take one variable—be it gender or race or, in a very farfetched link, class: by those lights Anita Hill was jealous of Thomas's career prominence and couldn't bear his going onto the Supreme Court—as supreme, as primary, as the bottom line.

Postmodern identity would seem to have it all over the legal subject here. In the churning froth of mobile and multiple sexual identities, of transgressive reformulations of object and subject, in the postmodern wash of identity, the legal subject who came to the fore was an impossible monolith, a female monster. In providing a critique of this monstrous result, one brand of postmodernism could be seen as a utopian theory seeking to undermine all such binaries and divisions, installing the play of differences in their stead. Thinkers like Craig Owens and others have wanted to suggest that postmodernity itself is the "discourse of others," of those who have been disenfranchised from the cultural system, and in particular he cites the prominence of sexual difference in postmodern art of the last fifteen years and of the female artists who have participated in making postmodernism what it is—for him, a questioning of all difference and a dissolving of natural or essentialized hierarchies.[13]

A postmodernism of this variety has been given the name *resistance* postmodernism, and to this I would register a serious caveat—not to the possibility of resistance but to its linkage with the postmodern. Viewed in this light, postmodernism becomes a critical tool kit, a set of techniques to deploy at will, generally in the realm of textual culture. That vision renders postmodernism with overly broad brush strokes, as providing internal options of a reactionary or progressive kind. What that is ordinarily going to mean is an overinvestment in discursive gestures, the often fatuous assumption that an alteration of textual style or nomenclature or the decentering of a discourse in some purely symbolic way sends shock waves to the heart of social domination. That very locution, of course, is disavowed by postmodernism anyway, since no "heart" or core of hegemony can be posited. This insight could quite profitably be tailored to an understanding of the law, of the legal subject, not as a monolithic construct but as a permeable membrane within which innumerable sites of conflict and innumerable forms of struggle can be seen to exist.

The real problem is that postmodern feminist theory has a different identity politics from that of feminism in the domain of the (legal) subject,

13. See Craig Owens, "The Discourse of Others," in *The Anti-Aesthetic*, ed. Hal Foster (Port Townsend, Wash.: Bay Press, 1983), 57–77.

in the public arena of image, protest, the woman on trial. It is fashionable to refer slightingly to an academic feminism of theory and writing, in contrast to a grass-roots feminism of marching and political action that does the real work of feminism. That division will no longer suffice, but not on the grounds that theory and practice can no longer be distinguished. "Academic feminism" is itself splintered into many domains, as is feminism in the supposedly real world outside the academy. Postmodern feminism is trying to catch up to a reality we barely have a name for, the postmodern situation of a theory of identity that seeks to overcome the limitations of fixed, immutable, and hierarchical identities, with a feminism still involved in a straightforward identity politics. Postmodern feminism is itself caught in those same nets. A singular feminist movement no longer exists, and postmodern theory embraces the fragmentation of multiple locales, sites, and dissolved identities. Trying to negotiate the new space for feminist theory involves seeing how much we still operate with incongruent and incompatible models. When identity politics is pushed up to the limit line of its politics of image, there is a price to pay politically. That price is the substitution of an identity politics for a relational politics, a multiple political dynamic that can see itself at work in the world in the back and forth of actual political engagement. Instead, an identity politics that becomes entrenched will more and more focus on the symbolic imagery of naming or of being named. Postmodern feminism can readily fall into that discursive trap by its concentration on symbolic imagery, so that pointing to the insubstantiality of identity can come back to haunt its own theoretical precincts. We live in a moment of contradiction, where finding our way across a sophisticated theoretical bridge to a viable politics beyond identities, including female identity, looks difficult. Female identities are now, as always, on trial, as in the case of Anita Hill. The mistake would be to collapse that postmodern spectacle into one discernible identity with one political response. Hill is a strong, brave woman, and an articulate law professor; she is heroic but is not a feminist heroine. Her transformation into precisely that, through awards and speeches in the feminist media, is a retroactive canonization, an indication of how image-driven feminist politics is today. To see her as such is to identify too much, and in the wrong ways—a symptom of the identi-fixations a postmodern feminism needs to outgrow.

Feminism and Postmodernism—Another View

Mary Poovey

The summer of 1991 witnessed a spate of popular movies with a strikingly similar theme. Each of these movies features a more or less middle-aged white man who is moderately to wildly successful in a high-pressure, high-prestige occupation. Suddenly, because of the vagaries of his own body tissue, random violence, or a desire to forestall the onset of age, these men find themselves humbled, frustrated, and, as a result, miraculously humanized. In *Regarding Henry*, an amoral lawyer needs a bullet in the brain to rediscover his own ethics; in *The Doctor*, a heartless surgeon recovers his ability to care after a bout with a tumor; in *Doc Hollywood*, a cynical plastic surgeon finds love through mandatory community service in a small South Carolina town; and in *City Slickers*, a joyless New York professional delivers a calf and discovers the meaning of life. In the summer of 1991, the wilderness was located not in Wyoming but in corporate America; the enemy was not the "red man" but the system, the rat race

I would like to thank Cora Kaplan, Emily Martin, and Joan Scott for discussions about various versions of this essay. I am especially grateful to Judith Butler for helping me clarify the logic of my argument.

that has run even the most successful man ragged and stripped him of his ability to feel.

No doubt these movies about masculine resuscitation are more salutary than the body-count movies of the summer before. The fantasy nature of their happy endings, however, seems to me as surely a barometer of anxiety as was the testosterone rush of *The Terminator*, *Total Recall*, and *Die Hard*. When you put the 1991 born-again movies alongside the biggest money-maker of the year, *Terminator 2: Judgment Day*, the anxiety becomes clearer and, to my mind, more poignant. Like its predecessor, *Terminator 2* is about a cyborg, a cybernetically engineered, computer-driven, machine-man, who can break human limbs with a snap of his fingers and who can withstand blasts from an AK-47 at close range. Unlike his namesake predecessor, however, this Terminator is a good guy. He takes orders from a little boy (with a knowing wink at *Kindergarten Cop*), he learns, he makes (clumsy) jokes, he even evokes (and almost expresses) feelings. This Terminator, in fact, is, in some ways, more human than the woman he is forced to work with. Whereas Schwarzenegger's character has softened considerably in the sequel to the first Terminator movie, Linda Hamilton's Sarah Connor has become as emotionally hard as her muscles. This machine can never be a man, but because he is so faithful, so reliable, and because he chooses at the end to sacrifice himself for the boy, this Terminator can stand in for the father the boy has never known and, in so doing, he can symbolically father the human race, which, without him, would have ceased to exist.

In this essay, I want to work from the complex of feelings of which the anxiety implicit in these movies is one expression to the structural contradiction that underwrites it. Put most bluntly, the fear is about ceasing to be human—whether because a man is so successful that nothing but money comes to matter or because the impenetrable, inexorable workings of the multinational, computer-run megacorporation have reduced him to a machine-man. I do not think that this anxiety is limited to white men with stethoscopes and expense accounts. I will argue, in fact, that it is another version of this same fear that is holding a certain definition of feminism in place, that is holding up feminism, in both senses of this phrase. I do think, however, that one defense against this fear—and therefore a telling articulation of it—is clearest in some (white) men's fantasies about women and minorities. This defense displaces the fear that the very nature of the human is at risk with the specific anxiety that some people—specifically, white men—are being denied the opportunity to realize themselves because other people—primarily women—have been given unfair access to the opportunities that used to belong to men. I also want to argue, however, that behind the fear that is displaced by the blame is a structural contradiction within the liberal, democratic version of humanism, made visible by the changes we call postmodernism, that renders all psychological responses inadequate to the problem at hand. Indeed, I will argue that the fact that most responses to the changes that have begun to transform U.S. society are psychological signals a failure of the political. I will also propose that some kind of political resuscitation of feminism is necessary to analyze this contradiction and to define the changes that are now bringing it to light.

First, let me follow the logic of the scapegoating defense against fear. To do so, I'll look at an essay about one of the signs of the changes with which dehumanization is associated—the growing problem of homelessness. Written by Peter Martin and published in the *Nation* in July 1991, "The Prejudice against Men" argues that "the problem of chronic homelessness is essentially a problem of *single adult men*."[1] "Out of all single homeless adults, 78 percent are men," Martin explains; "out of all homeless adults, more than 64 percent are single men; and out of all homeless people—adults or children—58 percent are single men." After one factors in programs intended to help get people off the streets, Martin concludes, one is left with the " 'chronically homeless,' of whom four-fifths are men. Seen that way, homelessness emerges as a problem involving what happens to men without money, or men in trouble."

The sex differential among the homeless, according to Martin, is partly a result of federal programs like AFDC, Aid to Families with Dependent Children. Because AFDC generally denies relief to a household that includes an adult male, this program sets up a situation of unequal competition that discriminates against men: "The regulations as they now stand actually force men to compete with the state for women."[2] Part of the problem, however, as Martin elaborates his argument, is not that men must compete with the state but that the state establishes an inequality between men and *women*, in which women retain a capacity that these men no longer have—the ability to choose. The language of choice pervades Martin's representations of women. In relation to the AFDC policy, for ex-

1. Peter Martin, "The Prejudice against Men," *Nation*, 8 July 1991, 46. Subsequent quotations in this paragraph are cited from this page.
2. Martin, "Prejudice," 47, 46. Subsequent quotations in this paragraph are cited from these pages.

ample, he writes: "Given the choice between receiving aid for themselves and their children and living with men, what do you think most women do?" In relation to work, Martin declares that "women, especially when young, have one final option denied to men. They can take on the 'labor' of being wives and companions to men or bearing children, and in return they will often be supported or 'taken care of' by someone else."

In ascribing choice to women, Martin is exploiting the feminist-humanist vocabulary, turning back as an accusation that which, in another arena, some women are struggling to retain as a right. The fact that he can do so should alert women to the danger for feminism of the assumptions that inform an argument like Martin's. Such an argument reveals the sexism inherent in the tradition of humanism that has developed alongside, and as part of, the rationalistic, democratizing epistemology dominant during the last two and a half centuries. It also suggests that when feminism takes up the language of this humanism we carry over its sexism, too. This is the first hint of the structural contradiction I want to explore. Even though the humanist subject seems to be without gender, it is always already gendered as *masculine*, for, within this tradition, the self-determining, rational subject always stands opposed to the subject-in-nature, which is gendered feminine. Martin's charge that women are, and ought to act like, humanist subjects, then, signals the contradiction that women now suffer: On the one hand, since the late eighteenth century, women have been excluded from the humanist subject position and have been defined by their reproductive capacity; on the other hand, as the crisis of late capitalism becomes more pressing in the West, the humanist subject position has opened to those who were previously excluded from it. As part of this profoundly mixed blessing, those who have enjoyed the benefits of humanism—largely white men—have begun to blame its increasingly obvious liabilities on those latecomers who have been admitted only because capitalism's demand for cheap and flexible labor knows, but does not respect, the "barrier" of sex.

I will return in a moment to explore this contradiction in more detail, but before I do so, let me stay with Martin's defense. Essentially, this defense is articulated in psychological and gendered terms. Martin's analysis, in other words, suggests that he experiences the dehumanization that accompanies the crisis of late capitalism as emasculation. In fact, as his argument draws to a close, Martin defines as the root of the problem of homelessness not a failing economy or inadequate safeguards for labor but a cultural denigration of men. "To put it simply," Martin writes, "men are neither supposed nor allowed to be dependent. They are expected to take care of both others *and* themselves. And when they cannot do it, or 'will not' do it, the built-in assumption at the heart of the culture is that they are *less than men* and therefore not worthy of help."[3]

Martin's analysis reveals that he thinks that the problem is who gets to be a humanist subject and that the gendering of the humanist subject is only a symptom of the current crisis. According to Martin, when women acquire the rights associated with humanism and push men out, masculinity comes under threat. Against Martin, I argue that the problem is not who gets to be a humanist subject but that the Enlightenment version of humanism, with its vocabulary of rights and choice, feelings and equality, continues to be produced as a solution to the crisis at hand. The problem with humanism is that the state apparatus that Martin accuses of depriving men of choice actually constructs subject positions in such a way that choice seems to exist for some when, actually, it is available to no one. Gendered meanings obscure this contradiction: Up until the moment when infrastructural changes open the humanist subject position to those who were previously excluded, gender functions as a "natural" principle of inequality, making the relative freedom of men seem absolute by contrast to the "natural" dependence of women. Martin's charge that women have brought about, or at least benefited from, a fundamental change in who is allowed to choose—like the charge leveled by the Right that "quotas" make equal opportunity impossible for white men—is naïve and misplaced. The changes that the United States is experiencing are actually more far-reaching, and ultimately even more threatening, than Martin imagines. Martin is right, however, in thinking that these changes have something to do with gender. In order to extend Martin's analysis of the relationship between these changes and gender, I shall look more closely at some of the other ways these changes are being conceptualized.

Homelessness is only one symptom in the United States of what David Harvey has called "the condition of postmodernity."[4] The changes for

3. Martin, "Prejudice," 47–48.

4. See David Harvey, *The Condition of Postmodernity: An Enquiry into the Origins of Cultural Change* (Oxford: Basil Blackwell, 1989). Other helpful discussions of postmodernity include Fredric Jameson, "Postmodernism, or the Cultural Logic of Late Capitalism," *New Left Review* 146 (July–August 1984): 53–92; Andreas Huyssen, *After the Great Divide: Modernism, Mass Culture, Postmodernism* (Bloomington: Indiana University Press, 1986); and Christopher Norris, *What's Wrong with Postmodernism: Critical Theory and the Ends of Philosophy* (Baltimore: Johns Hopkins University Press, 1990). Among the many discussions of feminism and postmodernity, see Donna Haraway, "Mani-

which postmodernity stands include not just observable alterations in the U.S. economy and welfare system but transformations in the global economy, as well: I have in mind both the creation of a part-time "homework" economy at the level of worldwide production and the forging of the corporate conglomerate at the level of global management. These changes also include technological innovations in the electronic storage, retrieval, and transmission of information; medical advances in genetic research and synthetic proteins; and the steady march of new diseases across the planet. While they can be theorized at this macrolevel, the effects of these changes are also being registered more immediately, as challenges to the most basic units of humanist understanding—the individuality of the subject and the bodily integrity of the person. The changes occurring in people's perceptions of the body are being measured by anthropologist Emily Martin, whose fieldwork finds people in Baltimore speaking of their bodies not as self-contained entities bounded by a shield-like skin but as systems that interact with the ecosystem that contains them. Here is one of the descriptions Emily Martin has recorded: "I think your immune system, for me, [it's] more that you have a whole network of things that affect you, and you order those things to, to work the most efficient way, and that you have to make choices in what you do with yourself and your life, and where you live and what you eat, for that to work. And it's all intertwined, so no one thing is going to save you from Illness."[5]

It may seem paradoxical that this informant conceptualizes these radical transformations in terms derived from humanism: She simply extends efficiency, flexibility, and choice from the autonomous humanist sub-

---

festo for Cyborgs: Science, Technology, and Socialist Feminism in the 1980s," *Socialist Review* 80 (vol. 15, no. 2) (March–April 1985): 65–107; Teresa L. Ebert, "The 'Difference' of Postmodern Feminism," *College English* 53, no. 8 (1991): 886–904; Judith Butler, *Gender Trouble: Feminism and the Subversion of Identity* (New York and London: Routledge, 1990); Judith Butler, "Contingent Feminism and the Question of 'Postmodernism,' " in *Feminists Theorize the Political*, ed. Judith Butler and Joan W. Scott (New York and London: Routledge, 1991), 3–21; and Linda Singer, "Feminism and Post-Modernism," in *Feminists Theorize the Political*, 464–75.

5. This quotation is from a personal interview with an unnamed person. Quoted in Emily Martin, "Producing New People, Reproducing a New Society: Gender, Death, and Reproduction" (unpublished essay, 1991), 6. My discussion of the changes in definitions of the body and in conceptualizations of the workplace is indebted to Martin's essay and to Donna Haraway, "The Biopolitics of Postmodern Bodies: Determinations of Self in Immune System Discourse," *differences* 1, no. 1 (Winter 1989): 3–43.

ject to the molecules and tissues of her body. Yet, it should come as no surprise that as individuals struggle to assimilate, to make sense of, the hitherto unimaginable changes that various theorists are describing, they use the images and systems of meaning that have provided order to the world as they have known it. Insofar as these changes are imagined at the level of the body, both humanism and gender provide crucial rubrics for conceptualizing new possibilities—just as these terms provide, for Peter Martin, a bulwark against having to accept the implications of radical change. In a moment, I will suggest that the reason postmodern challenges to humanist commonplaces mobilize assumptions about gender is more complex than just some natural bond between the body and sex, but in order to get to that argument, I need to give a few more examples of the variety of ways that responses to the postmodern condition are enlisting gendered meanings.

The cybernetic superiority of Terminator 2's adaptations to the vicissitudes of his environment—his body's ability to close flesh over bullet wounds, or one arm's capacity to peel back synthetic skin from the other to perform electronic surgery—is a type of the trait that many analysts say will triumph in the postmodern world. As these analysts describe both the flexible, adaptive entity that will eventually emerge and the process by which the mass-production corporation will become a "learning organization," they frequently use images that carry gendered—or, more specifically, feminized—meanings. In *Developing a 21st Century Mind*, for example, Martha Sinetar describes the executives who will succeed in the transformed workplace as embodying traditionally feminine traits: They "enjoy, are easy with, the soft, shadowy underbelly of human existence, however illogical it may seem. Feelings, intuitive hunches, moods, dreams, personal preferences are their allies. They court the world of the 'irrational.'"[6] As one "human resource management executive" describes the process by which the new corporate entity will come into existence, he pictures himself playing a feminized role:

> The old way of operating must end or die for the realization of the new to emerge from its remains. The Phoenix analogy is useful here. The transformed organization rises out of the ashes of its old form to take on a new direction, one that raises its performance capability to a much greater level of functioning, sophistication and response. . . . Empowering the human spirit, managing emotions and changing beliefs about reality seem to be essential ingredients to the process. . . . Transformation involves both birth and death. There can be profound

6. Martha Sinetar, *Developing a 21st Century Mind* (New York: Villard, 1991), 13.

> pain in seeing the process through . . . as change agents, we cannot walk into any organization and "do transformation." We can, however, . . . assist by facilitating the conditions to help it along, much like a midwife assisting a natural birth. She supports, encourages and guides the process; she does not do the birthing for the mother.[7]

The fantasies of rebirth in the films with which I began participate in this effort to forge new myths for success by appropriating the traits associated with femininity, as do spokesmen for the men's movement, like Robert Bly and Sam Keen. Thus, the hero of *City Slickers* plays midwife to a calf to heal himself, and Robert Bly encourages his would-be Iron John to "overcome . . . his fear of wildness, irrationality, . . . intuition, emotion, the body, and nature."[8]

It is by no means obvious that the corporate executives' appropriation of feminine traits to negotiate the transition to postmodernity will be any more beneficial to women than is the humanist defense against postmodernism. Indeed, I suggest that both humanism and postmodernism have the capacity to subordinate women—the former, in ways with which we are all too familiar; the latter, in ways we have yet to imagine. Because the potential for sex oppression demonstrated by humanism also exists within postmodernism, and because gendered meanings are being used to ease this transition, it behooves feminists now to examine both the ways that feminized traits are being appropriated to facilitate (or resist) material and conceptual changes and the consequences for women of these appropriations. In order to begin this project, I want to examine in some detail two recent legal cases that implicitly question the adequacy of the humanist subject as a response to or as a defense against postmodernity. Because each of these cases also centrally involves either sex or reproduction, they also illuminate both the complexities of the role gender plays in such responses and the underlying contradiction of humanism's construction of gender. While the legal negotiation about the humanist subject is not occurring exclusively in cases having to do with women or even sex,[9] I do think that such cases constitute the front line of defenses against change because of the particular position that women and reproduction occupy in relation to 'truth' or

7. Quoted in Martin, "Producing New People," 23.
8. Robert Bly, *Iron John: A Book about Men* (Reading, Mass.: Addison-Wesley, 1990), 14.
9. The case of *Moore v. The Regents of the University of California*, for example, focused on the question of whether an individual has a proprietary right over the tissues of his/her own body—whether, that is, tissues and organs are a part of the autonomous "self." The California Supreme Court ruled in 1990 that John Moore did not have proprietary rights to his spleen, which was surgically removed in 1976.

'nature'. While law is by no means the only arena where such negotiations are taking place—as my earlier examples should demonstrate—I do think that the law may be a critical arena for feminists to examine. I say this for the following reasons: (1) As an institution dedicated to maintaining continuity with the past, the law is particularly resistant to change. (2) The law stages the dynamics of social negotiation specifically in the form of contests and, therefore, makes these negotiations available to the public in the familiar, hence easily consumable, form of melodrama. (3) As its link to melodrama suggests, the law works not only by institutionalizing as *regulations* assumptions that elsewhere take the form of prejudices or beliefs but also by psychologizing responsibility, by shoring up its structural imposition of regulations with what feel like personal, private, unconscious feelings.

My first example is intended both to demonstrate how certain legal institutions function to reinforce the humanist juridical subject and to show how psychologized feelings reinforce the law's conservative tendencies. This case, which was widely publicized last summer, involved a charge that three male students at St. John's University had raped, sodomized, and sexually degraded a female student at a fraternity house after forcing her to drink vodka-laced orange soda. No one disputed that the sexual activity had taken place; the question at issue was the woman's consent. The defendants asserted that the woman had gone to the fraternity house willingly, that she had consumed the vodka knowingly, and that—explicitly or implicitly—she had consented to having sex. By contrast, the woman argued that not only had she not consented to having sex but she had been only intermittently conscious during the event. In July, the three defendants were acquitted of all charges by the jury, who explained that, because the woman's testimony contained contradictions and gaps, she must not have been telling the truth.

One set of assumptions implicit in this verdict underwrites the very institution of trial by jury. This assumption is that true stories will be recognizable as true because they are coherent, comprehensive, and comprehensible. Behind this belief lies the further assumption that coherent, comprehensive narratives can be generated by honest individuals because these persons are coherent, comprehending subjects. Even though these assumptions are basic to juridical humanism, however, they have, in the last few years and with increasing frequency, been set aside by juries who are persuaded by psychological research that asserts that victims of trauma often survive assault precisely by losing their coherence and their ability to comprehend—by falling briefly unconscious, by becoming confused, or even by repressing the memory of the event altogether.[10] Such juridical accommodation of what we might call a postmodern view of the subject has begun to erode the authority of humanism in all kinds of cases involving violent crime, with the exception of sexual assault. Juries are often willing to believe that memory lapses occur in violent crimes, notes Ann Burgess, a recognized authority on posttraumatic stress disorder, but they will not make the same allowance for sexual assault because they do not associate sex with violence and because they assume that women require "persuasion" before they consent to sex. "People tend to believe when people are robbed or held at gun point," Burgess comments, "[b]ut so many people still see rape as sex. They really don't see it as violence. But it's the violence that brings on the traumatic response."[11]

This is exactly what happened in the St. John's verdict. Even though the prosecutor argued that his client had momentarily lost consciousness during the assault, the jury held her to the standards of the humanist juridical subject. This occurred not because the jury assumed that all humans are equal before the law but because a set of assumptions about the gendered nature of the sex reinforced the humanist assumptions inherent in the law. These assumptions have become the staple fare of virtually all rape trials: The facts that the woman went to the fraternity house willingly and that she knew—even liked—her alleged assailants were used to argue that she willingly consented to having sex. In other words, once a woman enters an environment where sexual relations often occur, she is accepting—or even inviting—whatever sexual advances are made; she is renouncing the privileges of the humanist subject and accepting the subject position to which nature has assigned her.

Here, then, is the painful paradox that humanism imposes on women. On the one hand, because women are excluded from the humanist subject position in being associated with nature, they are not credited with full rationality; when a woman says "no" in relation to sex, she may as often mean "yes." On the other hand, because the law also assumes that the humanist subject exists apart from gendered meanings, the woman is held responsible for upholding the standards of rationality: She must tell a coherent story or tell no story at all. This unbearable contradiction also produces the psychological; that is, the double bind displaces what is really

10. See Bessel A. van der Kolk, *Psychological Trauma* (Washington: American Psychiatric Association Press, 1987).
11. "Bearing Witness to the Unbearable," *New York Times*, 28 July 1991.

a social contradiction onto the individual subject as the split between consciousness (rationality) and the unconscious (nature). When we analyze, or respond to, this contradiction in psychological terms, we reinforce this displacement: We substitute an explanation about the nature of "human subjectivity" for what could be a political critique. This double bind helps explain why women, like the accuser in the St. John's case, are so often held responsible for their own oppression.

My second example, the 1989 *Webster* decision about abortion, shows that this double bind results not from some incidental conjunction of assumptions about women and humanism but from the constitutive role that gender plays *in* juridical humanism. To explain this, I need to examine the *Webster* decision in some detail. The original case that resulted in the United States Supreme Court's *Webster* decision involved a Missouri statute, enacted in June 1986, and the charge brought by five health care professionals that this statute violated a woman's Fourteenth Amendment rights.[12] The Supreme Court upheld the original statute, arguing that the Court did not have to decide whether the controversial Missouri preamble, which declared that life begins at conception, is constitutional and that the statute's injunction against using public facilities to provide abortions places no obstacles in the path of a woman who wants an abortion. In other words, the lack of public facilities does not interfere with due process because it does not curtail a woman's right to choose.

Behind the specific provisions of the *Webster* ruling was a more general objection on the part of some justices to the 1972 *Roe v. Wade* decision legalizing abortion. This objection became clear in the ancillary opinion submitted by Justices Rehnquist, White, and Kennedy, which used the fact that medical tests are not capable of determining exact gestational age to attack *Roe*'s "rigid" trimester scheme. In *Roe v. Wade*, this trimester scheme, along with the associated concept of "potential human life," had been used to distinguish between the period in which a woman and the fer-

12. See *William L. Webster v. Reproductive Health Services, et al.*, 106 *U.S. Supreme Court Reports* (1989), 410–71. For provocative discussions of the abortion debate, see Ronald Dworkin, "The Future of Abortion," *New York Review of Books*, 28 Sept. 1989, 47–51; Catharine MacKinnon, "Privacy v. Equality: Beyond *Roe v. Wade*," in *Feminism Unmodified: Discourses on Life and Law* (Cambridge, Mass.: Harvard University Press, 1987), 93–116; Rosalind Pollack Petchesky, *Abortion and Woman's Choice: The State, Sexuality, and Reproductive Freedom* (Boston: Northeastern University Press, 1985); and Lawrence H. Tribe, *Abortion: The Clash of Absolutes* (New York: W. W. Norton & Co., 1990).

tilized egg constitute a single legal "person" (the woman) and the moment at which this single legal entity is recognized as two legal "persons," one of whom (the "potential life" of the fetus) deserves protection by the state.[13] In 1989, Justices Rehnquist, White, and Kennedy objected to the "web of legal rules" by which *Roe* had attempted to establish a distinction between these periods, arguing instead that because there is no medical basis for certainty, the state has an interest in "potential human life" *throughout* a woman's pregnancy. In so doing, these justices implicitly argued that a fetus is, from the moment of conception, a "person" with rights commensurate with those of a pregnant woman. They argued, in other words, that the fetus is, from the moment of conception and before the differentiation of sex, a humanist subject.

The reasoning set out in the *Webster* decision demonstrates conclusively that it was the intention of the Supreme Court to uphold constitutional individualism and the humanist juridical subject. At the same time, however, this reasoning also reveals both the strain that new medical technologies have placed on the humanist juridical subject and the crucial role that gender has always played within it. The first sign of this strain emerges with the Court's argument that state legislators have the right to decide when life begins. In advancing this opinion, the *Webster* decision essentially rendered the definition of life a *political*, not a medical or a theological, decision; that is, it opened what had previously been an area policed by "expert"—even absolute—authority to public debate and the democratic process. (At the same time, of course, it also placed the judiciary *within* this political process, not outside it.) The second sign of stress has even more direct implications for the humanist subject, for in arguing that curtailing public funds for abortion leaves a pregnant woman "with the same choices as if the State had decided not to operate any hospitals at all,"[14] the *Webster* ruling exposed the limitations inherent in the concept that has become the centerpiece of the feminist agenda (and of the white male backlash, as well)—the notion of individual choice. If the state operates no public hospitals, after all, the individual woman will only be free to "choose" a private hospital, and this "choice" will be available only to women with sufficient money and then only if private doctors are trained and willing to perform abortions. The third sign that maintaining a humanist subject is becoming

13. For a more extensive development of this argument, see my essay "The Abortion Question and the Death of Man," in *Feminists Theorize the Political*, 239–56.

14. *William L. Webster v. Reproductive Health Services, et al.*, 106 *U.S. Supreme Court Reports*, 419.

increasingly difficult is also the point at which space has begun to open for what might eventually become a postmodern juridical subject. In adopting *Roe*'s language of "potential human life" but attacking the trimester scheme, the *Webster* decision implicitly argued that the Constitution's language of individualized rights is not adequate to accommodate all of the guises in which so-called persons appear. Both the pregnant woman and the fetus (or "potential human") challenge the legal entity of the "person"—the first because she is nonunitary; the second because, being neither autonomous nor embodied, it is incapable of self-determination or even independent life. This, in turn, creates the possibility for a nonunitary definition of the juridical subject, in which sex will be only intermittently acknowledged or tied to reproduction.[15]

The signs of stress evident in both of these cases have appeared, and have been foreclosed, in relation to female sexuality and reproduction because of the critical role gender—and women, in particular—plays in upholding the humanist subject. To explain this role more fully, let me return for a moment to the legal assumption that the St. John's case made clear: A legal "person" is an individual capable of telling, knowing, and acting on a coherent, self-consistent representation of reality, or "truth." Theoretically, that is, an individual becomes a "person" with legal rights when she or he is reasonable, coherent, and capable of moral discrimination. Also theoretically, this coherent person exists *before* she or he is recognized by the law and in spite of sex, color, or class; the law claims simply to reflect the reality that exists outside it. In actuality, however, the law does not reflect or recognize some preexisting reality; the law recognizes only those things and persons "that correspond to the definitions it constructs."[16] In practice, this means that what counts as reasonable, coherent, and moral is a function of the categories the law creates. It also means that what counts as a reasonable, coherent, and moral subject—the individual upon whom the law confers personhood—is a function of the categories the law uses to define coherence. Among these categories, as Judith Butler has recently argued, the "*regulatory*" categories of gender are particularly (although not exclusively) influential: "The 'coherence' and 'continuity' of the 'person' are not logical or analytical features of personhood but, rather, socially instituted

15. For a more elaborate discussion of these ideas, see my "The Abortion Question," 239–56.

16. Parveen Adams and Jeff Minson, "The 'Subject' of Feminism," *m/f* 2 (1978): 50.

and maintained norms of intelligibility" that are anchored by " 'intelligible' genders."[17]

Gender functions as the bedrock of the humanist juridical subject, then, because an orderly system of gender differences seems to be the basis of our cultural systems of meaning and, therefore, of the very notions of coherence and continuity. It is also important to note that gender is intelligible as an ordered (binary) system of meanings only because each gender is defined relationally, by its difference from an Other. Furthermore, genders attain their appearance of internal coherence and their definitive difference from each other by a process that entails both (imperfectly) homogenizing each term of the binary opposition (by marginalizing all other kinds of difference) and claiming a natural relation to the (supposedly binary) biological difference of sex. This is why I say that gender *seems* to be the basis of our cultural system of meaning: Gender, with its apparently natural, or biological, referent, masks the presence of other differences (among these, race) that are marginalized in order to foreground gender. Thus, the coherent, reasonable, moral "person," the humanist juridical subject who is the possessor of rights, is not the *basis* of law but the *effect* of a set of social institutions—including the law—that differentiates between people on the basis of a binary system of coherent genders, which (falsely) claims to derive its coherence from biological sex. Women play a crucial role in upholding this system, because their gender—the *feminine*—has been culturally assigned the same side of the binary opposition as *nature*. This link reveals that the system of gender is not only binary and relational; it is also differential and hierarchical (as each term of the binary opposition of gender is also both differential and hierarchical). That is, in the same sense that rights exist for some only when there are others from whom the entitled can claim those rights, so the properties of humanism, which include both rights and coherence, can obtain for some individuals only so long as there are others whose exclusion from rights and choice guarantees humanism.[18]

The role that a differential system of gender plays in humanism sets up the cruel contradiction I have been examining throughout this essay: Because women are human and because the law supposedly recognizes all

17. Butler, *Gender Trouble*, 16, 17.

18. For a discussion of the differential nature of rights, see Wai-Chee Dimock, "Rightful Subjectivity," *Yale Journal of Criticism* 4, no. 1 (1991): 25–51.

humans as rational subjects, women are included in and held responsible as humanist subjects. This is the case especially now, as changes in the infrastructure have forcibly opened the humanist subject position to women as a group. Because, however, the humanist subject and the laws that uphold it actually depend upon a binary and differential organization of gender (and, within gender, upon such differential determinants as race), women are also excluded (albeit differently) from the humanist subject position and (as a group) made the guardians of the entire cultural order. The cultural logic that seems to tie a woman's gender to her sex makes womanly women the guarantors of the oppositions that the humanist juridical subject institutionalizes. At the same time, this logic also makes the womanly woman the guardian of the stability of each term of the opposition. This explains why any alteration in the "natural" alignment of women and childbearing—and, by extension, of women and the home—is so threatening to the basis of masculine identity, as we saw in Peter Martin's essay.

This logic also explains why any challenge to the definition of *woman* ushers in fears about the definition of *life* and mobilizes the threat of dehumanization with which I began. We see this fear again in two controversies that have sprung up alongside the abortion debate. The first concerns the question of who will determine what counts as life. We have already seen the *Webster* decision politicize this determination, but this politicization remained relatively uncontroversial on the Right because the Missouri legislature was understood to have based its determination that life begins at conception on religious authority. More recently, in January 1991, Catholic ethicists began to dispute even this basis for discrimination, noting that, despite the decree of the Church that "from fertilization the biological identity of a new human individual is already constituted," new scientific evidence reveals that the pre-embryo lacks the "determinate and irreversible individuality" that is "a necessary, if not sufficient, condition for it to be a human person."[19] The second of these controversies concerns the other extreme of "life." As early as July 1990 (and with increasing vehemence since the publication of the national bestseller *Final Exit*), the National Right to Life Committee began to argue that when *Roe v. Wade* extended the constitutional right to privacy to the realm of reproduction it set the stage for legalizing euthanasia. "*Roe v. Wade* was a precedent for killing people," one spokesperson recently declared, "and its impact has gone far

19. "Catholic Scholars, Citing New Data, Widen Debate on When Life Begins," *New York Times*, 15 Jan. 1991.

beyond abortion. We had warned years ago that euthanasia would be the next step."[20]

The emergence of such controversies—alongside, and as part of, the legal contests and the cinematic anxieties I have been discussing—indicates that even though women are assigned responsibility under the law, the feminine is also seen as the last frontier of nature, the last guarantor of identity, masculinity, and life itself. At the same time, however, these controversies and the anxieties behind mass-cultural fantasies also suggest that the contradiction I have been examining is no longer capable of sustaining itself; in other words, the alignment of (female) sex and (feminine) gender can no longer be taken for granted. *This* suggests that the specter of dehumanization I have associated with the postmodern is massively overdetermined. At one level, it is a response to material, infrastructural changes.[21] At another level, it is a response to the destabilization of the imaginary relation between sex and gender and to the imaginary homogenization of sex that is itself a symptom of these infrastructural changes. One outcome of this overdetermined logic of infra- and superstructural causes and effects is the other phenomenon with which I have been associating postmodernism: the appropriation of feminized traits to maximize success in a world conceptualized as an inhumane system. As the alignment of (female) sex and (feminine) gender has increasingly come to seem like a cultural organization, feminized traits have floated free from their female referent. These traits have become available for the kind of appropriation we see in a movie like *City Slickers* or in the management expert's description of the process of corporate transformation. They have become available, in other words, to help usher in the postmodern world.

Thus, we have the paradox of gender that emerges from the fundamental contradiction within humanism that I have been examining. On the one hand, because gendered meanings (particularly those meanings coded "feminine") have historically been accorded a natural, biological relation to sex, gender can be mobilized to resist the changes that are bringing in the postmodern condition. On the other hand, because the very changes that

20. "Foes of Abortion View 'Right to Die' as Second Battle Over Life and Death," *New York Times*, 31 July 1990.

21. The entry of increasing numbers of women into the work force has been instrumental in disturbing the relationship between sex and gender as has the transformation of work itself to accommodate both women and changes in the global relations of production and consumption. At the same time, of course, developments in reproductive technology have problematized the relationship between sex, conception, and "life."

people are resisting by invoking traditional gender definitions are altering perceptions of the relationship between sex and gender, gendered meanings are also available to describe, even to facilitate, these changes. This paradox seems to me to unravel the twisted skein of meanings contained in a film like *Terminator 2*, in which a human woman is masculinized in order to fight alongside a cybernetic humanoid, whose hypermasculinity is underwritten by feminine compassion. It also seems to me to illuminate the complex effects of the *Webster* decision, which is indisputably a setback for women who desire control over reproduction at the same time that, in theory at least, it provides an opening for a postmodern juridical subject that might be both heterogeneous and only intermittently defined by sex.

Recently, the American public was subjected to an ugly demonstration of the contradiction I have been examining, and I want to conclude by discussing this very briefly. When law professor Anita Hill made the allegation that then nominee to the Supreme Court Clarence Thomas had made sexually insinuating comments that rendered her places of employment hostile environments for her as a woman, she was attempting to use one forum constitutionally designated to adjudicate the claims of humanist juridical subjects to make her story known. The responses her testimony provoked, however, especially from the Republicans on the Senate Judiciary Committee, mobilized the double bind I have been discussing. On the one hand, Hill was cast out of the position of humanist subject by being hystericized: She was called "schizophrenic" and a "scorned woman," accused of fantasizing and of reading *The Exorcist* for prurient sexual details. On the other hand, she was also held up to the standards of the rational subject: She had the choice, senators charged, to leave Thomas's employment when he went to the EEOC; she had the choice to tell. In choosing to move with him and in remaining silent, they charged, Anita Hill either acted irrationally (and, therefore, deserved what she got) or else proved that nothing was wrong (and, therefore, merited the blame they were assigning to her). What the senators could not—or would not—see is that the responses Hill described are those given by the structural contradiction I have been discussing: On the one hand, she became the nonrational subject to which gendered meanings assigned her (she did not tell); on the other hand, she acted rationally, as the humanist subject should (she did not leave her job).

If, as I have been suggesting, we are now witnessing the emergence of one of the fundamental contradictions of humanism as a consequence and expression of the condition of postmodernity, then I think that feminism must assist—not fight—this historical transformation. I think that feminism must stop trying to resuscitate the humanist subject. We must move abortion out of the center of the feminist agenda and move choice away from the heart of our campaign for reproductive options. I say this because all arguments that keep sex at the center of legal defenses and social meanings—even arguments that are explicitly defenses of women—seem to me to support the humanist assumption that women should stand in for nature and to uphold the binary organization of gender. They do so because they endorse the cultural assumption that is the ground of sexism—the notion that sex is the most important determinant of difference. At the same time, I think that a feminism that elevates sex over all other determinants of difference inevitably, and inadvertently, participates in other forms of oppression, which invariably arise in a cultural logic that privileges sex over other demarcations of identity. In privileging sex, in other words, feminism, like humanism, marginalizes all other forms of difference that would fracture the gendered binary—differences like race, age, class, religion, or sexual preference. Indeed, the complexities of the Hill/Thomas hearings, like those of the St. John's case (where the accuser was also black), need to be read more systematically through race than I have been able to do in this essay. Meaningful analysis of the role that race continues to play in reinforcing the structural contradictions of gender was preempted in the Hill/Thomas debate when Thomas alleged racism. Why a black man was believed when he alleged racism, while a black woman was discredited when she alleged sexual harassment, is a question that cries out for serious attention.

What feminism needs now is some way to take account of the shifting meanings of sex that does not make sex the fixed, or the only, center of analysis. Feminists need to reconceptualize sex and gender, to see these as dynamic, relational categories—relational to each other and to other determinants of difference—not as the fundamental basis of the humanist subject. Such an account of sex might help render obsolete the gendered and race-specific meanings by which Anita Hill was discredited. At the very least, it might expose the fact that these meanings are complicit with the political interests that members of the Judiciary Committee were advancing. Such an account might move us beyond a psychological account of Hill's behavior and a psychological response to it to some more fully politicized understanding and organized resistance.

I suppose that, realistically, what I am calling for is a more flexible feminism, not a rejection of feminism altogether. At the same time, however, we need to guard against simply endorsing flexibility for its own sake, for to do so is to run the risk of reproducing those images that are already being co-opted by corporate analysts. Thus, there is the uncanny similarity between the call of feminist Chela Sandoval for a Third World feminism, which combines "grace, flexibility, and strength," and sociologist Rosabeth Moss Kantor's description of the new megacorporation, which combines the "power of a giant with the agility of a dancer."[22] In order to avoid simply participating in the production of such images, feminists must begin to analyze the paradox I have been discussing, by which the relationship between gender and sex is currently being used both to resist and support the arrival of that rough beast, the condition of postmodernity. Perhaps as more people analyze this paradox, the contradiction that it expresses will become more visible, and it will then not be so easy to hold women responsible for our own oppression. Of course, it still will not be obvious what new configurations of power postmodernism will usher in. I hope, in offering these observations, that feminists can begin to develop new terms that will help shape the articulations of power institutionalized by, or alongside, postmodernity—instead of defending out of fear a humanist subject that is sexist to its very core.

22. Here is Sandoval's description: "Differential consciousness requires grace, flexibility and strength: enough strength to confidently commit to a well-defined structure of identity for one hour, day, week, month, year; enough flexibility to self-consciously transform that identity according to the requisites of another oppositional ideological tactic if readings of power's formation require it; enough grace to recognize alliance with others committed to egalitarian social relations and race, gender, and class justice, when their readings of power call for alternative oppositional stands" (from "U.S. Third World Feminism: The Theory and Method of Oppositional Consciousness in the Postmodern World," *Genders* 10 [Spring 1991]: 15). The Kantor quotation comes from *When Giants Learn to Dance* (New York: Simon and Schuster, 1989), 33. I do want to register my agreement with Sandoval's basic point, however, that "what U.S. Third World feminism demands is a new subjectivity, a political revision that denies any one ideology as the final answer, while instead positing a *tactical subjectivity* with the capacity to recenter depending upon the kinds of oppression to be confronted" (4).

Feminisms and Feminizations in the Postmodern

David Simpson

Judith Lowder Newton has made the interesting and very credible claim that the notorious "New Historicism" about which we have all been so exercised in recent years is a remasculinization of the defining procedures of the feminist movement. She proposes that the attack on objectivity and the corollary interest in subjectivity and cultural construction, the preoccupation with power and representation, and the collapse of any distinction between the literary and the nonliterary, between the center and the margins, may all be rediscovered in the "mother roots" of feminist theory.[1] For Newton, the repression or disavowal of these origins represents a masculine appropriation of feminine labor, but also a deviation away from the progressive component of that labor, a tendency to "deny or to mute radically the possibility of change and agency both" (165).

One does not have to (and Newton does not) suppose that feminist theory was the single and exclusive origin of New Historical method in order to recognize the case for at least displacement or nonengagement,

1. Judith Lowder Newton, "History as Usual? Feminism and the 'New Historicism,'" in *The New Historicism*, ed. H. Aram Veeser (New York and London: Routledge, 1988), 153.

and perhaps for outright appropriation. The New Historicist might well claim the status of coworker rather than capitalist by appealing to his or her (but mostly his) laborious journey through the work of Foucault; and he might further propose that he is marketing a quite different product, one not at all deployable for radical social action (though not all New Historicists are devotees of the strong containment model of culture). I would guess that all these relations pertain: appropriator, coworker, and competitor. Regardless of the intentions of particular New Historicists, there is no doubt that the function of New Historicism in the literary critical academy has been to provide an *established* alternative to feminism, as well as to Marxism and deconstruction. It is not just our collective desire for novelty that has made this initiative, and not another, the fashionable movement of the 1980s and early 1990s. And, like so many persuasive alternatives, New Historicism contains assimilations and reorganizations of the energies it functions to replace.

But New Historicism is not at issue in this essay except as an instance of the postmodern, whose larger relation to feminism and to feminization I want to explore. That New Historicism is such an instance will, I hope, not be a controversial claim. It may be a pale version of the excesses of pomo culture as manifested in architecture and the creative arts or the fashion industry, but it is the best that many of us academics can hope for. In its denial of a rational method for drawing the line between subject and object, in its predilection for anecdote and its distaste for totality, and in its very obvious appetite for describing the culture of the body, it does belong on the map of the postmodern. In particular, it occupies an important place on the trade routes between the disciplines in the contemporary academy, both as importer and exporter. It takes in the ethnography of a Clifford Geertz and the philosophy of a Richard Rorty at the same time as it gives back the very literary criticism from which they and others like them have themselves previously borrowed. It belongs, then, very definitely in the ethos of postmodernity, both for its circulation of academic stocks (there may be no bonds) and also in its methodological priorities.

The debates about this postmodernity have tended to devolve around decisions between long and short durational models and between continuous or discontinuous development (evolution or revolution). (I leave aside the other preoccupations with the radical or conformist effect of the postmodern; they all entail, in some way, hypotheses about pedigree and chronology.) For some of us, like David Harvey, the postmodern proper began quite recently (in his case with the stock market crises and financial revolutions of the 1970s).[2] Fredric Jameson suggests a somewhat longer pedigree in proposing the postmodern as the successor of aesthetic and political modernism, which still sought to direct modernization into universally progressive directions and retained a critique of the commodity. Postmodernism accepts and even celebrates commodification, and its subsumption of the aesthetic, and is "what you have when the modernization process is complete and nature is gone for good."[3] The determining principle here is *late* capitalism. Jameson remains flexible on when and how this is to be defined within the spheres of unevenly developing cultural sectors, but it is generally recent: for instance, it may have happened in the late 1950s (4). My argument here will not seek to propose any precise emergence of a postmodern, since I do not in fact think that there is *a* single postmodern. But it will ask the question of whether the methods and priorities associated with postmodernism might not be better understood as a moment of significant punctuation in the equilibrium of modernity itself, so that postmodernism's declared reaction against high modernism is itself contained within a long durational evolution containing both.

It is indeed hard to have this argument about periodization with complete clarity or honesty. The long durational model risks collapse into Hegelianism, while the radical originality model can look like mere presentism, a function of the advertising industry as much as of the academy. Both have their uses for describing different components of what is called "the" postmodern. And both, I think, need to be held in play for any adequate account of the place of feminisms in the postmodern. Feminism has a long history, and one which proves that even a history written by the winners can record its deviant moments and roads not taken or plowed over. In its rhetorical identity for us now, *feminism* tends to serve as a description of very recent intellectual-political efforts, those mounted since the 1960s by and on behalf of women. But one can identify one or another kind of feminism as emerging in counterpoint to almost every shift in the dynamics of modernization since the Renaissance and perhaps earlier. As such, these feminisms have often attempted a resistance to *feminization*, to the gendering of certain undesirable or disavowed social and personal characteristics as the natural properties of women, and the imputed or acquired attributes of certain groups of negatively regendered men.

2. David Harvey, *The Condition of Postmodernity* (London: Basil Blackwell, 1989).
3. Fredric Jameson, *Postmodernism, or, The Cultural Logic of Late Capitalism* (Durham: Duke University Press, 1991), ix.

The argument for the function of feminization within modernity has been made in at least two important books, for America and Britain respectively. Ann Douglas's *Feminization of American Culture* made the case for a formative relation between sentimentalization, consumerism, and literature in the American nineteenth century as constitutive of the syndrome of feminization and of modern "mass" culture. She also proposed that the feminization of culture went along with an actual "feminine disestablishment" whereby women increasingly moved and were moved from being producers to being consumers.[4] Subsequently, Nancy Armstrong, in her *Desire and Domestic Fiction*, has found in eighteenth-century Britain a similar conjunction of social-textual energies whereby the very notion of the modern subjectivity came into being as a feminized entity: "The modern individual was first and foremost a woman."[5] Like Douglas, Armstrong specifies the new modern (and feminized) individual as middle-class and partly formed by (as she is formative of) the cultural artifact called "British literature" (20–21).

These two books summarize a great deal of evidence for the coevolution of feminization and of the modern notions of literature and of subjectivity. That their respective samples are a century or so and an ocean apart does not matter, since they are exploring a long-durational syndrome whose credibility depends less upon a precise moment of absolute origin than on a general articulation of modernity. Philosophers have often looked to Montaigne and Descartes for its exemplary expression (sometimes called an "origin"), while literary and cultural historians have tended to focus on what we recognize as the Renaissance for similar epitomes.[6] One could, and others surely have, proposed earlier symptomatic moments. The emergence of capitalism and of consumerism, upon which the syndrome may well depend, has always required for its analysis a famously labile chronology.

4. Ann Douglas, *The Feminization of American Culture* (New York: Alfred A. Knopf, 1977). In her sense of a disjunction between culture and its social-economic environment, Douglas opens the question of the relation between what I am calling feminisms and feminizations.
5. Nancy Armstrong, *Desire and Domestic Fiction: A Political History of the Novel* (New York: Oxford University Press, 1987), 8.
6. See, among others, Joel Fineman, *Shakespeare's Perjured Eye: The Invention of Poetic Subjectivity in the Sonnets* (Berkeley and Los Angeles: University of California Press, 1986); Catherine Belsey, *The Subject of Tragedy: Identity and Difference in Renaissance Drama* (London and New York: Methuen, 1985); and Francis Barker, *The Tremulous Private Body: Essays on Subjection* (London and New York: Methuen, 1984).

This necessary largeness or looseness of focus allows us some broad but I think workable assertions: that feminization has been a dominant subject-effect for the bourgeois or "middle" classes upon and through whom the processes of modernization have been carried out; that feminisms have often arisen in critical reaction to it; that our current notions of *literature*, and simultaneously of literary *criticism*, have developed within that same cultural evolution, as feminized media; so that those aspects of the postmodern that make central the literary are potentially continuing a long tradition of feminized subjection and subjectivity. The relation of femin*ism* to the (feminized) postmodern must then be inspected and perhaps contested; the desire to challenge must be set within a possible history of complicity, not to preempt the plausibility of challenge (in the manner of one kind of New Historicism), but in hopes of plotting just where the mines are buried in the minefield, and thus in hopes for a better future. If any feminism, in other words, is to mount a critical alliance with the postmodern, it must beware of unacknowledged complicities with those postmodern priorities that are arguably the legacies of a traditional feminization process, legacies often apparent, I suggest, in the postmodern preference for the "literary" method.

The literary-centered postmodern is not, of course, the only postmodern. Cyborgs, computers, virtual reality machines, and rewritten DNA models all seem at least to propose a technological postmodern that has on the surface little to do with the traditions of literary criticism. This "hard" postmodern seems to offer a world free of feeling, introspection, and bewildering hermeneutic speculations about subject-object relations and responsibilities. And yet it might be suggested that the very appeal of these models, models declaring or assuming the death of the subject, are dialectical formations, limit statements of the desire to be, finally and after all the promises, free of subjectivity. For in the nontechnological postmodern, subjectivity is everywhere, more than ever before. And the mode of subjectivity is *literary*. When Paul de Man called attention to "literature" as that which recognized the fictionality or language-bound identity of its own statements, he was repeating (albeit in the disguise of a technological ambition) the traditional understanding of literature as other than science, as dominated by a critical element of subjectivity, and not by any assumption of systematic access to a world of natural things.

One can find, across a whole field of disciplines, instances of a common pattern of methodological and ethical priorities that read as analogues of the New Historicism and/or feminism effect in literary criticism (an effect which, I have suggested, *risks* the attribution of deep familiarity). In political theory, the massive appeal of Laclau and Mouffe may be attributed to their disinclination for the "Jacobin imaginary" of grand theory and their recommendation of an immersion in "that infinite intertextuality of emancipatory discourses in which the plurality of the social takes shape."[7] (Note the assumption that the social *is* plural, which is not the same as saying it ought to be.) In a similar spirit, Judith Butler speaks of gender as "a complexity whose totality is permanently deferred," and of its social inscription as an "open coalition . . . an open assemblage that permits of multiple convergences and divergences without obedience to a normative telos of definitional closure."[8] And Evelyn Fox Keller writes about a scientific method called "dynamic objectivity" that is "not unlike empathy" in its assumption of a "connectivity with" the world and tells about the "many worlds" quantum theorists for whom "the universe is seen as continually splitting into a multitude of mutually unobservable but equally real worlds."[9]

These instances stand for a multitude of others in their recognition of all knowledge as situated knowledge, and of the need to recognize the likely asymmetry of different persons' situatednesses. Feminist scientists such as Keller and Donna Haraway are reluctant to give up completely on an objectivity that they still find potentially liberating albeit traditionally appropriated for masculine interests. Writers and scholars not working within a scientific tradition are often more relaxed about giving up on rationality and objectivity, hoping instead for some empirical resolution, in performed experience, of the tension between different interests. Their hope seems to be that the recognition of situatedness, and the admission thereof, can head off some of its more negative possible consequences, as if declaring that one has a position or an interest could be a way of achieving a useful methodological honesty, or at least a protective humility. It can also, of course, be a persuasive marketing tactic for a readership prone to conflating personal sincerity with analytic power.

I call these understandings "literary" not because they are explicitly derived from a literary vocabulary but because they share with that vo-

7. Ernesto Laclau and Chantal Mouffe, *Hegemony and Socialist Strategy: Towards a Radical Democratic Politics*, trans. Winston Moore and Paul Cammack (London: Verso, 1985), 2, 5.

8. Judith Butler, *Gender Trouble: Feminism and the Subversion of Identity* (New York and London: Routledge, 1990), 16.

9. Evelyn Fox Keller, *Reflections on Gender and Science* (New Haven and London: Yale University Press, 1985), 117, 147.

cabulary a recognition and celebration of the imprecision that comes from admitting one's subject-positionality. Moreover, the debt of the postmodern to the literary is sometimes explicit. It is so for Richard Rorty, the exemplary postmodern philosopher writing in English (rather than in French), who understands our present condition as lived within "the autonomy and supremacy of the literary culture" and who affirmatively infers from Nietzsche an understanding of history as "the history of successive metaphors" so that we should allow ourselves to "see the poet, in the generic sense of the maker of new words, the shaper of new languages, as the vanguard of the species."[10]

Modernity, then, for Rorty, devolves in and through the hegemony of the literary, precisely at the point when philosophy and theology have failed to satisfy. One could propose a number of exemplary formulations of this shift: Hume, Rousseau, Friedrich Schlegel, Wordsworth, Kierkegaard, Nietzsche, Wittgenstein would all suffice to illustrate some aspect of this emphasis. Hegel, however, would not quite do, since his solution to the unignorable problem of subjectivity, of situatedness, is designed certainly to acknowledge but also to defeat the sheer occasionality of historical experience. In this sense his work is the anticipatory antithesis to much of what is now recognized as the postmodern, in that it strives to preserve the (as we now say) "master narrative" marching through a sea of contingency and redundancy. Marx continues to be debated as falling on one side or the other (sometimes both) of this divide. Adorno elegantly articulated its existence, and his is a useful account for the disambiguation of feminism and feminization.

Adorno's *Negative Dialectics* "attempts by means of logical consistency to substitute for the unity principle, and for the paramountcy of the supra-ordinated concept, the idea of what would be outside the sway of such unity."[11] After Hegel, philosophy is obliged "ruthlessly to criticize itself," but it must do so by attention to everything in which Hegel was not interested (3, 8). Philosophy now must admit its inability to prescribe the particular, and to reduce what it interprets to "the concept"—a term (*Begriff*) having a specific history through Kant, Hegel, and beyond (11, 14). This imposes a "playful element" upon philosophy which is equivalent to the literary; thus

10. Richard Rorty, *Consequences of Pragmatism (Essays, 1972–1980)* (Minneapolis: University of Minnesota Press, 1982), 150; *Contingency, Irony, and Solidarity* (Cambridge: Cambridge University Press, 1989), 20.

11. Theodor W. Adorno, *Negative Dialectics*, trans. E. B. Ashton (New York: Continuum, 1973), xx.

the "element of the *homme de lettres*, disparaged by a petty bourgeois scientific ethos, is indispensable to thought" (14, 29).

Philosophy thus now knows "no fixed sequence of question and answer." Its questions are shaped by experience, so as to "catch up with the experience" (63). It would be wrong to assimilate lines like these to some strong identity with American pragmatism, of the sort that marks Rorty's project. Adorno remains, in complex yet undeniable ways, a Marxist.[12] And thus the recognition of philosophy's necessary incoherence is not so much matter for celebration as for understanding. In other words, the kind of knowing that the familiarized subject lays claim to is a form of not knowing, or of denying an alternative knowledge.

How about the postmodern, and its apparently alternative replication of feminized positionalities? What does it mean to be free in response to a posited constraint, spontaneous in reaction to a perceived discipline, localized in the face of an attributed totalizing tendency? How can a critical feminism distinguish its place in this sea of traditionally feminized attributes? To endorse the values of mass culture or to collapse the distinction between elite and mass culture is, as Andreas Huyssen's work has shown, to endorse that which has previously been feminized.[13] There is a dialectic here, and I suggest that it appears in the exemplary articulations of the whole period of capitalist modernization. Hegel will do for one side of this dialectic of modernity (and parts of him would even do for the other side): the master-narrative, masculinized version of the inevitable subjectivity of and in history. But the other side was there too, and its mode of self-representation was commonly the literary as such, before high modernism sought to remasculinize a part of the literary for elite identification. The oscillation between the two, the operation of the dialectic, may indeed be claimed as the very engine of bourgeois experience, always *between* interest and disinterest, ideology and science, nomadism and a sense of place. Between, again, feminine and masculine. And the languages within which the eighteenth-century middle class recognized itself were heavily marked by both the appeal and the fear of feminized cultural roles. Literature, incrementally gravitating toward the domestic, feminized sphere, and away

12. Fredric Jameson's *Late Marxism: Adorno, or the Persistence of the Dialectic* (London and New York: Verso, 1990) attempts to adjust our focus to a poststructuralist component in Adorno's Marxism, which still "stands or falls with the concept of 'totality' " (9).
13. Andreas Huyssen, *After the Great Divide: Modernism, Mass Culture, Postmodernism* (Bloomington and Indianapolis: Indiana University Press, 1986), 44–62.

from the public sphere, has devised various ways of countering its subsumption (for instance its projection of anarchist-erotic energies in the likes of Blake and Shelley), but it has never definitively escaped from the web.

The eighteenth-century obsession with the feminization of culture and politics under capitalism is vividly apparent in the debates about commerce and luxury, about divided labor and surplus production, about the domestic and the colonialist economies—the debates within and alongside which the modern idea of literature was being defined. These debates had been ongoing in Western culture at least since Lycurgus wrote into the Spartan constitution a ban on commerce in the cause of preserving civic virtue. But various eighteenth-century commentators, faced with the social and political consequences of empire, capitalized agriculture, and imparkment, found themselves repeating the arguments with special conviction. As wealth came more and more from the colonies and the stock market, and as cultivation at home became more efficient, the defenders of a ruralist (and masculinist) political ideal became more and more defensive. Power was seen to be moving from country to city, and what came back to the country was the iconography of surplus wealth: parks and mansions occupied for half the year by stock market millionaires, feminized personalities.

The increased concentration of surplus wealth in the hands of an aristocracy and a burgeoning middle class was seen as replacing an economy of need (masculinist subsistence) by an economy of desire (feminized superfluity). Once we have met our needs, we are free to develop desires, and desire is infinite. William Paley can stand for many others as he observes that trade does not depend on need: it does not matter "how superfluous the articles which it furnishes are; whether the want of them be real or imaginary; whether it be founded in nature or in opinion, in fashion, habit, or emulation; it is enough that they be actually desires and sought after."[14] Whig economists such as Adam Smith thought that the luxury cycle (and all nonnecessities were defined as luxuries) would prove a creative stimulus for national wealth as well as a force for social bonding. Opponents predicted only the collapse of society itself. Luxury and desire together were the feminized components of social-economic life: unstable, unpredictable, superfluous, and experienced as constant process rather than as finished product. Smollett's Matthew Bramble saw unrestrained commerce as begetting "a spirit of licentiousness, insolence and faction, that keeps

14. William Paley, *The Principles of Moral and Political Philosophy*, 20th ed., 2 vols. (London, 1814), 2: 374.

the community in continual ferment, and in time destroys all the distinctions of civil society; so that universal anarchy and uproar must ensue." Visiting old friends in the English countryside, Bramble discovers and relates three instances of "female vanity" having impoverished previously functional estates, turning them from production to consumption and display, and thence to bankruptcy.[15] The feminization of credit and luxury, versions of the traditional feminization of *fortuna*, was a commonplace in eighteenth-century moral and political philosophy and political economy.[16]

This was the field of reference within which modern literature took on shape and cultural definition. And literature was commonly cast as itself a luxury. Books designated as "literature" were, after all, expensive items and required leisure for their consumption. The role of literature was in this way already feminized, and that feminization was further exacerbated by the extraordinary and much-discussed growth in the numbers of women writers and women readers. This situation brought about a visible tension between a masculinized literature, premissed on the classics, on Milton, and on epic poetry and seeking to limit its availability by difficulty and high seriousness, and a feminized mode imaged in the vernacular and in the novel and lyric poetry. This tension explains why the major Romantics were often so ambivalent about whether their work could or should have a common rather than a specialist reader. Rousseau, in one of his voices, made clear the relation between literature and national decline:

> A taste for letters, for philosophy and the fine arts, enervates both body and soul. A confinement to the closet makes men delicate, and weakens their constitution; and the soul preserves with difficulty its vigour when that of the body is lost.[17]

In other words, men become women when they develop a taste for literature.

The feminization of literature was not, of course, uncontested. Words-

15. Tobias Smollett, *Humphry Clinker*, ed. James L. Thorson (New York and London: Norton, 1983), 258, 271.

16. For extended treatments of this trope, see J. G. A. Pocock, *The Machiavellian Moment: Florentine Political Thought and the Atlantic Republican Tradition* (Princeton: Princeton University Press, 1975), especially 401–505; and John Sekora, *Luxury: The Concept in Western Thought, Eden to Smollett* (Baltimore: Johns Hopkins University Press, 1977).

17. Preface to *Narcissus, or the Self-Admirer*, in *The Miscellaneous Works of Mr. J. J. Rousseau*, 5 vols. (London, 1767), 2: 135. See also my *Romanticism, Nationalism, and the Revolt against Theory* (Chicago and London: University of Chicago Press, 1993), especially 126–71.

worth's famous outcries against popular novels and plays and high modernism's reaffirmation of sheer difficulty and massive intellectuality are just two instances of a masculinizing reaction. But the struggle has always occurred from within an already feminized general construction of the literary mode. Literary criticism, as an appendix or companion to literature, has experienced the same struggles. Its attempted diversions into theory have often been gestures of remasculinization, and have been resisted by an establishment whose lexicon is dominantly feminized: intuition, exceptionality, sympathy, empathy, lived experience, and so forth.[18] (This is one part of an explanation of the contested relation between feminism and theory as traditionally understood, though the mix is now rather different.)

These connections between luxury, literature, and the feminization of culture are not, I suggest, at all redundant for an analysis of the contemporary situation. Their dynamics are not categorically different from those adduced by theorists of the postmodern between political/aesthetic formations and the determinations of late capitalism. Junk bonds and simulacra may have replaced such terms as *commerce* and *desire*, but the moral concerns exist in the same sorts of connection with economic determinations. And we are still having the argument about what, within the large range of things called postmodern, is merely a reproduction of ideology and what is a critique of it. I have suggested that in its enthusiastic embrace of the priorities of the *literary* mode, the postmodern gesture may also be inheriting a culturally sanctioned ethic of imprecision (as antitotality, local knowledge, conversation, or whatever) that is a function rather than a critique of feminization. This raises the question of a role for critical feminism, as that which must by definition or aspiration set out to critique feminization.

It seems unlikely that any answer to this predicament is to be had in general. Feminism is not a unitary movement defined by commonly agreed methods. On the contrary, it is as riven with disagreement as is the larger culture in which it functions, and it seems certain that a yet wider array of choices would open up to anyone who knows more than I do about what lies outside the narrow Anglo-American context, or what remains relatively unknown within it. Feminisms do arguably have a common goal in the lib-

18. This is a more accurate summary of the British than of the American academy, where masculine or at least theoretical establishments have at least briefly been in place. But they have never been uncontested, and have never achieved an enduring hegemony, despite the more general acceptance of professional-technical methods in America than in Britain. In both cultures, theory itself now stands against masculinization. The question is for whom will it be feminist and for whom merely feminized.

eration or improvement of the lives of women: their telos is as much in action as in theory. And this activist priority has been seen as visibly and at least superficially at odds with the postmodern predilection for the aesthetic and the discursive as its proper spheres of attention.[19] But even within activist feminisms there are radical disagreements about what will produce positive change, about what is revolution and what is mere reproduction. The problems raised by the postmodern rhetoric will likely reappear, in other words, in every feminist initiative that seeks to theorize itself at any level, though they are likely to remain less obsessive outside the academy than in it. Similarly and reciprocally, the postmodern has replicated many of feminism's internal debates in its own efforts at self-definition.[20]

The long-durational model I have sketched out here might suggest that there are no separate histories for feminism(s) and for postmodernism(s). The rhetoric of academic self-definition functions with a strongly presentist and individualist emphasis. We set up "isms" and then go about the task of distinguishing them from other "isms," often on grounds that are improvisational rather than structural, and functions of competitive rather than historical categories. The exclusionary gestures still seem to come mostly from the men, it must be said, so that the syndrome of gendered disavowal Judith Newton saw in the New Historicists may also describe the more general postmodern debate. Harvey is quite innocent of feminist work, and Jameson accords it only a single albeit laudatory mention, without discussion (*Postmodernism*, 107). If disavowal is one side of the coin, the other may well be uncritical espousal of the feminized, masquerading as the feminist. Sabina Lovibond has issued a timely reminder that the same Nietzsche who is for many commentators the founding father of the ethical-methodological emphases of the postmodernists also made a clear association between the emancipation from reason and a desired extinction of feminism.[21] She has argued against a simple rejection of the Enlightenment and against any naive embrace of localism or of analysis merely within the "parish boundaries" (22).

A critical feminism, then, must search out a position within a culture

19. See, for instance, Linda Hutcheon, *The Politics of Postmodernism* (London and New York: Routledge, 1989), 168, who notes feminism's commitment to "real social change" and contrasts postmodernism's downplaying of "strategies of resistance."

20. See Steven Best and Douglas Kellner, *Postmodern Theory* (New York: Guilford Press, 1991), 205.

21. Sabina Lovibond, "Feminism and Postmodernism," *New Left Review* 178 (1989): 5–28. See especially 16–18.

of modernity still governed by a dialectic of masculinization and feminization. Given this, no simple assertion of spontaneity and empathy and no mere abdication of authority ought to be respected as by definition constructive. The methodological analogue is that no mere assertion of the repressive masculinity of totalities and grand theories is enough to constitute a real alternative. To repeat this language is just to repeat a traditional positionality: literary, feminized, against theory. To admit situatedness is not a solution, merely the beginning of the problem. Here is Gayatri Spivak making exactly this point:

> I have invoked my positionality in this awkward way so as to accentuate the fact that calling the place of the investigator into question remains a meaningless piety in many recent critiques of the sovereign subject. Thus, although I will attempt to foreground the precariousness of my position throughout, I know such gestures can never suffice.[22]

Not only does this not suffice, Spivak goes on to explain, it may actually inhibit and subsist as "an interested desire to conserve the subject of the West." The confession of pluralized subject-positions may serve to provide "a cover for this subject of knowledge" (271). This is no mere wordplay. For there is indeed a way in which the now monotonous reiteration of who one is and where one is coming from is accompanied by an almost audible sigh of relief, as if one is thereby exonerated from responsibility or culpability. If I speak only for and as myself, then I cannot go wrong, I do no damage. This gesture of authentication may be suspected on a number of grounds. When it functions to imply identity, then it displaces any encounter with the problems of poststructuralist theory; and when it implies recognition of the equality of all differences, then it mystifies, as Spivak aptly notices, the actual distinctions of power and opportunity distinguishing not only the "subject of the West" from others in the global sphere, but also the subject of the subculture from other subcultures. To propose situatedness as an alternative to theory is then to deprive ourselves of the one language through which situatedness itself might be understood. Situatedness above all things desperately requires theorization.

These paradoxes, and others like them, have led to some fairly sig-

22. Gayatri Chakravorty Spivak, "Can the Subaltern Speak?" in *Marxism and the Interpretation of Culture*, ed. Cary Nelson and Lawrence Grossberg (Urbana and Chicago: University of Illinois Press, 1988), 271.

nificant divisions among those who seek a place for feminisms within the postmodern. The more self-conscious critics are, like Spivak, very much aware of the pitfalls of embracing a postmodernity founded in inherited feminization. They see that it is not enough to preach the value of detail against theory, of emotion against reason, of "community" against society. Patricia Waugh has argued, following Lovibond, that "if feminism can learn from Postmodernism it has finally to resist the logic of its arguments or at least to attempt to combine them with a modified adherence to an epistemological anchorage in the discourses of Enlightened modernity."[23] Nancy Fraser, coming from the other direction, has supplemented Habermas's enlightened-modern project with its missing gender component, about which Habermas himself says "virtually nothing," and which significantly redefines the understanding of consumer and welfare culture that is to be gained from his work.[24]

The quest for an alliance between a critical feminism and a demystified postmodernism has thus been initiated. Lovibond looks forward to a "friendly relationship" (11), though she insists on a place for reckoning with false consciousness and with the traditions of Enlightenment modernism as components of her feminism (25–26, 28). Fraser and Nicholson have proposed a potential synthesis of a nonessentialist feminism with a postmodern theory that would produce a "pragmatic and fallibilistic" procedure based in alliances rather than in hypothetical unities and identities.[25] Others continue to stress the differences between what they see as feminism and as postmodernism. Waugh believes that feminism needs "coherent subjects" (125) in order to pursue an activist agenda, not least because women have never had them, have never been in control of the master subject whose viability is the object of the postmodern critique.

It seems to me that this debate might usefully be refigured within the long-durational perspective I have been advocating, and taken out of the oppositional moment of presentist perceptions. The crucial third term to be

23. Patricia Waugh, *Practising Postmodernism, Reading Modernism* (London: Edward Arnold, 1992), 120.

24. Nancy Fraser, "What's Critical about Critical Theory? The Case of Habermas and Gender," in *Feminism as Critique: On the Politics of Gender*, ed. Seyla Benhabib and Drucilla Cornell (Minneapolis: University of Minnesota Press, 1987), 31–56. The citation is from p. 32.

25. Nancy Fraser and Linda Nicholson, "Social Criticism without Philosophy: An Encounter between Feminism and Postmodernism," *Theory, Culture and Society* 5 (1988): 373–94. The citation is found on p. 391.

added to the discussion would then be that of *feminization*, which would be the important principle against which feminism would want to define itself. Some of what is called the postmodern would embody this feminization, while some other of its attributions might not. To recast the debate in this way would be to deconstruct, or at least to investigate, such recourses as Waugh's to a notion of "western *patriarchal* grand narratives" (128), whose disappearance would leave an untroubled space for the constitution of integrally feminine subjects. I have suggested that the feminine subject has not been excluded from the Enlightenment project so much as written in dialectically and subordinately and thus made available to both women and men (literary men, for instance) in various, culturally mediated ways. Inclusion is a much more efficient form of repression than exclusion in these instances.

A long-durational history might not prove to be the ultimate history for the postmodern or for critical feminism's place within or beside it. But it might at least toss the salad in some new way and ask different questions of those who are searching for definitions of what they do or detest. I would not want to suggest that there can in principle be nothing new about the postmodern. To do so would be to answer the reifications of presentism with those of historicism. But it is when the postmodern ethic emerges as piety, as the way to go, as affirmative, as celebration, that I find it most suspicious. I return to Adorno, who notes the ubiquity of "the idol of a pure present" as an "endeavor to strip thought of its historic dimension" (*Negative Dialectics*, 53). Politicians are obliged to use the rhetoric of solutions. For us, the "intellectuals," solutions are obliged to be processed through thought and tested by skepticism, not with the result of disavowing all solutions (though that too is a besetting academic strategy), but in hopes of enabling the better ones. Much of what is called postmodern theory looks like affirmation, or its fellow traveler, despair. Between the two, there is a place for a skepticism that is not alienation but engagement. Adorno again:

> Thought as such, before all particular contents, is an act of negation, of resistance to that which is forced upon it; this is what thought has inherited from its archetype, the relation between labor and material. Today, when ideologues tend more than ever to encourage thought to be positive, they cleverly note that positivity runs precisely counter to thought and that it takes friendly persuasion by social authority to accustom thought to positivity.

Thought, here, is critical action, "a revolt against being importuned to bow to every immediate thing" (19). If the schematic history I have here proposed is of any use, it will be because it *is* a history, not an immediate thing but a mediated tradition. And as such it is not readily available in the easeful, insouciant manner of so much of the New Historicism, nor reducible to that other postmodern commitment to contingent opportunism—to what is of use to us now, and to hand. This history has to be worked for and worked over. It does not determine either the possibility or the impossibility of a postmodern feminism that is not itself a version of the feminization of the postmodern. It simply asks us to think a little harder than usual about where we are coming from.

Feminism and the Politics of Postmodernism

Linda Nicholson

The discussion of the relation between feminism and postmodernism/poststructuralism has generated a surprising degree of intense feeling among feminists. In the United States, the only recent discussion that has exhibited the same degree of passion has been the sexuality debates, wherein the nature of the subject matter could account for at least part of the intensity. Why has this most academic of discussions generated so much intensity of feeling?

In this essay, I shall try to uncover some of the reasons for this passion, and I shall also attempt to resolve some of the conflicts. My initial focus will be on postmodernism, not poststructuralism, because the context of my own thinking is philosophy and social theory, wherein the term *postmodernism* is more frequently employed. The term *poststructuralism* is more commonly used by those working in the context of literary criticism and theory. There are other reasons, however, for my desire at least initially to phrase the encounter as one between feminism and postmodernism. As I shall argue later, there are certain problems within the historical legacy of poststructuralism that have contributed to skewing the discussion among feminists in nonhelpful ways.

Let me begin by elucidating the meaning I give to *postmodernism*. The term has been used in such a diverse way by so many, working in a variety of contexts, that it is necessary to clarify my own understanding of this term. I will also describe some of the reasons I found myself drawn to many of the positions that seemed to fall under this rubric.

Part of my attraction to the term *postmodernism* followed from its ability to bring together various positions I had adopted but had not previously perceived as connected. As a philosopher, I was attracted to Jean-François Lyotard's use of the term to signify a critique of foundationalism. Such a critique was certainly emerging within contemporary British and North American philosophy, most notably in the writings of Richard Rorty, but had not yet been given an identifying label. Lyotard, in *The Postmodern Condition*, provided that label.[1] While the specific philosophers Lyotard chose to pick out as most clearly representing a foundational perspective differed from those Rorty pointed to, the types of arguments being advanced seemed similar enough to warrant the use of a common identifying term. Thus, both writers saw as centrally problematic the requirement that philosophical claims be grounded in basic, or foundational, truths. On the basis of such truths, systematic accounts could then be constructed, whether that meant, in the case of a philosopher such as Descartes, an accounting of the validity of sense perception, or, in the case of Marx, an accounting of the motor force of history. Lyotard, Rorty, and, in some respects, Foucault suggested that a mode of doing philosophy that sought to identify certain basic truths and to build up grand explanatory systems around such truths was suspect.

Part of what was problematic about this mode of doing philosophy was its commitment to identifying that which was universal. Thus, writers such as Rorty and Lyotard pointed to the locality and historical specificity of that which in previous philosophy had been described as universal and as universally foundational. This aspect of their arguments greatly resonated with my own historicist leanings. These leanings—ironically, in regard to Lyotard's critique of Marxism—derived from my own previous identification with Marxism. It was, after all, Marx who so prominently railed against bourgeois theorists for their false claims to universality and for their inability

1. Jean-François Lyotard, *The Postmodern Condition*, trans. Geoff Bennington and Brian Massumi (Minneapolis: University of Minnesota Press, 1984). Rorty's position emerges clearly in many of his essays collected in *The Consequences of Pragmatism* (Minneapolis: University of Minnesota Press, 1982).

to understand the historical specificity of their own ideas. Marx's insistence that we understand the dominant ideas of a culture as rooted in the specific conditions of that culture had left a powerful impression upon my own thinking about the nature of philosophy and social theory. That impression related well to these more contemporary arguments about the locality of philosophical claims.

While I recognized my own attraction to the idea of historical specificity in philosophy and social theory as rooted in prior attachments to Marxism, I also had come to understand, with writers such as Lyotard and Baudrillard, that Marx's own theory was crucially ambiguous in regard to upholding this position.[2] Marx's theory endorsed the ideas of historical change and diversity with respect to many aspects of human life: familial structures, religious beliefs, economic organization, and the like. Framing this theory of change, however, was also an implicit commitment to certain universals and to the idea that certain categories could cross-culturally organize such diversity. Thus, for example, the category of production served for Marx in such a way, being used as a means to explain and to organize social life across cultures and throughout history.

Like many feminists, I had come to see that this focus on production within Marxism provided a crucial obstacle in Marxism's abilities to explain and to help remove many forms of women's oppression. In my book *Gender and History*, I noted how Marx, and many Marxists, equivocated in their use of the term *production*.[3] While theoretically the term referred to any activity conducive to human reproduction, Marxists most frequently understood it in accord with its predominant meaning in capitalist societies: as an activity taking place outside the home in the form of wage labor. Such a use situated oppression outside the home. Moreover, since the theory claimed to account for all aspects of social life, this use constructed Marxism as not only irrelevant to explaining important aspects of women's oppression but, indeed, as an obstacle in the attempt to develop such explanations.

What was interesting to me in this analysis of Marxism's inadequacies for feminism was that it was as a consequence of Marxism's reliance on a single category to explain social life across history and diverse cultures that it had become so politically oppressive. As I elaborated in *Gender and*

2. Lyotard, *The Postmodern Condition*; Jean Baudrillard, *The Mirror of Production*, trans. Mark Poster (St. Louis: Telos Press, 1975). See also Linda Nicholson, *Gender and History* (New York: Columbia University Press, 1986), chap. 6, 167–200.
3. Nicholson, *Gender and History*, 172–79.

History, it was Marxism's very failure to appreciate the rootedness of many of its own explanatory categories—such as the categories of production, labor, economy, and class—within the hegemonic value system and belief structure of its times that also made it politically oppressive for feminists. Moreover, similar arguments could be developed to describe the inadequacies of Marxism in relation to other social movements, such as movements against racism or movements of gays and lesbians. Here, too, the failure of Marxism to recognize the rootedness of many of its organizing categories in the context of a nineteenth-century, Western, European, industrial worldview could account for the limitations of the theory in contributing to such struggles.

This conclusion about the failures of Marxism meant that there might be something political involved in my allegiance to the idea that philosophy and social theory need to recognize the historical specificity of their own claims. And this suspicion became further confirmed in thinking about liberal theory in Western culture since the Enlightenment.

While it might be said that the nineteenth-century writings of Hegel and Marx represented an intensification of the idea of the importance of history in social theory, a certain turning to history can also be identified in the late seventeenth- and eighteenth-century writers of the Enlightenment. In the writings of Voltaire and Condorcet, for example, there was a strong notion of progress, of human ideas and social organization potentially changing so as to lead to greater happiness. Certainly the ideas of potential human change and perfectability had contributed to much of what might be described as emancipatory in liberal theory, to, for example, its ideas about human betterment and equality. If, however, one can say that in a writer such as Marx, a focus on historical change was mitigated by an implicit commitment to certain universals, this was even more strongly the case with those who constructed liberal social theory. For many of these writers, the existence of such ideals as truth and beauty, which possessed universal meaning, and the human faculty of reason, which provided the means to achieve these ideals, made progress possible.

Again, such liberal ideals certainly contributed to much of what I would today describe as emancipatory, as did Marx's categories make their own important contributions to goals I share. It is now possible, however, to identify some of the negative political consequences that also followed from liberalism as a worldview.

For one, because the meaning of such ideals as truth and beauty were conceptualized universally, that is ahistorically, history could be constructed in evolutionary terms, with some societies being described as more "primitive" in their attainment of such ideals. Philosophical universalism contributed to the type of cultural arrogance that helped legitimize the colonialism of eighteenth-, nineteenth-, and twentieth-century Europe and North America. In this context, the emergence of cultural relativism within anthropological theory in the early twentieth century, as evidenced in the writings of such figures as Malinowski and Mead, must be interpreted as at least in part a political reaction against such arrogance.

Moreover, such arrogance was not confined to the ways in which Western Europeans and North Americans treated others outside their societies. During the course of the nineteenth and twentieth centuries, as science increasingly came to be viewed as the sole bearer of truth, those who spoke in the name of science came to possess the kind of power that permitted their own visions of the good life to become hegemonic. Thus, doctors could appeal to science in order to legitimize the elimination of midwives and practitioners of herbal arts from the domain of medicine. Throughout that century, and into the twentieth century, certain legitimization of social inequality rested upon the view that some, and not others, followed correct standards of morality, attained truth through education, and employed the right criteria in making aesthetic judgments. In short, the ideals of the good, the true, and the beautiful had a lot to account for.

Any accounting must, however, also include reference to that faculty that was attributed the ability to attain such ideals—specifically, reason. Enough has been written about the uses and abuses of reason within modernity to make me wary of saying more here. It is sufficient in this context to underline the many battles feminists have had to engage in with the idea of this faculty during the course of feminism's history. Such battles include those struggles engaged in by eighteenth- and nineteenth-century women whose social class might otherwise have provided them with education except for the description of reason as male. More relevant for contemporary feminists are the ways in which a more recent description of reason as without gender, race, class, or any cultural attribute precludes recognition of the ways in which contemporary education still serves distinct gendered, racial, class, and other dominant group aims. Thus, it is reason's accomplice, "objectivity," that continues to serve as a principal weapon in the ongoing struggle to limit the influence of women's studies, black studies, gay and lesbian studies, and the like in the academy.

Again, however, I saw the philosophical writings of many of those who could be described as postmodern adding to the discreditation of such aspects of the heritage of liberalism. Some of the contributions replicate themes that have been part of much twentieth-century critical theory. Thus, Lyotard's attack on the dominance of instrumental reason replicated ideas put forth earlier in the century by writers such as Horkheimer, Marcuse, and the early Habermas. Similarly, Foucault's analyses of the powers of science in organizing and constructing bodies and their pleasures during the course of modernity paralleled ideas put forth by others in the twentieth century but also extended such ideas in new directions. What I identified as one of the distinctive contributions of "the postmodern turn" was its direct assault on the idea of universal criteria of judgment. This seemed to take historicism in new and important directions.[4]

The historicism I earlier identified as one of the important legacies of Marx's writings has received support from many forms of intellectual discourse during the twentieth century: from Karl Mannheim's construction of "the sociology of knowledge" to later work by philosophers of science on the value- and theory-laden aspects of scientific inquiry. Some British and North American philosophers sought to prevent such claims from contesting the idea of universality in regard to truth by insisting on a distinction between what was labeled "the context of discovery" and "the context of justification." While it had become increasingly difficult to deny the importance of historical context in affecting the creation of hypotheses and ideas, surely history could be judged irrelevant in assessing the truth of such ideas.

For me, one powerful aspect of postmodernism in philosophy was the questioning of this distinction. The counterposition here was that history not only provides us with the context to understand the emergence of specific claims to knowledge but also supplies us with the context to understand the emergence of the criteria by which such claims are evaluated. Thus, both in Rorty's rejection of Truth with a capital *T* for truth with a small *t* and in Lyotard's insistence on the locality, plurality, and immanence of procedures of legitimation, I perceived crucial means for undermining the context of discovery/context of justification distinction.[5] It had become increasingly apparent to me that the hope of attaining universal criteria of justification,

4. See Steven Seidman, "Postmodern Social Theory as Narrative with a Moral Intent," in Steven Seidman and David Wagner, eds., *Postmodernism and Social Theory* (New York: Basil Blackwell, 1992), 47–81.

5. To be sure, these positions can be linked to earlier claims in the philosophy of science, to those of Feyerabend, for example. Rorty and Lyotard seemed to represent an important extension of Feyerabend by taking the discussion beyond that of science to the more general topic of truth.

whether that be in regard to truth, beauty, or standards of morality, was an unachievable goal. Those attempts that had been made in the history of philosophy to provide such criteria—for example, those of Kant—most often suffered from the liabilities noteworthy in his theory of morality: Such criteria either were so general as to provide inadequate assistance in resolving particular conflicts or, by their specificity, they revealed an inadequacy as universal criteria. Rather, it seemed that the only function the belief in the possibility of such criteria served was a political one, providing existing claimants to truth, beauty, or justice with the unwarranted premise that their assertions rested upon such a foundational base.

Moreover, my perception of such political aspects of foundationalism seemed also strengthened through the explicit, postmodern identification of knowledge judgments with power. To be sure, this move had its antecedents in prior intellectual/theoretical movements. Thus, feminists, with other political activists, had begun to question not only the claims to objectivity made within the academy, the media, and the publishing industry but also the feasibility of objectivity as a normative ideal. Such activists had also come to extend the terrain of power from the state to all institutions of ordinary life, including those involved in the production of knowledge. These insights had led to the intuition that claims to knowledge represent a form of power. One of Foucault's contributions was a theoretical elaboration for such intuitions.

In sum, I saw the arguments of postmodernists to be politically useful for feminists in a variety of ways. They enabled feminists to counteract the totalizing perspectives within both the hegemonic culture of liberalism and within certain versions of Marxism. When liberals or Marxists argued that their visions of the good life and models of explanation were those around which feminists should subordinate their claims, feminists now had useful philosophical weapons with which to respond. Postmodernism undermined the theoretical arrogance of these two political perspectives by showing that the foundations upon which each rested were themselves without ultimate justification and, like any other worldview, could be judged only within the context of historically specific values. From the perspective of values integral to much of contemporary feminism, each could be judged useful in some respects, but each could also be shown to be limited.

It was, however, not only the theoretical arrogance of liberalism and Marxism for which I saw postmodernism as a useful antidote. Such arrogance seemed also to be present in certain aspects of feminist theory itself. The manifestations of such arrogance were more subtle than in other political theories of modernity. Thus, only sometimes did feminists claim that their theories were about the nature of human society as a whole or about that which was true for all of human history. But, particularly in the early days of feminist theory, many accounts that aimed for explanations of male/female relations across large sweeps of history were proposed.[6] Moreover, and this is a tendency that continues, many feminist writings have included statements containing terms such as *man*, *woman*, *sex*, *sexism*, *rape*, *body*, *nature*, *mothering* without any historical or societal qualifiers attached. The claims containing such terms have often been meant to refer to large sweeps of history, and the terms themselves have been understood as possessing similar meanings throughout this history. Invariably, however, the meanings attached to such terms have reflected the meanings these terms possess in contemporary Western culture, particularly among dominant social groups. Thus, even when no explicit theory was being proposed, such writings often contained implicit theories. Both such explicit and implicit theories, by their ethnocentrism and by their disregard for differences across history and cultures, seemed to involve significant chunks of feminist writings in the kind of theoretical arrogance present in both liberal and Marxist social theory.

Of course, such arrogance has also been strongly mitigated by the continual admonishments from feminist anthropologists, feminist historians, and socialist feminists to acknowledge historical diversity. It has also been strongly mitigated by those political currents within feminism that have demanded the recognition of diversity among women with regard to race, ethnicity, sexual orientation, class, and so on. To all of these countertendencies, I saw postmodernist, philosophical writings as constituting one additional resource.

In sum, postmodernism appeared to me an important movement for helping feminists uncover that which was theoretically problematic in much modern political and social theory. Postmodernism was also useful in helping feminism eradicate those elements within itself that prevented an adequate theorization of differences among women. This did not mean that feminists should accept everything written by those who were described as postmodern. As Nancy Fraser and I argue in "Social Criticism without Philosophy," it was necessary for feminists to read such writings critically,

6. Nancy Fraser and Linda Nicholson, "Social Criticism without Philosophy: An Encounter between Feminism and Postmodernism," in *Feminism/Postmodernism*, ed. Linda Nicholson (New York: Routledge, 1990), 19–38.

to accept what was useful from a feminist perspective, and to reject that which was incompatible with feminist purposes.[7]

What I soon encountered, however, was a much greater lack of consensus among feminists on this issue than I would have guessed. Certainly, I found many who were thinking along similar lines as I was. On the other hand, I also found not only disagreement but disagreement with strong feelings attached. In the remainder of this essay, I would like to summarize some of what I regard as the most philosophically sophisticated of these objections. I would also like to suggest ways to resolve some of the strains between postmodern feminists and their feminist critics.

The Argument against Feminism as Negativity and Feminism as Nominalism

Within feminist discussions, the term *postmodernism* is often used interchangeably with *poststructuralism*. It is, however, more frequently the latter term that is the specific focus of the feminist attack. Thus, I would now like to examine some of the best of these attacks and raise questions about their applicability to postmodernism and, specifically, to the type of position I have elaborated above.

One of the most interesting critiques of feminist poststructuralism is provided by Linda Alcoff. Alcoff argues that Derrida's articulation of deconstruction involves the uncovering of what is most frequently understood as a binary opposition between such terms as *man/woman*, *subject/object*, and *culture/nature*, in which one side has been constituted as superior to the other. Undermining the dominating power of the superior term involves rejecting the organizing system in which such oppositions are constituted: for Derrida, logocentrism. In this context, *woman* becomes constructed as the rupture of, the absolute negation of, logocentrism. As Alcoff points out, however, this leaves feminism unable to articulate anything positive or substantive in the idea of *woman* and, thus, unable to assert itself as a political project with any positive meaning:

> For Derrida, women have always been defined as a subjugated difference within a binary opposition: man/woman, culture/nature, positive/negative, analytic/intuitive. To assert an essential gender difference as cultural feminists do is to reinvoke this oppositional

7. Fraser and Nicholson, "Social Criticism without Philosophy," 19–26.

> structure. The only way to break out of this structure, and in fact to subvert the structure itself, is to assert total difference, to be that which cannot be pinned down or subjugated within a dichotomous hierarchy. Paradoxically, it is to be what is not. Thus feminists cannot demarcate a definitive category of "woman" without eliminating all possibility for the defeat of logocentrism and its oppressive power. . . . Following Foucault and Derrida, an effective feminism could only be a wholly negative feminism, deconstructing everything and refusing to construct anything.[8]

A variation of Linda Alcoff's argument is made by Susan Bordo. Bordo claims that the poststructuralist ideals of endless movement, of endless possibilities of interpretation and perspective, leave the feminist reader or activist without a place to stand:

> I have no dispute with this epistemological critique or with the metaphor of the world-as-text as a means of undermining various claims to authoritative, transcendent insight into the nature of reality. The question remains, however, how the human knower is to negotiate this infinitely perspectival, destabilized world. Deconstructionism answers with constant vigilant suspicion of all determinate readings of culture and a partner aesthetic of ceaseless textual play as an alternative ideal. Here is where deconstruction may slip into its own fantasy of escape from human locatedness—by supposing that the critic can become wholly protean by adopting endlessly shifting, seemingly inexhaustible vantage points, none of which are "owned" by either the critic or the author of a text under examination.[9]

Moreover, according to Bordo, when deconstructionism turns its focus to the issue of differences among women, the consequence is a theoretical perspective that allows no room for generalizations of any kind. We are left with a type of theoretical nominalism, a methodological position surely inadequate to feminism's political needs.

How am I, as a feminist who sees the important philosophical benefits the postmodern position contributes to feminism, to answer these important and persuasively articulated arguments? My response is to distinguish

8. Linda Alcoff, "Cultural Feminism versus Poststructuralism: The Identity Crisis in Feminist Theory," *Signs* 13, no. 3 (1988): 417–18.

9. Susan Bordo, "Feminism, Postmodernism, and Gender-Skepticism," in *Feminism/Postmodernism*, 142.

such a reading of poststructuralism from many of the positions I have described as postmodern. One of the reasons I am able to make this distinction is that the philosophical positions I had described earlier as postmodern are highly compatible with a very different theory of language than the one attributed here to poststructuralism.[10] Rather, the theory of language I see as harmonious with the type of postmodernism previously articulated is one that stems from the writings of the later Wittgenstein and that is congruous, in many respects, with the American philosophical tradition of pragmatism.

To elaborate this position, I would like to draw on an essay by Nancy Fraser, in which she makes a distinction between two models of theorizing language that have emerged in France: a structuralist model that studies language as a symbolic system, and a pragmatic model that studies language as a set of historically situated practices. The former model lends itself to what she describes as "symbolicism"—that is, the tendency to homogenize and reify the diversity and historical variety of language practices into a monolithic and all-pervasive symbolic order and to set such an order apart from human action and context. Because such a model abstracts the issue of language from practice and context, it proves unable to satisfy a variety of feminist political needs. As Fraser argues, a pragmatic model whose theory of language is focused on discourses, not structures, and that understands the latter as concrete, historically situated practices, is preferable. Such a model provides the following advantages for feminist politics:

> First, it treats discourses as contingent, positing that they arise, alter and disappear over time. Thus, the model lends itself to historical contextualization; and it allows us to thematize change. Second, the pragmatic approach understands signification as action rather than as representation. It is concerned with how people "do things with words." Thus, the model allows us to see speaking subjects not simply as effects of structures and systems, but rather as socially situated agents. Third, the pragmatic model treats discourses in the plural. It starts from the assumption that there are a plurality of different discourses in society, therefore a plurality of communicative sites from which to speak. Because it posits that individuals assume different discursive positions as they move from one discursive frame

10. And to Derrida, in particular. Even if the argument is put forth that this represents a problematic reading of Derrida, the issue remains over the stance one should take toward such a position.

> to another, this model lends itself to a theorization of social identities as non-monolithic. Next, the pragmatic approach rejects the assumption that the totality of social meanings in circulation constitutes a single, coherent, self-reproducing "symbolic system." Instead, it allows for conflicts among social schemas of interpretation and among the agents who deploy them. Finally, because it links the study of discourses to the study of society, the pragmatic approach allows us to focus on power and inequality.[11]

Fraser claims that the problems of a structuralist model are not limited to structuralists per se. Rather, they can be found in at least some of those writers who, while claiming a distance from structuralism, in many respects, embody it. For example, Fraser points to Lacan and argues that insofar as he posits a fixed, monolithic symbolic system and differentiates identities in binary terms (i.e., in relation to the possession or lack of the phallus), the "symbolicism" that is a feature of structuralism is also a feature of his own writings. Fraser notes similar tendencies in the writings of Kristeva.

It seems easy, however, to generalize many of Fraser's arguments to the above construction of poststructuralism. The concept of "logocentrism" so posited also construes language as a monolithic symbolic system. In such a context, the operation of male domination within language becomes an all or nothing affair: One either participates in it or one rebels against it in the limited, negative ways that Alcoff and Bordo describe. In neither case is an opening provided for the study of the very specific forms in which sexism is differently embodied in different languages, for examination of the historical shifts in sexism within any one language over time, or for analysis of the relation between such specific manifestations of sexism within language and the operation of sexism in other practices. Because language itself is identified with oppression, resistance to oppression can only be formulated as antilanguage. We are left with no cues on "how to do things with words" in the fight against sexism.

The question thus becomes: What is a postmodern approach to language that avoids the essentialist arrogance of much modernist, and some feminist, discourse but that also does not reduce feminism to silence or to a purely negative stance? The answer, I claim, is a discourse that recognizes

11. Nancy Fraser, "The Uses and Abuses of French Discourse Theories for Feminist Politics," in *Revaluing French Feminism*, ed. Nancy Fraser and Sandra Bartky (Bloomington: Indiana University Press, 1992), 177–94.

itself as historically situated, as motivated by values and, thus, political interests, and as a human practice without transcendent justification.

To elaborate this position, let me begin by clarifying what I mean by a discourse that recognizes itself as historically situated. In "Social Criticism without Philosophy," Nancy Fraser and I distinguish between feminist appeals to categories such as *mothering, sexuality*, and *reproduction* and feminist use of a category such as *the modern, restricted, male-headed, nuclear family*.[12] Whereas the latter category explicitly situates itself within a particular time period, the former categories, because of their implicit associations with biological functions, convey the possibility of a transhistorical reference. Moreover, the explicit historicity of a category such as *the modern, restricted, male-headed, nuclear family* suggests further questioning about the range of its applicability, about, for example, the geographical region to which it can be applied, the range of subgroups within that region to which it is applicable, and so on. On the other hand, with categories such as *sexuality* and *mothering*, we are much less likely to raise such questions, again because of widespread assumptions that these categories describe something "natural" and, thus, endemic to human society per se. In sum, because a category such as *the modern, restricted, male-headed, nuclear family* already presents itself as framed within a certain time period, it is easier to raise questions about the validity of this temporal frame, as well as about the need to apply other frames, than with categories that present themselves as without frames of any sort.

In response, it might be argued that the distinction Fraser and I make is too vague to provide adequate direction. What does it mean to differentiate "correct" framing from framing that is still subject to the charge of essentialism? While terms such as *mothering* or *sexuality* are more liable to the dangers of transhistorical projection than others, terms that carry fewer biological associations, such as *domestic* and *public*, have been accused of being used in essentialist ways.[13] Moreover, since the possibility of overgeneralization always exists, a feminist who wishes to avoid the charge of essentialism would seem to be reduced to nominalism, to describing particular events at particular points in time. This point is made by Susan Bordo, who argues that this type of methodological demand threatens to destroy the political organizing categories of race and class, as well as those of gender:

12. Fraser and Nicholson, "Social Criticism without Philosophy," 34.

13. Michelle Zimbalist Rosaldo, "The Use and Abuse of Anthropology: Reflections on Feminism and Cross-Cultural Understanding," *Signs* 5, no. 3 (1980): 389–417.

> For (although race, class, and gender are privileged by current intellectual convention), the inflections that modify experience are endless, and *some* item of difference can always be produced which will shatter any proposed generalizations. If generalization is only permitted in the *absence* of multiple inflections or interpretive possibilities, then cultural generalizations of *any* sort—about race, about class, about historical eras—are ruled out. What remains is a universe composed entirely of counterexamples, in which the way men and women see the world is purely as *particular* individuals, shaped by the unique configurations that form that particularity.[14]

My response is to admit that, certainly, there are no rules that can be invoked to diffuse the possibility of essentialism. That does not, however, negate the importance of an attitude, a sensitivity, a continual recognition of the dangers of historical projection, and an awareness that such dangers directly increase with the generality of one's claims. Thus, such an attitude does not entail limiting oneself to descriptions of particular phenomena at particular points in time; it entails, rather, continuously weighing the political reasons for specific generalizations against the degree to which such generalizations risk these dangers. Moreover, as there are no rules for indicating where qualification needs to stop, so also are there no rules to differentiate stopping points that are important from those that are not. Here, too, the needs of the historically specific situation must set the frame for decision making. These last points invoke the second of what I described as crucial elements of a postmodern discourse: that it recognize itself as political. One problem with Bordo's objection is that its conceptualization of discourse is still embedded in an objectivist framework: Either there are rules for distinguishing the important qualification from the unimportant qualification, or all qualifications are equally important. Of course, theoretically, all qualifications can *become* important. If, however, we think of discourse as a human practice carried out in the service of historically specific purposes, then it becomes easier to understand both the necessity for being attentive to the qualifications we are making, or failing to make, and also that there can be no rules for guiding such attentiveness. As Fraser and I note, a major problem with feminist uses of categories such as *mothering, sexuality*, and *reproduction* is that such uses project the meanings these activities hold for contemporary Western, white, middle-class women onto the lives of women

14. Bordo, "Feminism, Postmodernism, and Gender-Skepticism," 150–51.

of different classes, cultural backgrounds, and historical periods.[15] A point of our argument is to awaken sensitivity to the ways in which even feminist language can be implicated in the processes of cultural domination. This does not, however, mean that once such a sensitivity is awakened there are simple measures available to prevent such dominance from reappearing in even a qualified discourse. If we recognize discourse as guided by historically and culturally specific purposes, all categories will bear some marks of the needs of their creators. We can only mitigate the political dangers of this feature of discourse by becoming aware of those forms in which its ability to oppress is more likely to occur than in others.[16] Finally, our best safeguard may ultimately lie not with the kinds of discourse we rule acceptable or not but with the more practical issue of who is able to take part in discourse—that is, with the question of access "to the means of communication."[17]

This model of discourse is, however, also subject to critique from a different direction. In describing discourse as political and as shaped by the historically specific needs of its diverse participants, I can imagine some will claim that I have reduced the issue of truth to the issue of power. Discourse, as I have described it, is merely a power struggle, with no criteria available to rule against offensive positions. Thus, such a model of discourse allows for no distinction between reason and power and rests upon a theory of truth that is thoroughly relativistic.

Again, the force of this type of objection largely follows from the continued power of a representational model to shape our thinking. When one conceptualizes discourse not as representational but as a process of human interaction, such objections lose much of their strength.

For one, to say that the process of deciding which categories to employ or how thoroughly qualified our categories need to be is a political decision, shaped by historically specific needs and purposes, is not to deny the simultaneous presence of rules of discourse that are, at least in some cases, also adhered to by those of opposing purposes and needs. Such rules will vary both in terms of their historical specificity and in relation to the range of discourses they govern. Thus, we might differentiate the rule of noncontradiction from the rules governing most academic discourses in the late twentieth century, as well as from those governing specific disciplines.

15. Fraser and Nicholson, "Social Criticism without Philosophy," 31, 33.

16. For further elaboration of this point, see Steven Seidman, "The End of Sociological Theory: The Postmodern Hope," *Sociological Theory* 9, no. 2 (1991): 131–57.

17. For a helpful discussion of this issue, see Nancy Fraser, *Unruly Practices* (Minneapolis: University of Minnesota Press, 1989), chap. 8, 161–87.

Such rules do much to organize discourse in contexts of contestation. To be sure, such rules may themselves become the subject of contestation; or, it may be the case that in any particular discursive conflict, there may be no rule readily available to arbitrate the conflict. The degree to which such real-life situations present themselves, however, seems unrelated to any philosophical pronouncement I, or anyone else, might make. In other words, to say that discursive conflict may, indeed, sometimes be political—that is, not resolvable through appeal to intersubjectively agreed upon rules—is to make a claim whose validity appears independent of anything philosophers might say about the strength or weakness of relativism as a philosophical position.

This last point underlines one of the most important features of the model of discourse I am here endorsing: that discourse be construed as a process of human interaction and not as a structure susceptible to abstract formalization. It is only by construing discourse in structural terms that one is inclined to speak of the existence or nonexistence of criteria of legitimation or procedural rules that transcend specific localities. Any claim, however, that rejects such criteria, or rules, seems also to imply relativism. But if one conceptualizes discourse not as a structure but as a process of interaction, the issue of relativism must take on a different meaning. Most importantly, if one perceives discourse as a communicative process, then the absence of rules mitigating communicative breakdown emerges as a life possibility rather than as a position to be endorsed or not. As a life possibility, the question of whether it is resolvable in any given instance appears obviously an open one—that is, not a question for which one can provide an absolute answer. Finally, then, to think about discourse as a communicative process is not to endorse or reject relativism but to reconceptualize relativism as communicative breakdown, a real-life possibility whose outcome can never be stipulated in advance.

• • • •

If there are any common threads in the above, they can be summarized in my view that postmodernism represents not so much a set of discursive rules different from those found in modernism as a different type of approach to such issues as discourse, knowledge, truth, and validity. First, postmodernism can be characterized by the rejection of epistemic arrogance for an endorsement of epistemic humility. Such humility entails a recognition that our ways of viewing the world are mediated by the contexts out of which we operate. This means that not only are our specific beliefs and emotions about the world a product of our historical circumstances but so are the means by which we come to those beliefs and emotions and by which we resolve conflict when dissent is present. This does not entail the position that there are no solutions to epistemic dilemmas, merely that there are no final ones.

Moreover, the kind of postmodernism I am endorsing here represents a reconceptualization of discourse from that of a structure to that of a process of interaction. Such a reconceptualization brings with it a blurring of the lines that have previously divided issues concerning the criteria for arbitrating claims of truth and falsity from issues concerning the contexts by which such criteria are established. Thus, questions concerning access to discourse, both in relation to issues of substance and in relation to how such issues get to be talked about, take their place beside questions of truth and validity. For me, then, what postmodernism adds to feminism is an expansion of the widely held feminist dictum "The personal is political" to include the dictum "The epistemic is political," as well.

Ambiguity and Alienation in *The Second Sex*

Toril Moi

Divided, torn, disadvantaged: for women the stakes are higher; there are more victories and more defeats for them than for men.
—Simone de Beauvoir, *The Force of Circumstance* (translation amended)

Preliminary Note

The article that follows is an excerpt from a much longer discussion of alienation and the body in *The Second Sex*, taken from chapter 6 of my forthcoming book on Simone de Beauvoir.[1] The excerpt printed here is preceded by a discussion of the relationship between *The Second Sex* and *The*

1. Page references to frequently quoted texts by Beauvoir appear in parentheses in the text and notes. I use the following abbreviations: *SS* = *The Second Sex*, trans. H. M. Parshley (Harmondsworth: Penguin, 1984); *DSa* = *Le Deuxième Sexe*, Coll. Folio, vol. 1 (Paris: Gallimard, 1949); *DSb* = *Le Deuxième Sexe*, vol. 2; *FC* = *The Force of Circumstance*, trans. Richard Howard (Harmondsworth: Penguin, 1987); *FCa* = *La Force des choses*, Coll. Folio, vol. 1 (Paris: Gallimard, 1963); *FCb* = *La Force des choses*, vol. 2; TA = Translation Amended. I provide references to the English translation first, followed by references to the French original.

Ethics of Ambiguity, and by an analysis of the rhetoric—the language—of philosophy in *The Second Sex*. It is followed by a detailed study of Beauvoir's analysis of female desire. Drawing these threads together, the chapter concludes by examining the philosophical implications of Beauvoir's analysis of what I like to call *patriarchal femininity*. One of my conclusions in this chapter is that Beauvoir actually succeeds in dismantling the patriarchal paradigm of universal masculinity in philosophy. I am afraid that the excerpt published here only forms one of the steps on the way to that conclusion. I nevertheless hope that it can be read on its own as a close textual analysis of the concept of alienation in Beauvoir's theory. As this excerpt makes clear, this concept is bound up with the idea of the body: it is imperative to integrate any discussion of alienation with an exploration of Beauvoir's understanding of the body. I should perhaps also say that in my own readings of Beauvoir I try to produce a dialectical understanding of her contradictions and ambiguities. It follows that I don't consider every contradiction to be unproductive. It also follows that any single concept, such as that of alienation, should be examined in its interaction with other crucial concepts in Beauvoir's texts. This is why Beauvoir's account of female sexuality—or female psychosexual development—should not be taken to represent the whole of her analysis of women's oppression. In order to grasp the political implications of her epochal essay, it is also necessary to explore the strength and limitations of her understanding of freedom. That is the task I try to carry out in chapter 7 of my book.

Ambiguity

In *The Ethics of Ambiguity* (1947) Beauvoir presents a general philosophy of existence.[2] Her fundamental assumptions in this book also form the starting point for her next essay, *The Second Sex* (1949). According to Beauvoir's 1947 essay, men and women share the same human condition. We are all split, all threatened by the "fall" into immanence, and we are all mortal. In this sense, no human being ever coincides with him- or herself: we are all lack of being. In order to escape from the tension and anguish (*angoisse*) of this ambiguity, we may all be tempted to take refuge in the havens of bad faith. Starting where *The Ethics of Ambiguity* ends,

2. Simone de Beauvoir, *The Ethics of Ambiguity*, trans. Bernard Frechtman (New York: Citadel Press, 1976). *Pour une morale de l'ambiguïte*, Coll. Idées (Paris: Gallimard, 1947).

The Second Sex launches its inquiry into women's condition by focusing on the question of difference:

> Now, what specifically defines the situation of woman is that she—a free and autonomous being like all human creatures—nevertheless discovers and chooses herself in a world where men compel her to assume the status of the Other.[3] They propose to turn her into an object and to doom her to immanence since her transcendence is for ever to be transcended by another consciousness which is essential and sovereign. The drama of woman lies in this conflict between the fundamental aspirations of every subject—which always posits itself as essential—and the demands of a situation which constitutes her as inessential. (*SS*, 29; *DSa*, 31; TA)

This is perhaps the single most important passage in *The Second Sex*, above all because Beauvoir here poses a radically new theory of sexual difference. While we are all split and ambiguous, she argues, women are *more* split and ambiguous than men. For Simone de Beauvoir, then, women are fundamentally characterized by *ambiguity* and *conflict*. The specific contradiction of women's situation is caused by the conflict between their status as free and autonomous human beings and the fact that they are socialized in a world in which men consistently cast them as Other to their One, as objects to their subjects. The effect is to produce women as subjects painfully torn between freedom and alienation, transcendence and immanence, subject-being and object-being. This fundamental contradiction, or split, in which the general ontological ambiguity of human beings is repeated and reinforced by the social pressures brought to bear on women, is *specific to women under patriarchy*. For Beauvoir, at least initially, there is nothing ahistorical about this: when oppressive power relations cease to exist, women will be no more split and contradictory than men. As I will go on to show, however, Beauvoir's analysis implies that while the major contradictions of women's situation may disappear, women will in fact always remain somewhat more ambiguous than men.

Again Beauvoir's theory is clearly metaphorical: the social oppression of women, she implies, *mirrors* or *repeats* the ontological ambiguity of existence.[4] Paradoxically enough, on this point Beauvoir's analysis gains in

3. In this crucial spot, the Folio edition reads "s'assumer *contre* l'Autre" (*DSa*, 31). Introducing a wholly erroneous idea of opposition, this misprint may give rise to many misunderstandings. Fortunately, the original *édition Blanche* correctly prints "s'assumer *comme* l'Autre" (31).

4. At this point, one may well ask why it is not the other way around: could one not

potential strength from its metaphorical structure: it is precisely the absence of any purely logical link between the two levels of analysis that leaves us free to reject the one without having to deny the other as well. In this way, Beauvoir's careful account of women torn between freedom and alienation under patriarchy may well be experienced as convincing, even by readers radically at odds with Sartre's theory of consciousness.

The oppression of women, Beauvoir argues, is in some ways similar to the oppression of other social groups, such as that of Jews or American blacks. Members of such groups are also treated as objects by members of the ruling caste or race. Yet women's situation remains fundamentally different, above all because women are scattered across *all* social groups and thus have been unable to form a society of their own: "The bond that unites her to her oppressors is not comparable to any other," Beauvoir insists (*SS*, 19; *DSa*, 19).[5] The effect of this social situation is that women tend to feel solidarity with men in their own social group rather than with women in general. This is why, unlike every other oppressed group, women have been unable to cast themselves as historical subjects opposing their oppressors: under patriarchy, there are no female ghettos, no female compounds in which to organize a collective uprising: "Women," Beauvoir writes in 1949, "do not say 'We' . . . they do not authentically posit themselves as Subject" (*SS*, 19; *DSa*, 19). The specificity of women's oppression consists precisely in the absence of a female collectivity capable of perceiving itself as a historical subject opposed to other social groups. This is why no other oppressed group experiences the same kind of contradiction between freedom and alienation. Beauvoir, in other words, is not interested in producing a competitive hierarchy of oppression. Her point is not that women necessarily are *more*, or *more painfully*, oppressed than every other group but simply that the oppression of women is a highly specific *kind* of oppression.

argue that the ontological ambiguity mirrors the social conditions of existence? Taking ontology—the general theory of human freedom—as the starting point for her analysis, Beauvoir herself would clearly not condone such a reversal. Given what I call elsewhere the metaphorical structure of her argument—the fact that she never spells out the exact relationship between the two levels of the argument—nothing prevents the reader from preferring such a reading to that of Beauvoir herself.

5. To argue, as Elisabeth Spelman does in her *Inessential Woman*, that Beauvoir's comparison of women with blacks and Jews is sexist because it implies that Beauvoir excludes the existence of black and Jewish women from her categories is to make the mistake of taking a statement about *oppression* (that is, about power relations) for a statement about *identity*. What Beauvoir is saying is that the relationship of men to women may, in some ways (not all), be seen as homologous to that of whites to blacks, anti-Semites to Jews, bourgeoisie to working class. In such a statement there is absolutely no implication

Rich and varied, Beauvoir's own vocabulary of ambiguity and conflict ranges from ambivalence, distance, divorce, and split to alienation, contradiction, and mutilation. But every ambiguity is not negative: as readers of *The Second Sex*, we must not make the paradoxical mistake of taking the value of ambiguity to be given once and for all. For Beauvoir, the word *ambiguous* often means "dialectical" and describes a fundamental contradiction underpinning an apparently stable and coherent phenomenon. In *The Second Sex*, every conflict is potentially both productive and destructive: in some cases, one aspect wins out; in others, the tension remains unresolved. The advantage of Beauvoir's position is that it enables her to draw up a highly complex map of women's situation in the world, one that is never blind to the way in which women occasionally reap paradoxical advantages from their very powerlessness. As a whole, however, *The Second Sex* amply demonstrates that such spurious spin-offs remain precarious and unpredictable: for Beauvoir, the effects of sexism are overwhelmingly destructive for men as well as for women.

Every one of the descriptions of women's "lived experience" in *The Second Sex* serves to reinforce Beauvoir's theory of the fundamental contradiction of women's situation. Unfortunately, the sheer mass of material makes it impossible to discuss the whole range of her analyses: her brilliant account of the antinomies of housework, or the absolutely stunning defense of abortion rights (see the chapters entitled "The Married Woman" and "The Mother"), for instance, ought still to be required reading for us all, yet they will not be discussed here. Instead, I have chosen to explore the single most important—and by far the most complex—example of contradictions and ambiguity in *The Second Sex*: Beauvoir's account of female sexuality.

---

that these other groups do not contain women, nor that all women are white and non-Jewish: nothing prevents us from arguing that the position of a black Jewish woman, for instance, would form a particularly complex intersection of contradictory power relations. In her chapter on Beauvoir, Spelman also confuses the idea of otherness and the idea of objectification (Sartre's distinction between *autre-sujet* and *autre absolu*). Spelman's book, in general, is an excellent example of the consequences of treating the word *identity* as if it represented a simple logical unit and of mistaking the opposition of *inclusion* and *exclusion* for a theory of power relations. Such strategies tend to backfire: while criticizing Beauvoir's "exclusivism," Spelman herself excludes women from outside the United States from her categories. Thus, her eminently pedagogical figures illustrating different categories of people all have the suffix *American* appended to them (*Afro-American*, *Euro-American*, *Hispanic-American*, *Asian-American*, and so on). See Elisabeth Spelman, *Inessential Woman: Problems of Exclusion in Feminist Thought* (Boston: Beacon, 1988), 144–46.

By *sexuality* I understand the psychosexual, as well as the biological, aspects of female sexual existence, or, in other words, the interaction between desire and the body.

Alienation

"One is not born a woman, one becomes one," Beauvoir writes (*SS*, 295; *DSb*, 13; TA). The question, of course, is *how*. How does the little girl become a woman? In her impressive history of psychoanalysis in France, Elisabeth Roudinesco credits Simone de Beauvoir with being the first French writer to link the question of sexuality to that of political emancipation.[6] Beauvoir's interest in the various psychoanalytic perspectives on femininity was so great, Roudinesco tells us, that a year before finishing her book, she rang up Lacan in order to ask his advice on the issue: "Flattered, Lacan announces that they would need five or six months of conversation in order to sort out the problem. Simone doesn't want to spend that much time listening to Lacan for a book which was already very well researched. She proposes four meetings. He refuses."[7] It is not surprising that Lacan was flattered by Beauvoir's request: in Paris in 1948, Beauvoir possessed

6. Elisabeth Roudinesco, *La Bataille de cent ans. Histoire de la psychanalyse en France. 2: 1925–1985* (Paris: Seuil, 1986). The fact that Beauvoir explicitly rejects Freudian psychoanalysis in the first part of *The Second Sex* does not prevent her from producing a relatively psychoanalytical account of women's psychosexual development. As far as I can see, her rejection of psychoanalysis is based on the Sartrean grounds that the unconscious does not exist and that to claim that human dreams and actions have sexual signification is to posit the existence of essential meanings. When it comes to the phenomenological description of women's fantasies or behavior, however, Beauvoir is perfectly happy to accept psychoanalytical evidence.

7. Roudinesco, *La Bataille de cent ans*, 517. Beauvoir met Lacan during the Occupation, at a series of rather wild parties organized by Picasso, Camus, and Leiris, among others. In *Simone de Beauvoir: A Biography* (New York: Summit, 1990), Deirdre Bair claims that when writing *The Second Sex*, Beauvoir "went sporadically to hear Jacques Lacan lecture" (390), but this is not very likely. According to Elisabeth Roudinesco, Lacan's earliest seminars were held at Sylvia Bataille's apartment, from 1951 to 1953 (see Roudinesco, *La Bataille de cent ans*, 306). In his essay "De nos antécédents" (About our antecedents), Lacan himself claims that he started his teaching in 1951: "No real teaching other than that routinely provided saw the light of day before we started our own in 1951, in a purely private capacity" (Jacques Lacan, *Écrits* [Paris: Seuil, 1966], 71). According to David Macey, the subject of that first seminar was Freud's *Dora* (see David Macey, *Lacan in Contexts* [London: Verso, 1988], 223). If Beauvoir ever attended Lacan's seminars, then, it must have been well after finishing *The Second Sex* in 1949.

much more intellectual capital than he; in other words, she was famous, he was not.

Given this highly Lacanian disagreement on timing, the tantalizingly transgressive fantasy of a Lacanian *Second Sex* has to remain in the imaginary. Although she never sat at Lacan's feet, Beauvoir nevertheless quotes his early work on *Les Complexes familiaux dans la formation de l'individu*, and much of her account of early childhood and femininity reads as a kind of free elaboration on Lacan's notion of the alienation of the ego in the other in the mirror stage.[8]

The term *alienation*, in fact, turns up everywhere in *The Second Sex*. Mobilized to explain everything from female sexuality to narcissism and mysticism, the concept plays a key role in Beauvoir's theory of sexual difference. It is unfortunate indeed that this fact fails to come across in the English translation of *The Second Sex*. In Parshley's version, the word *aliénation* tends to get translated as 'projection', except in passages with a certain anthropological flavor, where it remains 'alienation'. *Aliénation*, however, also shows up as 'identification', and on one occasion it even masquerades as 'being beside herself'. As a result, English-language readers are prevented from tracing the philosophical logic—in this case particularly the Hegelian and/or Lacanian overtones—of Beauvoir's analysis. In my own text, I amend all relevant quotations, and I also signal particularly aberrant translations in footnotes.[9]

According to Beauvoir, the little child reacts to the crisis of weaning by experiencing "the original drama of every existent: that of his relation to

8. I don't mean to suggest that Lacan's concept of alienation is radically original or that it is the only source of Beauvoir's development of the concept. Eva Lundgren-Gothlin makes a plausible case for the influence of Kojève on Beauvoir in her *Kön och existens: Studier i Simone de Beauvoirs Le Deuxième Sexe* (Gothenburg: Daidalos, 1991), 89–94. Beauvoir herself tells of a drunken afternoon in 1945 spent discussing Kojève with Queneau (*FC*, 43; *FCa*, 56–57). Given that Lacan's concept of the mirror stage also displays the traces of Kojève's reading of Hegel, Beauvoir's own readings of Hegel may well have predisposed her to feeling particular affinities for this aspect of Lacanian theory. Nor should it be forgotten that Lacan himself—as every other intellectual in postwar France—was influenced by Sartre.

9. I don't think, as some have argued, that this is an effect of *conscious* sexism on the part of the translator. Rather, it demonstrates the fact that he was utterly unfamiliar with existentialist philosophical vocabulary. The general effect of Parshley's translation of *The Second Sex* is to divest the book of the philosophical rigor it has in French. When Beauvoir consistently uses the phrase *s'affirmer comme sujet*, for example, Parshley translates vaguely and variably as "assume a subjective attitude," or "affirm his subjective exis-

the Other" (*SS*, 296; *DSb*, 14; TA). This drama is characterized by existential anguish caused by the experience of *délaissement*, or what Heidegger would call *Überlassenheit*, often translated as 'abandonment' in English. Already at this early stage, the little child dreams of escaping her freedom either by merging with the cosmic all or by becoming a thing, an in-itself:

> In carnal form [the child] discovers finiteness, solitude, abandonment in a strange world. He endeavours to compensate for this catastrophe by alienating his existence in an image, the reality and value of which others will establish. It appears that he may begin to affirm his identity at the time when he recognizes his reflection in a mirror—a time which coincides with that of weaning.[10] His ego blends so completely into this reflected image that it is formed only through its own alienation [*il ne se forme qu'en s'aliénant*]. . . . He is already an autonomous subject transcending himself towards the outer world, but he encounters himself only in an alienated form. (*SS*, 296–97; *DSb*, 15; TA)

Initially, then, all children are equally alienated. This is not surprising, since the wish to alienate oneself in another person or thing, according to Beauvoir, is fundamental to all human beings: "Primitive people are alienated in mana, in the totem; civilized people in their individual souls, in their egos, their names, their property, their work. Here is to be found the primary temptation to inauthenticity" (*SS*, 79; *DSa*, 90). But sexual difference soon

---

tence" (*SS*, 19, and *SS*, 21). The word *situation*, heavy with philosophical connotations for Beauvoir, is not perceived as philosophical at all by Parshley, who translates *cas* as "situation" and *situation* as "situation" or "circumstances," and so on. The same tendency to turn Beauvoir's philosophical prose into everyday language is to be found in the English translations of her memoirs, particularly *The Prime of Life* and *The Force of Circumstance*. The effect is clearly to divest her of philosophy and thus to diminish her as an intellectual. The sexism involved in this process has more to do with the English-language publishers' perception and marketing of Beauvoir as a popular woman writer, rather than as a serious intellectual, than with the sexism of individual translators.

10. At this point, Beauvoir inserts a footnote quoting Lacan's *Complexes familiaux*. It is interesting to note that Lacan's essay introduces the notion of alienation in the other, not in relation to the mother but in the context of a discussion of jealousy as a fundamental social structure. As often happens, Beauvoir's actual quotation is slightly inaccurate: "The ego retains the ambiguous aspect [*figure*] of a spectacle," she quotes (*SS*, 297; *DSb*, 15), whereas Lacan actually refers to the "ambiguous *structure* of the spectacle" (Lacan, *Les Complexes familiaux dans la formation de l'individu: Essai d'analyse d'une fonction en psychologie* [1938; reprint, Paris: Navarin, 1984], 45); my emphasis.

transforms the situation. For little boys, Beauvoir argues, it is much easier to find an object in which to alienate themselves than for little girls: admirably suited to the role as idealized *alter ego*, the penis quickly becomes every little boy's very own totem pole: "The penis is singularly adapted for playing this role of 'double' for the little boy—it is for him at once a foreign object and himself," Beauvoir claims. Projecting themselves into the penis, little boys invest it with the whole charge of their transcendence (*SS*, 79; *DSa*, 91).[11] For Beauvoir, then, phallic imagery represents transcendence, not sexuality.[12]

A little girl, however, has a more difficult time. Given that she has no penis, she has no tangible object in which to alienate herself: "But the little girl cannot incarnate herself in any part of herself," Beauvoir writes (*SS*, 306; *DSb*, 27). Similar in many respects to Freud's analysis of femininity, Beauvoir's account differs, as we shall see, in its explicit denial of *lack* and in its emphasis on the tactile rather than the visual. For Freud, girls experience themselves as inferior because they *see* the penis and conclude that they themselves are lacking; for Beauvoir they are different (not necessarily inferior) because they have nothing to *touch*. Because her sex organs are impossible to grab hold of (*empoigner*), it is as if they do not exist: "In a sense she has no sex organ," Beauvoir writes.

> She does not experience this absence as a lack; evidently her body is, for her, quite complete; but she finds herself situated in the world differently from the boy; and a constellation of factors can transform this difference, in her eyes, into an inferiority. (*SS*, 300; *DSb*, 19)

Deprived of an obvious object of alienation, the little girl ends up alienating herself in herself:

> Not having that *alter ego*, the little girl does not alienate herself in a material thing and cannot retrieve her integrity [*ne se récupère pas*]. On this account she is led to make an object of her whole self, to set herself up as the Other. The question of whether she has or has

11. Beauvoir also uses the term *phallus*. In general, she tends to use *penis* and *phallus* as interchangeable terms, mostly in the sense of "penis."

12. This is true for Sartre, too. When I claim that their metaphors of transcendence are phallic, Sartre and Beauvoir would claim that it is the phallus that is transcendent, not the other way around. For my argument, however, it does not matter very much which way round the comparison is made: my point is that in their texts, projection and erection get involved in extensive metaphorical exchanges.

> not compared herself with boys is secondary; the important point is that, even if she is unaware of it, the absence of the penis prevents her from becoming conscious of herself as a sexual being. From this flow many consequences. (*SS*, 80; *DSa*, 91; TA)

Objects for themselves, regardless of whether they know about the penis's existence or not, little girls are radically split, yet irredeemably caught up in their own alienated self-image. But this is not all. On the evidence of this surprising passage, little girls are forced *by their anatomy* to alienate themselves in themselves. Furthermore, Beauvoir claims, they fail to "recover" or "retrieve" (*récupérer*) themselves. In my view, these remarks offer a condensed version of the whole of Beauvoir's theory of alienation. As such, they have a series of wide-ranging and complex implications that I will now go on to explore.

Much like Lacan, Beauvoir casts the moment of alienation as constitutive of the subject, but, unlike Lacan, she believes that the subject only comes into authentic being if it completes the dialectical movement and goes on to *recover* (*récupérer*), or reintegrate, the alienated image of itself (the double, the *alter ego*) back into its own subjectivity. Drawing on this Hegelian logic, Beauvoir insists that little boys easily achieve the required synthesis, whereas little girls fail to recover themselves. Why, then, do little boys easily "recover" their own transcendence? For Beauvoir, the answer is to be found in the anatomical and physiological properties of the penis. Eminently detachable, the penis is nevertheless not quite detached from the body. Projecting his transcendence into the penis, the boy projects it into an object that is part of his body yet has a strange life of its own: "The function of urination and later of erection are processes midway between the voluntary and involuntary," Beauvoir writes; the penis is "a capricious and as it were foreign source of pleasure that is felt subjectively. . . . The penis is regarded by the subject as at once himself and other than himself" (*SS*, 79; *DSa*, 90). Not so foreign and distant as to appear entirely without connections with the boy, yet not so close as to prevent a clear-cut distinction between the boy's subjectivity and his own projected transcendence, the penis, according to Beauvoir, enables the boy to *recognize* himself in his *alter ego*: "Because he has an *alter ego* in whom he recognizes himself, the little boy can boldly assume his subjectivity," she writes. "The very object in which he alienates himself becomes a symbol of autonomy, of transcendence, of power" (*SS*, 306; *DSb*, 27; TA).

In my view, the word *recognition* here must be taken to allude to the

Hegelian *Anerkennung*. Loosely inspired by Hegel, Beauvoir would seem to imply that there can be no recognition without the positing of a subject and an other. By being relatively other (thus allowing the positing of a subject-other distinction), yet not quite other (thus making recognition of oneself in the other easier), the penis facilitates the recuperation of the boy's alienated transcendence back into his subjectivity. Recuperating his sense of transcendence for himself, the boy escapes his alienation: his penis totem becomes the very instrument that in the end allows him to "assume his subjectivity" and act authentically.

To say that there is something Hegelian about Beauvoir's argument here is not to claim that she is being particularly orthodox or consistent. Freely developing the themes of recognition and the dialectical triad, Beauvoir entirely forgets that for Hegel recognition presupposes the reciprocal exchange between two *subjects*. As far as I can see, however, Beauvoir never actually claims that the penis speaks back. Confronted with the alluring idea that it is not only the little boy who must recognize himself in his penis, but the penis that must recognize itself in the boy, Hegel himself might have had some difficulty in recognizing his own theory.[13]

Whatever the vicissitudes of the penis may be, little girls have a harder time of it. As we have seen, Beauvoir holds that the girl's anatomy makes her alienate herself in her whole body, not just in a semi-detached object, such as the penis. Even if she is given a doll to play with, the situation doesn't change. Dolls are passive things representing the whole body, and as such they encourage the little girl to "alienate herself in her whole person and to regard this as an inert given object," Beauvoir claims (*SS*, 306; *DSb*, 27; TA). In her alienated state, the little girl apparently becomes "passive" and "inert." Why is this the outcome of the girl's alienation? The "alienated" penis, after all, was perceived by the boy as a proud image of transcendence. Why does this not happen to the girl's whole body? Where does *her* transcendence go?

On this point, Beauvoir's text is not particularly easy to follow. I take her to argue that the girl's alienation sets up an ambiguous split between herself and her alienated image of herself. "Woman, like man, *is* her body," Beauvoir writes about the adult woman, "but her body is something other than herself" (*SS*, 61; *DSa*, 67). This, one may remember, is an exact quotation of her description of the boy's alienated penis. The adult woman, then,

13. Vigdis Songe-Møller helped me fully to appreciate the comic aspects of Beauvoir's use of Hegel.

has still not achieved the dialectical reintegration of her transcendence. The reason why she fails to do so is that, paradoxically, she wasn't alienated enough in the first place. Precisely because her body *is* herself, one might say, it is difficult for the girl to distinguish between the alienated body and her transcendent consciousness of that body. Or, in other words, the difference between the whole body and the penis is that the body can never be considered simply an object in the world for its own "owner": the body, after all, *is* our mode of existing in the world: "To be present in the world implies strictly that there exists a body which is at once a material thing in the world and a point of view towards this world," Beauvoir writes (*SS*, 39; *DSa*, 40).

Alienating herself in her body, the little girl alienates her transcendence in a "thing" that remains ambiguously part of her own original transcendence. Her alienation, we might say, creates a murky mixture of transcendence, thingness, and the alienated *image* of a body-ego. The very ambiguity of this amalgam of the in-itself and the for-itself recalls Sartre's horrified vision of the "sticky" or "slimy," as that which is eternally ambiguous and always threatening to engulf the for-itself. Permitting no clear-cut positing of a subject and an other, this ambivalent mixture prevents the girl from achieving the dialectical reintegration of her alienated transcendence which, apparently, is so easy for the boy. For her, in other words, there is no unambiguous opposition between the two first moments of the dialectic: this is what makes it so hard for her to "recover" her alienated transcendence in a new synthesis.

It does not follow from this that the little girl has no sense of herself as a transcendence at all. If that were the case, she would be *entirely* alienated, which is precisely what she is not. Instead, Beauvoir appears to suggest that there is an ever present tension—or even struggle—between the little girl's transcendent subjectivity and her complicated and ambivalent alienation.[14] On this theory, the girl's psychological structures must be pictured as a complex and mobile *process* rather than as a static and fixed *image*. But on this reading, Beauvoir's account of the girl's alienation transforms and extends her own highly reified initial concept of alienation: rather

14. It follows from this analysis that I cannot agree with Moira Gatens's claim in *Feminism and Philosophy: Perspectives on Difference and Equality* (Cambridge: Polity, 1991) that for Simone de Beauvoir, the "female body and femininity quite simply *are* absolutely Other to the human subject, irrespective of the sex of that subject" (58). I also think it is rather too easy simply to assert, as Gatens does, that the inconsistencies and difficulties in *The Second Sex* are the result of Beauvoir's "intellectual dishonesty" (59).

unwittingly, I think, Beauvoir here manages to challenge the limitations of her original point of departure. The result is that her theory of female subjectivity is far more interesting and original than her rather too neat and tidy account of male psychological structures.[15]

Towards the end of *The Second Sex*, Beauvoir argues that the process of alienation is constitutive of narcissism. (On this point, one may add, her position is entirely compatible with that of Lacan.) "Narcissism is a well-defined process of alienation," Beauvoir writes, "in which the ego is regarded as an absolute end and the subject takes refuge from itself in it" (*SS*, 641; *DSb*, 525; TA). For the narcissistic subject, her ego or self is nothing but an alienated and idealized *image* of herself, another *alter ego* or double in danger in the world. As far as I can see, the difference between the narcissistic and the non-narcissistic woman is that the latter conserves a sense of ambiguity or contradiction, whereas the former persuades herself that she *is* the image projected by her alienation. This is why narcissism, according to Beauvoir, represents a supreme effort to "accomplish the impossible synthesis of the *en-soi* and the *pour-soi*": the "successful" narcissist really believes that she is God (*SS*, 644; *DSb*, 529).

For Beauvoir as for Sartre, alienation is transcendence attempting to turn itself into an object. Alienating ourselves in another thing or person, we deprive ourselves of the power to act for or by ourselves. Deprived of agency, our alienated transcendence is defenselessly delivered up to the dangers of the world. For Beauvoir, there is thus no need to mobilize a specific theory of castration anxiety to explain why little boys feel that their penis is constantly endangered. To worry about the safety of one's penis, however, is infinitely preferable to feeling obscurely threatened in one's whole person, as little girls do:

> The diffuse apprehension felt by the little girl in regard to her "insides" . . . will often be retained for life. She is extremely concerned about everything that happens inside her, she is from the start much more opaque to her own eyes, more profoundly immersed in the obscure mystery of life, than is the male. (*SS*, 305–6; *DSb*, 27)

In this passage, as everywhere else in *The Second Sex*, Beauvoir's subtle and incisive exploration of women's situation is juxtaposed to a far too sanguine view of masculinity. In the light of her own belief in the influ-

15. Beauvoir herself would certainly disagree with my value judgment here. As I go on to show, she idealizes the male configuration, perhaps precisely because she perceives it as more "neatly" philosophical.

ence of social factors on the development of sexual difference, she hugely overestimates the convenience of the penis as a foolproof instrument of alienation and reintegration. Every little boy or every adult male does not, after all, come across as an authentically transcendent subject. Beauvoir's admiration of masculinity is such that she even assumes that girls brought up by men rather than by women "very largely escape the defects of femininity" (*SS*, 308; *DSb*, 30).

While there are strong biographical reasons for her misjudgment on this point, rhetorically speaking, the main source of Beauvoir's idealization of the penis would seem to be metaphorical. Littered with references to the powerful symbolic effects of urination from a standing rather than from a crouching position, her text repeatedly emphasizes the penis's capacity for quasi-independent motion, as well as for the projection of liquids over a certain distance. What fascinates her above all is the idea that the male organ moves and, moreover, that it is *upwardly mobile*, particularly in its grandiose projection of urine: "Every stream of water in the air seems like a miracle, a defiance of gravity: to direct, to govern it, is to win a small victory over the laws of nature," Beauvoir claims, quoting Sartre and Bachelard to substantiate her point (*SS*, 301–2; *DSb*, 22).[16]

Strikingly original in her approach, Beauvoir in fact sees sexual difference as the result of different modes of alienation. At first glance, however, it looks as if the development of different forms of alienation depends entirely on the anatomical presence or absence of the penis. The question is whether this really is a correct reading of Beauvoir's position. Insisting that hers is a theory of the *social* construction of femininity and masculinity, Beauvoir herself categorically refuses the idea of a biological "destiny." On the contrary, she argues, it is the social context that gives meaning to biological and psychological factors: "True human privilege is based upon anatomical privilege only in virtue of the total situation [*la situation saisie dans sa totalité*]" (*SS*, 80; *DSa*, 91). It is only when the girl discovers that men have power in the world and women do not that she risks mistaking her difference for inferiority: "She sees that it is not the women, but the men who control the world. It is this revelation—much more than the discovery of the penis—which irresistibly alters her conception of herself" (*SS*, 314; *DSb*, 38).

Given the right social encouragement, Beauvoir argues, girls may

16. Interestingly enough, the same belief in the transcendent qualities of any form of movement makes her recommend sports and other forms of physical training as an excellent way to help girls develop a sense of themselves as subjects.

still manage to recover their transcendence. While the penis is a privileged possession in early childhood, after the age of eight or nine it holds onto its prestige only because it is socially valorized. Social practices, not biology, encourage little girls to remain sunk in passivity and narcissism, and force little boys to become active subjects. It is because little boys are treated more harshly than girls, and not because they intrinsically *are* less self-indulgent, that they are better equipped to project themselves into the competitive world of concrete action (*SS*, 306–7; *DSb*, 28–29). In my view, Beauvoir's theory of alienation actually implies that social factors have *greater* influence on girls than on boys: precisely because girls' transcendence is precariously balanced between complete alienation and authentic subjectivity, it doesn't take much to push the girl in either direction. Less pronounced in boys, one might argue, this ambiguity makes girls particularly susceptible to social pressure:

> Along with the authentic demand of the subject who wants sovereign freedom, there is in the existent an inauthentic longing for resignation and escape; the delights of passivity are made to seem desirable to the young girl by parents and teachers, books and myths, women and men; she is taught to enjoy them from earliest childhood; the temptation becomes more and more insidious; and she is the more fatally bound to yield to those delights as the flight of her transcendence is dashed against harsher obstacles. (*SS*, 325; *DSb*, 53)

I take her constant appeal to social factors to be one of the strongest points of Beauvoir's position. But when it comes to explaining exactly how we are to understand the relationship between the anatomical and the social, Beauvoir's discourse becomes curiously slippery. Not to have a penis, for instance, is not necessarily a handicap: "If woman should succeed in establishing herself as subject, she would invent equivalents of the phallus; in fact, the doll, incarnating the promise of the baby that is to come in the future, can become a possession more precious than the penis" (*SS*, 80; *DSa*, 91). Dolls, it now appears, do not necessarily cause alienated passivity after all: "The boy, too, can cherish a teddy bear, or a puppet into which he projects himself [*se projette*]; it is within the totality of their lives that each factor—penis or doll—takes on its importance" (*SS*, 307; *DSb*, 29). There is something circular about Beauvoir's argument here. For if the very form of the little girl's body encourages a sticky and incomplete mode of alienation in the first place, the little girl will find it difficult, indeed, to "establish herself as a subject." If "equivalents of the phallus" are what is needed in order to become an authentic subject, it is hard to see why women would want them *after* they have managed to become subjects in their own right anyway. In my view, Beauvoir's hesitations over the subject of dolls signal her own uneasy feeling that her original formulation of the girl's alienation privileges anatomy more than she would wish. Her contradictory feelings about the role of dolls, then, reveal a deeper theoretical difficulty: that of finding a way of linking an anatomical and psychological argument with a sociological one.

The fact that Beauvoir fails explicitly to raise this problem causes her to overlook an important gap in her own account of alienation. Attentive readers may already have noticed that her text moves directly from the Lacanian idea of the alienation of the child in the gaze of the other to the rather different idea that boys and girls alienate themselves in their bodies. Unfortunately, Beauvoir makes no attempt to relate Lacan's theory to her own. For her, apparently, the two simply coexist. Failing to perceive this as a problem, Beauvoir also misses out on a crucial opportunity to bridge the gap in her own theory, for instance by suggesting that it is the gaze of the other that originally invests the child's alienated image of itself with the phallocentric values it then goes on to repeat in its own work of alienation. By giving her own theory a slightly more Lacanian twist on this point, she would have managed, at least in my view, to produce a better account of the relationship between the biological and the psychosocial than she actually does.

It is unfortunate, to say the least, that Beauvoir makes her subtle theory of femininity function as a foil to her rather less sophisticated theory of masculinity. It is not difficult to show that Beauvoir's idealization of the phallus in fact contradicts Sartre's own account of masculine desire and transcendence.[17] Nowhere is she on a greater collision course with Sartre than in her idealized account of masculinity: there is a nice paradox in the fact that in the very passages where she unconsciously seeks to pay tribute to Sartre, she entirely betrays his philosophical logic.

In Beauvoir's theory of alienation, I appreciate above all her effort to think dialectically, her courageous attempt fully to grasp the contradictions of women's position. The strength of Beauvoir's theory of alienation as constitutive of sexual difference is not only that it manages to suggest—albeit somewhat imperfectly—that patriarchal power structures are at work

17. I go on to demonstrate that this is the case in the next section of the chapter of which this essay is an excerpt.

in the very construction of female subjectivity but also that it attempts to show exactly *how* this process works. Emphasizing the social pressures brought to bear on the little girl, Beauvoir also indicates that different practices will yield different results: hers is not at all a theory of intrinsic sexual differences. Providing the basis for a sophisticated analysis of women's difficulties in conceiving of themselves as social and sexual subjects under patriarchy, Beauvoir's theory also implies that it is both unjust and unrealistic to underestimate the difficulty involved in becoming a free woman. Given Beauvoir's logic, for a woman to be able to oppose the order that oppresses her is much harder than for a man to do so; under patriarchy, women's achievements therefore become rather more impressive than comparable male feats. As she puts it in *The Force of Circumstance*: "For women the stakes are higher; there are more victories and more defeats for them than for men" (*FC*, 203; *FCa*, 268; TA).

Screwing the System: Sexwork, Race, and the Law

Anne McClintock

A prostitute tells me that a magistrate who pays her to beat him confessed that he gets an erection every time he sentences a prostitute in court. This essay is about the magistrate's sentence, the magistrate's erection, and the prostitute who spilled the beans.

• • • •

In 1760, a French *philosophe* coined the term *fetichisme* for "primitive" religion. Marx took the term *commodity fetish* and the idea of "primitive" *magic* to express the central social form of the modern industrial economy. In 1887, Freud transferred fetishism to the realm of sexuality and to the domain of erotic perversions.[1] Religion (the ordering of time and the transcendent), sexuality (the ordering of the body), and money (the ordering of the economy) took shape around the idea of fetishism, displacing

1. I am gratefully indebted to William Pietz's three excellent essays on fetishism: "The Problem of the Fetish I," *Res* 9 (Spring 1985): 5–17; "The Problem of the Fetish II," *Res* 13 (Spring 1987): 23–46; "The Problem of the Fetish III," *Res* 16 (Autumn 1988): 105–24.

what the Enlightenment imagination could not incorporate onto the domain of the "primitive," the zone of racial and sexual "degeneration." Imperialism returned to inhabit the liberal enterprise as its concealed, but central, logic.

"The erotic deviant is not the only fetishist familiar to us. Think of the primitive," says William Pietz.[2] Yet, this could be said in another way. By thinking of the "primitive" (inventing the "primitive"), the idea of erotic deviance was constituted in Europe to serve a specifically modern form of social dominance. By the latter half of the nineteenth century, the analogy between erotic deviance and racial deviance emerged as a necessary element in the formation of the modern European imagination. The invention of racial fetishism became central to the regime of sexual surveillance, while the policing of "degenerate sexuality" became central to the policing of the "dangerous classes": the working class, the colonized, prostitutes, the Irish, Jews, gays and lesbians, criminals, alcoholics, and the insane. Erotic "deviants" were figured as racial "deviants," atavistic throwbacks to a racially "primitive" moment in human prehistory, surviving ominously in the heart of the imperial metropolis. At the same time, colonized peoples were figured as sexual deviants, the living embodiments of a primordial erotic promiscuity and excess.[3]

For Freud, the erotic fetish is akin "to the fetishes in which savages believe that their gods are embodied."[4] Yet, Freud is the first to define fetishism as a question of male sexuality alone. As Naomi Schor has pointed out, "It is an article of faith with Freud and Freudians that *fetishism is the male perversion par excellence*. The traditional psychoanalytical literature on the subject states over and over again that there are no female fetishists; female fetishism is, in the rhetoric of psychoanalysis, an oxymoron."[5] Lacan, too, notes, after Freud, "the absence in women of fetishism."[6] By reducing

2. Pietz, "Fetish I," 5.

3. See Sander L. Gilman, *Difference and Pathology: Stereotypes of Sexuality, Race, and Madness* (Ithaca: Cornell University Press, 1985). See also Nancy Stepan, *The Idea of Race in Science* (London: Macmillan, 1982).

4. Sigmund Freud, *Three Essays on the Theory of Sexuality*, vol. 7 of *The Standard Edition of the Complete Psychological Works of Sigmund Freud*, trans. James Strachey (London: Hogarth, 1953–1966).

5. Naomi Schor, "Female Fetishism: The Case of George Sand," in *The Female Body in Western Culture*, ed. Susan R. Suleiman (Cambridge: Harvard University Press, 1986), 365.

6. Jacques Lacan, "Guiding Remarks for a Congress on Feminine Sexuality," in *Feminine Sexuality: Jacques Lacan and Ecole Freudienne*, ed. Juliet Mitchell and Jacqueline Rose, trans. Jacqueline Rose (New York: W. W. Norton, 1982), 96.

fetishism, however, to a single, male poetics of the flesh and a privileged, Western narrative of origins, the traditional psychoanalytic theory of fetishism does not admit either race or class as formative categories crucial to the etiology of fetishism.

Foucault argues, in a different vein, that the historical notion of sex "made it possible to group together, in an artificial unity, anatomical elements, biological functions, conducts, sensations and pleasures, and it enabled one to make use of this fictitious unity as a causal principle, an omnipresent meaning, a secret to be discovered everywhere: sex was thus able to function as a universal signifier and as a universal signified."[7] By privileging sex as the invented principle of social unity, however, Foucault conceals the degree to which, in the nineteenth century, a racial fetishism in analogy with sexual fetishism became the organizing prototype for other social "deviations."

Far from being a purely sexual icon, fetishism is a memorial to contradictions in social value that can take a number of historical guises. The fetish stands at the crossroads of a crisis in historical value, as the symbolic displacement and embodiment in one object of incompatible codes in social meaning, which the individual cannot resolve at a personal level. The fetish is thus destined to recur with ritualistic repetition.

The fetish is haunted by historical memory. As a composite symbolic object, the fetish or fetishized person embodies the traumatic coincidence of historical memories held in contradiction. In this article, I explore the racial and sexual fetishizing of prostitutes and argue that the problem of social value embodied in the whore stigma is the historical contradiction between women's paid and unpaid work.

The moment of paying a female prostitute is structured around a paradox. The client touches the prostitute's hand in a fleeting moment of physical intimacy in the exchange of cash, a ritual exchange that confirms and guarantees each time the man's apparent economic mastery over the woman's sexuality, work, and time. At the same time, however, the moment of paying confirms precisely the opposite: the man's dependence on the woman's sexual power and skill.

Prostitutes stand at the flash points of marriage and market, taking sex into the streets and money into the bedroom. Flagrantly and publicly demanding money for sexual services that men expect for free, prostitutes insist on exhibiting their sexwork as having economic *value*. The whore

7. Michel Foucault, *History of Sexuality; Volume 1: An Introduction* (New York: Vintage, 1980), 154.

stigma reflects deeply felt anxieties about women trespassing the dangerous boundaries between private and public. Streetwalkers display their sexual and economic values in the crowd—that social element permanently on the edge of breakdown—and thereby give the lie to the rational control of "deviance" and disorder. Hence the fetishistic investment of the law in violently policing the prostitute's body.

The Law and the Whore

In 1981, in Britain, Peter Sutcliffe (or, the Yorkshire Ripper, as the tabloid press dubbed him) was brought to trial for the mutilation and murder over a six-year period of at least thirteen women, some of whom were prostitutes. Sutcliffe first claimed that he had killed because he wanted to "kill a woman, any woman."[8] Later, he claimed that God had graced him with a "divine mission"[9] to purge the earth of prostitutes: "scum who cannot justify their existence."[10] Sutcliffe's defense rested on the construction of prostitutes as inherently *unlike* all other women and as culpably complicit in their own murder. He claimed he was able to tell that his victims were prostitutes "by the way they walked. He knew they were not innocent."[11] For Sutcliffe, the prostitutes' guilt could be read off their bodies as a stigma of the flesh, their culpability revealed unambiguously in the lineaments of their limbs, an anatomical allegory signifying sin.

Most troubling, however, was the systematic continuity between Sutcliffe's mission to exterminate prostitutes and the public sentiment voiced by the tabloids, the police statements, and the judiciary itself that the prostitutes were, indeed, somehow *not* innocent. During the extraordinary trial that followed, a legal discourse, a psychiatric discourse, and a journalistic discourse took shape around the preordained verdict of the murdered prostitutes' guilt in the eyes of the law. Throughout the trial, distinctions were repeatedly made between "innocent" victims (nonprostitutes) and "disreputable," or "blemished," victims (prostitutes).[12] Indeed, the police investigation into the murders began in earnest only when the fifth victim was killed,

8. See Wendy Holloway, " 'I Just Wanted To Kill a Woman.' Why? The Ripper and Male Sexuality," *Feminist Review* 9 (October 1981): 33–40.

9. *The Guardian* (London), 19 May 1981. Quoted in Holloway, " 'I Just Wanted To Kill a Woman.' Why?" 36.

10. Quoted in Holloway, " 'I Just Wanted To Kill a Woman.' Why?" 38.

11. *The Guardian* (London), 7 May 1981. Quoted in Holloway, " 'I Just Wanted To Kill a Woman.' Why?" 39.

12. Holloway, " 'I Just Wanted To Kill a Woman.' Why?" 39. See also Andrew Ross, "Dem-

and she turned out *not* to be a prostitute. A police poster read: "The next victim may be innocent."[13] The judge, moreover, offered the jury the following extraordinary advice. If Sutcliffe *was* deluded into believing that he had killed only prostitutes, "then the correct verdict was probably manslaughter," not murder.[14] The distinction between prostitutes and other women was finally summed up in Attorney General Sir Michael Havers's notorious comment: "Some were prostitutes, but perhaps the saddest part of this case is that some were not."[15]

On 28 January 1987, at the height of the celebrated trial of Madame Cyn Payne (charged with exercising control over prostitutes for the purpose of gain), Sergeant David Broadwell dragged into court a large, clear, plastic bag and exposed to the titillated courtroom the taboo paraphernalia of S/M: whips, belts, chains, a dog collar, and assorted sticks and leather items.[16] For days, police and witnesses had been describing the "naughtinesses" at Payne's party: spankings; lesbian shows; elderly gentlemen cross-dressed in women's evening clothes; policemen in drag; and lawyers, businessmen, and even a Peer of the Realm waiting in queues on the stairs for sex.

The prostitution trial, conducted in a blaze of publicity, exposes its own structuring paradox, staging in public, as a vicarious spectacle, that which it renders criminally deviant outside the juridical domain. Through the mechanism of the prostitution trial, contradictions in the distribution of money, pleasure, and power are isolated as crimes and are then performed again in the theatrical ceremony of the trial as confession. The judiciary is a system of ordered procedures for the production of "truth" (facts, verdicts, the rational sentence). The judge's wig (like the prostitute's wig) signifies a separation between subjective identity and body, and thereby guarantees the impartiality of the trial.

---

onstrating Sexual Difference," in *Men in Feminism*, ed. Alice Jardine and Paul Smith (New York: Methuen, 1987), 49.

13. Quoted in Ross, "Demonstrating Sexual Difference," 49.

14. *The Guardian* (London), 21 May 1981. Quoted in Holloway, "'I Just Wanted To Kill a Woman.' Why?" 34.

15. *West Indian World*, 6 June 1981. Quoted in Holloway, "'I Just Wanted To Kill a Woman.' Why?" 39. As Ross notes, Sutcliffe's mission "to kill all prostitutes was *recognized*, notoriously, at all levels of interpretation, from that of the popular press to that of the professional lawyer, as a moral mission, and was therefore less culpable than the asocial desire to kill all women" (see "Demonstrating Sexual Difference," 48).

16. See Gloria Walker and Lynn Daly, *Sexplicitly Yours: The Trial of Cynthia Payne* (London: Penguin, 1987).

The law is also a regime for disqualifying alternative discourses: the disenfranchised, feminists, and prostitutes who might spill the beans.[17] The more prostitutes are obliged to speak of their actions in public, the more they incriminate themselves. By ordering the unspeakable to be spoken in public, however, and by obsessively displaying dirty pictures, filmed evidence, confessions, and exhibits, the prostitution trial reveals itself as structured around the very fetishism it sets itself to isolate and punish. Under his scarlet robe, the judge has an erection.

The prostitution trial is not only a regime of truth for demonstrating the proper circulation of money and property but also a technology of violence, setting in motion the violent constraint of women's bodies: floggings, dunkings, jailings, and exile. The institution of the fine serves the purpose of restoring the economic exchange subverted by the prostitute. If the prostitute makes the judge pay for sexual services that she should offer for free, then by fining the prostitute the judge returns illicit female money back into male circulation.

At the outset, the "sciences of man"—philosophy, Marxism, psychoanalysis, anthropology—sought to contain the "primitive" possibility of the "perversions" by a projection backward in time to the "prehistory" of racial "degeneration." Commercial S/M (the collaborative organization of fetishism) does the opposite: It insists on playing the role of the "primitive" (slave, female, baby) as a *character* in the historical time of modernity. If the prostitution trial isolates and organizes deviant sexual *pleasure* for *punishment*, commercial S/M is the dialectical opposite of the trial, organizing the *punishment* of sexual deviance for *pleasure*.[18] S/M performs the social idea of the *primitive irrational* as a dramatic *script*, a theatrical, public performance in the heart of Western reason. The paraphernalia of S/M (boots, whips, chains, uniforms) are the paraphernalia of state power, public punishment converted to private pleasure. S/M plays imperialism backward, visibly and outrageously staging racial and gender differences, ecstasy, the irrational, and the alienation of the body as at the center of Western individualism. Commercial S/M reveals the logic of liberal individualism and refuses it as

17. See Susan Edwards, *Female Sexuality and the Law* (Oxford: Martin Robertson, 1981), and Carol Smart, *Feminism and the Power of the Law* (London: Routledge, 1989).
18. Let me emphasize that I refer here to the specific phenomenon of ritualized, commercial S/M, wherein the exchange of cash takes place in the context of a consensual agreement. It is crucial to distinguish between consensual S/M and nonconsensual violence and sexual sadism. These mark a continuum rather than two exclusive poles, and there are relationships that waver perilously across the twilight middle.

fate but does so without stepping outside the enchantment of its magic circle.

If the prostitution trial redistributes illicit female money back into licit male circulation, commercial S/M performed by a woman enacts the reverse: staging the contradictions of women's unpaid sexual and domestic work as *unnatural*—as theater—and insisting (strictly) on payment. The paradox and scandal of S/M is its flagrant exposure in the form of a spectacle of the conceptual and political limits of the liberal ideal of the autonomous individual. The outrage of S/M is its provocative confession that the dynamics of power are reversible.

The act of paying a female prostitute flagrantly announces the *unnaturalness* and fictive inventiveness of the ancestral edict that women do not own property in their own persons. Historically, male law has attempted, with great vigilance and inclemency, to police the contradiction between male dependence on female sexual power and male juridical definitions of women as naturally and universally the property of men.

In 1855, in New York, the Trinity Church vestryman, George Templeton Strong, confided to his diary that "what the Mayor seeks to abolish and abate is not the terrible evil of prostitution . . . but simply the scandal and the offense of the peripatetic whorearchy."[19] Indeed, states have seldom sought to abolish prostitution outright; rather, they have sought to curb sexworkers' control of the trade.

Of what sin are prostitutes guilty? What, precisely, is the scandal of the whorearchy?

The Scandal of the Whorearchy: Prostitution and Property

In 1986, Pasadena Superior Court Judge Gilbert C. Alston presided over the trial of Daniel Zabuski, who was charged with the violent rape and sodomy of Rhoda Dacosta, a prostitute. Alston dismissed the charges on the grounds that a whore cannot be raped. He based his judgment not on standard procedural grounds of legally relevant evidence, nor on the construction of a credible, juridically sound case, but on the grounds that, as he put it, "a whore is a whore is a whore."[20] For Alston, all prostitutes share a common identity that makes them essentially and universally unrapeable.

19. Quoted in Arlene Carmen and Howard Moody, *Working Women: The Subterranean World of Street Prostitution* (New York: Harper and Row, 1985), 6.

20. "Judge Rules Prostitutes Can't Be Raped," *Whisper* 1, no. 2 (Spring 1986): 1. See also *Sex Work: Writings by Women in the Sex Industry*, ed. Frederique Delacoste and Priscilla Alexander (Pittsburgh: Cleis Press, 1987), 185.

In San Francisco recently, the Oakland police chief admitted to closing rape cases of prostitutes without proper investigation simply because the victims were prostitutes. David P. Lambkin, a detective with the Los Angeles police, admitted that rape of prostitutes is on the increase, but he added: "It's hard enough to make a rape case with a legitimate victim."[21] "Sure," said Lieutenant Vito Spano, head of the sex crimes unit in Brooklyn, "sure they get victimized, but they are their own worst enemies."[22] What does the male judiciary see in prostitutes that puts them outside the protection of the law?

Until very recently, two categories of women have been deemed unrapeable by law: wives and prostitutes. Indeed, Friedrich Engels first suggested that prostitution and marriage find their social meaning in dialectical relation to each other.[23] Rape is not illegal, it is regulated. Judge Alston's notion that a whore cannot be raped finds its logic in an ancient tradition that defines rape not as an affront to women but as an affront to male property rights. Historically, female chastity has had property value for men. In surviving law codes of the Mesopotamian valley, for example, women were legislated as the property of fathers, husbands, brothers, or sons, so that rape was figured not as the violation of women but as the ruination of male property value.[24] Until late in the nineteenth century, under the common-law doctrine of coverture, a woman's sexual property passed into a man's hands at marriage; so did her labor, her inheritance, and her children. Under coverture, a wife, like a slave, was civilly dead. In the eighteenth century, in Britain, Sir M. Hale's notorious injunction gave a husband de jure sanction to rape his wife by the legal category of *conjugal rights*.[25] Until October

21. Jane Gross, "Prostitutes and Addicts: Special Victims of Rape," *New York Times*, 12 Oct. 1990, 14.

22. Gross, "Prostitutes and Addicts," 14.

23. Friedrich Engels, *The Origin of the Family, Private Property, and the State* (New York: International Publishers, 1972), 129–30, 138–39.

24. Vern Bullough and Bonnie Bullough, *Women and Prostitution: A Social History* (Buffalo: Prometheus, 1987), 16. In medieval Europe, likewise, customary law gave the husband the right to execute his wife if she committed adultery, and rape was seen as the tarnishing of male property value (115). See also Gerda Lerner, "The Origin of Prostitution in Ancient Mesopotamia," *Signs* 1, no. 2 (1986): 236–54.

25. Hale laid down that "the husband cannot be guilty of a rape committed by himself upon his lawful wife, for by their mutual matrimonial consent and contract the wife hath given up herself in this kind unto her husband, which she cannot retract" (Sir M. Hale, *The History of the Pleas of the Crown* [London: Sollom Emlyn, 1778], vol. 1, chap. 58, 628). Until 1884, in Britain, a wife could be forcibly incarcerated in a state prison for re-

1991, it was legal for a man to rape his wife in Britain, except in Scotland. It is still legal in many states in the United States and in most countries around the world.

The rape trial serves to police contradictions inherent in the judiciary's own laws, isolating points of conflict in the distribution of male property rights over the bodies of women. Central to the idea of the modern, universal citizen is John Locke's famous formulation: "Every Man has a *Property* in his own *Person*."[26] Yet, the principle that individuals own property in their own persons is immediately contradicted by the fact that women do not, whereupon a fissure opens in the ideology of individualism. The rape trial serves to isolate and close the fissure, which is identified as a crime: a rape, a theft, adultery, prostitution.

"A woman," Judge Alston explains, "who goes out on the street and makes a whore out of herself opens herself up to anybody."[27] The logic of rape law is as follows: Since rape is a crime against a man's property in the woman, a wife cannot be raped by her husband, for a man cannot rob himself of his own property. Similarly, since rape is a crime against a man's property, and since the prostitute is a *common prostitute*, the prostitute no longer has private property value for men. By "opening herself up" to any man, the prostitute ruins her potential value as private property for a single man and becomes, by definition, unrapeable.

A prostitute who removes her body from the stock of male property, and claims it for her own, removes her body from the sphere of male law, which exists to negotiate the distribution and circulation between men of property and power. Historically, most regimes have legislated that a woman's relation to the rights and resources of the state are indirect, mediated through a social relation to a man (father, husband, or nearest male kin). By publicly selling sexual services that men expect for free, prostitutes transgress the fundamental structure of the male traffic in women. Therefore, as Judge Alston put it, a prostitute "steps outside the protection of the law."[28] As a result, she is also disqualified from speaking for herself before the law. Alston adds: "Who the hell would believe a prostitute in the witness

---

fusing conjugal rights (see Carole Pateman, *The Sexual Contract* [Oxford: Polity Press, 1988], 123).

26. John Locke, *Two Treatises of Government*, ed. P. Laslett (Cambridge: Cambridge University Press, 1967), vol. 2, 183, 81–82.

27. "Judge Rules Prostitutes Can't Be Raped," 1.

28. "Judge Rules Prostitutes Can't Be Raped," 1.

stand anyway?"[29] Marx's injunction could hardly be more apposite: "They cannot represent themselves; they must be represented."[30]

A standard Latin term for prostitute, *meretrix* means "she who earns."[31] Since prostitution, in European history, is theft by a woman of sexual property that rightfully belongs to a man, some of the earliest laws against prostitution were laws to curb the kind of money and property women could accumulate.[32] Hence the analogy between the terms *common land* and *common prostitute*. Until very recently, marital law enclosed a woman's "private parts" and transferred them from the father to the husband. The wife, by law, did not possess the title deeds to her sexual property but served only as custodian and gatekeeper to ensure that the grounds remained private. In the sexual commonage of the prostitute, however, the body fluids and liquid assets of men from different classes and races mix promiscuously.

It is, therefore, not surprising that prostitutes are traditionally associated with challenges to rule, with figures of rebellion, revolt, insurrection, and the criminal appropriation of property. The scandal of the whorearchy amounts to flagrant female interference in male contests over property and power. Not for nothing did Parisian public health official Parent-Duchatelet call prostitutes "the most dangerous people in society."[33]

29. "Judge Rules Prostitutes Can't Be Raped," 1.

30. Karl Marx, "The Eighteenth Brumaire of Louis Bonaparte," in *Selected Works* (New York: International Publishers, 1973), 417.

31. Bullough and Bullough, *Women and Prostitution*, 48.

32. At the end of the first century A.D., Emperor Domitian tried to rule against prostitutes receiving inheritances and legacies. In Roman law, a prostitute was canonically barred from accusing others of crime, was forbidden to inherit property, and could not represent herself in court. Medieval Byzantine church legislation forbade a prostitute from owning property. In the Visigothic kingdom in Spain, prostitutes who persisted in their trade received three hundred lashes. In 1254, Louis IX decreed that all prostitutes be placed beyond the protection of the king's law and that all their personal goods, clothing, furs, tunics, and linen chemises be seized (Bullough and Bullough, *Women and Prostitution*, 48, 55, 116, 120, 122).

33. Alexandre-Jean-Baptiste Parent-Duchatelet, *De la prostitution de la ville de Paris* (Paris: J. B. Bailliere, 1836), quoted in Louise White, *The Comforts of Home: Prostitution in Colonial Nairobi* (Chicago: University of Chicago Press, 1990), 2.

Black Markets: Prostitution and Race

In late Victorian Britain, the imagery for representing sexuality was drawn from the sphere of economic activity.[34] Sexual problems were figured as fiscal problems and were imaged by metaphors of accumulation, production, and excessive expenditure.[35] As Foucault has suggested, the middle class lacked the means, and therefore had to invent the means, for defining itself as a class. Sexual reproduction and economic production became deeply symbolically linked. Sexuality (one's relation to one's body and to the bodies of others) became the language for expressing one's relation to class (one's relation to labor and to the labor of others). The middle class figured itself as different from both the aristocracy and the working class by virtue of its sexual restraint (its monogamy) and its economic moderation (its thrift). The bank, as the economic institution for managing the accumulation and distribution of capital, found its accomplice in monogamous marriage as the social institution for managing the accumulation and distribution of reproductive power and property. A contradiction in the form of gender, however, opened in the formation of class identity, for monogamy was monogamy for women only, and saving and accumulating property were for men only. In order to foreclose the contradiction, *nature* was reinvented to guarantee gender *difference* within class *identity*. The primary symbolic means for the reinvention of nature was the idea of *race*, and the primary arena was empire. The invention of *imperial nature*, moreover, would guarantee that the "universal" quintessence of Enlightenment individualism would belong only to propertied men of European descent.

The relation between the "normal" male control of reproduction and sexual pleasure in marriage, and the "normal" bourgeois control of capital was legitimized and made natural by reference to a third term: the "abnormal" zone of racial "degeneration." Illicit money and illicit sexuality were seen to relate to each other by negative analogy to race. The internal, historical contradiction *within* the modern social formation was thereby displaced and represented as a natural difference *across* the time and space

34. See Steven Marcus, *The Other Victorians: A Study of Sexuality and Pornography in Mid-Nineteenth Century England* (New York: New American Library, 1974), xiii.
35. Women "saved" themselves for marriage, or "cheapened" themselves in promiscuity; men "wasted" or "spent" themselves in masturbation or homosexuality. See Sander Gilman, *Difference and Pathology: Stereotypes of Sexuality, Race, and Madness*. See also Gilman in *The Anatomy of Racism*, ed. David Goldberg (Minneapolis: University of Minnesota Press, 1990).

of empire: the difference between the "enlightened" present and the "primitive" past. The movement across the space of empire was thus figured as a movement backward in time.

Prostitutes became associated with black and colonized peoples within a discourse on racial degeneration that figured them as transgressing the natural distributions of money, sexual power, and property, and as thereby fatally threatening the fiscal and libidinal economy of the imperial state. Prostitutes, who stepped beyond the edicts of heterosexual marriage and the doctrine that women did not work for profit, were figured as atavistic throwbacks to a primordial phase of racial development, their "racial deviance" written visibly on the body in the stigmata of female sexual deviance: exaggerated posteriors, mutant genitals and ears, excessive sexual appetites, disheveled hair, and other sundry "racial" stigmata.

Gambling, likewise, as Sander Gilman points out, took its place in a vocabulary that metaphorically intertwined money, sexuality, and race. If commercial S/M was the dialectical twin of the sex trial, the gambling hall was the dialectical twin of the bank. Gambling was the institutional display of organized commodity fetishism: the flagrant exhibition of the capitalist superstition that money can breed itself autochthonously without labor. The organized dream of gambling was the orgasmic excess of pure exchange value from which all labor has been voided. Similarly, masturbation (autoerotic and outside the heterosexual reproductive economy) was widely condemned in sexual treatises as interfering with a man's ability to work and accumulate capital. Homosexuality and clitoral eroticism, similarly, stood outside the reproductive economy and outside the narrative teleology of racial evolution, and were both figured as precipitating a steady decline into "racial" degeneration, visibly expressed in the stigmata of hairy hands, shambling gait, mental deficiency, and irrationality.

In the symbolic triangle of deviant money, deviant sexuality, and deviant race, the so-called degenerate classes—the militant working class, the colonized, prostitutes, gays and lesbians, gamblers, the Irish, and the Jews (particularly those who lived in the East End of London, on the cusp of empire)—were metaphorically bound in a regime of surveillance figured by images of sexual pathology and racial aberration.

In Victorian iconography, the fetish emblem of dirt was compulsively drawn on to police the boundaries between "normal" sexuality and "normal" market relations. "Dirty" sex—masturbation, prostitution, lesbian and gay sexuality, and the host of Victorian "perversions"—transgressed the libidinal economy of heterosexual reproduction within the monogamous marital relation ("clean" sex, which has value). Likewise, "dirty" money—associated with prostitutes, Jews, gamblers, and thieves—transgressed the fiscal economy of the male-dominated, market exchange ("clean" money, which has value). The bodily relation to dirt expressed a social relation to labor. Because it was the surplus evidence of human work, dirt was a Victorian scandal. Dirt was the visible residue that stubbornly remained after the process of industrial rationality had done its work. Smeared on clothes, hands, and faces, dirt was the memory trace of human labor, the evidence that the production of industrial wealth, and the creation of liberal rationality, lay in the hands and bodies of the working class and the colonized. For this reason, Victorian dirt entered the symbolic realm of fetishism with great force, and the body of the prostitute, standing on the street corner of marriage and market, became subject to vigilant and violent policing.

In late Victorian Britain, the infamous Contagious Diseases Acts gave British police the right to forcibly impose physical examinations on women suspected of working as prostitutes in designated garrison towns in Britain and its colonies. The initial impetus for the Acts came from blows to male self-esteem in the arena of empire, in resurgent militancy in India, South Africa, Ireland, and elsewhere. The argument ran that the real threat to the potency of the imperial army lay in the sexual bodies of transgressive women. If working women could be cordoned off, the purity of the army and the imperial body politic could be assured. With the Acts, the policing of female sexuality became both metaphor and means for policing unruly working-class and colonized peoples at large.

If the Western discourse on degeneration sees the white prostitute as a racial deviant, and colonized people as inherently sexually degenerate, the prostitute in the colonies brings the discourse on deviance to its conceptual limit. If all colonized people are the embodiment of degeneration, there is no way to represent the special case of the prostitute. How can she be defined as sexually abnormal if all colonized people are already quintessentially abnormal? In the colonies, the relation between prostitution and female property, between paid and unpaid female work, comes critically to the fore.

In colonial Kenya, for example, prostitution emerged from the collision of natural catastrophe and colonialism, from the disruptions of African agriculture and African resistance to colonial wage labor.[36] Yet, as Louise

36. See Louise White, *The Comforts of Home*. I am gratefully indebted to White's groundbreaking book. For a fuller discussion of White's book, see my review "The Scandal of the Whorearchy," *Transition* 52 (1991): 92–99.

White shows, the history of colonial prostitution was not a litany of victims. Working prostitutes were Kenya's "urban pioneers," some of the first residents to live year-round in Nairobi. Kenyan prostitutes themselves defined sexwork as a defiant form of labor. Dodging colonial wage labor, many of the women used the cash they earned from "digging with their backs" to buy cattle and build houses and to found the "nearly revolutionary notion" that women can control their own money and property as independent heads of households.[37]

As White shows, *malaya* prostitution mimicked marriage, the radical difference being that women exchanged for money the domestic, emotional, and sexual services that wives performed unpaid.[38] Fostering values of female and community loyalty, the prostitutes helped maintain African communities and struggled to shape the colonial urban scene to meet African women's needs.

In precolonial society, the daughter's marriage was the source of the father's accumulation of property and power. Since women did the bulk of the work and were the chief reproducers of life and labor, their work was the single most valuable resource apart from the land itself. In cattle-marriage societies, livestock were the symbolic coinage of women's labor power. More wives meant greater wealth and more cattle for men, and cattle marriage was the fundamental institution by which women's labor power was metamorphosed into male political power. Through male control of female sexuality and marriage, cattle and cash were redistributed through male familial networks.

Through prostitution, however, women began to buy their own property. Many of the *malaya* prostitutes were runaway wives who came to the city to escape forced marriages. Instead of sending their money back to the male-headed homestead, women bought livestock and houses and became independent heads of households, moving a whole cycle of new, female family formation into the new urban centers. If marriage was a source of fathers' accumulation, prostitution became the source of daughters' accumulation. As Kayaya Thababu put it: "At home, what could I do? Grow crops for my husband or my father. In Nairobi I can earn my own money, for myself."[39] By the early 1930s, half of the landlords in Pumwani, Nairobi's black township, were women.[40]

37. White, *The Comforts of Home*, 34.

38. Unlike the *watambezi*, or streetwalking prostitutes, *malaya* prostitutes worked from their homes, exchanging both domestic and sexual services for cash.

39. White, *The Comforts of Home*, 51.

40. White, *The Comforts of Home*, 64.

Many of the women, moreover, consciously refused to pass their property back through the male system, disinheriting fathers and brothers and keeping their money and their bodies for themselves. *Malaya* prostitution expressed a clear rejection of traditional male family ties. Windfalls went into helping women friends, and the women designated female heirs to ensure that their property did not pass back into the patrilineage, thereby creating new, explicitly female lineages. Not surprisingly, many men took umbrage at the women's temerity, and the prostitutes had to negotiate constantly to keep their property out of the hands of irate fathers, brothers, ex-husbands, and the state.

Indeed, the colonial state's response to Nairobi prostitution was riven with paradox. On the one hand, prostitution was essential to the smooth running of a migrant labor economy, saving the state the cost of servicing African men, as well as forestalling the perils of settled African communities taking root in the urban areas. On the other hand, the earnings of the prostitutes also allowed women and men to elude the depredations of colonial wage labor. Settlers constantly carped at African scoundrels and slothful layabouts who lived off women's earnings and were thereby able to refuse to work for whites.

In colonial Kenya, as elsewhere, the state objected less to prostitution itself than to the women's scandalous accumulation of money and property.[41] In a world where colonials sought constantly to control the lives of Africans through housing, marriage, and migrant labor, prostitutes owning property and passing on the values of community, self-respect, and gender loyalty were a constant affront to the white male management of power.

In many parts of Africa, the state's ambiguous relation to prostitution has endured after independence. In the 1970s and 1980s, in Zimbabwe, Gabon, Zambia, Tanzania, Mozambique, and Burkina Faso, for example, police launched massive assaults on single, independently working women in putative attempts to "clean" the cities of prostitution. Yet, the real threat to the state was not prostitution but the general specter of economically independent women, who were fetishized and demonized by the whore stigma in order to license state violence. As Paola Tabet puts it, "Control of women in marriage and exploitation of their labor is based on male monopoly of resources and means of production. When women have access to other forms of income, marriage and direct male control are threatened."[42] In

41. White, *The Comforts of Home*, 219.

42. See Paola Tabet, "I'm the Meat, I'm the Knife. Sexual Service, Migration, and Re-

1983, in Zimbabwe, for example, the Mugabe government ordered massive roundups of women who could not demonstrate an immediate relation to a man. Women walking alone on the streets, living alone in flats in Harare, or raising children independently as single mothers were arrested as prostitutes and sent to camps, where they were subjected to appalling abuse. The roundups were repeated during the recent Commonwealth Summit.

Prostitution is a realm of contradiction. In the colonies, prostitution may very well have confirmed colonial fantasies about white men's privileged access to the bodies of black women, but prostitution also confused racial segregation and the racial and gendered distributions of money. The fact that men had access to prostitution did not mean that they had control over prostitutes. Prostitutes obliged white men to pay far better than usual for African women's work and, at least temporarily, subjected white men to African women's control. Prostitutes dictated the times and terms of the exchange, what services they offered, and how much they charged.[43]

In contemporary Britain, Europe, and the United States, the policing of prostitutes as racial degenerates persists in at least three ways. Prostitutes continue to be figured as atavistic throwbacks to racial "degeneracy." In 1969, a British pamphlet, for example, widely read by probation officers, condemned prostitution as "a primitive and regressive manifestation."[44] Poor, black, immigrant, and migrant prostitutes are subjected to systematic, and especially violent, harassment. The police, moreover, use the control of prostitutes as a cover for policing black, minority, immigrant, and working-class communities, both male and female. Defining zones of the city as sexually deviant, the police attempt to penetrate and subdue the black body politic. As a statement from the English Collective of Prostitutes protested, "Women are pushed from area to area, and even from city to city, but the police remain in the area after the women have left."[45]

Through prostitution laws, space is criminalized and enters the realm of law. In Britain, the recent, notorious Kerb Crawling Bill is no exception. In 1985, under the guise of protecting women, it became a crime for men to engage in "persistent kerb crawling" (soliciting women for sex). In 1990,

---

pression in Some African Societies," in *The Vindication of the Rights of Whores*, ed. Gail Pheterson, Preface by Margo St. James (Seattle: Seal Press, 1989), 204–23.

43. As White points out, women controlled the price, the type, the time, and the length and intensity of the services they preferred to exchange.

44. Quoted in Pateman, *The Sexual Contract*, 194.

45. English Collective of Prostitutes' Statement, Kings Cross, London, 10 July 1987.

under the Sexual Offenses Bill, Sir William Shelton proposed the removal of the term *persistent*, in order to make it possible for a single officer without a witness to charge any man simply suspected of talking to a prostitute (hence the term *sus law*). Prostitutes argue that the new bill, far from protecting women from violent clients, only deepens the dangers. Nervous johns do not have time to dawdle, so women do not have time to check them out or negotiate for safe sex. As a result, some women have been badly battered and murdered. As a Kings Cross prostitute complained: "If the law can nick them straight away, everything will be done so fast you won't have a chance, especially at night. With some of the nuts you get around here, it's a frightening prospect."[46] At the same time, the bill has been widely used as a "sus" law to arrest and harass black, immigrant, and minority men for unrelated reasons. In London, many black and immigrant men have been stopped, arrested, charged with stealing their own bicycles, or harassed and beaten up simply for talking to a woman who is "suspected" of being a prostitute. White, middle-class men, like Prosecutor Allan Green, however, are let off with a fraternal slap on the wrist.[47]

Prostitutes who are poor and black bear the most vicious brunt of the law. In 1982, in London, police abuse of black, immigrant, and minority prostitutes became so widespread that women occupied the Church of the Holy Cross to draw public attention to their plight. In the United States, while only 40 percent of streetwalkers are women of color, they make up 55 percent of those sentenced to jail.[48] In New York, police hold "trick tournaments," lining black and white prostitutes on either side of a road and forcing them to run races against each other. Those who lose go to jail.[49]

Generally speaking, in Britain, Europe, and the United States, black and white prostitutes experience the metropolis in different ways. A racial geography of sex maps the city and divides the sex industry. In the exchange of commercial sex, the private (white) spaces of escort services and

46. See Jo Grant, "Streets Apart," *The Guardian* (London), 3 July 1990, 14.

47. Chief Prosecutor Allan Green was arrested for kerb crawling near the Kings Cross Station in 1991. In 1985, the Campaign against Kerb Crawling Legislation was launched by a coalition of sexworkers, anti-rape, black, and civil rights groups to lobby members of Parliament and make their objections known to the press. On Friday, 11 May 1990, after a rowdy and acrimonious debate, Member of Parliament Ken Livingston talked the Sexual Offenses Bill down. The bill, however, comes up every Friday, and will be passed unless one MP opposes it.

48. Delacoste and Alexander, *Sex Work*, 197.

49. Arlene Carmen and Howard Moody, *Working Women: The Subterranean World of Street Prostitution* (New York: Harper and Row, 1985), 146.

clubs are tacitly condoned, while the public (black) spaces of streetwalking and car sex are more violent, more heavily policed, and more profoundly stigmatized. In the 1970s, in New York, massage parlors on the East Side were run by white men who overwhelmingly employed white women and were comparatively safer and more comfortable than the less opulent black parlors on the West Side. Black and Asian women in the United States find it harder to get work as go-go dancers and escort women than white and Latina women do. In Nevada, until the 1960s, black women could not enter casinos. Today, many bar owners, hotel keepers, and landlords either do not allow black prostitutes to use their premises or they charge them punitively inflated rents. Police are far more tolerant of less overt sexwork, largely because the customers are drawn from the white, middle, and professional classes. By licensing indoor work, and harassing street work, police isolate the poorest women, who cannot afford to pay high rents and who have the least access to health care, social resources, and legal aid. The police thereby ensure that poor, black women pay the heaviest price for the criminalization of sexwork.

The whore stigma polices the racial divide, stigmatizing and endangering the lives of women of color, as well as perpetuating racism within the sex industry and among some white prostitutes. At the same time, in Britain, Europe, and the United States, clients are overwhelmingly white, married, and middle class, while most of the men arrested are men of color, are gay, or are transvestite.

"It's a Business Doing Pleasure with You": Prostitution Is Work

Prostitutes around the world are now becoming their own media advocates and political activists, radically challenging the stigma of sexual and racial deviance.[50] Since the 1970s, hundreds of prostitution organizations have burgeoned worldwide, from Hawaii to Austria, from Canada to the Philippines, from Zimbabwe to the Netherlands. In 1986, prostitutes from around the world met in Brussels at an extraordinary session of the European Parliament, where they launched the Second World Whores' Congress. Drawn from over sixteen countries and representing millions of

50. See Delacoste and Alexander, *Sex Work*. See also Dolores French, *Working: My Life as a Prostitute* (New York: E. P. Dutton, 1988), and *Good Girls/Bad Girls: Feminists and Sex Trade Workers Face to Face*, ed. Laurie Bell (Toronto: Seal Press, 1987).

sexworkers worldwide, the prostitutes drew up a Whores' Charter, calling for the decriminalization of sexwork and an end to all violations of sexworker rights.[51]

In October 1991, sexworkers from sixteen countries met in Frankfurt at the First European Prostitutes' Congress to call for the recognition of voluntary prostitution as a profession in the European Charter and for full rights as workers under European labor law.[52] To the consternation of many governments, and some feminists, prostitutes called not for the abolition of prostitution but for the redistribution of sexual pleasure, power, and profit; for the transformation of land and property rights; for the removal of foreign armies; and for the right of women and men to work voluntarily in the sex trade under safe, unregulated, and respected conditions.[53]

Many men, however, prefer to find whores in their beds than in their parliaments, and attempts by sexworkers to organize have met with unswerving violence. An Irish organizer was burnt to death, and Thai organizers have been murdered. Ecuadoran brothel owners rotate prostitutes regularly to prevent them from organizing.[54] Yet by and large, the international Left has been largely indifferent to the issue, while the abolitionist tendency among some feminists has been nothing short of calamitous for working prostitutes.

Most prostitutes insist that the first target of their international organizing is the state and the law. Prostitutes argue that the laws punish, rather than protect, women, especially women of color. Where sexwork is a crime, clients can rape, rob, and batter women with impunity. Murderers know the weight of a prostitute's life in the scales of the law. As Dallas Judge Jack Hampton admitted, "I'd be hard put to give somebody life for killing a prostitute."[55] Not surprisingly, more prostitutes are murdered in the United States, where prostitution is still a crime, than anywhere else in the world.

Prostitutes denounce the laws that shunt them into dangerous, desolate docklands, meatpacking districts, and railway yards, unable to organize for decent conditions or against coercion. Where prostitution is a crime, women cannot demand police protection or claim legal recourse for robbery

51. For a full account of the congress, see Pheterson, *Vindication of the Rights of Whores*.
52. See Anne McClintock, "Down by Law," *The Guardian* (London), 23 Oct. 1991, 20.
53. See Anne McClintock, "Meanwhile Back at the Chicken Ranch," *The Guardian* (London), 12 May 1992, 36.
54. Pheterson, *Vindication of the Rights of Whores*, 7.
55. Lisa Belkin, "Report Clears Judge of Bias in Remarks about Homosexuals," *New York Times*, 2 Nov. 1989, A25.

or coercion, for they thereby expose themselves as implicated in a criminalized trade. Where sexwork is a crime, prostitutes are forced by landlords to pay exorbitant rents or are driven to work the freezing and dangerous streets. Prostitutes cannot claim social welfare or life insurance, health care or maternity benefits, childcare or pensions. Where prostitution is a crime, migrant women are evicted from their homes, are denied work papers, and are detained and deported. Every cent of a prostitute's earnings is criminally contaminated. The property and possessions of prostitutes are often forfeited, and mothers, brothers, friends, and lovers can be flung into prison for living off immoral earnings. Most cruelly, a prostitute cannot keep her children. Most prostitutes are mothers, and most are in the game for their children. In many countries, however, social workers have the power to take a prostitute's children out of "moral danger" into "care." In these ways, the state curtails women's power, diverting illicit female money back into the coffers of male circulation and curtailing the emergence of independent female heads of family.

Sexwork that benefits the male state, however, is tolerated and administered by a system of international euphemisms: massage parlors, escort agencies, bars, rest and recreation resorts, and so on, which are run not by hookers but by male "entertainment managers." In Thailand, for example, prostitution inhabits a twilight realm of legal ambiguity. The law makes prostitution a crime, but the green light is given to male "tour operators" and "entertainment managers," whose operations are sanctioned and defined as the "personal service sector."

Most prostitutes regard legalized prostitution as legalized abuse. Despite its benign ring, legalization places prostitution under criminal law instead of commercial law, where it is tightly curbed by the state and administered by the police. Instead, prostitutes want the law off their bodies and are calling for the decriminalization of the profession and the repeal of all legislation not ordinarily applicable to a business or trade.

Legalization puts women's bodies firmly in men's hands. In the aptly named Chicken Ranch, a legalized brothel in Nevada, prostitutes are forced to work three weeks at a stretch, servicing any man who picks them, at any time of the day or night, a dizzying and dispiriting carousel of faceless tricks. In many of the legalized brothels and clubs in Europe, Lisbet, a German prostitute, told me, "Women have no right to refuse men and often no right to use a condom."

Under legalization, the profits of women's work clatter into men's pockets. The state becomes a licit pimp, penning prostitutes in brothels and levying punitive taxes at rates higher than other workers. In Germany, legalized prostitutes pay 56 percent of their earnings in taxes, but, unlike other taxpayers, they are not eligible for any social benefits whatsoever. Under legalization, the state controls prostitutes' work and leisure, preventing organization and often making it very hard for them to leave the trade if they wish. Most prostitutes prefer to work illegally rather than submit to the abusive and humiliating ordeals of state-controlled brothels.

French prostitutes cannot live with a husband, wife, lover, or child, as anyone under their roof can be charged with "cohabitation." Italian prostitutes cannot help their husbands or wives pay the rent or give their parents money, as they can be charged with living off "immoral earnings." In Britain, engaging in prostitution is not a crime (which lets the johns off the hook), but virtually every aspect of a prostitute's work is criminalized. Two women working together for safety can be charged with keeping a brothel. In Switzerland, if a woman decides to leave the trade and seek other work, she first has to get a "good girl" letter from the police to prove her good conduct. To get the letter, she has to wait three years without working as a prostitute to prove her good conduct. Until then, she cannot legally find other work. In Frankfurt, zoning laws force women to work the deserted harbor area, where they can be tortured and dumped in the water without a stir. In Canada, prostitution is not a crime, but "communicating for the purposes of prostitution" is. Prostitutes can be penalized for organizing and informing each other of dangerous tricks or corrupt police. Austrian prostitutes have to report to the police simply to go on holiday. Some of the most appalling conditions prevail in India. Between 1980 and 1984, not a single landlord was arrested for illegally pandering to prostitutes, but 44,633 prostitutes were arrested for soliciting in Bombay alone.

As Dolores French, author, activist, and prostitute, told me in a private interview, "Legalizing prostitution sees women as a controlled substance—controlled by men." The international prostitutes' movement thus calls for the *decriminalization*, not the *legalization*, of their work. Prostitutes demand that their work be respected as a social service for both men and women and that it be brought under commercial law like other professions. Why, they ask, can masseurs command respect and gratitude for servicing naked clients in comfortable rooms, while prostitutes are criminalized? If their work were decriminalized, prostitutes could ply their trade in safety and respect, paying normal rent and taxes, in houses as clean and comfortable as those of the average therapist or chiropractor.

Prostitutes insist it is not the exchange of money that demeans them but the conditions under which the exchange is made. They demand, as a priority, the right to choose and refuse their clients, rejecting men who are in any way disrespectful or offensive, drunk, or simply unsavory. No respect, they say, no sex. Prostitutes also want the right to stipulate what services they offer. Some prefer to give handshandies, others prefer vanilla sex. Some prefer to work with their mouths, others with a whip. Some refuse to undress. Most refuse anal sex. Many refuse to kiss. All demand that they be free to negotiate these preferences safely and professionally with their clients and that the prostitutes have the final say on the terms.

Some clients are experts at anger, venting on whores their misogyny and sexual despair. If sexwork were decriminalized, prostitutes could work in conjunction with trained therapists, offering counseling referral for clients in need. Prostitutes could also organize collectively, educating each other, their clients, and the public about sexual pleasure and sexual health.

Prostitutes scoff at the notion that the criminal laws are there to protect them. Why, they ask, are men arrested for paying prostitutes but not arrested for raping them? Prostitution catches the law with its pants down. In the eyes of the prostitute, the emperor has no clothes: Those who make the prostitution laws are often the ones who break the laws. Police are ambiguous exterminating angels, curbing and harassing a trade they don't really want to destroy. Prostitutes insist that the police are their greatest scourge, demanding freebies, raping them in vans and in precincts, and interfering with safe sex practices by puncturing holes in condoms and confiscating bleach. In the states of Washington and Arizona, cops are legally allowed to have sex with prostitutes in order to entrap them. In New York, police are on record for confiscating women's shoes in the winter and forcing them to walk home barefoot through the icy streets.

Prostitutes are calling internationally for the end to all police harassment and to the forced testing of prostitutes for HIV.[56] In the current climate of sexual paranoia, prostitutes are being demonized as deadly nightshades, fatally infecting good family men. A hue and cry has gone up around the world, with public officials clamoring for prostitutes to be force-tested for HIV and corralled into quarantine. Officials, however, have been far less gung ho about throwing a cordon sanitaire of arrests, tests, and quarantine around johns, perhaps because so many of these good public servants are johns themselves.

Since most johns are husbands, the current call for legalization stems

56. See Delacoste and Alexander, "Prostitutes Are Being Scapegoated for Heterosexual AIDS," in *Sex Work*, 248–63. See also Anne McClintock, "Safe Sluts," *Village Voice*, 20 Aug. 1991.

less from recognition of prostitutes' rights than from the illusion that herding prostitutes into brothels and force-testing them for HIV will protect good family men from infection. Force-testing prostitutes, however, only fosters the illusion that either partner is then safe without a condom.

As prostitutes tirelessly point out, it is not the exchange of cash but high-risk behaviors that transmit disease. Moreover, safe sex, not testing, prevents HIV. As Jasmin, a German prostitute, told me in a private interview, "Testing is always too late." Most sexworkers, except, perhaps, for the very young, the very desperate, and those denied access to condoms, insist that men use condoms for all services, including handshandies and oral sex. As a result, studies show that, contrary to popular stigma, cases of HIV for prostitutes who are not also IV drug users remain consistently low.

Of greater concern than a safe sex slut is a client who refuses a condom. For prostitutes, the onus is on the woman to get the rubber on the man. As Jasmin told me, "Some men ask me: 'I want it without a condom.' I say: 'You can't pay me what my life is worth. Get out of here.'" Thus, the European Congress report on AIDS demanded that managers of clubs, brothels, and Eros Centers who forcibly prevent prostitutes from using condoms should be punished by criminal law for attempted homicide.

Speakers at the European Congress voiced greatest concern for the plight of migrant workers in the new Europe. In 1992, borders within the "European Fortress" will be opened to all workers but not to prostitutes. Unless prostitutes are recognized as workers like everyone else, migrant prostitutes, in particular, will suffer the increasing indignities of arrests, deportation, and racist assaults. Prostitutes are more aware than anyone else of the ordeals of forced prostitution. They insist that decriminalizing voluntary sexwork will make it far easier to detect and destroy forced prostitution.

The United Nations has estimated that by the year 2000 tourism will be the most important economic activity in the world.[57] The international politics of Third World debt and the international pursuit of commercial sex have become deeply entwined, turning sex tourism into a surefire, coin-spinning venture—with most of the profits clattering into the coffers of the multinationals. Sex tourism is creating both a new kind of economic dependence and a new kind of international refusal. In many countries, tourism has replaced products, such as bauxite and sugar, as the leading earner

57. See Thanh-Dam Truong, *Sex, Money, and Morality: Prostitution and Tourism in Southeast Asia* (London: Zed, 1990). For a more detailed discussion of this book, see my review in the *Times Literary Supplement*, 16 Aug. 1991, 10.

of foreign exchange. The militarization of sexuality and the sexualization of the military have deep international implications, as well. Millions of women and men work in countries officially designated as R and R sites for the U.S. military, in the burgeoning cruise ship industry, and in tourist hotels, clubs, and resorts. Sex tourism depends on powerful constructions of race and gender: on the militarization of masculinity, on foreign businessmen willing to invest in sexual travel, and on a racial geography of sex that persuades privileged men that women in economically disempowered countries will be more sexually available and pliant.[58] As Life Travel assured male adventurers in Thailand, "Taking a woman here is as easy as buying a package of cigarettes."[59] Sex tourism depends on women and men available to sell their services and on a network of international companies willing to foster local bureaucratic structures, to organize sex tours, and to prevent sexworkers from organizing.

The boy's-own adventure of sex travel is as much about empire as it is about sun, sex, and souvenirs. Foreign sunseekers fly to Southeast Asia with airlines that promise to embody the feminine quintessence of their nation: "Singapore girl, you're a great way to fly." As Thai Airline advertised, "Some say it's our beautiful wide-bodied DC-10s that cause so many heads to turn. . . . We think our beautiful slim-bodied hostesses have a lot to do with it."[60] Multinationals, borrowing the R and R idea from the U.S. military, regularly send male employees on package tours to be sexually serviced by women billed as "little slaves who give real Thai warmth."[61] As yet, there are no package tours for female executives from Tokyo, Dallas, and Ryad; and company wives chafing under the sexual ennui of marriage do not light out in droves for a "taste" of the Orient.

The current social context of most prostitution—pleasure for men and work for women—well-nigh guarantees its sexism. Men enjoy privileged access to sexual pleasure, to porn, and to prostitution, not to mention that hardy perennial, the double standard. Women's desire, by contrast, has been crimped and confined to history's sad museum of corsets, chastity belts, and the virginity cult. Contexts, however, can be changed, and empowering prostitutes empowers all women. Dolores French suggested

58. Cynthia Enloe, *Bananas, Beaches, and Bases: Making Feminist Sense of International Politics* (Berkeley: University of California Press, 1990).
59. Quoted in Thanh-Dam Truong, *Sex, Money, and Morality*, 178.
60. Quoted in Thanh-Dam Truong, *Sex, Money, and Morality*, 179.
61. Quoted in Thanh-Dam Truong, *Sex, Money, and Morality*, 178.

to me in a private interview that many women fear prostitutes because they make women feel tricked. Prostitutes call men's bluff, challenging the gendered distribution of power and profit by flagrantly demanding money for nonreciprocal sex that many women give for free.

History changes the meaning of the sexual body. There is no one privileged narrative of prostitution, nor is there any one politically correct politics of prostitution. Some sexworkers ply their trade in opulent hotels, some in parked cars, some in bars and cafés, some in agricultural plantations and migrant worker hostels, some on cruise liners, some at R and R sites for the U.S. military. Sexworkers do not share the same reasons for entering the trade, nor do they experience the work in the same way. Not all sexworkers are women; not all customers are men. The enormous trade in gay commercial sex complicates the notion that prostitution is no more than the embodiment of female bondage. By some men's accounts, commercial sex for women—arguably one of the deepest taboos of all—is on the increase. What is crucial, however, is that prostitutes themselves define the conditions for organizing their work to suit their own local needs and contexts.

Perpetuating the image of prostitutes as either broken baby dolls or fatal Frankenhookers serves only to heighten the climate of violence and hypocrisy under which so many women live. Indeed, the feminist critique of prostitutes is to my mind theoretically misbegotten and strategically unsound, short-circuiting sexworkers' efforts (many of whom are feminists themselves) to transform the trade to meet their own needs. Whatever else it is, female prostitution is the erasure of a woman's sexual desire in exchange for cash. It is, however, no different in that respect from most other forms of women's work. Prostitution that is not tightly controlled by men differs from most women's work in that it is far better paid, has flexible working hours, and gives women considerable economic independence from men. As a result, working-class women and women of color are able to educate themselves, find social mobility, and raise their children in the comfort and security usually given to only good white girls.

It seems crucial, therefore, to remain alert to the nuances and paradoxes of prostitution rather than to patronize prostitutes as embodiments of female sexual degradation or to glamorize them as unambiguous heroines of female revolt. Sexwork is a gendered form of work that takes its myriad meanings from the different societies in which it emerges.

Would feminists who condemn prostitutes for becoming complicit in commodity fetishism, for example, make the same criticism of black South

African mine workers who drag from the earth the very stuff of commodity fetishism? Doesn't the argument that prostitutes sell themselves bear an uncanny and perilous resemblance to the sanctioned male view that a woman's identity is *equivalent* to her sexuality? Prostitutes do not sell themselves; rather, like all workers (including feminists), they exchange specific services for cash and carefully negotiate with their clients what services they provide, at what rate, and for how long.

The whore stigma disciplines all women. As one prostitute told me in a private conversation, "It's the stigma that hurts, not the sex. The sex is easy. Facing the world's hate is what breaks me down." The license to despise a prostitute is a license to despise any woman who takes sex, money, and mobility into her hands. If tricks are at liberty to abuse whores, chances are they will abuse other women. Empowering whores empowers all women, and educating men to respect prostitutes educates men to respect all women.

Society demonizes sexworkers because they demand more money than women should for services men expect for free. Prostitutes screw the system, dangerously interfering in the male distribution of property, power, and profit. As Margo St. James puts it, "In private the whore has power. The great fear for men, who are running things, is that if whores have a voice, suddenly good women are going to find out how much their time is worth, and how to ask for money."[62] By organizing for decriminalization, prostitutes are organizing to put control of women's work back in women's hands.

62. "The Reclamation of Whores," in Bell, *Good Girls/Bad Girls*, 82.

Bodies and God: Poststructuralist Feminists Return to the Fold of Spiritual Materialism

Kathryn Bond Stockton

> In contemporary feminist theory, no issue is more vexed than that of determining the relations between the feminine body as a figure in discourse and as material presence or biological entity. The debates surrounding this question in recent years have been the most highly charged, but also perhaps the most fruitful.
>
> —Mary Jacobus, Evelyn Fox Keller, Sally Shuttleworth, in their introduction to *Body/Politics: Women and the Discourses of Science*

> What if matter had always, already, had a part but was yet invisible, beyond the senses, moving in ways alien to any fixed reflection.
>
> —Luce Irigaray, *Speculum of the Other Woman*

Poststructuralists and Victorians

Poststructuralist feminists are the new Victorians. What 'God' was to Victorian thinkers, 'the body' is to poststructuralist feminists: an object of

I gratefully acknowledge Melanee Cherry, Barry Weller, and Srinivas Aravamudan for their astute criticisms of this essay's earlier drafts. Many thanks to Margie Ferguson, Jennifer Wicke, and Meg Sachse for superb editorial support.

doubt and speculation but also a necessary fiction and an object of faith.[1] Cultivating belief in 'real bodies' as 'material presence', poststructuralist feminists now want to compensate for deconstructive excesses and extreme forms of social constructionism, both of which so heavily stress how language constructs human beings and their world.[2] That is to say, poststructuralist feminists are becoming believers as they return to the fold of materialism.[3]

What can *materialism* mean to poststructuralists? Materialism is now difficult to think; it is the opaque impasse poststructuralists have reached. I don't mean materialism in the sense of ideologies by which we live out our relations to the real (ideology as "a material practice," Althusser would say).[4] Few would deny that materialism in this sense is laced with construc-

1. When I refer to *poststructuralist* feminists or *poststructuralists* in this essay, I will be referring to those theorists both who live in the postmodern age (post–World War II) and who consciously borrow heavily from deconstruction. Although I considered using the term *postmodern* in this way—as signaling both a period designation and a theoretical orientation—I decided to choose (what might be regarded as) a narrower term. I wish, in this way, to mark my awareness that some theorists (mostly European) still distinguish between the terms *postmodern* and *poststructuralist* as a way to distinguish philosophically oriented forms of deconstruction (which they call *poststructuralist*) from the postmodern playfulness of Lyotard and Baudrillard.

2. Let me, from the outset, call attention to a typographical dilemma that relates to my essay's argument. In accordance with the *Chicago Manual of Style*, I am required to enclose philosophical terms in single quotation marks ('being', 'nonbeing', and 'the divine' are examples this style book furnishes). Words used as words are italicized (such as all the words in this paragraph I have marked instead with single quotation marks); words used ironically are enclosed in double quotation marks, along with material quoted from texts. My dilemma is this: I wish to mark several terms in this essay as terms poststructuralists now consistently interrogate—terms such as 'God', but also terms such as 'body', 'reality', 'man', 'woman', 'objectivity', and 'biology', which have not traditionally been deemed philosophical but which have been deemed so over the course of poststructuralist discussions. Even so, the reader will notice that in the case of 'body', 'real', and 'reality' I will at times let quotation marks drop. By this move I wish to emphasize that the body outside quotation marks (real bodies that exist apart from cultural markings) forms the object of poststructuralist feminist belief.

3. I use the word *return* to describe these feminists' reconsideration of what may look like positivist materialist claims, even though they return as poststructuralists. I use this term because *going back* and reexamining prior theories and assumptions is how these feminists seem to view what they are doing.

4. Althusser explains: "Where only a single subject (such and such an individual) is concerned, the existence of the ideas of his [ideological] belief is material in that his ideas are his material actions inserted into material practices governed by material rituals which are

tions. I mean materialism in its strongest sense: the material onto which we map our constructions, 'matter on its own terms' that might resist or pressure our constructions, or prove independent of them altogether. This materialism is the nondiscursive something poststructuralist feminists now want to embrace, the extradiscursive something they confess necessarily eludes them. This materialism stands as a God that might be approached through fictions and faith but never glimpsed naked. Real bodies are what never appear.

I want to speculate on this strange eclipse, as if to keep vigil with this newly emerging feminist tendency to spiritualize bodies, to endow bodies with sacred enigmas and mystical escapes—all in order to gesture toward bodies that stand apart from the constructions that render them. Poststructuralist feminists like Jane Gallop, for example, admit that bodies elaborately present themselves as objects for construction. Yet, Gallop argues, bodies resist domination by the mind. The body is "a bodily enigma," "an inscrutable given," and "points to an outside—beyond/before language."[5] "The body is enigmatic," moreover, "because it is not a creation of the mind" and "will never be totally dominated by man-made meaning" (*TTB*, 18, 19).

Gallop exemplifies the poststructuralist feminist who, *in the act* of making problematic what (we think) Victorians often took for granted—the body's presence—ends up sounding like a Victorian believer. Stranger yet, poststructuralist feminists write versions of a *spiritual* materialism that remarkably echo Victorian discussions of bodies and God.[6] For instance, we find the Victorian Thomas Carlyle bent around conundrums that do not die out in the nineteenth century but that surface, resurgent, to plague poststructuralists. This bend is particularly true of Carlyle's discussion of bodies

---

themselves defined by the material ideological apparatus from which derives the ideas of that subject" (see Louis Althusser, *Lenin and Philosophy and Other Essays*, trans. Ben Brewster [New York: Monthly Review Press, 1971], 169). Alex Callinicos provides this gloss: "Despite the repetition of the word 'material' like an incantation, we can see that the materiality of a set of ideological beliefs derives from the fact that they are, firstly, embodied in particular social practices, and, secondly, the products of what Althusser calls an Ideological State Apparatus (ISA)" (see Alex Callinicos, *Althusser's Marxism* [London: Pluto Press Ltd., 1976], 63–64).

5. Jane Gallop, *Thinking Through the Body* (New York: Columbia University Press, 1988), 13, 16. All further references to this text will be abbreviated *TTB*.

6. Thinking I had coined the phrase *spiritual materialism*, I was intrigued to discover that the phrase has also been used by Chogyam Trungpa in his book *Cutting Through Spiritual Materialism* (Berkeley: Shambhala, 1973).

as "mystic unfathomable Visibilities." I seek to illuminate this unexpected join between poststructuralist feminists and Victorian intellectuals, such as Carlyle. By doing so, I believe, we can better locate the conceptual dilemmas these feminists face in their returns to materialism and can better understand why spiritualizing gestures suggest themselves to feminists as ways to produce escapes *back* to bodies.

Three exemplars of this feminist curve have emerged in Donna Haraway, Jane Gallop, and Luce Irigaray. Admittedly, Haraway and Gallop, along with Irigaray, are among those feminists I seek when I look to be shaken into feminist disturbance. Gallop and Haraway present, moreover, an intriguing pair, since they would not be, to my mind, likely candidates for spiritual gestures. Yet, both of these feminists, entirely sympathetic to, familiar with, and shaped by poststructuralist theory and its largely constructionist slant, now worry about where the body might stand apart from, or at times against, the representations that encode it at every turn. Unfolding their worry, we will find that Haraway and Gallop evince a more oblique form of spiritual materialism. They, unlike Irigaray, do not overtly use Christian discourse in order to leverage their returns upon the body. In this way, we could distinguish between greater and lesser spiritual materialisms, or, as I prefer to regard them, materialisms which are oblique or overt in their spiritualizing character. Nonetheless, however we may cut between Gallop and Haraway on the one hand, and Irigaray (and Carlyle) on the other, I want to suggest that the antitranscendental bent of poststructuralist feminists only masks their deep dependence upon the kinds of gestures commonly deemed spiritual in Victorian writings. Most likely, it is precisely because of their differences that I have been struck by these feminists' surprising convergence on the plane of spiritual materialism.

Haraway, a biologist and philosopher of science, is clearly seeking new ways to conceptualize 'objectivity' and 'biology'; she thinks we lose too much if we see "the body itself" as only "a blank page for social inscriptions" without seeing how our bodies, by being agents themselves, resist linguistic capture.[7] Gallop, a psychoanalytic theorist and literary critic of French and American texts (quite removed from Haraway, in this respect), continues to explore the linguistic and materialist issues she has pondered for over a

7. Haraway captured feminists' attention with her now-legendary essay "A Manifesto for Cyborgs: Science, Technology, and Socialist Feminism in the 1980s," *Socialist Review* 80, no. 2 (March–April 1985): 65–107. The publication of her masterpiece on primatology, *Primate Visions: Gender, Race, and Nature in the World of Modern Science* (New York: Routledge, 1989), has only strengthened her position as a leading theoretical voice.

decade: the frictions between bodies and language and between political and psychoanalytic categories.[8] Hence her attempt in *Thinking Through the Body* to make *bedfellows* (her term) of Adrienne Rich and Roland Barthes, and to explore "the impossibility in our cultural tradition of separating an earnest attempt to listen to the material from an agenda for better control" (*TTB*, 4). For both Haraway and Gallop, political responsibility to real bodies and political rage against "agenda[s] for better control" (Gallop) spur their different "attempt[s] to listen to the material."[9] This responsibility and rage is shared by Irigaray, the widely read deconstructive feminist philosopher and psychoanalyst, steeped in French intellectual traditions. Irigaray is almost always read as an essentialist, sometimes dismissed but only superficially understood as a mystic, rarely seriously deemed a materialist, and never read as a spiritual materialist, as I primarily wish to read her. It is curious to me that her materialism always gets reduced to essentialism, since her early works clearly evince Gallop and Haraway's same strong concerns for (female) bodies that resist constructions and agendas for control.

It is time to scrutinize materialism in poststructuralist feminist thought and the undeniable ways in which spiritualizing means have come to justify materialist ends. As a poststructuralist feminist schooled in theologies and spiritual traditions, I confess my fascination with these feminist returns. I confess again: Though I am not necessarily arguing for their claims, I continue to find these feminists inspiring. The problems and limits that stem from these versions of spiritual materialism reveal, I suggest, some of the most telling concerns we encounter in feminist studies.

At first glance, of course, the subversive possibilities of resubmitting to anything spiritual would not appear promising. In the discussions of many poststructuralist theorists, whether Marxists or feminists, "god-talk," as Har-

8. Gallop's career began with her book on Sade (*Intersections: A Reading of Sade with Bataille, Blanchot, and Klossowski* [Lincoln: University of Nebraska Press, 1981]). Her next two books focused squarely on psychoanalytic theory: *The Daughter's Seduction: Feminism and Psychoanalysis* (Ithaca: Cornell University Press, 1982) and *Reading Lacan* (Ithaca: Cornell University Press, 1985). *Thinking Through the Body* follows as an extended meditation on and challenge to the mind-body split, containing a collection of Gallop's feminist essays written over a ten-year span.

9. On the issue of control, Haraway confesses her "nervousness about the sex/gender distinction in the recent history of feminist theory," by means of which "sex is 'resourced' for its representation as gender, which 'we' can control." See Donna Haraway, "Situated Knowledges: The Science Question in Feminism and the Privilege of Partial Perspective," *Feminist Studies* 14 (Fall 1988): 592. All further references to this text will be abbreviated SK.

away tags it, serves as the most convenient foil to subversive theorizing. Clearly, I am kicking against the goads when I argue that some materialist theories may be read as forms of spiritual discourse. My efforts in this direction are not meant to criticize feminists, as if I were upbraiding them for writing spiritualities. Nor is my goal to argue for a more pristine poststructuralist stance. My aim is to dramatize a difficulty, daunting even for poststructuralists: how to depart from forms of faith or mysticisms when we are anxious to envision movements beyond oppression. Hopes and desire for escape, even at this historical juncture, often find their way, and quite unknowingly, into recaptures of spiritual schemas.

Unbind *spiritual*. The connotations of *religious doctrine* and *religious practices* would seem to be implied, and, indeed, *spiritual* can include such meanings. Yet, *spiritual discourse* is not merely language-use bound to religious institutions or to the representations of traditionally religious behaviors. Spiritual discourse is discourse on what exceeds human sign systems; discourse on where human meanings fail; discourse on escapes from discourse; and, most importantly, culturally constructed discourse on escapes from culture, though from the present standpoint these escapes are always incomplete and deferred.[10] *Spiritual* can illumine both Victorians' and poststructuralists' reliance on general categories of inscrutabilities.

10. Readers may wonder how Judeo-Christian people of the Book can be linked to the failure of human meaning and to discourse on what exceeds human sign systems. Let me underscore, then, how much the sense of both Old and New Testament revelations carries the sense of inscrutable communications—whether it be the opaque revelation of Yahweh ("I AM THAT I AM " [Exodus 3:14]) or the puzzling statements by and about Jesus that make the opacity of his Person the Word that escapes full human comprehension. By their enigmatic qualities, these revelations purposely and divinely cause human meanings to fail their familiar transparencies—all in order to open onto meaning that can appear only as discourse in excess of established discourse.

Let me say, in addition, that lest it seem that I slip imprecisely in this definition between the terms *exceeds*, *fails*, and *escapes* (and I could easily add *eludes*), these are terms that are used synonymously both by the poststructuralist feminists in this essay and by those who write on mysticism generally. For evidence with regard to mysticism, see Evelyn Underhill, *Mysticism* (New York: New American Library, 1974), 3–37. Since, for the purposes of length, I have kept my quotations from Gallop and Haraway short, see the full texts of Gallop's "Thinking Through the Body" (*TTB*, 1–9) and "The Bodily Enigma" (*TTB*, 11–20), and Haraway's "Situated Knowledges." Gallop's page four, for example, uses the terms *failure*, *exceeds*, and *impossibility* in fairly close succession (and in opposition to the term *transparent* on her previous page). Both Gallop and Haraway, to be sure, distance themselves from the term *transcendence*, even while they continue to use the terms listed above; in the mystical literature a term like *escape* is consistently used in apposition to the term *transcend* (see Underhill, *Mysticism*, 33).

Two points of clarification are required here. First, one might wonder to what extent these features of spiritual discourse prove unique to spiritual discourse. In other words, might some poststructuralists argue that my definition of spiritual discourse could also be cited for literary discourse? I am not convinced that the difference matters. It may not matter because I simply want to show that the poststructuralist stance on language (with its stress on the failure of language fully to capture materiality) makes poststructuralist gestures toward real bodies correspond to gestures Victorians called spiritual. When they bend back to bodies, poststructuralists almost inevitably repeat a Judeo-Christian problematic, since they must invest in beliefs in something real that escapes and exceeds human sign systems. At the very least, the poststructuralist distinction between a hidden material 'reality' and a hidden spiritual 'reality' must fall into question. My second clarification concerns what could seem a too neat correspondence. That is to say, the correspondence I note here does not make Victorian spiritualizing the same as that of poststructuralists. True, for many Victorian intellectuals, among them Carlyle (a major contributor to Victorian religious thought), spirituality lies equally close, if not closer, to conceptions of enigma/inscrutability/escape than it does to the religious doctrines of their day. Unlike poststructuralist thinkers, however, many Victorian intellectuals hold their spiritual discourse in obvious tension with or against the more traditional religious contexts out of which they write. Poststructuralists, by contrast, are generally so dismissive of religion in terms of institutions and practice that their spiritualizing seems idiosyncratic, cut free from the dominant strands of Judeo-Christian traditions—even when it is not.

Unbend the poststructuralist investment in writing escapes back to bodies. This particular impetus for escapes emerges from a sense that the dominant culture's allowed relations to 'one's own body' (especially if one lives under a 'woman' sign) are not desirable. Desire for escape from the constructions and commodifications of the body accompany, furthermore, a desire to produce those bodies elsewhere, in some other cultural space, where bodies might be returned upon, and so touched upon, on different terms and in different ways.[11]

11. We see this impetus for an escape-as-return in other significant (and overlapping) quarters of theorizing. Michele Wallace, for example, revisits Houston Baker's trope of the black hole as a way of conceiving how black feminist creativity escapes prevailing classifications and interpretations (even those that prevail among white feminists and African American men): "An object or energy," she writes, "enters the black hole, is infinitely compressed to zero volume, as Baker reported, then it passes through to another dimension, whereupon the object or energy reassumes volume, mass, form, direction, velocity,

This is where humanist concepts of alienation join hands with poststructuralist concepts of indeterminacy. Before poststructuralism, *alienation* conveyed the sense that the dominant culture's allowed relations to one's own body fundamentally conflicted with one's real self—from which one was alienated.[12] Now, in a postmodern period that is as wary of real selves as real bodies, we cannot use any determinate sense of an original or essential self by which to mark (as we desperately need to do) our alienations. The most we seem able to perform is a scream against our constructions—to say they don't suit us. If we do not like their opposite, more privileged constructions any better (masculine instead of feminine ones, for example) but desire to appear *outside the system* of currently available alternatives, then we are left indeterminate. Indeterminacy becomes, in this way, our mode of resistance to those determinate selves we know that we do not want to be.

This projection outside known systems seems at least obliquely spiritualizing (as it seems to me in Gallop and Haraway); in its move to exceed discourses we know, this projection outside can overtly employ (as Irigaray, to be sure, overtly employs) spiritual discourse (as I have defined it, discourse on an escape from discourse). This faith in escape for the sake of our bodies, as the necessary precondition for *non-alienated embodiment*, calls forth poststructuralist logic concerning materialism as a hidden God. That is to say, it parallels poststructuralist moves to believe in a materiality that, like God, escapes our constructions, while still rendering this 'matter on its own terms', like God, inaccessible to view.

Hope in Failure: Feminists' *Felix Culpa*

The spiritualizing going on around us in "theory" involves us in failures of human meaning; it immerses us in (discursive) attempts to escape from discourse. No wonder we find dramatically reemerging in feminist forms the Christian doctrine of *felix culpa*, or, "the happy fall"—the doctrine that proclaims that human failure makes possible a greater good. (For

all the properties of visibility and concreteness, but in another, perhaps unimaginable, dimension." See Michele Wallace, *Invisibility Blues: From Pop to Theory* (London: Verso, 1990), 218.

12. Marx, of course, is the famous example here. For a discussion of "the alienation of labor," which demonstrates that "labor is *external* to the worker, i.e., it does not belong to his essential being," see Karl Marx, *Economic and Philosophic Manuscripts of 1844* (Moscow: Foreign Languages Publishing House), 68–81. For a feminist version of alienation, see Catherine MacKinnon, "Feminism, Marxism, Method, and the State: An Agenda for Theory," *Signs* 7, no. 3 (1982): 515–44.

Christians, for example, humanity's fall makes possible the greater good of Christ's appearing.) Indeed, feminists of poststructuralist stripes are investing in failure for the sake of our future, for what failure might eventually make luminous by screening off our current sights. Now more than ever, poststructuralist feminists are losing their hope in 'positive' projects that directly deliver 'the' feminine difference, and they are placing hope, instead, in the failure of the dominant constructions that would *fix* them.[13] Feminine specificity, given this scenario, has more to do with escape (what 'she' is not, or what 'she' is elsewhere) than with essence (what 'she' is), for we need escapes from fixed constructions if we are to produce new bodies and selves.

Feminists, to be sure, have long desired the failure of (masculine) meanings. Yet, the advent of poststructuralism has made feminists newly cautious toward, if not downright resistant to, any fixed feminist meanings. One senses this leeriness in Jacqueline Rose's 1983 essay "Femininity and Its Discontents." Arguing against what she saw at that time as "the present discarding of psychoanalysis in favor of forms of analysis felt as more material in their substance and immediately political in their effects," Rose was arguing for a psychoanalysis (namely, Freud's) that lets us put feminist hope in the failure of who we are as 'women' and 'men':

> The unconscious constantly reveals the "failure" of identity. Because there is no continuity of psychic life, so there is no stability of sexual identity, no position for women (or for men) which is ever simply achieved. . . . "Failure" is not a moment to be regretted in a process of adaptation. . . . Instead "failure" is something endlessly repeated and relived moment by moment throughout our individual histories. . . . Feminism's affinity with psychoanalysis rests above all, I would argue, with this recognition that there is a resistance to identity at the very heart of psychic life.[14]

Feminist poststructuralist theorizing is still full of attempts to "unthink" and "render impossible" the versions of bodies and selves that we

13. I use *fix* in this sentence in two senses: (1) dominant gender constructions attempt to "fix" women in order to make them "right" and proper in appearance, behavior, language, and occupation; (2) dominant constructions attempt to "fix" women to assured and familiar positions in culture. This doubleness constitutes what we might call women's "fix" (their bind and, sometimes, their addiction).

14. Jacqueline Rose, *Sexuality in the Field of Vision* (London: Verso Press, 1986), 83, 90–91.

have known, even the feminist versions that we have come to prefer.[15] Hence, Mary Ann Doane acknowledges that "all feminist positions are in some sense uninhabitable," echoing Elizabeth Weed's comments on the "impossible . . . relation of *women* to feminism."[16] Ellen Rooney, in a similar vein, seeks "the possibility of a political gesture that is not rooted in identity" (*CT*, 239). In fact, the desire to escape fixed gestures—toward politics or identities—runs so strong in these feminists that even their materialist cautions against escape end with imagining some vision of it. Donna Haraway, for example, in her effort to stress materialities, seeks escape from escapes like Christian "salvation history" (*CT*, 175). Yet, she ends her cyborg essay by envisioning what reads like a feminist embrace of Christian Pentecost: "a dream *not of a common language*, but of a powerful infidel *heteroglossia* . . . a feminist speaking in tongues" (*CT*, 204; my emphasis). In "Post-Utopian Difference," Mary Ann Doane actually critiques *as utopian* Rose's feminist hope in failed identities. We can cling to "the constant failure of sexual identity, its instability, or even its impossibility," but we must remember, Doane would caution, that this belief is a utopian gesture, for "identity in the realm of the social may be oppressive but insofar as patriarchy seems to work . . . it [identity] cannot be seen either as a failure or an impossibility" (*CT*, 76). With this materialist caution in mind, Doane ends her essay by seeming to reaffirm utopia (but utopian beliefs recognized as utopian):

> My critique of psychoanalysis is not a critique of utopian thinking—to the contrary—but of its misrecognition (as authoritative science). . . . Utopias open up a space for non-essentialized identities—they authorize certain positions rather than others, certain politics rather than others. A utopia is the sighting (in terms of the gaze) and siting (in terms of emplacement) of another possibility. The chance of escaping the same. (*CT*, 78)[17]

15. Throughout his book *Altarity* (Chicago: University of Chicago Press, 1987), Mark Taylor associates poststructuralist "unthinking," "not knowing," and "saying the unsayable" with religious and theological categories. Since his book does not address materialism, however, he does not make these further links.

16. Mary Ann Doane, "Post-Utopian Difference," in *Coming to Terms: Feminism/Theory/Politics*, ed. Elizabeth Weed (New York: Routledge, 1989), 209. All further references to this text will be abbreviated *CT*. See also Elizabeth Weed, "A Man's Place," in *Men in Feminism*, ed. Alice Jardine and Paul Smith (New York: Methuen, 1987), 74.

17. For a consideration of the theological roots and theological implications of particular utopian schemes, see Peter S. Hawkins's *Getting Nowhere: Christian Hope and Utopian Dream* (Cambridge, Mass.: Cowley Publications, 1985). Hawkins helpfully reminds us of how the word "utopia" was conceived: "[Thomas More] coined a word that withdrew with

Escapes remain crucial to Haraway and Doane, in spite of their strong stands against some escapes: Both feminists desperately want out of the material relations we have known, even as both desperately desire new materialities we would embody. Unforeseen, and as yet unrepresented, *embodiments* and *"emplacements"* (as Doane would have it) are what they seek.

Here is the crucial context in which to read Luce Irigaray. Gallop, as usual, has put the matter well. In discussing Irigaray's focus on women's genital lips, she locates in Irigaray's theorizing "the tension between a feminist investment in the referential body and an aspiration to poetics" (*TTB*, 95) ("poetics" is Gallop's term for constructions). Irigaray's "referential illusion," Gallop claims, "might just save (post)modernist poetics from the absurd appearance of asserting the nonreferentiality of language and move it into a more complex encounter with *the anxiety produced by the absence of any certain access to the referent*" (*TTB*, 95–96; my emphasis). Aside from noting that if we substituted "God" for "the referent," this last phrase could apply aptly to Victorian thinkers, I want to emphasize something that Gallop was among the first to notice: Irigaray poeticizes the body that many readers think she essentializes.[18] This point looms radiant among Irigaray's poststructuralist supporters, though they often stress her "strategic" essentialism, arguing that she "risks" biological reference for the sake of making different bodies appear.[19] This slant is ultimately misleading, I believe. A

---

one hand the credibility it extended with the other. He achieved this verbal sleight-of-hand by taking the Greek noun for 'place,' *topos*, and prefixing it with a mysteriously ambivalent 'u.' His learned audience was quick to enjoy the confusion, because More's prefix could be played out in either of two directions. It could be taken as the Greek 'eu,' meaning good, ideal, perfect, or, on the other hand, taken as 'ou,' indicating an absence or deficiency. A linguistic hermaphrodite from birth, 'utopia' might point either to the happy place of one's dreams ('eu-topia') or to no place at all ('ou-topia'). Better yet, it might suggest both realities at once" (5). Based on Hawkins's account, one could say that utopia is a knotting of the good with the absent—a happy gap, until it meets fulfillment. For another theological address to utopia, see "Critique and Justification of Utopia" by the German theologian Paul Tillich (in *Utopias and Utopian Thought*, ed. Frank Manuel [Boston: Houghton Mifflin, 1965]).

18. My book on spiritual materialism and desire between women (Stanford University Press, forthcoming) explores Brontë and Eliot as examples of such Victorian thinkers.

19. See Naomi Schor, "This Essentialism Which Is Not One: Coming to Grips with Irigaray," *Differences* 1, no. 2 (Summer 1989): 38–58; Diana Fuss, *Essentially Speaking: Feminism, Nature, Difference* (New York: Routledge, 1989); Margaret Whitford, "Luce Irigaray and the Female Imaginary: Speaking as a Woman," *Radical Philosophy* 43 (Summer 1986): 3–8.

stress on strategic essentialism bears the rhetorical effect of reemphasizing Irigaray's closeness to the body rather than the ways in which she elaborately *mystifies* it—especially through blatant mystical conceptions. It is not that Irigaray is too close to the body in some assured, or even strategically essentialist, manner; it is perhaps the opposite: The impetus for Irigaray's "referential illusion" (a form of faith?) is her anxiety that we cannot, with certainty, anymore assume access to the referent—and some form of *access*, not just failure, is what she desires.

Far from alone, then, Irigaray is like Doane, like Haraway, like Gallop, in wanting to escape (back) to feminine bodies—to the bodily enigmas that, in Gallop's terms, exist "beyond/before language" by virtue of how they resist words' captures. Irigaray's uniqueness lies, if anywhere, in the explicitness with which she spiritualizes—not just poeticizes—the bodies she would grasp. Pointedly mystical moves, which effectively locate lack and God between 'woman's' genital lips (no small moves, these), make possible her bold belief in women's bodies that escape the dominant constructions that would suture them.[20] Irigaray, on some level, seems to understand, and even to dramatize, what I propose calling real-bodies mysticism. This is the belief (not the certainty) that real bodies may exist on their own terms but that we can reach them only *by the same visionary means that separate us from their 'reality'*.

Real-Bodies Mysticism

For poststructuralist feminists, this separation from 'reality' remains one of the most familiar dilemmas—so much so that in the introduction to *Body/Politics: Women and the Discourses of Science*, Jacobus, Fox Keller, and Shuttleworth cite this dilemma as their central issue, offering the statement in my essay's first epigraph. These feminists wish to hold in "tension" (and Gallop used this word exactly) discursive figures "and" material presences. This implied duality, however, cannot be so easily held, if imagined (in spite of the "and" that serves both to separate and to join

20. I mean *suture* in both its ordinary language sense of "sewing up" and its more technical theoretical sense of "that moment when the subject inserts itself into the symbolic register in the guise of a signifier, and in so doing gains meaning at the expense of being." For the latter definition, see Kaja Silverman, *The Subject of Semiotics* (New York: Oxford, 1983), 200. Both senses suit Irigaray, because she associates women's oppression within the symbolic register (where her body appears only in terms of lack) with the "sewing up" of women's genital lips.

these terms). Even in stating the problem, one can point *only through discourse* to that bodily aspect—"material presence or biological entity"—that exceeds, escapes, or stands partly separate from "a figure in discourse."

Materialism in its discursive shades has shadowed theorists for quite some time. One detects worry over things-in-themselves as early as Barthes's famous structuralist essay "Myth Today." Concluding, Barthes wonders if we can ever know objects apart from the myths by which their cultures grasp them:

> It seems that this is a difficulty pertaining to our times: there is as yet only one possible choice, and this choice can bear only on two equally extreme methods: either to posit a reality which is entirely permeable to history, and ideologize; or, conversely, to posit a reality which is *ultimately* impenetrable, irreducible, and, in this case, poetize. . . . The fact that we cannot manage to achieve more than an unstable grasp of reality doubtless gives the measure of our present alienation. . . . For if we penetrate the object, we liberate it but we destroy it; and if we acknowledge its full weight, we respect it, but we restore it to a state which is still mystified. It would seem that we are condemned for some time yet always to speak *excessively* about reality.[21]

Barthes is discussing what later becomes the debate between full-blown linguistic constructionists (who "posit a reality which is entirely permeable to history") and essentialists, or at least believers in objects that might, at some point, in some way, resist full linguistic construction (who "posit a reality which is *ultimately* impenetrable, irreducible"). His most important insight comes as he approaches his closing, when he recognizes that to pull apart an object's myths is to lose the very object itself ("we liberate it but we destroy it"), for *nothing that we can reach* remains beneath our demystifying penetrations. Extreme constructionism loses its object. Conversely, Barthes notes that to believe that the object does exist, somewhere on its own terms, is to leave it mystified or to mystify anew ("we respect it, but we restore it to a state which is still mystified"). Materialist respect for objects that exist apart from our myths can only serve to "poetize" and thus still "mystify" the very objects materialists or poets would want to deliver in "inalienable" form. Importantly, Barthes's use of *poetize* here should not be confused with Gallop's use of *poeticize*. For Gallop, *poeticize* refers to the

21. Roland Barthes, *Mythologies*, trans. Annette Lavers (New York: Hill and Wang, 1957), 159.

use we make of language's metaphorical properties—its discursive figures. Barthes's *poetize* means nearly the opposite (if one could hold these concepts apart): We poetize when we (think we) point to a reality that exists outside our discursive figures. Truly, then, this distinction collapses, since we can only poetize by poeticizing in a mystical vein.

In fact, Barthes's last point—"that we are condemned for some time yet always to speak *excessively* about reality"—makes clear that every materialist *must* "poetize," must mystify, and even must make mystical, I would claim, the nondiscursive reality for which they would reserve some conceptual, discursive, and material space. On poststructuralist terrain, one cannot speak of "the tension between a feminist investment in the referential body and an aspiration to poetics," as Gallop does for Irigaray, without confessing that these two conceptions cannot rest side by side. One can only lean upon the other, and only one—"an aspiration to poetics"—can ever appear. The most real, most referential thing, cannot be seen.

The legacy of poststructuralist dicta, warning that referents never appear, proves startling in its effects. Theorists have become so squeamish about pointing to the body or to a reality outside of language that they have taken to submitting *the body itself* and *reality* to quotation marks. Here is an oxymoronic confession that they are pointing to an outside to language from within its domain. By contrast, the terms *material conditions*, *material effects*, and *material limits*—increasingly used in our critical climate—are not standardly marked with quotation marks. Even so, in the introduction to her book *Uneven Developments: The Ideological Work of Gender in Mid-Victorian England*, Mary Poovey finds it necessary to qualify even *material conditions*:

> Despite my assumption that the conditions that produce both texts and (partly through them) individual subjects are material in the ever elusive last instance, I also maintain that this famous last instance *is* ever elusive—precisely because the material and economic relations of production can only make themselves known through representations. . . . I return in a moment to the compromise I have tried to strike in my organization of each chapter, but the effect of the self-consciousness I voice here will have to carry over into the rest of the book, where I occasionally represent the "real" as if it were a linear development that could shed both textualization and the quotation marks that signify that it is always a social construction.[22]

22. Mary Poovey, *Uneven Developments: The Ideological Work of Gender in Mid-Victorian England* (Chicago: University of Chicago Press, 1988), 18.

What is material, we note, has become perhaps the most "elusive" (and remains an "ever elusive") category in deconstructive thought. Representations are endlessly available, whereas materiality and bodies elude, demanding now belief, self-conscious confession, and quotation marks that the 'real' cannot shed.

In Haraway's 1988 essay "Situated Knowledges: The Science Question in Feminism and the Privilege of Partial Perspective," she reveals a familiar nervousness about where extreme constructionism—especially deconstruction—has left us vis-à-vis 'reality' (which Haraway, at the start, italicizes, letting italics drop as she states her desires):

> The strong program in the sociology of knowledge joins with the lovely and nasty tools of semiology and deconstruction to insist on the rhetorical nature of truth, including scientific truth. . . . So much for those of us who would still like to talk about *reality* with more confidence than we allow to the Christian Right when they discuss the Second Coming and their being raptured out of the final destruction of the world. We would like to think our appeals to real worlds are more than a desperate lurch away from cynicism and an act of faith like any other cult's. (SK, 577)

What makes Haraway nervous is twofold: (1) since deconstruction, we cannot intelligently talk about reality without sounding like (very conservative) religious believers whose appeals to hidden realities, beyond worldly constructions, must always constitute "an act of faith"; (2) we need to talk about reality, real bodies, and real worlds if we are to hold each other "responsible" (a key word for Haraway) for how we learn to see a world of bodies and things that are agents themselves.

Haraway wants the fruits of real-bodies mysticism, minus mysticism. She eschews any "act of faith" that relies on *escapes* from embodiment. She states: "To lose authoritative biological accounts of sex, which set up productive tensions with gender, seems to be to lose too much; it seems to be to lose not just analytic power within a particular Western tradition but also the body itself as anything but a blank page for social inscriptions, including those of biological discourse" (SK, 591). What Haraway wants is something very close to the "tension" that Gallop and the editors of *Body/ Politics* outline: the tension between discursive figures and material presences. Not surprisingly, Haraway's statement of the problem, reminiscent of Gallop's and the editors', depends largely on an unexamined "and" (which she italicizes) that joins and separates both sides of the equation (and keeps both sides within the same sentence!):

> So, I think my problem, and "our" problem, is how to have *simultaneously* an account of radical historical contingency for all knowledge claims and knowing subjects, a critical practice for recognizing our own "semiotic technologies" for making meanings, *and* a no-nonsense commitment to faithful accounts of a "real" world, one that can be partially shared and that is friendly to earthwide projects of finite freedom, adequate material abundance, modest meaning in suffering, and limited happiness. (SK, 579; Haraway's emphasis)

Perhaps Haraway is not telling us how to perform this tension—only stating that it should be our goal. Still, I would argue that her call to "commitment to faithful accounts," particularly in her listing of "earthwide projects"—"*finite* freedom, *adequate* material abundance, *modest* meaning in suffering, and *limited* happiness" (my emphasis)—lends a clue: Poststructuralist humility will save the day and will enable a reliance on escape to sneak in through the back door.

What I mean is this: Haraway's stress on particularity, limits, modesty, finitude, accountability, responsibility, and noninnocence (central to her essay's thematic embrace of things "partial") spells a twist that resembles Christian believers' required humility before God, since God represents a domain of possibility and agency beyond believers' control. With this panegyric to "partial" perspectives, Haraway is able to stress the benefits of our acknowledging our limits, over and against our seeking forms of disembodied transcendence, for this human humility is *what would make possible*, in her scheme, a world (and bodies) that transcend(s) us. We limit ourselves so that our world (and our bodies) can escape us and return to us (at least in part) outside our constructions. In taking a stand against transcendence, Haraway thus makes a certain kind of transcendence possible. Small wonder that her essay ends by tying our humility to the possible appearance of something other than our selves:

> The approach I am recommending is not a version of "realism," which has proved a rather poor way of engaging with the world's active agency. . . . Ecofeminists have perhaps been most insistent on some version of the world as active subject, not as resource to be mapped and appropriated in bourgeois, Marxist, or masculinist projects. Acknowledging the agency of the world in knowledge makes room for some unsettling possibilities, including a sense of the world's independent sense of humor. . . . The Coyote or Trickster, as embodied in Southwest native American accounts, suggests the situation we are

> in when we give up mastery but keep searching for fidelity, knowing all the while that we will be hoodwinked. I think these are useful myths for scientists who might be our allies. Feminist objectivity makes room for surprises and ironies at the heart of all knowledge production; we are not in charge of the world. . . . Perhaps our hopes for accountability, for politics, for ecofeminism, turn on revisioning the world as coding trickster with whom we must learn to converse. (SK, 593–96)

How far are we here from a Victorian version of a Christian God? Institutionally and practically, it appears that we are quite far, so that Haraway might rightfully balk at the question. Discursively, however, some points of contact remain striking: The world, like God, is deemed an active subject with an independent sense of humor, which may prove uncomfortable to human projects; the world, like God, demands that we "give up mastery but keep searching for fidelity, knowing all the while that we will be hoodwinked," for "we are not in charge of the world"; the world, like God, demands that our hopes be expressed in conversations with what, or with someone who, remains outside our ability to bind everything with words.[23]

I have tried to show that Haraway speaks against transcendence on behalf of materialism. Yet, her very gestures that would script a poststructuralist materialism depend upon escapes that would return us to bodies that surprise us. I want to argue something similar for Gallop in *Thinking Through the Body*, for Gallop stresses that side of the duality that poststructuralists only recently have stressed: "the body as insubordinate to man-made meaning"; the body as "enigmatic because it is not a creation of the mind" (*TTB*, 18). This is no naïve return to bodies, assuming linguistic, or material, transparency. Gallop rejects the notion that there could appear "such a thing as a 'body itself,' unmediated by textuality" (*TTB*, 93). What she does explore is the body's resistance to linguistic domination:

> The human being cannot help but try to make sense out of his own idiosyncratic body shape: tall or short, fat or thin, male or female, to name but a few of the least subtle morphological distinctions. Outside the theological model there is no possibility of verifying an inter-

23. As Robert Caserio has suggested to me, Robert Browning offers intriguing possibilities for imagining Victorian versions of God as a coding trickster. See, in particular, Browning's poem "Caliban Upon Setebos; or, Natural Theology in the Island." One might even notice that Caliban's natural theology meets and intersects with the theology of Browning's St. John (see "A Death in the Desert").

> pretation: no author to have intended a sense in composing such a body. . . . By "body" I mean here: perceivable givens that the human being knows as "hers" without knowing their significance to her. In such a way a taste for a certain food or a certain color, a distaste for another, are pieces of the bodily enigma. We can, a posteriori, form an esthetic, consistent system of values (rules for Good Taste) to rationalize our insistent, idiosyncratic tastes. But the system is a guess at the puzzle, a response to the inscrutable given. (*TTB*, 12–13)

From the start, one might argue that Gallop has trouble pointing to "morphological distinctions"—"tall or short, fat or thin, [especially] male or female"—that are not already the result of culturally specific codes; this difficulty seems most dramatically apparent in her appeal to "a taste for a certain food or a certain color," as well as in a later list of tastes, predilections, and repulsions (which could be *fully* culturally induced in some cases, though perhaps not in all). Of course, Gallop's trouble surrounding "morphological distinctions" points to the very issue I have been discussing all along: the difficulty of indicating in language whatever we want to designate as falling outside it.

Not surprisingly, Gallop seems most convincing on the body, from a deconstructive standpoint, at those points where she discourses on escapes from discourse, where the 'body' (in quotation marks, we note) "means all that in the organism which exceeds and antedates consciousness or reason or interpretation," where 'body' means "perceivable givens that the human being knows as 'hers' without knowing their significance to her." This last phrase, in fact, sounds like Lacan on St. Theresa ("it is clear that the essential testimony of the mystics is that they are experiencing it [the "*jouissance* which goes beyond"] but know nothing about it").[24] True, Gallop defines the body against "theological models," linking theology to (beliefs, I guess, in) verifiable interpretations, puzzle-masters, correct divinations, and final guarantees of intended meaning—even though theology can only ever command faith in these things. Clearly, however, Gallop's antitheological return to the body proves itself a spiritualizing project of major magnitude, for she *defines* the body in terms of escape, the failure of meaning, and the impossibility of human sign systems ("that which *exceeds* and

24. Jacques Lacan, "God and the Jouissance of ~~the~~ Woman," in *Feminine Sexuality: Jacques Lacan and the Ecole Freudienne*, ed. Juliet Mitchell and Jacqueline Rose, trans. Jacqueline Rose (New York: Norton, 1985), 147.

antedates consciousness or reason or interpretation"). Precisely, as she puts it, the body is an "inscrutable" given. The same gesture, then, that makes the body seem like it is solidly there, renders it elusive. The best argument for its material resistance to our domination is its propensity to escape our efforts at capture. We believe, however, that the bodily puzzle remains as something that Gallop rather mystically calls "the mark of an enigmatic silence (sign of an impossible transcendence)" (*TTB*, 14).

"Mystic Unfathomable Visibilities"

This material perplexity that preoccupies Gallop and Haraway is emergent already in Thomas Carlyle. In fact, in Carlyle, this dilemma outlines the conceptual surprises we encounter now in feminists who would shed the linguistic garments that constrain them—shedding them through forms of cloaking and concealment. Carlyle, that is, better than any theorist I know, represents the kind of spiritual materialism to which poststructuralist feminists are returning, either obliquely or overtly. In Carlyle, too, as in poststructuralists, *materialism has to do with concealment*: Carlyle's historical enigmas, akin to Gallop's bodily enigmas, show resistance to our conceptual control, thus heightening their existence apart from us. Most important of all, consulting Carlyle who uses avowedly spiritual discourse, we can sense the collapse between 'spiritual' and 'material' borders in which poststructuralists, despite their deconstructions, still invest so much distinction.

Some issues in Carlyle's *Past and Present* light up this collapse. This is a book as focused on the need to escape intolerable material relations (produced by the Corn Laws and the Poor Law Amendment Act of 1834) as are feminist visions. This book, too, envisions an *alternative materiality*, but one that directs our hope to a historical past, not the future. The historical past limns itself as a beckoning *enigma*, a puzzle that promises a material presence to be approached and followed. Yet, troubling senses of inaccessibility seem wedded to Carlyle's hope in history: The Past is a "dim indubitable fact," whose dimness seems a function of approaching "a fact" that always recedes, "*far off* on the edge of *far* horizons, towards which we are to steer *incessantly* for life."[25] For Carlyle, as much as for any poststructuralist, history has gotten difficult. Even written voices from the past repel in their "remote," "exotic," "extraneous" characters, as Car-

25. Thomas Carlyle, *Past and Present*, ed. Richard D. Altick (Boston: Houghton Mifflin, 1965), 41; my emphasis. All further references to this text will be abbreviated *PP*.

lyle discovers when he reads the notebooks of a twelfth-century monk. "We have a longing," writes Carlyle, "to cross-question him, to force from him an explanation of much"; "but no; Jocelin, though he talks with such clear familiarity, like a next-door neighbor, will not answer any question: that is the peculiarity of him, dead these six hundred and fifty years, and quite deaf to us, though still so audible!" (*PP*, 49–50). In history's character as "inscrutable and certain" (Carlyle's phrase), these *historical enigmas*, as one might call them, bear a discursive resemblance to the "bodily enigmas" that Gallop discusses, rather mystically, as "inscrutable givens." Because history resists us, because it is *not* transparent, it asserts, we believe, a materiality that exceeds us.

How fitting for Carlyle's sense of history, and for the poststructuralist debates that concern us, that Carlyle concludes his journey into the historical past with a monk's report of a bodily enigma. The story involves Abbot Samson's wish to glimpse the body of the martyr St. Edmund. Carlyle quotes his monk, Jocelin, on this secret sacred event, from which he, Jocelin, was unhappily excluded and heard about only through witnesses:

> "These coverings being lifted off, they found now the Sacred Body all wrapped in linen. . . . But here the Abbot stopped; saying he durst not proceed farther, or look at the sacred flesh naked. [Yet] proceeding, he touched the eyes; and the nose, which was very massive and prominent . . . and then he touched the breast and arms; and raising the left arm he touched the fingers, and placed his own fingers between the sacred fingers. And proceeding he found the feet standing stiff up, like the feet of a man dead yesterday; and he touched the toes and counted them. . . . And now it was agreed that the other Brethren should be called forward to see the miracles." (*PP*, 124)

Here is testimony: The most naked materiality seems the most holy, the most mysterious, the most difficult to grasp—something that Irigaray will dramatically demonstrate. In fact, the passage illuminates a difficulty more than it illuminates a body: the difficulty of grasping naked flesh. Where the description becomes most particular (the reference to the nose as massive), or most intent on the act of grasping (placing fingers between the sacred fingers, counting the toes), we receive the strongest sense of a bodily enigma that defies our captures. Carlyle caps this instructive scene with his own gloss on bodily enigmas:

> Stupid blockheads, to reverence their St. Edmund's dead Body in this manner? Yes, brother;—and yet, on the whole, who knows how

to reverence the Body of a Man? . . . For the Highest God dwells visible in that mystic unfathomable Visibility, which calls itself "I" on the Earth. (*PP*, 126)

Surprisingly, we can couple Carlyle's spiritual materialism, so evident in this passage, with his own brand of full-blown constructionism. By so doing, we can understand why Gallop and Haraway, who seem primarily constructionists, participate in spiritual materialism. Carlyle's view of the body as a "mystic unfathomable Visibility" (a phrase that could describe some poststructuralist conceptions of 'the body' apart from social constructions) points in two directions simultaneously: toward concealment and toward revelation. The interconnections between these terms prove quite intricate. What the body reveals most easily are the fabrications—in Carlyle's terms, the "garments," or "clothes"—by which we know it. This is, in large part, what his earlier book *Sartor Resartus* had explored: "The whole external Universe and what it holds is but Clothing," dressed up by society and religious institutions in every manner of word, symbol, and human conception.[26] Since, however, "the Tailor is not only a Man, but something of a Creator or Divinity," there is another side to the revelation of human constructions.[27] Every "garment" (every person or thing) reveals not only the set of human tailorings by which we know it, but it also *reveals* a divine *concealment*. What is revealed, what "*super*naturalism [brings] home to the very dullest," is concealment itself; and this concealment bespeaks a spiritual reality that "dwells visible in that mystic unfathomable Visibility" (*PP*, 126). Again, we graze poststructuralist formulations, except that it is spiritual discourse that renders the concealment that poststructuralists stress as material. Thus, explains Gallop, "by 'body' I mean here: perceivable givens [Visibility] that the human being knows as 'hers' without knowing their significance to her [mystic, unfathomable]" (*TTB*, 13). Or, as Lacan will say: "The essential testimony of the mystics is that they are experiencing it but know nothing about it."

There is further evidence that Carlyle's spiritual materialism sits close to his own social constructionist tendencies. Having ended his historical review with a "mystic unfathomable Visibility" (St. Edmund's body), Carlyle closes Book II of *Past and Present*, "The Ancient Monk," by taking a turn that looks like a version of extreme constructionism:

26. Thomas Carlyle, *Sartor Resartus*, ed. Kerry McSweeney and Peter Sabor (New York: Oxford University Press, 1987), 57.
27. Carlyle, *Sartor*, 219.

> What a singular shape of a Man, shape of a Time, have we in this Abbot Samson and his history; how strangely do modes, creeds, formularies, and that date and place of a man's birth, modify the figure of the man!
>
> Formulas too, as we call them, have a *reality* in Human Life. They are real as the very *skin* and *muscular tissue* of a Man's Life; and a most blessed indispensable thing, so long as they have *vitality* withal, and are a *living* skin and tissue to him! . . . And yet, again, when a man's Formulas become *dead* . . . till no *heart* any longer can be felt beating through them, so thick, callous, calcified are they . . . yes, then, you may say, his usefulness once more is quite obstructed. (*PP*, 128)

Carlyle not only appears a precursor to poststructuralist analysts who would claim that everything is fashioned by discourse; he also sounds faintly like Althusser on how ideologies hail us into subjectivities (asks Carlyle: "This English Nationality . . . has it not made for thee a skin or second-skin, adhesive actually as thy natural skin?" [*PP*, 129]). "Formulas" are real and inescapable (as are ideologies and subjectivities for Althusser). What we need, suggests Carlyle, are better formulas, since "blessed [is] he who has a skin and tissues, so it be a living one, and the heart-pulse everywhere discernible through it" (*PP*, 130–31). Happily, historical retrospection provides some: "Monachism [*sic*], Feudalism, with a real King Plantagenet, with real Abbots Samson, and their other living realities, how blessed!—" (*PP*, 131). Seemingly, the *only* thing Carlyle can promise is other (possibly better) formulas, more distant and provocative.

Yet, Carlyle is not this fully constructionist, as we have seen. The clue to what might escape these formulas is his almost unnoticeable reference to "the heart-pulse," which he mentions twice: "When a man's Formulas become *dead* . . . till no *heart* any longer can be felt beating through them . . . his usefulness once more is quite obstructed"; "blessed he who has a skin and tissues, so it be a living one, and the heart-pulse everywhere discernible through it." The sense of something not commonly seen but *felt* beating or pulsing *through* skin is vital for Carlyle. This pulse, or beat, however, indicates a mysterious sign of a reality that can best prove its presence when it starts to *fail*—when "no *heart* any longer can be felt."[28] For bodily and

28. In fact, in Carlyle's *Past and Present*, *dead* things—dead languages, dead bodies, dead Formulas, dead hearts—are largely what signify history and materiality as mystery: "The language of it is not foreign only but dead: Monk-Latin lies across not the British Channel, but the ninefold Stygian Marshes, Stream of Lethe, and one knows not where!";

historical objects seem most real and most referential not where they reveal something recognizable (for this revelation would prove their confinement within the "garments" by which we know them) but where they conceal something from us.[29] These are concealments constructions cannot capture—except for mystical formulas, which tell us that there is something that cannot be told.

'God' between Their Lips: In Search of Symbolic Holes Women Can Feel

Here—on the question of perceivable concealments that only mystical formulas can capture—is the link to the deconstructive feminist Irigaray. For the sake of making different (female) bodies appear, Irigaray renders these bodies opaque but seeks to lavish upon them concealments that they might wear. More arresting still, in offering us her spiritual materialism, Irigaray puts 'God' between women's lips.

By means of this puzzle I want to make bold that with all that has been written in reference to Irigaray, we have not fully realized the interest of her materialist dilemmas (for my purposes, her theories in *Speculum of the Other Woman* and *This Sex Which Is Not One*). In fact, in a major study of Irigaray, Margaret Whitford confirms that materialist address to Irigaray is particularly needed now: "The question of Irigaray and materialism still awaits a thorough elucidation, which will take into account the fact that 'materialism' is a political term, over which there is contest for rights and possession."[30] I concur with Whitford and would add that Irigaray's materi-

---

"That is the peculiarity of [Jocelin], dead these six hundred and fifty years, and quite deaf to us, though still so audible!"; "The body of one Dead;—a temple where the Hero-soul once was and now is not: Oh, all mystery, all pity, all mute *awe* and wonder" (*PP*, 46, 49, 126).

29. Gallop says something quite close to this, in fact, when she discusses confusion and contradiction: "To read for and affirm confusion, contradiction is to insist on thinking in the body in history. Those confusions mark the sites where thinking is literally knotted to the subject's historical and material place" (*TTB*, 132). Scientists would seem to know this knotting well, since they encounter the body and matter at those places where every known scientific formula or construction fails to explain what they are observing. It is precisely this failure, however, that convinces us that bodies and matter do push back against even our most subtle, precise formulations.

30. Readers of Irigaray are now fortunate to possess Margaret Whitford's indispensable study, *Luce Irigaray: Philosophy in the Feminine* (New York: Routledge, 1991), a book which had not yet appeared when I first submitted this essay for publication. Whitford's is

alist dilemmas are more nuanced than the few discussions of them have suggested. But this is true as well of Irigaray's other assigned designations. Irigaray has been called an essentialist, but, as I have already said, she may be more aptly deemed a *believer*: She believes in bodies (and labors) whose essence, if anything, is escape.[31] More generously, she has been called a "strategic" essentialist but may be more fairly regarded as an *opaque essentialist*, and a very mystical one at that, since mysticism, she asserts, "is the only place in the history of the West in which woman speaks and acts so publicly."[32] She has been called a theorist of plenitude but may be more powerfully read as a feminist theologian of lack, for whom the happy fall may be found between a woman's lips—the same place, importantly, she locates 'God'.[33]

By virtue of her stance as a believer, a mystic opaque essentialist, and a feminist theologian of lack, I take Irigaray as the premiere test case for spiritual materialism. Her theorizing, for a start, unambiguously exposes how spiritual discourse engenders discourse on materialities that dominant constructions fail to capture. Yet Irigaray's happy fall is specific. She puts a version of *felix culpa*, "the happy fall" (lack, separation, failure), between the lips, representing the self-caress of the lips as made possible by the

---

clearly the most detailed study of Irigaray to date and a major contribution to our understanding of Irigaray as a philosopher of sexual difference. Although there is not much discussion in her book of Irigaray as materialist or even of Irigaray's theory of desire, I find in Whitford important confirmation for a point that touches on the issues I address: Irigaray, she argues, is trying "to effect change in the symbolic order. . . . She is not pre-Lacanian, but post-Lacanian" (14). Whitford is superb on this point. See 196 n. 20 for the quotation in the text above.

31. For the essentialist designation, see, for example, Monique Plaza, "'Phallomorphic Power' and the Psychology of 'Woman'," *Ideology and Consciousness* 4 (Autumn 1978): 57–76; and Toril Moi, *Sexual/Textual Politics: Feminist Literary Theory* (New York: Methuen, 1985), 143.

32. Luce Irigaray, *Speculum of the Other Woman*, trans. Gillian C. Gill (Ithaca: Cornell University Press, 1985), 191. All further references to this text will be abbreviated *S*. For the strategic essentialist reading of Irigaray, see those critics cited in note 19.

33. In a recent major study of Irigaray, Elizabeth Grosz continually reads Irigaray against the grain of loss. Discussing Irigaray on mother-daughter relations, for example, Grosz examines the dynamics of "When Our Lips Speak Together" (the concluding essay to *This Sex Which Is Not One*). Writes Grosz: "The 'we' here does not subsume or merge one identity with another but *fuses* them *without residue or loss* to either. . . . This is a space of exchange *without debt, without loss, without guilt*, a space women can inhabit *without giving up a part of themselves*" (see Elizabeth Grosz, *Sexual Subversions: Three French Feminists* [Sydney: Allen & Unwin, 1989], 126; my emphases). I desire to provide an alternative to this reading.

slit, 'woman's' nothing, her (supposed) castration, that divides her genitals. More intriguingly, Irigaray locates not only lack, but also 'God', between the lips: She *implants escape within the genitals* and makes what she terms "unformable apartness" (*S*, 235) their most essential biological feature. This is why, too—as much as Irigaray shares Marx's need for faith in 'natural' objects, 'matter on its own terms' before it is mystified through commodifications—her materialism breaks from Marx's: She elaborately mystifies the female body, using blatantly mystical terms to bolster it against mystifications that are far more alienating than her own.

I want to convey how Irigaray's stance as an *opaque essentialist* (my term) is tied to her stance as a *feminist theologian of lack* (my term, again). At bottom lies my central claim: Irigaray wants to say that something of women's bodies is concealed without saying exactly what this something is. This something, however, is closer to a crack, a seam, a slit, than it is to something we deem substantial. Irigaray's opaque essentialism, her tendency to make visible the body's opacity, thus enables her to perform two operations at once: She can complain against women's alienation from their bodies (by arguing that something is concealed by constructions), and she can forge a deconstructive pact to leave the body's essence indeterminate (by arguing that what is concealed is a crack). What we might conclude from Irigaray's simultaneous embrace of alienation and indeterminacy is a maxim like this: Women are alienated not from some past body they have known but from a *future* body owed to them. These are bodies women have not yet been allowed to see, to fashion, or to listen for, even though these bodies *already* resist their dominant constructions, particularly where these bodies appear as holes in the dominant Symbolic.

My focus on holes should remind the reader that for Irigaray these issues center on genitals—understandably so, since the body's genitals are still the prime site for the cultural readings that fashion boys and girls. Here is the import of Irigaray's famous, and much contested, figure of the lips: The lips represent Irigaray's address to the *matter* of castration. Do women, she seems to query, possess anything to be *seen materially* at the genital level? Or are "woman's erogenous zones," as their culture paints them, a "hole-envelope"?[34]

It is a common mistake to begin discussion of Irigaray's lips with the tired, overworked issue of essentialism. Perhaps it is time to say directly

34. Luce Irigaray, *This Sex Which Is Not One*, trans. Catherine Porter with Carolyn Burke (Ithaca: Cornell University Press, 1985), 23. All further references to this text will be abbreviated *TS*.

that I want to make Irigaray ride new rims, on the lip of old extremities. This push appears in my portrait of her as opaque essentialist and feminist theologian of lack who puts 'God' between the lips. These formulations are my own manufacture. I'm suggesting how to read her, moreover, in order to usher the question of material concealments, perceivable concealments, into an explicitly gendered domain. The question of castration, to which the lips speak, leads us to a border we have not yet broached: What bodies in dominant Western culture are *privileged* to claim a material concealment?

We can probe this concern by taking up an issue Irigaray knows well. I am referring to Lacan's notion of primary castration: the child's loss of direct material access to its body when it enters language. One of Lacan's central insights and revisions of Freud, and one that shapes Lacan's distinctive slant on human tragedy, is that both 'boys' and 'girls' lose unmediated contact with their bodies when they become speaking subjects caught in the "defiles" of signification. Lacan puts it this way: "What by its very nature remains *concealed* from the subject [is] that self-sacrifice, *that pound of flesh* which is mortgaged [engagé] in his relationship to the signifier."[35]

Lacan links this "pound of flesh" to the production of sexual difference that attends the child's castration through language, for children do not enter the Symbolic (language/law/culture) on equal terms. 'Boys', by virtue of a cultural reading that assigns to their genitals *a valued and visible materiality*, enter the Symbolic as privileged subjects who "sacrifice" their "pound of flesh" for Symbolic rites. 'Girls', by virtue of a cultural reading that assigns to their genitals *an unhappy lack and missing materiality*, enter the Symbolic as underprivileged subjects who "sacrifice" their inferior bodies for inferior rights within the Symbolic. Cultural readings clearly determine, then, *how* bodies mortgage materiality for culture. Indeed, these differential doors to privilege are why so many poststructuralist feminists have argued that the phallus—the privileged signifier of what I am calling Symbolic rites—cannot be easily separated from the penis. Witness Kaja Silverman, who spells out the privilege that attends the boy's castration through language:

> Lacan suggests . . . that the male subject "pays" for his symbolic privileges with a currency not available to the female subject—that he "mortgages" the penis for the phallus. In other words, during

35. Jacques Lacan, "Desire and the Interpretation of Desire in *Hamlet*," trans. James Hulbert, *Yale French Studies* 55/56 (1977): 28; my emphases.

> his entry into the symbolic order he gains access to those privileges which constitute the phallus, but forfeits direct access to his own sexuality, a forfeiture of which the penis is representative. . . . What woman lacks within the Lacanian scheme is the phallus-as-lost-penis, the "amputated" or "castrated" appendage which assures the male subject access to the phallus-as-symbolic-legacy.[36]

Here is a material concealment, "a pound of flesh," worth its weight in gold, since this particular material concealment (whatever the penis as a pound of flesh might be if not "concealed" by discourse) can be cashed in for cultural coins.

Now we see what lies at stake in achieving a certain kind of *access to lack*, along with a material concealment one can point to, and why Irigaray might seek to acquire lack and concealment *on behalf of women*. What emerges from Silverman, so important for my essay, is precisely this: The phallus signifies lack and material concealment *while* transmitting privileges to dominant men that remain, perniciously, unavailable to women. Dominant men's associations with *veiled* lack appear to empower them, whereas women, who by assigned cultural readings *figure lack*, mortgage their bodies for the phallus (that is, for signification) free of charge, with no symbolic payoff. In this way, so perverse is the game, the Symbolic offers to dominant men the fabrication that they have lost nothing in language and that they are genitally superior to women who are lacking, materially, the sign of success (the penis). This Symbolic myth, of course, offers *the* reading children learn to apply to their bodies ('he' has one, 'she' doesn't). In other words, men's lack gets them privilege along with the means by which to veil their lack; women possess no empowering passage to the lack they are made *by the Symbolic* to wear. For according to dominant cultural constructions, the penis, against some feminists' splendid hopes for failure, is not deemed lost, or latent, or lacking—rather, 'woman' is, and her genitals are, too. What women are lacking, *within the Symbolic*, is the privilege of a material concealment.

Clearly, it would be in 'her' interests to unveil 'his' lack—to show that the fullness of the penis is a fraud, as Gallop, joined by Rose and others, tries to do.[37] But 'her' lack? Should 'she' reach for veils or revela-

36. Silverman, *Subject of Semiotics*, 185, 186, 188.

37. See Gallop's "Of Phallic Proportions: Lacanian Conceit," in *The Daughter's Seduction: Feminism and Psychoanalysis* (Ithaca: Cornell University Press, 1982), 29 and

tions? One might expect, under these circumstances, that Irigaray would offer to women their own plenitude—spectacular, pregnant, perhaps, in its fullness—and grant them something to be seen as genitals. The lips have surely been read this way, as part of a plurality of sex organs Irigaray wants to make visible. There is, however, another way to interpret her lips. By focusing there, Irigaray attempts to gain a more empowered conduction both to materiality *and* to lack *at the same time*. We can read women's genital lips in the guise of a perceivable concealment:

> As for woman, she touches herself in and of herself without any need for mediation, and before there is any way to distinguish activity from passivity. Woman "touches herself" all the time, and moreover no one can forbid her to do so, for her genitals are formed of two lips in continuous contact. Thus within herself, she is already two—but not divisible into one(s)—that caress each other. (*TS*, 24)

The lips tell us that something is there. The lips tell us that women's bodies are not the "hole-envelope" the Symbolic currently fashions them to be. The lips also say that the signal feature of what is there is what Irigaray calls "an unformable apartness" (lack, separation). This failure to fuse is a happy gap, a *felix culpa*, that was there "in the beginning," making the contact between lips possible. Irigaray here turns full face onto masculine theory by arresting Lacan's narrative with an image, with a material concealment of 'woman's' own.[38] "Reopen[ing] paths into . . . [a] logos that connotes [woman] as castrated" (*S*, 142), Irigaray makes visible what was supposed to remain invisible: 'woman's' genitals. Yet the lips wear their material concealment for all to see, for it is the lack of closure between her lips—'woman's' nothing-to-see—that forms "two lips in continuous contact," a nearness made possible by a space, a lack, a gap that allows 'woman' constantly to caress herself. This radical valuation of lips invests in 'woman's' slit—a dangerous expenditure. Nonetheless, castration, by this alternate logic of loss, converts to (auto)erotic pleasure.

---

throughout, for her discussion of how Lacan purposely inflates the phallus as privileged signifier so as to undermine the penis, to make it fall short of impossible phallic qualities. See Jacqueline Rose's "Introduction II," in *Feminine Sexuality*, for her discussion of Lacan's attack on "the order of the visible" that would seem to privilege the penis.

38. I am obliquely making reference here to feminist film theory's founding moment in Laura Mulvey's famous essay "Visual Pleasure and Narrative Cinema," in which she asserts that (feminine) image arrests (masculine) narrative (see Mulvey's *Visual and Other Pleasures* [Bloomington: Indiana University Press, 1989], 19–22).

Strangely, the question of belief enters in here, showcased in a Derrida passage on castration:

> "Woman"—her name made epoch—no more believes in castration's exact opposite, anti-castration, than she does in castration itself. . . . Unable to seduce or to give vent to desire without it, "woman" is in need of castration's effect. But evidently she does not believe in it. She who, unbelieving, still plays with castration, she is "woman." She takes aim and amuses herself (en joue) with it as she would with a new concept or structure of belief, but even as she plays she is gleefully anticipating her laughter, her mockery of man.[39]

The way Derrida poses castration in terms of amusement and *belief* suits Irigaray. This slant, in fact, may provide the terms for understanding that Irigaray does not refuse castration (a mistake Jacqueline Rose and others make in reading her) but refuses to believe in its standard associations with the female body. I want to underscore Derrida's notion that 'woman' "amuses herself . . . with [castration]." But if Derrida helps us to grasp 'woman' as an unbeliever, I will stress Irigaray's stance as a believer and the new structure of belief she creates by "converting" castration into affirmation (not the same as anti-castration). What Irigaray believes in, I will argue, is a material concealment that she can simultaneously reveal and *preserve* by making what she reveals a crack.

Irigaray's mystical, lyrical essay "La Mysterique" envisions how divine resistance to familiar visibilities might operate to make a different body seen, though seen opaquely. Here we find Irigaray's most elaborate demonstration of how she ties escapes back to feminine bodies: Irigaray brilliantly imagines 'God' (using the term under erasure) between women's lips. In this way, she conducts us from the psychoanalytic landscape, with its focus on the phallus, to a bodily landscape with its focus on the lips. She accomplishes this shift by passing us over a theological terrain where 'God' casts 'His' lot with lack. To make this move, Irigaray must be relying upon 'God' as the most respectable, and certainly the most elegant, absence in Judeo-Christian traditions. Even in the most incarnational theologies—Catholicism, for example, which invests most heavily in the body of Christ, endowed with sacramental mystery, nonetheless—'God' is a sacred space, the one we must humbly allow, in the final analysis, to remain resistant to

39. Jacques Derrida, *Spurs: Nietzsche's Styles/Eperons: Les Styles de Nietzsche*, trans. Barbara Harlow (Chicago: University of Chicago Press, 1979), 61.

us. As elegantly absent Person, or figure for material concealment, 'God' designates whatever resists our attempts at securing our bodies and world.

Visible concealment and escape once again become friends to bodies that would make their opacities seen and known. Irigaray's own hope in failure (for the sake of our bodies) appears when she stresses the need *as subjects and objects* to escape from sight. "But as the eye is already guardian to the reason," writes Irigaray, "the first necessity is to slip away unseen . . . and in fact without seeing much either," for "her eye has become accustomed to obvious 'truths' that actually hide what she is seeking" (*S*, 192–93). Irigaray even directly invokes the opacity of objects, especially bodies, that we must learn to see. She speaks of "the opaque barrier that every body presents to the light" (*S*, 193). She also queries in ways that touch upon Haraway, Gallop, and Carlyle's tendencies to define matter *in terms of* escape: "What if matter had always, already, had a part but was yet invisible, beyond the senses, moving in ways alien to any fixed reflection" (*S*, 197). This passage makes "matter" sound indistinguishable from even traditional explanations of 'God'.

If matter's opacity defies linguistic capture, then this is a defiance that mysticism, with its stress on sacred silence or inarticulate utterance, is well designed to make perceivable. Hence, Irigaray on the female mystic's failure to speak:

> But she cannot specify exactly what she wants. Words begin to fail her. She senses something *remains to be said* that resists all speech, that can at best be stammered out. . . . So the best plan is to abstain from all discourse, to keep quiet, or else utter only a sound so inarticulate that it barely forms a *song*. While all the while keeping an attentive ear open for any hint or tremor coming back. (*S*, 193; Irigaray's emphasis)

This is a particularly opaque essentialism, if it can count as essentialism at all ("for it is no longer a matter of longing for some determinable attribute, some mode of essence, some face of presence" [*S*, 193]). Irigaray's "attentive ear open for any hint or tremor coming back," along with her "expectant expectancy, absence of project and projections" (*S*, 194), may remind us of Gallop's "attempt to listen to the material" apart "from an agenda for better control." Both theorists stress escapes *on behalf of* "any hint or tremor coming back," and on behalf of materialities that might resist our learned visions (note Irigaray's invocation of "song" and Gallop's stress on listening).

We need to come closer to something I have claimed: that Irigaray puts 'God' between women's lips. What is the clue to this puzzling assertion? The hint, I suggest, is itself "the hint or tremor [that comes] back," that tells us some material resistance, some material escape, is taking place. This "hint or tremor" of material escape Irigaray, I would offer, codes as 'God'; more substantial yet, she makes this tremor felt between a woman's genital lips, implanting escape, as I earlier argued, within the genitals. Thus, if Irigaray seeks, as she says, "the possibility of a different relation to the transcendental" (*TS*, 153), then "God," she writes, "knows women so well that he never touches them directly, but always in that fleeting stealth of a fantasy that evades all representation: between two unities who thus imperceptibly take pleasure in each other" (*S*, 236). This declaration implies 'God's' touch between the autoerotic lips. Given the suggestion that this touch is not direct but caught up, rather, in a "fleeting stealth," and given that the lips, as we know from Irigaray, touch by means of apartness, 'God', by this logic, *becomes spacing*. 'God' is the gap, at the gap, in the gap; 'God' *is* the gap of a woman's pleasure between the lips, "opening up a crack in the cave (*une antr' ouverture*) so that she may penetrate herself once more" (*S*, 192). *'God' is figured as the material resistance of 'woman's' body* to representations that have neglected her pleasure. This material resistance eludes her in terms of specificities, but she can perceive this resistance as concealed in mystical encounters.

I want to pierce the mystery of Irigaray's mysticism: to show how her own mystical interests are strongly staked to lack—who wears it, who suffers for it, and who envisions economies based upon it.[40] Mystical discourse, by this account, may provide for Irigaray a way of affirming, so as to use differently, the lack assigned to 'woman'. As much as women might like to flee God, Irigaray implies, they must retreat upon the mystical, because "this is the only place in the history of the West in which woman speaks and acts so publicly" (*S*, 191). We, as readers, then, are asked to enter into Irigaray's mystical discourse sympathetically, reverently, and, as women—even spiritual women—are so good at, expectantly.

Irigaray comes to a different 'God' and a different relationship between 'God' and 'woman' than traditional Christian theology has rendered. Irigaray speaks of "that most female of men, the Son"—Christ—a 'man' who lines up with 'woman'. In fact, 'God' figures a masculine body that

40. For other discussions of Irigaray's mysticism, see Toril Moi's *Sexual/Textual Politics*, 135–37, but especially Elizabeth Grosz's *Sexual Subversions*, 140–83.

wears its lack—its wounds unveiled—for all to see. Irigaray plays jubilantly upon the mystic's holiness, celebrating 'his' holes that tell 'woman' glorious things about 'her' own:

> And that one man, at least, has understood her so well that he died in the most awful suffering. . . . And she never ceases to look upon his nakedness, open for all to see, upon the gashes in his virgin flesh. . . . Could it be true that not every wound need remain secret, that not every laceration was shameful? Could a sore be *holy*? Ecstasy is there in that glorious slit where she curls up as if in her nest, where she rests as if she had found her home—and He is also in her. . . . In this way, you see me and I see you, finally I see myself seeing you in this fathomless wound which is the source of our wondering comprehension and exhilaration. And to know myself I scarcely need a "soul," I have only to gaze upon the gaping space in your loving body. (*S*, 199–200)

This is Irigaray at her recapturing best, mapping lack onto the masculine body so that she can *afford* to reclaim lack for women. She makes the Christian tradition give back what Christ on the cross has borrowed from the feminine: a "gaping space" in the body worth gazing upon.[41] 'Woman's' "slit," here pronounced "glorious," mirrors Christ's "fathomless wound." The wound itself acts as a mirror, enabling 'woman' to reflect upon her folds. In this way, the wound tells all, making possible her peculiar ability to feel a hole she now inhabits *as* a mystery and *as* a revelation *in* a secret. The wound is a place (from which) to see a material opacity revealed by a gash.

41. To be sure, Christ has sometimes been gendered female by previous writers; see especially Caroline Walker Bynum, *Jesus as Mother: Studies in the Spirituality of the High Middle Ages* (Berkeley: University of California Press, 1982). Moreover, when Christ is being implicitly sexualized in relation to the father, theologians—presumably, to avoid homosexual overtones—gender Christ as a Bride who takes the place of the Church (or Eve) on the marriage bed of the cross. Christ, in this way, can play the role of Bridegroom only by first becoming a Bride. Consider, for example, Augustine on the crucifixion: "[Christ] came to the marriage bed of the cross, and there, in mounting it, He consummated his marriage. And when He perceived the sighs of the creature, He lovingly gave himself up to the torment in the place of His bride . . . and He joined the woman to Himself for ever." The Victorian Coventry Patmore depends upon this same tradition in *The Unknown Eros*: "In season due, on His sweet-fearful bed, / Rock'd by an earthquake, curtain'd by eclipse, / Thou shareds't the spousal rapture of the sharp spear's head / And thy bliss pale / Wrought for our boon what Eve's did for our bale." Both passages are quoted from M. H. Abrams, *Natural Supernaturalism: Tradition and Revolution in Romantic Literature* (New York: Norton, 1971), 45, 487 n. 57.

Irigaray renders this mystical version of perceivable concealment as a fold, where "He is also in her": "She is closed over this mystery where the love placed within her is hidden, revealing itself in this secret of desire" (*S*, 200). This "secret of desire" shifts bodily boundaries even as the pronouns shift and bleed. The "He" who bleeds into "you," bleeds into "her," who bleeds into "me." Such a plea (and *pli*, in French, means "a fold") for the other that folds the other into the lips requires, we can see, a God who bleeds. Irigaray takes on castration, then, to its most excessive degree, complete with Freud's fatal look upon nakedness that reveals the "shameful" "secret" of the "gaping space"—a secret and a sacred lack that 'woman' shares with Christ, reminiscent of the mystics' stigmata that function as speaking wounds. Irigaray takes castration to the crypt, where she makes castration convert into autoerotic concealments. There might well be "exhilaration" in these bodies' hidden, but perceivable, material folds.

If Irigaray gets mystical when discussing sexual economies, she attempts to be pointedly materialist in her Marxist essays, in which she theorizes women's bodies as commodities ("Women on the Market" and "Commodities among Themselves," in *This Sex Which Is Not One*). In these essays, Irigaray appears to agree with Marx's critiques of capitalism as she fashions feminist analogies to his commodities analysis. While doing so, however, Irigaray conveniently forgets (or possibly does not realize) that she, in an essay like "La Mysterique," has repeated some of the very moves that Marx would censure. She proves particularly contradictory on the question of what Marx complains is "the mystical character of commodities"—the alienation of objects through abstractions. Indeed, Irigaray's contradictions on this question are so central to her own dramatic real-bodies mysticism that they provide a fitting climax to my essay.

Women don't exchange, they are exchanged. Irigaray begins "Women on the Market" with this fundamental point that she takes on loan from Lévi-Strauss.[42] This point, in fact, when she connects it to those she borrows from Marx on the bodies of commodities, forms the nerve of her argument. Women, she asserts, when socialized into a "normal" femininity, play the role of commodities in the dominant (masculine sexual) economy, metaphorically (and sometimes literally) bought and sold on the marriage market.[43] 'Woman's' "price," moreover, is set not according to her body's

42. See, in particular, the first two pages of Irigaray's "Women on the Market" (*TS*, 170–71) for her repetition and questioning of Lévi-Strauss.

43. Irigaray does not consider men's bodies as commodities. Considerations of nondominant men demand that we take up these complications.

'own properties' (an essential Irigarayan problem) but according to what counts in a phallic economy: 'woman's' ability to mirror men's "needs/desires" and thus to copy the "fabricated" standards set for women as reproductive and sexual vessels (*TS*, 176).

Like Marx, Irigaray, in her righteous anger over commodifications, leans heavily upon a natural/alienated opposition: "A commodity—a woman—is divided into two irreconcilable 'bodies': her 'natural' body [notice Irigaray's use of quotation marks] and her socially valued, exchangeable body, which is a particularly mimetic expression of masculine values" (*TS*, 180). The real surprise appears when Irigaray begins to depend upon Marx's critique of commodities' "mystical character"—though this surprise depends upon how one reads Irigaray's seeming essentialism. If one reads Irigaray as conventionally essentialist, one is not amazed that she laments with Marx that (the bodies of) commodities are treated as abstractions, abstractions that obscure their "coarse materiality":

> *Marx*: The value of commodities is the very opposite of the coarse materiality of their substance, not an atom of matter enters into its composition. Turn and examine a single commodity, by itself, as we will. Yet in so far as it remains an object of value, it seems impossible to grasp it.
> *Irigaray*: When women are exchanged, woman's body must be treated as an *abstraction*. The exchange operation cannot take place in terms of some intrinsic, immanent value of the commodity. . . .
> *Marx*: The fact that it is value, is made manifest by its equality with the coat, just as the sheep's nature of a Christian is shown in his resemblance to the Lamb of God.
> *Irigaray*: Each commodity may become equivalent to every other from the viewpoint of that sublime standard. . . . They are exchanged by means of the general equivalent—as Christians love each other in God, to borrow a theological metaphor dear to Marx.
> *Marx*: The mystical character of commodities does not originate, therefore, in their use value.
> *Irigaray*: *This phenomenon has no analogy except in the religious world*. (*TS*, 175–76; 178; 181; 182–83)

Wedding her analysis to Marx, this stinging censure of making materialities mystical comes with contradictions from the author of "La Mysterique." Irigaray herself puts 'God' between the lips—a mystical abstraction of sublime proportions—in order to enable 'woman's' "coarse materiality" to appear, albeit opaquely. Her agreement with Marx, while contradictory, is nonetheless wise. Believing along with Marx that use values and real bodies do exist, though they are never seen truly unclothed in capitalist economies, Irigaray can strongly register an alienation under capitalism.

As I stressed earlier, before deconstruction *alienation* was a concept that marked a conflict with one's real body or self; but since deconstruction, with its break from any notion of authentic selves or bodies, we have found it less possible to use any determinate sense of original selves or bodies by which we might mark our alienations. We are left with conceiving alienation, then, as alienation from *new* possibilities, not from original ones. This is an alienation from a future we might discover, not from a familiar, essential past that we have known. This is an unhappy alienation from what could prove a happier one. This is an alienation *from whatever exists outside of capitalism*. This alienation can best be marked, then, by positing, *as a form of belief*, what must exist below, behind, or inside the bodies that commodities are currently required to wear. This is real-bodies mysticism Marxist-style, wherein one can only hope to split the good mystical stuff (real bodies and their uses) from bad mysticism (commodification of the bodies we know to masculine capitalist ends).

As is Irigaray's way, what she gives as complaint bleeds into possibility:

> [A commodified] body becomes a transparent body, *pure phenomenality of value*. But this transparency constitutes a supplement to the material opacity of the commodity. (*TS*, 179)
> The value of a woman [apart from her transparent value as commodity] always escapes: black continent, hole in the symbolic, breach in discourse. . . . It is only in the operation of exchange among women that something of this—something enigmatic, to be sure—can be felt. (*TS*, 176)

Irigaray's opposition, transparency/opacity, offers evidence once again that representations (here, commodifications) are particularly available ("transparent," in this case), while the bodies and objects that are made to wear these transparent supplements elude through their "material opacity." For this reason, Irigaray must concern herself with making 'woman's' material opacity *seen* and *felt as opacity*. Of course, Irigaray well knows the complications that lie in wait: 'Woman's' (material) value may escape the Symbolic as a "hole," but, to a large extent, this escape is reappropriated *by* the Symbolic and made *internal* to the workings of the system. Thus 'woman's' value as a commodity seems to *include* her enigmatic escapes from the system that also contains her: 'Woman' gets commodified, bought, and sold *as an enigma*. Irigaray, however, cannot finally let herself believe in such a total containment. She invests, therefore, in 'woman's' hole. By so doing, she registers two objectives: First, she registers resistance to totalizing masculine values (since she preserves the sense of 'woman's' escape from the dominant Symbolic); second, she registers hope for making women "feel" this "something enigmatic" in ways that might empower them, leading, as she says, to "a new critique of the political economy" (*TS*, 191).

Irigaray seeks, then, to *give a form to "material opacity"* that women can invest in for themselves, without falling back upon the masculine value of transparent selves that relate as rivals. It is not surprising that Irigaray believes "it is only in the operation of exchange among women that something of this—something enigmatic, to be sure—can be felt." Given the cultural and economic status of women as commodities exchanged among men, alternative exchanges between men and women are sometimes hard to see and feel.[44] Exchanges between women (or, as in mysticism, between the feminine mystic and 'God') can, at times, provide at least a *partial isolation* from the circuits of the masculine sexual economy and thus lend a more vivid backdrop against which *to see a material opacity as opaque*.

Perhaps for this reason, Irigaray ends her Marxist essays with the female homosexual's "inconceivable" desire for women. Here is an enigma that psychoanalysis—Freud, explicitly—has been made to feel as a "difficulty," she writes, "so foreign to his 'theory' " (*TS*, 195). "Hence the fault, the infraction, the misconduct, and the challenge that female homosexuality entails" (*TS*, 194). The female homosexual writes a happy fall for feminists, since psychoanalysis under Freud is itself forced to feel an opacity. As much as he attempts to force the explanation of the female homosexual's "masculinity complex," Freud cannot, even by his own terms, account for 'her' to his satisfaction. Women's desire, turned toward each other, can potentially make them feel the Symbolic hole between them, that each, as commodity, mirrors for the other. Feeling this hole, they might erect for themselves their own material opacity that defies their culture's attempts to deliver them as fully bought and sold. Something might even accrue from this cipher—"a certain economy of abundance," says Irigaray, but an economy, I would add, that, according to her own most cherished theories, is solidly based upon fracture and loss.

Unhappily, I cannot follow these final issues to their destination. To do

44. This problem of making *visible, readable*, alternative exchanges runs parallel to the problem of fashioning for women a visible renunciation. How can their willing embrace of loss be read as resisting their prescribed role as "woman" when read against the background of traditional coupling that enjoins this part upon them?

so would involve us in the complicated circuits of the invisibilities of women's labor and women's desire and of Irigaray's attempts to address these forms of material concealment by making desire a form of labor. We would have to take stock of how pleasurable loss can be produced between bodies, attending to the dangers of reproducing familiar fractures based upon inequities. We would have to examine what Irigaray cannot see: how women are positioned asymmetrically as commodities, so that exchanges between them are always susceptible of *partial* accounts along other axes (those of class, race, religion, age, appearance, etc.). These implications raise serious questions for alternative exchanges that would count so dramatically upon discernible loss.[45]

These are questions for further examinations of material concealments and what to make of them. My purpose in this essay, I confess, has proved a relatively simple one, though its exposition is necessarily dense. My purpose is simple because I simply want to discover poststructuralist feminists in the moves—spiritual moves—that return them to seemingly materialist commitments to bodies and objects outside/beyond discourse. My exposition is dense because so much resistance *from* poststructuralists lies in wait for those who would wander too close either to materialism or to spirituality.

To conclude, the fix for feminists is this: If escapes, though partial, from dominant constructions do take place, if subordinates to systems are never fully constrained by the boundaries that write their relations, what 'body' gets touched when the boundaries are broken? Is it enough to believe—to have faith—that some freer body is being touched upon? Can one touch a body that one must, in order to touch it, locate in the impossible place of a discourse that escapes the discourses that we know? Is this necessary detour of one's culturally constructed body—through an other body that one cannot, must not, know by means of dominant constructions—the ultimate act of political, mystical autoeroticism? The question remains (and I believe it bears a spiritual materialist stamp): How can we bend ourselves toward the impossible bodies and selves we must believe *now* that we can be? And how can we keep from fully arriving at this material destination, so that we do not fully overtake ourselves, capture ourselves, enslave ourselves, but continue to yearn after a telos that recedes from our desire to fix it?

45. I address these complications in my book on spiritual materialism and desire between women in Irigaray, Brontë, and Eliot. In particular, I explore how Victorian women novelists help us to see, better than any theorists I have read, the limits to Irigaray's splendid visions.

"In the Golden Chariot Things Will Be Better"

Salwa Bakr

Translated by Barbara Harlow

Introduction by Barbara Harlow

Aziza the Alexandrian is a prisoner in the women's prison in Egypt, serving a life sentence for the murder of her mother's husband. Aziza, the main character in Salwa Bakr's recent novel *The Golden Chariot Won't Ascend to the Heavens* (1991), assassinated the man who had seduced her following her mother's death, when, despite his apparent promises to Aziza, he took another woman as his new wife. Aziza, meanwhile, plans to leave the prison in a golden chariot destined for the heavens, but she does not intend to leave alone. Bakr's novel describes not only Aziza's liberation project but also the life histories of the other women prisoners whom she has elected to accompany her in the chariot.

"In the Golden Chariot Things Will Be Better" is a chapter from Bakr's book *The Golden Chariot Won't Ascend to the Heavens* (Salwa Bakr, *Al-'araba al-dhabiyya la tus'adu ila-l-sama'* [Cairo: Sina li-l-nashr, 1991]). The translator thanks Hatem Natsheh for his help with the hard places and many of the easy ones, as well.

Um Ragab, for example, became a pickpocket in order to support her children. Hana killed her husband, after forty-five years as his sexual slave and domestic, by leaving on the gas under a cooking pot. Azima "the Tall"—too tall, that is, to get married—who became a *nadabba* (professional mourner), then a vocal performer at religious celebrations, and, finally, a popular singer, killed her abusive lover. Aida, who is from Upper Egypt, is in prison on her brother's account, having taken, on her mother's orders, the blame for his honor and revenge killing of Aida's battering husband. Huda, at sixteen, a drug addict and mother of two, is the youngest prisoner. Zaynab Mansur, referred to in the company as "madame," is the best educated and most cultured among the prisoners. The story of Dr. Bahiga Abd al-Haq, in prison for alleged "malpractice," describes the painful difficulties and contradictions of lower-class women who have succeeded in entering the professional ranks. Shafiqa had been a beggar. Um al-Khayr, a peasant, is likened to a Pharaonic goddess. And so on. Twelve prisoners in all are to accompany Aziza in that "golden chariot to the heavens."

The chapter translated here tells the stories of Gamalat, a thief who assaulted her sister's would-be "boyfriend," and Huda, the youthful drug addict and prostitute, and accounts for, as well, the story of the only political prisoner who passes briefly through the prison. For Aziza, one political prisoner's story is like another, and they are not very interesting, and she dismisses this one, too, as more of the same. The place of the anonymous political prisoner in the chapter is significant, however, both to Aziza's project and to Bakr's narrative. If the "politicals" remain isolated, as Aziza points out, from the "people," Aziza's own liberation project is itself still not consciously constructed as an effective political agenda or a collectively organized movement. The golden chariot remains an escape from, rather than a challenge to, the system, in which she, like Gamalat and the other women inmates—including the "politicals"—is imprisoned. The imposed silence of the political prisoner in the text, in turn, rearticulates critically and reflexively the probatory space of the novel itself.

Set in prison, Bakr's fictional narrative not only proposes a contemporary sociology of Egyptian women and gender relations through their "oral histories" but argues, as well, the necessary, if conflicted, connection between women's issues and their historical, political, institutional, and, especially, familial context. What the state, and with it the traditional order, construes as women's "crimes" punishable by law are recast as gender issues—abuses, determined by class, as well as by gender oppression—against the women themselves. Rather than the salvational "golden chariot to the heavens" Aziza imagines in prison, however, the novel suggests the necessity of emancipatory projects for social and political change grounded in the current historical conditions—both regional and global—and the material realities of women's lives. While Salwa Bakr has chosen the novel as the form and prison as the setting for this reexamination of women's location in the gender order and the various ways they resist this positioning, her text also mobilizes the political prisoner's silence in combining the generic and disciplinary diversity of personal account, ethnographic report, cultural critique, review essay, and political analysis, collectively suggesting the reciprocal and developing parameters, both academic and activist, social and political, for engaging with women's issues precisely through women's own engagement with these issues. That engagement is being waged on multiple fronts and in varied spaces, and often against official, and unofficial, opposition. In 1991, the Women's Health Book Collective in Cairo, for example, after more than five years of preparation, published their important volume *Hayat al-mar'a wa sihhahatu* (Women's life and health), based on *Our Bodies, Ourselves* but critically adapted to the specific circumstances of Egyptian women. The Arab Women's Solidarity Association, however, founded in 1985 by Nawal al-Saadawi, was closed by the Egyptian government early that same year. Meanwhile, in Nablus, in the occupied West Bank, the Palestinian writer Sahar Khalifeh has established the Women's Research and Training Center for young women. Across the "green line," in Israel, the Women's Organization for Political Prisoners (WOFPP) was created in the first years of the intifada to assist Palestinian women prisoners and their families materially and legally. Women across the Middle East—that is, from Morocco to the Gulf states—are continuing to engage with the social and political exigencies that continue to interrupt their lives.[1]

Aziza the Alexandrian dies in the last chapter of Salwa Bakr's novel, just as she is making final preparations for the departure of the "golden chariot." The chariot, as the novel's title concludes, "does not ascend to the heavens." Aziza's project, however, is even now being given many new organizational shapes and multiple innovative routes, while the skies themselves are being relocated on the ground in the shifting political, social, and cultural map of the Middle East and the international order.

1. For further discussion of some of these organizations, see the special issue on gender and politics, *Middle East Report* 173 (November/December 1991).

"In the Golden Chariot Things Will Be Better"

The old pavement of Aziza the Alexandrian's cell looked shiny clean despite its grayish white color, the result of time and much use. Gamalat had devoted herself to scrubbing it with water and liquid chloride, the only disinfectant and cleaner allowed and used like carbolic acid, whose strong clean smell Aziza preferred. But unfortunately this was forbidden, since it came in dark glass bottles rather than in the transparent plastic containers, which couldn't be used in any violent incidents that might break out among the women residents of the prison.

Aziza looked with satisfaction at the washed floor, with its dampness so agreeable in that hot season, and at the strip of foam matting rolled up in the corner, and reflected contentedly from her solitary iron bed on the political prisoner, one of those who get brought to the prison from time to time without any reasonable explanation for her sentencing or why the government should want to push her head in amongst their heads. This political prisoner seemed very nice to Aziza and had greeted her once while crossing the corridor when she was standing there with Azima the Tall. Aziza plucked up her courage and approached her in order to learn her story. The political smiled a broad welcoming smile. Aziza guessed that she must be either a Communist or from the Muslim Brotherhood, since those were the only kinds of politicals that Aziza had met during her stay in prison.

She concluded, somewhat hastily, that the political must be a Communist, since she wasn't veiled and appeared even rather cheerful and ordinary. Aziza reproached herself that she could no longer understand things at first glance as she used to be able to when her mind was alert and her thinking active. When she conversed with her, though, the girl spoke the same language that Aziza had heard from the other Communists she had met time and again in the prison without ever understanding anything of it or grasping the reasons behind all the intellectual and emotional pain that these women bring on themselves. Most of the ones that Aziza had met were well educated and respected, with decent jobs and comfortable living circumstances, and were much better off than most people. And she noticed that they received quite splendid visitors every day or two and cartons of cigarettes.

Aziza sighed heavily when she had heard the girl's story, which had nothing new in it for her. She had heard its like many times before. Her opinion, that these stories were joyless and without hope, remained the same. They were just stories. The people are in one world and these politicals are in another, that's for sure, because they know nothing about the life of the poor that they are always talking about. But then, when she looked into the political's cell, she saw that there was no bed in it, and she noticed the damp foam mat on the floor. When the political asked her about her own story, Aziza told her just a brief part of it. The young woman smiled again and appeased Aziza with the offer of a full pack of Marlboros as a gift. That generosity caused Aziza to reconsider her reactions, and when she went back to her room, she decided to give the young woman her own iron bed. For Aziza, it didn't matter whether she slept on a bed raised off the ground or on a mattress placed directly on the pavement, especially since it was summer and hot. And then Aziza considered whether she might not invite her to the heavens when the time came for the golden chariot with its winged horses to ascend. Aziza followed through on her first thought, though, and asked Gamalat and Azima the *nadabba* [a professional mourner] to take the bed and to put it in the political's cell. As for her second consideration, the government aborted it when it released the girl after just a month of detention. Aziza regretted that she hadn't told her about the heavenly ascent in the beginning, before the question of her release came up, since the political girl would, of course, accept that release and wouldn't then be able to leave the prison together with the passengers in the chariot to the beautiful heavenly world, which had no comparison on earth.

After thinking a bit, however, Aziza thanked God for the girl's departure, since if she had really joined in the chariot, she would certainly never be able to stop talking politics and agitating everyone else against the miserable prison conditions, and this would only make the government rearrest her, even if the chariot had already departed for the clouds of the heavens. The government had many planes and could easily send one of them to arrest the girl, and this could delay, or even destroy, the project of the ascent.

Aziza looked around the wide room and checked the arrangement of the few things in it—her old dresses, her comb and hairpins, and some plastic cups and plates. Satisfied that everything was clean and in place just as she liked it, she looked at Gamalat, who had done all that, and said to her, "*Insha'allah* [literally, "God willing," an expression used frequently in conversation], Gamalat, thank you . . . my soul feels better now."

Gamalat smiled happily, which made her round face light up like the shiny wrapping of children's candy, and answered Aziza, "Are you really happy with it, moon?" Aziza glanced around the room once again with the kind of feigned disdain, which she had often noticed in her old life on the part of those superior to her, was silent awhile, and said, "Fine . . . now wash out the trash can, please, and put it back where it belongs and come eat something."

Gamalat went out to wash the trash can in the communal bathroom at the end of the long corridor of cells. Aziza began to prepare for her a bit of bread and a piece of white cheese, which Azima the *nadabba* had given her, together with a Cleopatra cigarette, the local kind, not for export, which had a lot of sawdust, perhaps out of some kind of concern for the health of the smokers. There was a homegrown guava, too, which Safiya Heroin had given her from the basket of guavas she distributed to her friends. They had been brought by her sons on a visit, and she couldn't really save them, since they would only spoil if she kept them too many days. All the while, Aziza was thinking about Gamalat's circumstances.

Gamalat returned and put the clean trash can in the corner of the room opposite the mattress and clothes. Then she came and squatted on the worn floor in front of Aziza and plunged into the bread and cheese. Still chewing, she said, "I want your opinion about something, Aunt Aziza." "Yes?" Aziza replied. Her eyes grew big and focused on the angelic face of Gamalat, thinking that Gamalat was about to open the question of the winged golden chariot and her wish to be included in its ascent to the heavens.

Gamalat stuffed the rest of the bread into her mouth now that there was no more cheese and went on, spitting out the small stones from her last mouthful: "You know, when I leave here, *insha'allah*, at the end of my sentence, I was thinking about changing my work. Stealing is coming to have too many problems, running and hurrying here and there and at the end of the day there is nothing for it. So I thought of working the way women originally worked. That would solve my headaches."

Gamalat looked at Aziza with wide, innocent eyes as she made this momentous statement, which she had never before told anyone. But she trusted her and felt secure and comfortable with her, in spite of all the rumors in the prison about Aziza's craziness. Gamalat preferred to serve her rather than the drug leaders, who showered favors on all those who worked with them and who, with all their money, bought everything in the prison, including the prison guards themselves. But Gamalat persisted, whatever her feelings about the craziness of Aziza, who sometimes would dart frightening glances at her, and then at others smile for no reason at all, during their conversations, with a warm and affectionate humanity. She was always changing, and if Gamalat one day asked her for something, she would give it to her if she could. Thus, Gamalat did not heed the warnings she heard about Aziza's peculiarity or that she might beat her or turn against her if she were angry or upset. Gamalat had found no one in the prison better than Aziza to serve and to attach herself to as a sister. Sisterhood between one prisoner and another was necessary, and they would become as sisters born from one womb, supportive and affectionate to each other, bound by their ordeal of defenselessness and the punishment of incarceration inside the walls. And so Gamalat disclosed her secret to Aziza and sought her advice about her intentions, to help her to live and to leave this place far behind. Aziza was older and understood the world better than she did, and she had a wise insight into people. Time had only reaffirmed her correctness.

Aziza bowed her head to the ground, thinking. At her prolonged silence, Gamalat resumed her talk in order to explain her point of view: "Prostitution is easy and secure, and the penalties are light if there's a police raid. If I worked at it a year or two, I would make some money and then get out of it all and open a small store or some business to support myself in peace."

Aziza didn't answer, but she was busy observing a large ant dragging a small bread crumb that Gamalat had let fall while eating a little while ago. Aziza watched the ant until it was just about to enter its hiding place in the hole at the bottom edge of the cell's old door, whose paint had peeled away, exposing the wood, dark black from much use, and said to it, "Come on up. It's more comfortable up here."

The ant responded by disappearing entirely into the hole. Gamalat, who didn't understand what Aziza meant by these words, pretended to be busy brushing back some strands of her smooth brown hair that had fallen across her cheeks, and then said, "Do you know, tomorrow they might bring us some meat. I wish I could find some fat red meat to boil into soup with vinegar and garlic. You and I could eat it together."

Aziza raised her head from the floor and asked Gamalat to go and make a cup of tea for the two of them. When she got up, Aziza watched her full body and soft, white legs and continued thinking about what she had said to her. This was new talk for her, of a kind that she had never uttered before, notwithstanding the long months of their attachment and sisterhood in this prison, and despite Aziza's sharp knowledge of the girl and her story and what had led to her imprisonment.

Aziza knew that Gamalat belonged to a family of gypsy thieves, professionals at pickpocketing and stealing, from grandfather to father, and that the men of the family plied their trade in Saudi Arabia and the Gulf, especially during the *hajj* [the pilgrimage to Mecca and Medina] when the crowds of humanity made an excellent field for their work. As for the motherless Gamalat and her sister, they lived where Gamalat could practice her own theft, in Tanta, particularly during the *mawlid* [a religious festival] of Said Badawi, when the crowds of people and their preoccupation with pleasure were at their peak, making theft easy and uncomplicated.

Gamalat, however, was arrested for a reason other than stealing. The matter involved her sister, three years younger than she and prettier, but less clever and intelligent as a result of brain damage during her difficult birth, which had also taken the life of her mother. This sister, with finer hair than Gamalat and captivating honey-colored eyes, fell prey to the pursuit of a young man who attempted to involve her in a relationship with him when he noticed that the two girls lived alone in a furnished apartment. Such an arrangement was socially disapproved of because of what Egyptian films had shown of the inhabitants of these apartments and their immorality, as well as their connection with the world of oil from which they took their rent and which was associated with acts both illegal and irreligious. [Wealthy visitors from the oil-rich Gulf states are well known in Egypt for their profligate use of Egyptian apartments, serving to inflate rental prices, as well as to debase traditional codes of morality.] The problem was that the idiot, if well-endowed, sister cared more about chewing gum and sweets than she did for that young man, for whose existence and pursuit she felt nothing, just as he never discovered her retardedness. But Gamalat worried that this person might be careless one day and do something with her sister that would have unwanted consequences. Then the problem Gamalat faced would become two problems, and she might have to arrange for a third, small creature, as well. This sister-cross that she carried continually on her back spoiled her life night and day. She accompanied her sister whenever she went out, and if she left her at home, she would have to make sure that the windows were well closed and would turn the key in the apartment door several times for fear that the idiot girl would open it or allow someone else to open it from outside. Nonetheless, Gamalat, whenever she was away from her sister, remained anxious about the danger her sister was exposed to in her absence, such as playing with a sharp tool or accidentally setting a fire in the house.

Gamalat really did try to get her sister to take part in supporting herself. She attempted to teach her the basics of stealing and the simple arts of pickpocketing, but her sister almost caused another problem for Gamalat once, when she went up to an old man walking in the street and, sticking a corncob she was eating in his chest, shouted at him to give her the change in his pocket. If the old man had not made a small joke about a naughty little girl in distress, the problem would have gotten bigger, only God knows how big.

Gamalat had warned the young man, who worked as an assistant in a women's hair salon on the ground floor of the same building she lived in with her sister, about the difficulties he was exposing the girl to. If he didn't go away and leave her and her sister alone, she would give him a good beating and make a spectacle of him in front of everyone around. But one day she was surprised to find the young man knocking at the door. When she opened it to chase him away and to tell him that he had nothing to do with these stupid matters that he had started with them, even coming to the door of the apartment, the young man, rather than withdrawing apologetically, forced the door open and tried to enter. What could Gamalat do, then, but take the hot iron she had been using to press a red silk blouse, which she had stolen from a well-known shop in the city, and, unplugging the iron, throw it at him? It hit him and gave him a concussion, according to the diagnosis of the doctors at the public hospital, since the iron had struck him directly on his head.

Aziza thought that the hairdresser might be the one who had tried to entice Gamalat, since Lula was a professional prostitute and madam, who had been in prison numerous times for the many networks of vice that she managed. Among her victims were university students, office employees, and women of some social standing. Aziza gave up that idea, however, because Gamalat hated Lula more than anything. She treated her with scorn once she discovered her eccentricity, even though Lula still clung to Gamalat for no apparent reason. When Lula saw Gamalat standing in the prison yard, she would want to touch her in a way that just wasn't natural. In the beginning, Gamalat would explain this as a kind of love and affection that made her happy, because it came from someone who felt sorry for her and took care of her. Then one day Gamalat was bathing in the prison bath and the water from the tap was very slow because the main water pipe had been broken for nearly a month. There was water, but not enough of it reached the bath. Gamalat asked Lula to bring her a bucket of water, and then when she brought it Lula offered to scrub Gamalat's back with the luffa and soap. That was how Gamalat discovered that Lula wanted to do more than just clean those areas that Gamalat couldn't reach herself. Their breaths met as Lula played with the details of Gamalat's body, which, despite its tendency to corpulence, was indeed lovely. Gamalat tried to push her away. She didn't need any more evidence of her immorality and lewdness, and if she didn't put a stop to it, it would be all over the prison, especially among those who liked to gossip about such things, like the hags in the older women's cell, and Um Ragab, who spied on the prisoners for the administration. For sure, that reputation had helped Aziza with them. Saniya Matar, however, the most famous drug dealer in the prison, serving a life sentence for smuggling drugs from outside the country by plane, grabbed the morsel happily and took Lula as one of her main lovers, but Gamalat never gave up her bitter scorn. It helped her to deal with Lula whenever she ran into her, poisoning her life and cornering her so that she couldn't respond, not because of good manners or a modest tongue, which, like the rest of her body, had never known modesty anyway, but because, despite the insults and harshness, she was really in love with a little girl and could not sleep at night.

Aziza never did know who was behind Gamalat's decision to change her profession or how she came to be persuaded to it. Aziza met Huda, the newest inmate in the scabies cell, who had arrived only the previous week, afterwards. Even though at sixteen Huda was the youngest woman-wife in the prison, the mother of two children, she, nevertheless, from her short and intense experience of life, could have persuaded Gamalat to change her profession to a better and more successful one.

Huda had come to her own low pass along unimaginably twisted routes. The beginning was years earlier, when she had first entered the police station with her mother, not as criminals being brought to justice but to report the murder of a hen. Her mother owned fourteen other hens, which she had raised since they were hatched and which had now become laying hens themselves. Huda's mother's complaint was against a neighbor who lived in a shack near her own in one of those sprawling areas of the city that had grown and grown until it almost resembled a large country town. Before that, Huda's mother had gone to the government hospital, not because of her eye, which she had lost in the fight with her mighty neighbor who had hit her straight in the eye with a brick big enough to gouge it out, but to persuade the naturally unconvinced doctor on duty to write a death certificate for the murdered hen, confirming that it had been violently slain, which she could present to the police, who would then take the necessary steps against the neighbor.

When the doctor refused to understand Huda's mother, maintaining that he didn't write medical certificates for hens but that he could write a certificate indicating the extent of the physical damage to her burst eye, she left, claiming that the government never understood the real essence of the problem, the truth of the matter, and went, instead, to the police station. Here, she was met at the door by an old sergeant who paid no attention to the mother's lost eye nor to the departed hen lying motionless wrapped in the edge of the woman's long, black veil. All his attention was fixed on the tender, white body of the little girl who stood just then clinging fearfully to her mother and watching cautiously what was going on around her. The sergeant offered to buy them a cold drink—something that did not usually happen in police stations—and, assuring the mother that he would avenge the wrong done to her, inquired about the girl and her situation. Not a quarter of an hour later, he had proposed to the mother that he marry the little girl standing at her side.

The mother forgot her lost eye, the departed hen, and the cruel neighbor at this astonishing and momentous occurrence. Never, ever, and in no way had she dreamed that she could possibly be related to someone with connections to the government or that she could receive such distinction. It did not, therefore, take her long to reflect before she agreed to marry off her daughter without delay, having, meanwhile, remarked with satisfaction the colored braid on the man's arm, indicating that he really was a sergeant and not just an ordinary soldier with no rank in the police force. Huda's mother figured that fate had thrown him in her path in order to lift her from her life among the lowest of the low and to bring her into the view of the world. The man was lavish and most serious in his behavior and had promised her thirty pounds as a dowry and the same amount again to prepare clothes and other necessities for the small wedding. He also announced his intention to present her with a gold bracelet from one of those wholesale shops specializing in the sale of copper jewelry plated with gold, guaranteed by a legal stamp, the kind that pleased the poor fellahin but that most others couldn't buy.

For two months, the sergeant prepared to become the husband of the little girl not yet thirteen years old. The obstacle of legal age determined by the government was overcome by purchasing for two pounds a certificate of age from a doctor who specialized in such illegal medical practices as abortion, repairing the lost virginity of girls ready for marriage, and issuing certificates of age for girls too young to marry legally. This then allowed the official authorized to perform marriages to issue the government documents and to issue, in turn, a marriage certificate to the sergeant. Despite the official's suspicions about the girl's age, the sergeant had the legal paper, together with the other papers, for the marriage contract, thereby removing him from any judiciary question or suspicion.

After just a year, Huda, from her esteemed husband, gave birth to a fine boy, who eventually came to resemble her. Another year later, there was a baby sister next to him, always crying and upset, because of the drug habit she had inherited from her mother, who was, in fact, an addict. From the beginning of their marriage, her husband had never come home in the evening without some opium or hashish in his pocket, seized in raids on the dens of drug traffickers or given to him by dealers in the neighborhood to ensure his implication and to buy his silence. When the husband came home less and less frequently and abandoned his small family for another woman whom he had met through his exciting work, which brought him into daily contact with dozens of different human types, Huda had to confront life on her own. She had to find a source of food for herself and her children, as well as another source for feeding the needs of her nervous system. This took her all too naturally to the ABCs of the matter and the easiest and most available profession in history for women.

Gamalat was not an inmate in the scabies cell, like Huda, but she did spend most of her time there because of their friendship. Most of the inmates in the prison avoided any interaction with the women who lived in that cell for fear that they would be contaminated by those packed into the scabies club by their destitution and poverty, which meant that they couldn't afford to buy even a cheap piece of soap, just enough to bathe and wash their clothes, to supplement the bit of soap issued them by the prison administration. The real portion they were supposed to get disappeared into the pockets of the concessionaires and the petty functionaries of the prison, and so the young bodies of most of the cell's residents became feeding grounds for tiny insects and microscopic vermin. Huda's boisterous desire for life, her friendliness, and her ability to make jokes all attracted Gamalat to her, in addition to the singing and dancing parties they joined in with the rest of the girls in the cell. Huda would attempt—unsuccessfully—to imitate Farid al-Atrash [a popular Egyptian singer], whom she liked a lot, but, in any case, she was the uncontested star of the parties in the scabies cell and its leader, in spite of her young age. Everyone else had to follow her orders, especially with regard to designating sleeping spaces, assigning cleaning duties, which didn't take much time because of the lack of cleaning materials, and collecting rags and scraps of paper in the prison yard in the afternoon to burn at night in the cell in the futile effort to drive away the disgusting mosquitoes who joined the other vermin in sucking the prisoners' blood. The smoke that rose from the burning of this garbage was not enough to keep away the mosquitoes, but it did give all the women chest ailments.

Aziza lit a cigarette and reflected sadly: How many men would lick the nectar of that tender body before her if Gamalat were to become one of those women who sold their bodies to any and every man who presented himself? Aziza thought about the old men, the tall and the short men, the ones with huge paunches and smoke-stained teeth, dirtied from taking drugs, all those who would squeeze the last drop of youthfulness from Gamalat's body and destroy her soul, bit by bit, until, in the end, she became a human deformity, worn out from so much use. She asked herself why such a young and pretty girl should have to endure all that ugliness and spend her life, which had only just begun, in a way that could only lead to a dead end. She wondered why Gamalat couldn't have a man as handsome as she, to whom she could give her heart and her body and who would give her everything a man can give a woman. Aziza went so far as to imagine what would become of Gamalat if she pursued this path she was contemplating, how, in the end, she would become a professional prostitute, selling her love to anyone who could pay for it, until one day she would become another Lula, a shrewd proprietress, not only selling her own body but managing the sale of the bodies of other women, as well.

At this point in her thinking, Aziza's sadness turned to defiant anger. Lifting her head, she fixed her eyes on the iron bars of the window and raised her voice in protest to the inscrutable higher power that she considered responsible for all that had happened and that would happen in the future to that good and lovely young woman with a soul as pure and innocent as the souls of children. Looking at the bit of sky draped in dark gray clouds, she said in sorrow and anger, "Do you hear? Do you see? The story breaks all bounds. We can't be silent about it any longer!" She went on in her anger and sorrow, "Fine, then. I swear on my mother's grave that the girl will leave with us. I won't leave here without her. But first she must have a hot bath with Finik soap, so no one will catch any disease. *Insha'allah*, she will be in good shape then and ever so sweet-smelling."

At that point she noticed Gamalat, who was busy scratching something between her fingers as Aziza spoke. She turned to where she was standing in the corner of the room and poured the tea into the two cups on the tray. She was late in pouring it out, and the color of the tea had turned a dark red, the color of rubies. Flirting with Aziza a bit, she spoke in surprise, calling her by the secret name that she had given her and that she liked to use in moments of happiness, "Allah, were you speaking to me, moon?"

Our Lady of MTV: Madonna's "Like a Prayer"

Carla Freccero

White academic feminists and feminist intellectuals are currently enacting the wanna-be syndrome of Madonna fans, analyzed, along with fashion, by Angela McRobbie, and more recently by Lisa Lewis, as the complex and specific mode of interpretation, appropriation, and revision belonging to "girl culture" in Britain and the United States.[1] What better way to construct an empowered performative female identity than to claim for ourselves a heroine who has successfully encoded sexiness, beauty, *and* power into a

The use of initial caps in writing "Black" is a deliberate political gesture on my part, referring not to a color but to a political designation.

1. Angela McRobbie, *Feminism and Youth Culture: From "Jackie" to "Just Seventeen"* (Boston: Unwin Hyman, 1991); Lisa Lewis, *Gender Politics and MTV: Voicing the Difference* (Philadelphia: Temple University Press, 1990). See also Simon Frith and Angela McRobbie, "Rock and Sexuality," *Screen Education* 29 (1978–1979): 3–19. I owe a debt of gratitude to numerous people who have assisted in this study of Madonna: Nancy Vickers, in particular, for her studies of the lyric tradition, MTV, and popular music; Tom Kalin (see "Media Kids: Tom Kalin on Pussy Power," *Artforum International* [September 1991]: 19–21); Charles Hamm; the audiences, mainly students, who have heard and criticized this paper; and Cirri Nottage and Melinda Weinstein, whose research assistance has been invaluable.

performing embodiment? You can have it all, Madonna suggests, and be credited with a mind, as well. For her girl fans, Madonna has suggested ways of appropriating rebellious masculine youth culture, both preserving and subverting femininity, mitigating the adolescent disempowerment of the female position. It is Madonna's ambition, hard work, and success, as she moves into her thirties, that her women fans appreciate. Thus, Lisa Lewis and Susan McClary, abandoning the intellectual feminist's suspicion of popular cultural representations of female empowerment, argue for a feminist reclamation of Madonna on solid intellectual and feminist, if overly celebratory, grounds.[2]

While impressed with their insights and sympathetic to their "defense" of Madonna against her detractors (all of whom, to my knowledge, deploy traditional élite or masculinist *topoi* in their attacks), I am skeptical of their and my own desire to appropriate Madonna for intellectuals, if only because "she" responds so easily to this desire and fits so well into the progressive white feminist fantasy I am about to explore in her text. Since I am interested in practicing cultural politics, in strategically locating and developing what Andrew Ross calls the "protopolitical" in popular culture, particularly in those media that have been derogatorily designated as "mass culture" or the "culture industry" by left- and right-wing intellectuals alike, it will be important to consider my investment in this reading, as a patrilineally Italian American academic, antiracist (multiculturalist) feminist, whose micropolitical positioning is peculiarly adapted to the cultural representations called *Madonna*.[3]

Much has been made of MTV's postmodern style: the fragmenting

2. See, in particular, Susan McClary, "Living to Tell: Madonna's Resurrection of the Fleshly," *Genders* 7 (March 1990): 1–21; and Lewis, *Gender Politics and MTV*.

3. Andrew Ross, *No Respect: Intellectuals and Popular Culture* (New York and London: Routledge, 1989); see also his "Hacking Away at the Counterculture," in *Technoculture*, ed. Constance Penley and Andrew Ross (Minneapolis: University of Minnesota Press, 1991), 107–34: "The significance of these cultures lies in their embryonic or *protopolitical* languages and technologies of opposition to dominant or parent systems of rules. If hackers lack a 'cause,' then they are certainly not the first youth culture to be characterized in this dismissive way. In particular, the left has suffered from the lack of a cultural politics capable of recognizing the power of cultural expressions that do not wear a mature political commitment on their sleeves" (122). For a critique of the too-rapid dismissal of neo–Frankfurt School leftist intellectuals' suspicion of mass culture, see Meaghan Morris, "Banality in Cultural Studies," in *Logics of Television: Essays in Cultural Criticism*, ed. Patricia Mellencamp (Bloomington: Indiana University Press, 1990), 14–43: "There is an active process going on in both of discrediting—by direct dismissal (Baudrillard) or covert

of images, the blurring of generic boundaries between commercial, program, concert, and station identification, the circulation of commodities wrenched from their marketplace context, the sense of play and carnival; the attention to fashion; and the de-centered appropriation of images without regard for context or history. Now, there is even a show called "Postmodern Videos." Its advertised de-centeredness, its "semiotic democracy" (John Fiske's term), its refusal of national boundaries, are, however, like postmodernism itself, far from innocent, and most comparisons that foreground MTV's postmodernism neglect its project, a sort of global cultural imperialism that is nowhere more clearly demonstrated than in its own self-advertisement: "ONE WORLD, ONE IMAGE, ONE CHANNEL: MTV." I call this *imperialism* because MTV is not a democratic medium, equally available to all cultures and nations for use, but a specific creation of the United States for the incorporation of "world music" into itself and for the creation of global desires to consume the products of U.S. popular culture.

The global preparation for Madonna's Pepsi commercial testifies both to MTV's success in having colonized cable and to some of the more concrete goals of this capitalist medium (for MTV models itself on television advertisements and airs commercials for songs and albums). A commercial appeared around the world, featuring an aborigine running across the plains of Australia (in reality, California) into a bar, arriving just in time to see, you guessed it, Madonna's Pepsi commercial version of "Like a Prayer." The commercial itself aired in forty countries on 2 March 1989. Madonna is, like George Michael and other relatively recent stars, one of the "corp-rock" generation, as the *Village Voice* puts it, untroubled by Neil Young's accusations of sell-out as they take directorial control over multinational commodity advertising to the tune of $3 to $5 million.[4]

I point out these things to emphasize that it is not a question of holding these stars to some kind of moral or political "standards"; the portrait of

---

inscription as Other (cultural studies)—the voices of grumpy feminists and cranky leftists ('Frankfurt School' can do duty for both). To discredit such voices is, as I understand it, one of the immediate political functions of the current boom in cultural studies (as distinct from the intentionality of projects invested by it). To discredit a voice is something very different from displacing an analysis which has become outdated, or revising a strategy which no longer serves its purpose. It is to character-ize a fictive position from which anything said can be dismissed as already heard" (25).

4. Leslie Savan, "Desperately Selling Soda," *Village Voice* 34, no. 11, 14 Mar. 1989, 47. See also Bill Zehme, "Madonna: The *Rolling Stone* Interview," *Rolling Stone*, 23 Mar. 1989, 52.

the folk/rock artist as an oppositional figure does not apply to the same extent in the domain of pop. Rather, if resistance, or opposition, is to be found, it is in the subordination of the multinationals' interests to the promotion of an individual; both George Michael and Madonna made long, seminarrative minimusic videos out of Coke and Pepsi bucks that de-centered the corporation's product (Diet Coke and Pepsi) relative to their own. Madonna's piece is that of an *auteur* inscribing a thoroughly private autobiography as a masterpiece of global interest in its own right.[5]

It is often said of the postmodern that its messages are both reactionary and leftist; certainly popular texts must occupy at least both those positions to be "truly" popular, for the clearer the *partis pris*, the narrower and more specific the addressee.[6] Madonna aims for a wider audience, the widest possible, as her changing image indicates. One song that quintessentially illustrates this political both/and position is Madonna's "Papa Don't Preach," a song about a girl who decides against having an abortion but articulates this decision in assertively pro-choice terms.[7]

I start from the position that these products of late capitalism are, with almost no embarrassment, reproducers of dominant ideologies; I then ask whether there is anything else to be found in them. Fiske, in his studies of television, of Madonna, and of television audiences, argues for a *reading* of television that emphasizes not only the dominant ideology's efforts to reproduce and maintain itself, not only the representation of hegemonic forces, but also the active and empowering pleasures that are negotiated

5. Lewis points out how the traditional opposition between rock and pop (serious/frivolous, political/apolitical, etc.) has often been used to marginalize female vocalists by trivializing the genre with which they are most frequently associated. See Lewis, *Gender Politics and MTV*, 29–33. For an analysis of the Madonna Pepsi commercial, see Nancy Vickers, "Maternalism and the Material Girl," in *Embodied Voices: Female Vocality in Western Culture*, ed. Leslie Dunn and Nancy Jones (Cambridge University Press, forthcoming).

6. John Fiske, "British Cultural Studies," in *Channels of Discourse: Television and Contemporary Criticism*, ed. Robert C. Allen (Chapel Hill: University of North Carolina Press, 1987), 254–89: "The television text can only be popular if it is open enough to admit a range of negotiated meanings, through which various social groups can find meaningful articulations of their own relationship to the dominant ideology. Any television text must, then, be polysemic, for the heterogeneity of the audience requires a corresponding heterogeneity of meanings in the text" (267).

7. For an interesting and suggestive survey of audience response to this video and to "Open Your Heart," see Jane D. Brown and Laurie Schulze, "The Effects of Race, Gender, and Fandom on Audience Interpretations of Madonna's Music Videos," *Journal of Communication* 40, no. 2 (Spring 1990): 88–102.

in television by subcultures, by the marginalized and subordinate. "Television and its programs do not have an 'effect' on people. Viewers and television interact," he asserts, which is another way of saying that viewing television is, for its viewers, an act of reading and that the cultural text is that which is produced by these acts of reading.[8] Television, Fiske argues, is an open text, one that enables "negotiated," resistive, and oppositional meanings to be read even as it promotes the values and serves the interests of the ruling classes. I propose to read the ways in which several of Madonna's music videos enable some oppositional readings, and I want to go a step further in describing a theologico-political discourse that moves into and out of focus in these videos. I want to make an argument for deliberately locating elements of resistance in cultural texts produced, as in this case, squarely within a patriarchal and capitalist hegemony. Of course, it is difficult to gauge whether such elements are indeed resistive, or whether, through their staging of rebellion, they, in fact, contribute to hegemony.

The *Village Voice*, given to a great deal of highbrow sneering when it comes to Madonna, remarks nastily of her autobiographical album, "Like a Prayer," "You don't need Joseph Campbell to untangle her personal mythos."[9] I am suggesting, however, that there is a specificity to Madonna's mythos and that the specific cultural semiotics of Madonna's lyric and visual

8. John Fiske, *Television Culture* (London and New York: Methuen, 1987), 19; see also his "British Cultural Studies," 260. Much of Fiske's discussion here is taken from Stuart Hall, "Encoding/Decoding," in *Culture, Media, Language*, ed. Stuart Hall et al. (London: Hutchinson, 1980): 128–39. I take to heart the critique offered by the "disgruntled" Morris in "Banality in Cultural Studies" with regard to Fiske's and others' "making the best of things" approach to popular culture as a way of salvaging leftist energy from mass media, yet I also find it necessary continually to rehearse arguments for attending at all seriously to elements of resistance within these texts. At the same time, my own project takes some distance from Fiske's particular approach to cultural studies and Madonna by its in-depth focus on an "ethnic" and "female" subcultural specificity. In this regard, it resembles more the "new philological" project of cultural critics such as Stephanie Hull, though our (political) conclusions diverge significantly ("Madonna's Vogue," Paper presented at session number 504: "Essentialism, Philology, and Popular Culture," Modern Language Association Annual Meeting, San Francisco, 29 Dec. 1991). In one of the most intellectually serious treatments of Madonna as a postmodern text, Ramona Curry cites Richard Dyer's discussion of stars as composite images and argues that one should read Madonna as an "intertextual conglomerate": "Meanings of any given text arise not predominantly in readers' experience of its construction but in their discursive interactions with it in the context of myriad associated texts" (see "Madonna from Marilyn to Marlene—Pastiche and/or Parody?" *Journal of Film and Video* 42, no. 2 [Summer 1990]: 15–30; in particular, 16).
9. Steve Anderson, "Forgive Me Father," *Village Voice*, 4 Apr. 1989, 67.

production are located within the history and popular spirituality of an Italian American cultural imagination. Robert Orsi, in *The Madonna of 115th Street: Faith and Community in Italian Harlem, 1880–1950*, describes the mythos of the immigrant community, its relationship to the homeland and to spirituality, as well as the relationship of the second generation (the immigrants' children) to this mythos, fundamentally centered on the *domus*, household or family, as its significant unit.[10] Orsi argues that one must understand Italian immigrant culture to understand the sometimes "strange" forms its popular piety takes. The visual images of "Like a Prayer," and those of an earlier video, "Open Your Heart," bring this Italian American culture into focus so as to articulate Madonna's feminocentric street theology. Critics of "Like a Prayer" accuse it of sacrilege and even heresy. Orsi notes that there is a similar response to the forms of popular spirituality in the communities he studied, and he adds, "There is a spirit of defiance in popular spirituality . . . it allows the people to claim their religious experience as their own and to affirm the validity of their values" (Orsi, 221). Furthermore, Orsi provides a key to the central role played by the Madonna, or heavenly mother (*mamma celeste*), in Madonna's theology and provides, as well, a key to her staging of a daughterly discourse within a patriarchal family context.

Madonna Louise Veronica Ciccone was born in 1958 and grew up in Pontiac, Michigan. Her father is a first-generation Italian American, whose parents came from the Abruzzi in the twenties or thirties to work in the steel mills of Pittsburgh. Like many Italian Americans of his generation, he was upwardly mobile. Silvio Ciccone went to college to become an engineer, and he moved to the Detroit area to work in the automotive industry. Like many "patriotic" Italian Americans, Silvio Ciccone served in the U.S. military. In interviews, Madonna talks about his ambition, his work ethic, and his will to succeed materially, all of which bequeathed a legacy that is embodied in the nickname critics give to Madonna and that is also the title of one of her most famous songs, "Material Girl."

Madonna takes her name from her mother, a French Canadian

10. Robert Anthony Orsi, *The Madonna of 115th Street: Faith and Community in Italian Harlem, 1880–1950* (New Haven and London: Yale University Press, 1985); hereafter cited in my text as Orsi. Luc Sante, in "Unlike a Virgin," *New Republic*, 20 Aug. and 27 Aug. 1990, 25–29, modifies his acerbic tone when he discusses Madonna's Catholicism: "If, at this point, there is any aspect of Madonna's act that seems independent of calculation, it is her preoccupation with the Catholic mysteries" (28). For a high theological reading of Madonna, especially "Like a Prayer," see Andrew Greeley, "Like a Catholic: Madonna's Challenge to Her Church," *America*, 13 May 1989, 447–49.

woman, who lived in Bay City and who died when the singer was six. Madonna is the third of six children, the oldest daughter. After high school, she won a dance scholarship to the University of Michigan, where she remained for a year or so. She then left for New York and "worked in a donut shop" until she joined the Alvin Ailey Dance Co., after which she went to Paris, where she began to sing. Hers is a typical and typically romanticized immigrant story, an American dream come true. She affirms this myth at the beginning of the Virgin Tour, where her voice-over prefaces the concert tape with the following story: "I went to New York. I had a dream. I wanted to be a big star. I didn't know anybody. I wanted to dance. I wanted to sing. I wanted to do all those things. I wanted to make people happy. I wanted to be famous. I wanted everybody to love me. I wanted to be a star. I worked really hard and my dream came true."[11]

The autobiographical album, "Like a Prayer," makes explicit the traces of a Roman Catholic Italian American family ethos in Madonna's work. Family is the major theme of the album: from "Till Death," an account of the violent dissolution of her marriage; to "Promise to Try," a child's hymn of mourning to the lost mother and an appeal for guidance to the Virgin herself; to "Oh Father," an indictment and a forgiving of the severe patriarch; to "Keep It Together," a song that asserts the necessity of family ties. The album also includes a distorted rendering of the Roman Catholic Act of Contrition that turns into a sort of child's parody of this frequently recited confessional prayer. The album itself is dedicated to her mother, who, she writes, "taught me how to pray." The cover playfully exploits Roman Catholic religious themes and reinscribes Madonna signifiers, most notably her navel, from her earlier work.[12] The album cover of "Like a Prayer," which reveals Madonna's naked midriff and the crotch of her partially unbuttoned blue jeans, imitates the Rolling Stones's "Sticky Fingers" album cover. Above the crotch is printed her name, Madonna, with the *o* (positioned where her navel should be) surrounded by a cruciform drawing of light and topped with a crown (the Virgin's, presumably).[13]

Understanding Madonna in this context depends on three aspects of

11. "Madonna Live: The Virgin Tour," Warner Music Video, Boy Toy, Inc., 1985.

12. For a meditation on Madonna's navel, see Harold Jaffe, *Madonna and Other Spectacles* (New York: PAJ Publications, 1988), 7–12.

13. The cover design also puns on the Elizabethan meaning of *o* as a designation for female genitals; on this cover, Madonna makes a joke about her phallic power by combining the Rolling Stones blue jeans, which "contain" the phallus, with the *o* of her own phallic absence.

these video texts. First, Madonna plays with the codes of femininity to undo dominant gender codes and to assert her own power and agency (and, by extension, that of women, in general), not by rejecting the feminine but by adopting it as masquerade; that is, by posing as feminine.[14] She takes on the patriarchal codes of femininity and adds an ironic twist that asserts her power to manipulate them. The second salient aspect of Madonna's text depends on understanding a subculture that goes unread, for the most part, by the dominant culture: a connectedness to Italy—in name, of course; in tradition; and in relation to theology, to femininity, and to exile, departure, and immigration. Madonna represents herself as doubly, if not triply, exiled: She has lost her homeland (as a second-generation immigrant), she is a woman, and she is motherless. She also figures herself in a relation of generational conflict (as the oppressed daughter) within the severely patriarchal structure of the household, represented by her Italian American father.[15] The inscription of the daughterly position is a market strategy, as well, for it sets up an identification with adolescent girls, who initially constituted the majority of Madonna's fans.

These motifs appear strikingly in two videos: "Papa Don't Preach" and "Open Your Heart." "Open Your Heart" presents an early version of Madonna's musings about her Italian heritage, explicitly brought out by the 1987 Ciao Italia tour, where she attempts rudimentary conversation in the language and makes a pilgrimage to the home of her Italian relatives. In this video, Madonna also works, dream-like, through her relationship to an actress she idolizes, Marlene Dietrich in the *Blue Angel*, and to Dietrich's

14. For the notion of femininity as masquerade, see Joan Riviere, "Womanliness as a Masquerade," and Stephen Heath, "Joan Riviere and the Masquerade," in *Formations of Fantasy*, ed. Victor Burgin, James Donald, and Cora Kaplan (1986; reprint, London and New York: Routledge, 1989), 35–61; see also Mary Russo, "Female Grotesques: Carnival and Theory," in *Feminist Studies/Critical Studies*, ed. Teresa de Lauretis (Bloomington: Indiana University Press, 1986), 213–29. Lewis (*Gender Politics and MTV*) convincingly argues the case for female empowerment and gender code manipulation in the works of several female pop musicians from the point of view of authorial control and production, on the one hand, to fan response and the issue of female address, on the other hand; Fiske ("British Cultural Studies") points to the evidence of female fan response; while McClary's study (*Feminine Endings: Music, Gender, and Sexuality* [Minneapolis: University of Minnesota Press, 1991]) traces, among other things, a genealogy of female musicianship and struggles for empowerment that "culminates" in Madonna.

15. This notion of the household could be extended to include not only the family but the music industry, as well, for this upstart female has not always been well received in the traditionally white male bastion that is MTV.

dark sister Liza Minnelli (another Italian American), in its remake, *Cabaret*. The relationship to Italy, to the father, and to her own commodification as a female sex object and a performing star are all deeply ambivalent.

The video opens with a small boy trying to gain admittance to a sort of cabaret/peep show that displays out front photographs of naked women (with black bars covering breasts and pubes) and a blue-tinted poster of Madonna, who wears a black wig. The ticket-taker will not admit the boy. We move inside, then, to Madonna's "strip show" number, where she manipulates a chair and sings, while onlookers sit in coin-operated booths that enable them to watch the show (this video also includes, for the first time in Madonna's videos, the gay spectator—a woman rather than a man). The video plays with the notion, made famous by Laura Mulvey, of the male gaze in cinema, the construction of the camera's "look" as male and its object as female. Madonna is clearly the object of these voyeuristic gazes, yet, at the same time, she fractures the monolithic nature of the camera's look with the opening and closing barriers of the booths, her direct countergaze into the camera's lens, and the cuts in the video to the little boy standing outside, placing his hands over the various body parts of the pinup women as if to cover them. Thus, the video makes the audience uncomfortably aware of the voyeuristic aspect of our enjoyment of the performance, while nevertheless staging that performance for us to watch. The camera cuts to the young boy, who, looking in a mirror, dances in a manner imitating Madonna's dance inside the cabaret, thus establishing an identification between them. When Madonna comes outside, she is dressed like the boy, with her hair similarly disheveled. McClary argues that "the young boy's game of impersonating the femme fatale and Madonna's transvestism at the end both refuse essentialist gender categories and turn sexual identity into a kind of play," a visual effect echoing the musical resistance to closure in the song itself.[16] Madonna gives the boy a chaste kiss, and they run off together. The ticket-taker runs after them and mouths some words that appear as subtitles in the video. The two "children" go skipping off into the distance.

The subtitles without translation, "Ritorna . . . ritorna . . . Madonna.

16. McClary, "Living to Tell," 13. See also Curry's reading of "Open Your Heart," which makes the argument that the video constructs an "alternative audience address" that champions "oppressed social and racial groups" (see "Madonna from Marilyn to Marlene," 19–20). Brown and Schulze found that white girls did not react to the pornographic performance as parody, although they did interpret the final scene as an escape into childhood innocence (see "The Effects of Race, Gender, and Fandom," 97–99).

Abbiamo ancora bisogno di te" ("Come back . . . come back . . . Madonna. We still need you") literalize Louis Althusser's description of how ideology functions by "hailing" the subject; here, Madonna is hailed by what is represented as Italian patriarchy. In the Virgin Concert Tour, her real-life dad comes on stage during the song and says, "Madonna get off that stage right now!" Madonna looks around and out into space, as if puzzled, and says: "Daddy, is that you?"

The father is figured as in the role of service to a clientele (he is a ticket-taker) and thus not in the dominant position, clueing us in on the immigrant or subcultural status of "Italian" in this context. "We" is, of course, a symbolic utterance: "We," uttered in Italian, suggests that the "we" has to do with being Italian, with "serving," and with profiting from the woman's prostitution. It is not, in other words, the "we" of the clientele. It is also a private message. Subtitles, which are meant to make what is foreign intelligible, here refuse to translate for the Anglophone viewer, staging, instead, the private in a public place; like the cabaret act and the children's flight from both it and the camera, subtitles permit voyeurism but reject voyeuristic mastery by the viewer. Meanwhile, what is also staged is the flight from an interior space (coded as "feminine" in music video) to the exterior (coded as "masculine" and "free"), with its explicitly drawn vanishing point.[17] The family triad of Madonna, child, and interpellating father, who is resisted and refused, uneasily alludes to the absent mother, who is both sacrifice (Madonna as commodity) and savior (fantasy of escape), the homeland, or motherland.

Madonna says that her father was socially ambitious, focusing on his own, and his children's, upward social mobility. This video stages Madonna's ironic resentment of the hostility and rejection she receives as a "bad woman" (whore, slut, skeezer, etc.) within the very culture that uses her for profit; and she marks that culture as Italian. The ambitions are figured as

17. Lewis discusses the coding in music videos of male and female spaces and the creation of female address videos through an initial appropriation of what is coded as "male space," primarily the street. See "Female Address in Music Video," *Journal of Communication Inquiry* 11, no. 1 (Winter 1987): 73–84; also "Form and Female Authorship in Music Video," *Communication* 9 (1987): 355–77. She develops this discussion at greater length in *Gender Politics and MTV*. For a feminist critique of subculture study that focuses on the street as a site of youth activity, see Angela McRobbie, "Settling Accounts with Subcultures: A Feminist Critique," *Screen Education* 34 (Spring 1980): 37–49. McClary, in "Living to Tell," 12–13, and Lewis, in *Gender Politics and MTV*, 141–43, also provide (different) interpretations of "Open Your Heart."

her father's. She stages, as well, the typical second-generation resentment of the make-it-in-America materialist mentality (*and* her willingness to serve those ends). Madonna is thus "martyred" to the male gaze, but she escapes into preadolescent innocence. Yet, this martyrdom is simultaneously a recognition of her power to rake in profit, to fix and fragment the male gaze, and to control men.

A third important aspect of Madonna's text is the way in which the relation to exile becomes displaced in "Like a Prayer," so that the position of exile without a home, pariah, or outsider comes to be occupied not by Italian immigrants but by African Americans. This displacement has become even more pronounced in her recent work, which consistently features Black gay dancers. This, too, has its microcultural history: Italian Harlem shared borders with Black Harlem in New York, as in many urban communities across the United States, and Italians and African Americans share a long American history of similarities and differences, conflicts and cooperations. For Madonna, there is, additionally, a personal narrative of guilt assuaged, in that Steven Bray, an African American R&B musician, composer, songwriter, and producer, gave her her first break into the business and established her on the R&B charts before she ever crossed over into pop. She subsequently abandoned him for a producer with more prestige but has since then provided him with opportunities for fame and has reunited with him to collaborate in songwriting.[18] Finally, of course, what traverses many white popular musicians' work is a sense of indebtedness and collective guilt about R&B, or Black, music, whose deliberate exclusion from avenues of mainstream stardom and, until recently, MTV itself, is well documented.[19]

"Like a Prayer" is the now-notorious video that occasioned Pepsi's withdrawal of the Madonna commercial featuring the same song but different visuals. Fundamentalist religious groups, in the United States and abroad, protested that the video was offensive, and they threatened to boycott Pepsi.[20] In part, their reaction stems from a long-standing dominant

18. Christopher Connelly, "Madonna Goes All the Way," *Rolling Stone*, 22 Nov. 1984, 15–20, 81. Subsequent to the making of "Vogue" and "Truth or Dare," there has been a dispute about Madonna's business relationship to dancers José Gutierrez and Luis Camacho; here, too, the politics of race plays a subtextual role. See "Madonna's Boyz Express Themselves to Jonathan Van Meter," *NYQ* 13, 26 Jan. 1992.

19. See the NAACP's pamphlet *"The Discordant Sound of Music": A Report on the Record Industry* (Baltimore: The National Association for the Advancement of Colored People, 23 Mar. 1987). I thank Nancy Vickers for providing me with this document.

20. James Cox, "Pepsi Cans Its Madonna Ad under Pressure," *USA Today*, 4 Apr. 1989;

culture hostility to Italian Catholic popular spirituality: statues coming to life, bleeding (an old tradition called *ecce homo*, whereby Christ's, or a saint's, face becomes bathed in blood), stigmata, sexuality coupled with religious worship, as well as the demystification involved in developing an intimate and personal reciprocal relationship to the divine (Orsi, 225). There is also the fact that Madonna is inserted as an active agent in a story and in a role reserved for men, and in so doing, she challenges the patriarchal stranglehold on the Catholic church. The video of "Like a Prayer" can also be read as an indictment of a white male patriarchal Christianity in the name of what has happened to "white" women and to Black men.

Here, then, is Madonna's (and the video's director, filmmaker Mary Lambert's) account of the plot for "Like a Prayer":

> A girl on the street witnesses an assault on a young woman. Afraid to get involved because she might get hurt, she is frozen in fear. A black man walking down the street also sees the incident and decides to help the woman. But just then, the police arrive and arrest him. As they take him away, she looks up and sees one of the gang members who assaulted the girl. He gives her a look that says she'll be dead if she tells. The girl runs, not knowing where to go, until she sees a church. She goes in and sees a saint in a cage who looks very much like the black man on the street, and says a prayer to help her make the right decision. He seems to be crying, but she is not sure. She lies down on a pew and falls into a dream in which she begins to tumble in space with no one to break her fall. Suddenly she is caught by a woman who represents earth and emotional strength and who tosses her back up and tells her to do the right thing. Still dreaming, she returns to the saint, and her religious and erotic feelings begin to stir. The saint becomes a man. She picks up a knife and cuts her hands. That's the guilt in Catholicism that if you do something that feels good you will be punished. As the choir sings, she reaches an orgasmic crescendo of sexual fulfillment intertwined with her love of God. She knows that nothing's going to happen to her if she does

---

Karen Phillips, "Madonna Canned: Pepsi Pulls the Plug on Controversial Ads," *New York Post*, 5 Apr. 1989; "Madonna's 'Like a Prayer' Clip Causes a Controversy," *Rolling Stone*, 20 Aug. 1989. Pepsi denied the charge (see Bruce Haring, "Pepsi Denies Pulling Madonna Spots," *Billboard*, 18 Mar. 1989), but this commercial, unlike George Michael's Diet Coke commercial, no longer appeared on television.

> what she believes is right. She wakes up, goes to the jail, tells the police the man is innocent, and he is freed. Then everybody takes a bow as if to say we all play a part in this little scenario.[21]

The puns, reversals, and circularities of this video, in combination with the lyrics, are dizzying. The name *Madonna* and "the voice" are constantly referred to yet never named: "When you call my name it's like a little prayer." The name is Madonna, heavenly mother, here also embodied in the singer herself. Calling the name Madonna is "like a little prayer," a prayer to the Virgin, "little," presumably, because the big one would be the "Our Father." Yet, it is "like a" prayer as well, suggesting the deep irreverence familiar to us from a former context, Madonna's "Like a Virgin." It is and it is not a prayer, the name-calling referring devoutly and daughter-like to the absent mother (whose name was Madonna) and narcissistically to the star herself. When she enters the church, she is singing: "I hear you call my name . . . and it feels like . . . Home," whereupon she closes the door to the church. Orsi mentions how the women of East Harlem called their church *la casa di mamma* (Momma's house), grafting together their real mothers in the lost homeland, Italy, and their heavenly mother (the Madonna) (Orsi, 206–7). Madonna does this, and goes a step further, returning the name Madonna to herself. The strange distortion of pronouns in the song can be attributed to this circularity: Madonna is both mother and child, both divine intervener and earthly supplicant.

After witnessing a double crime that is equated with a burning cross, Madonna falls into a dream. That this is a dream is of utmost importance, for it signals that the character Madonna is not really putting herself in the place of the redeemer but imagining herself as one (note the insistence on dreaming in the script). At this point, Madonna sings the words, "Oh God, I think I'm falling" and "Heaven help me," clichés that in the context of a dream flight and a divine encounter become literal. A Black woman

21. Cited by Stephen Holden, "Madonna Re-Creates Herself—Again," *New York Times*, Sunday, 19 Mar. 1989, Arts and Leisure section. There are many imagistic, verbal, and thematic resemblances between the video "Like a Prayer" and Mary Lambert's earlier film *Siesta*, starring Ellen Barkin, indicating that intertextuality occurs on the directorial level, as well, so that not only the star but also (at least) the director contributes to the composite, or conglomerate, text that is Madonna. The centering of female subjectivity in *Siesta* also supports an argument for Lambert's important role in constructing the structure of address in "Like a Prayer." I thank Nancy Vickers for drawing these similarities to my attention and Mary Lambert for her corroboration of my reading of these texts as feminocentric.

catches her; the woman is a figure of divinity (a heavenly mother) and assists Madonna. She plays this role throughout; meanwhile, similarities of hair, halo, and voice establish an identification between the two women.

Back at the church, Madonna encounters the black icon (apparently a representation of Saint Martin de Porres), who comes alive through the praying Madonna's faith and who, after conferring upon the character Madonna a chaste kiss (like the chaste kiss in "Open Your Heart"), leaves the church.[22] The scene of the encounter between mortal and saint epitomizes Orsi's description of "popular religion" and the hostile reactions it provokes from the established church:

> When used to describe popular Catholic religiosity, the term conjures up images of shrouds, bloody hearts, bilocating monks, talking Madonnas [!], weeping statues, boiling vials of blood—all the symbols which the masses of Catholic Europe have found to be so powerful over the centuries and which churchmen have denigrated, often while sharing in the same or similar devotions. (Orsi, xiv)

After the icon comes to life and departs from the church, Madonna picks up his dropped dagger and receives the stigmata that mark her as having a role to play in the narrative of redemption. Stigmata, with their obvious phallic connotation, are a sensual sign of contact with the divine, a kind of holy coupling, which the film *Agnes of God* has made clear in the popular filmic imagination. This reciprocity between the worshipper and the divine is a common feature of popular piety (Orsi, 230–31).

During the (second) scene of the crime, an identification is established (through the camera's line of sight, through hair color and style) between Madonna and the victim. The woman's death is compared to a crucifixion (arms out, Christlike knife wound in her left side) and, perhaps, to a rape.[23] Madonna first sings the lines, "In the midnight hour I can feel your power," in the scene with the icon; now these words are given a sinister reinterpretation, suggesting the collusion between patriarchal and racist power rather than the more traditionally lyric "seductive power" of woman. The woman cries out while the lyric line is "When you call my name." The look between the ringleader and Madonna sets up a complicity (one com-

22. Sante, "Unlike a Virgin," 28.

23. Freud refers to experiments finding sexual symbolism in dreams about stabbing and shooting in *The Interpretation of Dreams*, vols. 4 and 5 of *The Standard Edition of the Complete Psychological Works of Sigmund Freud*, trans. James Strachey (London: Hogarth Press, 1953), 419.

mits a crime, one remains silent about it) that is also a challenge. The scene sets up a parallel: White men rape/kill women, white men blame it on Black men; or, women are raped/killed for being on the streets at night, Black men are thrown in jail.

With the line, "Life is a mystery, everyone must stand alone," the scene cuts to Madonna singing in front of a field of burning crosses, a visual citation of the film *Mississippi Burning*, as is the young boy in the white choir gown (referring, perhaps, to the only Black person represented in the movie as speaking out against Klan violence), who beckons to Madonna. She prays. This scene, which marks the dramatic center of the video, uses the privileged "sign" of Madonna (the cross, or crucifix, which she always wears) to set up the religious and political discourses of the text.[24]

Back at the church, Madonna is brought into the community of worshippers by the female deity. With the laying on of hands, Madonna is "commissioned," or slain in the spirit; the community is an African American community. The scene of erotic union with the saint sets up the syntax for a sentence: We see the kiss; a burning cross; Madonna; a field of burning crosses; Madonna's face looking shocked; the bleeding eye of the icon, all of which seem to suggest: Black men have been martyred for kissing white women.

At this point, the dream ends, and the choir files out. The icon returns to its position, and the bars close in front of him. Madonna wakes up, and the camera cuts to the jail cell, which is the church, now without the altar and with the American flag in its stead. We see Madonna mouthing the words "He didn't do it" to the police, who then free the Black man. A red curtain closes on the scene, which fades to Madonna in the field of burning crosses. Next, the curtain rises on the church, with all the actors—the criminals and victim and police—gathered, seated or standing in the foreground. They take a bow; the camera moves in to focus on the Black woman. Madonna and her co-star, Leon Robinson, come center stage, holding hands, and they take a bow. The camera pulls back and the credit comes up: "Madonna/'Like a Prayer'/Like a Prayer/Sire Records." We see

24. *Home*, an important, if not central, term of the text, is repeated again in this scene (Madonna in the field of burning crosses), referring back to and reinterpreting the scene in which she enters the church. There, *home* seemed a relatively positive term, although the conflation between the church and the police station at the end of the video suggests an ambivalence about the positioning of the institution of the church. In this scene, however, *home* is ironic and constitutes an indictment of racist and patriarchal America.

the actors dancing, and the curtain comes down again. Finally, "The End" is written in script on the curtain.

• • • •

How can we read the political and spiritual in this melodramatic medieval morality play? On the one hand, there is the displacement of a predicament: A woman's disempowerment in relation to a religious tradition is displaced by a story about how a white woman, with the help of a female Black divinity, saves a Black man. Madonna stages the predicament of the Italian American immigrant daughter within the patriarchal institutions of family, church, and state and enacts a feminine fantasy of resolution and mediation, the quintessential Roman Catholic fantasy of sacrifice, redemption, and salvation. This feminine fantasy of resolution resembles that of the popular religious *feste* that constitute the spiritual experiences of the East Harlem women described by Orsi, as well as those of most southern Italian immigrant communities in cities all over the United States, with their specific focus on the divine intercession of the Virgin. It is the temporary empowerment of sacrifice that connects the woman to the Madonna and that allows her to play a central role within the Italian spiritual community. This role is also a trap, however, for it perpetuates an ethos of self-sacrifice and self-abnegation. The video suggests Madonna's rebellion against this entrapment by presenting the image of a successful heroine. In this fantasy of female empowerment, the mother, as divine intercessor, empowers the daughter to play the son's salvific role. The narrative attempts to break the cycle, whereby the mother's centrality to the *domus* also disempowers, by finding a place of empowerment as the mother, as the *mamma celeste*, the omnipotent woman—Madonna herself. In other contexts, Madonna will figure herself as playfully and parodically phallic, but here she remains emphatically feminine, even while enacting the son's castration in the stigmata.[25] Yet, the trace of a self-wounding sacrifice remains, for at the end

25. The *Rolling Stone* photographs of Madonna (Zehme, "Madonna: The *Rolling Stone* Interview") focus on the phallic Madonna with shots of her crotch and the now-infamous "phallic woman" gesture—first used parodically by Michael Jackson, then deployed (post-Madonna) by Roseanne Barr—of crotch-grabbing. On the parodic use of this gesture, and on Madonna's "imitation" of Michael Jackson, see Marjorie Garber, "Fetish Envy," *October* 54 (Fall 1990): 45–56. On Madonna's later phallicism, see also Sante, "Unlike a Virgin," 27: "Oh yes, and there were those male dancers adorned with breasts that flopped like so many pairs of flaccid phalli while her own looked like armor-plated projectiles."

of the play there is a corpse, the young woman, who is also a double for Madonna, thus reminding us that phallic power also kills.

There is clearly guilt here, a guilt Madonna shares with many white rock and pop musicians who have been making "Black America" the subject of their videos, for theirs is a musical tradition grounded on a violation and a theft, the appropriation of musical forms originating with African American musicians who were unable, in racist America, to profit. That appropriation made millions of dollars for these white musicians. But if we take seriously the cultural specificities of this particular white woman (Madonna), cultural specificities that may be applicable to communities larger than the private fantasies of one individual, then the mixture of religious traditions in the video and the intertwining of two political histories may constitute a different sort of text.

Orsi points out that southern Italian immigrants were often associated with Africans by their northern compatriots, by the Protestant majority, and by the established Catholic church.[26] Chromatically black Madonnas and saints abound in southern Italian and Catholic worship. The video, too, sets up a chromatic proximity through the racial indeterminacy of the woman who is killed and, most markedly, through hair: Madonna's hair is her natural brown (she says it makes her feel more Italian) and curled into ringlets, the female deity's hair is similarly brown and curly, while the female victim's hair is black and curly. The only blond characters are the white men who attack. Madonna says she grew up in a Black neighborhood and that her playmates and friends were Black. In a *Rolling Stone* interview, she notes apologetically that when she was little she wanted to be Black.[27] Likewise, there is a tradition of African Americans in northern urban

26. Orsi, *The Madonna of 115th Street*, 160: "Americans and American Catholics distinguished the northern Italian racial type ('Germanic') from the southern ('African'), a tendency that may have contributed to the identification of East Harlem with West Harlem. In 1912, Norman Thomas admitted that American-born Protestants in Harlem did not appreciate the presence of Italians in their churches." Sante cannot resist a racist remark about Madonna's ethnicity, though he says it isn't one: "In her 'Ciao Italia' video, decked out in various gymnastic outfits and body-pumping to the screams of tens of thousands in a soccer stadium in Turin, Madonna looks perfectly able to make the trains run on time. (Do not mistake this for an ethnic slur: her last name could just as easily be O'Flanagan and the setting Oslo or Kalamazoo.)" ("Unlike a Virgin," 27).

27. Zehme, "Madonna: The *Rolling Stone* Interview," 58: " 'When I was a little girl, I wished I was black. All my girlfriends were black. I was living in Pontiac, Michigan, and I was definitely the minority in the neighborhood. White people were scarce there. All of my friends were black, and all the music I listened to was black.' "

settings who identify themselves as "Italian" in order to pass or to protect themselves from the full force of U.S. racism in the majority community.

This fantasy thus attempts to reach out beyond the private ethnic imagination to create a bridge to another culture's popular piety, itself grounded in an experience of exile and oppression. McClary notes how the song merges the traditional solemnity of Catholic organ music with the joyous rhythm of gospel, thus musically reinforcing the fusion of the two communities.[28] More ethnographic research might reveal the ways in which these communities met or meet (East and West Harlem) in the neighborhoods of New York City or Detroit and might also reveal what is produced from the similarities in their family structures, spiritualities, and their historical experiences. The media, the press, and even resistive subcultural narratives, such as Spike Lee's film *Do the Right Thing*, suggest that the dominant representation of intercultural relations is a narrative of conflict. The alternative vision of community presented in this video challenges the complicity with hegemonic violence of Spike Lee's cultural politics. I wonder to what extent the rareness of this fantasy is related to the fact that it is a feminine fantasy of mediation, a woman's representation of the possibilities of connectedness rather than conflict. In other words, one difference between the cooperative interaction narrated here and the representations of violent conflict is that this representation is feminocentric and grounded in a spiritual vision. Points of contact between communities are imagined not only in terms of conflicting and competing ethnicities but also in terms of communicative openings, the affirming interactions and the potential for communication between contiguous cultural groups who also share some experiences of oppression within a majority community hostile to their presence.[29]

The visual bridges that connect the two communities are identity and

28. McClary, "Living to Tell," 14–15.

29. Mark D. Hulsether, writing for the Left progressive Christian journal *Christianity and Crisis*, forcefully affirms his sense of the radical message of "Like a Prayer": "This video is one of the most powerful statements of the basic themes from liberation theologies I have seen in the mainstream media. It sharply rejects racist perversions of Christianity such as the Ku Klux Klan; emphasizes Jesus' human solidarity or identity with victims of oppression; places the cross in the context of sociopolitical struggle and persecution; and presents the church as a place of collective empowerment toward transforming justice. In the context of racism, it promotes African-American culture and combats both police violence and the scapegoating of black males. In a way that converges with some feminist theology, it stresses the importance of the erotic in conceptualizing faith" (see "Madonna and Jesus," *Christianity and Crisis*, 15 July 1991, 234–36, especially 235).

icon. Identity connects Madonna and the Black priestess, the Madonna, a phallic woman, the "muse," who answers Madonna's prayers and assists her, who participates as her mirror in the narrative. The identification, furthermore, extends beyond two individuals; Madonna does not redeem alone, she seeks assistance from her Black double and from the community of worship whom the woman represents and leads. The icon is the Madonna icon par excellence: The cross, or crucifix, the calvary for African Americans, and the burning cross of the Ku Klux Klan all remind us that Catholics and African Americans (as well as Jews) were targets of this nationalist project conducted in the name of the cross. It is no wonder, then, that the first to speak out about this video, condemning its irreligiosity and sacrilege, were fundamentalist religious leaders and televangelists—Jimmy Swaggart, Donald Wildmon, Bishop Gracida of Texas, and the American Family Association.[30]

This story of how a white girl learns to "do the right thing" and succeeds, with the help of a Black woman and the Black community, depends on the scapegoat and the saved being Black and in a position of even more radical disempowerment relative to the police and to "America." As the recognition of a predicament, the narrative is politically progressive; in its resolution, however, it participates in the myth of the great white savior, marked here as a traditionally feminine wish fulfillment in its simultaneous desire for power and approval. The absent-mother-returned-as-divine-intercessor-become-Black mitigates that usurpation, covering also for the guilt of the white woman's erotic appropriation of the man she saves (the Black woman says "I'll take you there" just before the camera cuts to the kiss). The narrative itself signals this irony through the explicit reference to fantasy and dream as the contexts for wish fulfillment and through the framing device of the play, which distances the events from anything that might occur in "real life." Madonna's hyperfemininity in the video and her association with the children in the choir attempt to convince us that she is, indeed, a daughter, a mediator, and not the powerful superstar Madonna, so that we can "believe in" the power and agency of the other woman. But the governing irony of the text as a whole, an irony that remains unstated, is that the mother, the Madonna, *is* Madonna; the Black woman is "merely" a screen.

It is in its relation to the "Other woman" then, to use Gayatri Spivak's term, that the political blind spot in the narrative, and in its reception,

30. Cox, "Pepsi Cans Its Madonna Ad under Pressure."

appears.[31] We would not expect a Madonna commercial to assume any subject-position other than that of its protagonist, Madonna. Though in the media we can see interviews with Leon Robinson and hear him speak about his role, with regard to the other woman there is silence, so much silence that I do not know her name. This necessarily questions the gender/race empowerment of the representation in its interaction with a hegemonic racism that traditionally suppresses nonstereotypic representations of women of color. The erasure of the embodied African American woman, the Madonna of the narrative—Madonna's double—is even more marked, because she is the only character other than Madonna to have a solo part in the song. The Pepsi commercial merely reinforces the interchangeability of that image, for the gospel solo is sung not by the woman we see here but by a more stereotypical—maternal and desexualized—member of the choir who is, therefore, more "fitting" for the traditional worship setting of the service.

A bold fantasy of intercultural relatedness that will not obey the rules of the dominant culture's narrative of necessary interracial conflict; a fantasy of self-aggrandizement that recognizes itself as such; a world where women are both heroic and omnipotent, where female agency can be effective. A world, too, where the authorities are benign, where police will admit that they have made an honest mistake. A world where Black women approve of white women's desires for the leading role in the narrative of African American salvation. As Andrew Ross has insisted, "We cannot attribute any purity of political expression to popular culture, although we can locate its power to identify areas and desires that are relatively opposed, alongside those that are clearly complicit, to the official culture."[32] In celebrating the proto-political of Madonna's texts, academic feminists must recognize, as well, the self-aggrandizement these fantasies serve. Madonna is not, after all, a revolutionary feminist (*pace* Camille Paglia); she is a female multimillionaire.[33] MTV reveals its political inadequacies in the very postmodernism

31. Gayatri Chakravorty Spivak, "Imperialism and Sexual Difference," in *Contemporary Literary Criticism: Literary and Cultural Studies*, ed. Robert Con Davis and Ronald Schleifer (New York and London: Longman, 1989), 517–29.
32. Ross, *No Respect*, 10.
33. Camille Paglia, "Madonna—Finally, A Real Feminist," *New York Times*, 4 Dec. 1990. Both Paglia and Madonna are called feminists by the press, but feminists sui generis. In my own understanding of feminism this is not possible, since *feminism*, by any political definition, implies collective political struggle, distinguishing it from a liberal bourgeois ideology of individualism, even when the individual is marked as female.

of its premise: It is the individual, or the private subject, who makes cultural meaning, rather than communities or collectivities, and individuals may become empowered through those meanings.[34]

So why read MTV, and why read it in this way? For one thing, it's pleasurable—pleasurable because these texts are there to be read and talked and gossiped about publicly in the culture. They often bridge class gaps and, at least in my experience, have made for some interesting interracial, intergenerational, and interfaith conversations that have served as occasions for political debate. Almost anyone can participate in such debates and conversations, since Madonna, MTV, and television, in general, are available to the many rather than the few. If the news constructs, produces, and mediates hegemonic national fantasies under the guise of a reality principle, why not frankly confront and contest it with alternative fantasies explicitly produced in the name of pleasure?

At the same time, the Left cannot retreat into anachronistic puritanism with regard to what it calls the new opiate of (young) people—"mass" culture—or else it cedes a strategic terrain of cultural politics all too clearly recognized as such by the New Right. These texts may suggest strategies for the empowerment of the subordinated, marginal, and de-centered in advanced capitalist culture, strategies that are not anachronistic but born of the medium of advanced capital and the gaps that are produced within it. I am interested in the ways such strategies, and such technology, may be used to produce significant counterhegemonic forces within a culture whose ruling classes seem to have perfected the art of containment. If Gil Scott-Heron is correct in claiming that "the revolution will not be televised" (and I am no longer convinced that he is), it may, nevertheless, be the case that through strategic articulations of these popular cultural texts, something "like a" revolution can be imagined.

34. Perhaps this is a sign of capitalism's triumph from within the postmodern, for the construction of the private subject as addressee and agent seems to be simply the extension of bourgeois individualism.

Soft Boundaries and Relatedness: Paradigm for a Postmodern Feminist Musical Aesthetics

Claire Detels

This article was inspired by three converging academic developments: (1) the rising interdisciplinary influence of postmodern thought; (2) the emergence of feminist aesthetic theory in the literary and visual arts, developed in support of the feminist criticism in those fields;[1] and (3) the

I would like to acknowledge the assistance received at the 1991 Institute on "Philosophy and the Histories of the Arts," directed by Arthur Danto, co-directed by Anita Silvers, Gerrold Levinson, and Noel Carroll and sponsored by the American Society for Aesthetics and the National Endowment for the Humanities, in revising and completing this article. A shorter version of it was delivered at the 1991 Portland meeting of the American Society for Aesthetics.

1. See Toril Moi, *Sexual/Textual Politics: Feminist Literary Theory* (London: Methuen, 1985), for a concise description of the origins, development, and various camps and practitioners of feminist aesthetics. Also see Nancy K. Miller, ed., *The Poetics of Gender* (New York: Columbia University Press); and Josephine Donovan, ed., *Feminist Literary Criticism: Explorations in Theory*, 2d ed. (Lexington: University Press of Kentucky, 1989), for essays by and about many of the central figures of feminist literary theory. For theoretical essays on the visual arts, see Linda Nochlin, *Women, Art, and Power and Other Essays* (New York: Harper and Row, 1988); Griselda Pollock, *Vision and Difference: Femininity, Feminism, and the Histories of Art* (New York: Routledge, 1988); and a special issue of

recent flowering of feminist music criticism, offering a challenge to the positivistic mode of mainstream musicology and its overly reified conception of music, as especially seen in the theory, pedagogy, and production of Western art music.[2]

In view of the third development in particular, it appears the time may now be ripe for the emergence of a feminist musical aesthetics, featuring a new paradigm that can support the new feminist musical criticism by changing the terms of the musico-aesthetic debate, similar to the way in which new feminist paradigms and theoretical concepts have changed the aesthetic debate in the literary and visual arts.[3] The paradigm I am proposing is that of *soft boundaries and relatedness*, wherein the covert valuation of "hard" (i.e., clearly distinct) boundaries in traditional aesthetic definitions and judgments about music is superseded by the recognition of the need to consider relatedness of music and musical entities across "soft" (i.e., permeable) boundaries, including relatedness to social context and function. The soft boundary of the paradigm is not a hard-and-fast line or rule for defining and judging music as in traditional aesthetics but is similar to Heidegger's sense of boundary: "that from which something *begins its essential unfolding*."[4] As a result, the implicit critical focus of the paradigm is on how the unfolding proceeds within and across permeable boundaries, rather than on the definition and reification of the boundaries themselves. Or, in other words, the focus is necessarily the whole musical experience rather than any particularized musical entities.

In its attention to relationship, rather than singular fact or thing, the

---

Journal of Aesthetics and Art Criticism, entitled "Feminism and Traditional Aesthetics," 48, no. 4 (Fall 1990).

2. See Susan McClary, *Feminine Endings* (Minneapolis: University of Minnesota Press, 1991), 3–31, for a survey and discussion of the rise of feminist music criticism.

3. The need for new paradigms and theoretical concepts has been a consistent theme in feminist theory for the literary and visual arts, and notable success has been achieved with the paradigm of genderized perspective and such concepts as the "male gaze" and the gendered sadomasochism of narrative and representation in general. See Mary Deveraux, "Oppressive Texts, Resisting Readers, and the Gendered Spectator: The *New* Aesthetics," *Journal of Aesthetics and Art Criticism* 48, no. 4 (Fall 1990): 337–48. Deveraux discusses how the concept of the "male gaze" has literally changed the subject in art and film criticism. See also Teresa de Lauretis, *Technologies of Gender* (Bloomington: Indiana University Press, 1987), for some of her influential essays on the gender violence of narrative and representation in literature and film.

4. Martin Heidegger, *Basic Writings*, ed. David Farrell Krell (New York: Harper and Row, 1977), in chap. 8, "Building Dwelling Thinking," 332.

paradigm of soft boundaries and relatedness has ties to contemporary postmodern and feminist theory, hence its characterization here as a postmodern feminist paradigm. The ties to postmodernism are most obvious, for, as Jerome Klinkowitz has stated, the key to the postmodern habit of thought is "that the authentic phenomenon in any event is not *fact* but *relationship*."[5] The reorientation from fact to relationship has roots in existential and pragmatist philosophy,[6] but it has received particular emphasis in the French poststructuralist theory of, for example, Michel Foucault, Jean-François Lyotard, and Jacques Derrida, wherein the traditional "logocentric" claims to epistemological universality and objectivity have been deconstructed and replaced by a recognition of the validity of multiple perspectives of reality, each related to its own context.[7] Thus, postmodernism has become the philosophy of pluralism and relativity, or, as Lyotard puts it, that which "denies itself the solace of good forms."[8] In the case of music, that denial must extend to supposed norms of musical structure, as we shall see.

The connections of the paradigm of soft boundaries and relatedness to feminist theory are more difficult to define but just as important. Note, for example, that the identification of relatedness as a feminine-identified function started in Freudian psychoanalytic theory and was counterfeminist in some respects. Many feminist theorists, however, have also explored the connection between relatedness and the feminine and have found validity therein, usually more in terms of enculturation than nature.[9] Another tie

5. Jerome Klinkowitz, *Rosenberg, Barthes, Hassan: The Postmodern Habit of Thought* (Athens and London: University of Georgia Press, 1988), 8.

6. See Heidegger, *Basic Writings*. See also John Dewey, *Art as Experience* (New York: Minto, Balch and Co., 1934), whose focus on experience is becoming influential again in aesthetic circles; see, for example, Arnold Berleant's recent *Art and Engagement* (Philadelphia: Temple University Press, 1991), and Marcia Eaton's *Aesthetics and the Good Life* (London and Toronto: Associated University Presses, 1989).

7. See Jacques Derrida, "Structure, Sign and Play in the Discourse of the Social Sciences," in *The Structuralist Controversy: The Languages of Criticism and the Sciences of Man*, ed. Richard Macksey and Eugenio Donato (Baltimore and London: Johns Hopkins University Press, 1971), 247–65, for the definitive poststructuralist attack on Western logocentrism. Also see Jane Flax, *Thinking Fragments: Psychoanalysis, Feminism and Postmodernism in the Contemporary West* (Berkeley, Los Angeles, and Oxford: University of California Press, 1990), 187–221, for an insightful general discussion of the postmodern epistemologies of Derrida, Foucault, Lyotard, and Richard Rorty.

8. Jean-François Lyotard, *The Postmodern Condition: A Report on Knowledge*, trans. Geoff Bennington and Brian Massumi (Minneapolis: University of Minnesota Press, 1984), 81.

9. See, most notably, Carol Gilligan, *In a Different Voice: Psychological Theory and*

to feminist theory is in the implicit emphasis on experience and the body, an emphasis that leads away from reification and hierarchization toward a more communal, shared conception of art.[10]

In addition, the implicit pluralism of the paradigm has ties to feminist theory in that many feminists, like postmodernists, view traditional logocentric thinking as inherently monistic, hierarchic, and marginalistic because of its habitual binary divisions and the tendency to privilege one member of the binary pair over the other (as in the structuralist dyads of culture/nature, cooked/raw, and masculine/feminine). Such an observation is feminist, not just postmodern, because, as biological and cultural mothers, women have the role and consequent hardships of our society's primary Other, and they are thus best positioned to recognize and theorize on the functioning and ramifications of marginalization, in general.[11]

Although a relevant response to the hard boundaries of traditional Western thought and culture in general, the paradigm of soft boundaries and relatedness is especially well suited to the task of changing the subject in aesthetics because it directly reveals and counters the otherwise covert value of hard boundaries that have prevailed in aesthetic definitions and judgments going back to classical Greek culture and the categories of Aristotle. In the seventeenth century, these hard boundaries took the form of Cartesian dualism, which, according to Susan Bordo's critique, consisted largely of masculinist projections of rage and fear onto the feminine-identified, sensual realm of nature and the consequent attempts to control

---

Women's Development (Cambridge: Harvard University Press, 1981); and Nancy Chodorow, *The Reproduction of Mothering: Psychoanalysis and the Sociology of Gender* (Berkeley: University of California Press, 1978).

10. See, for instance, Jane Gallop, *Thinking Through the Body* (New York: Columbia University Press, 1988); and Heide Gottner-Abendroth, "Nine Principles of a Matriarchal Aesthetic," in *Feminist Aesthetics*, ed. Gisela Ecker, trans. Harriet Anderson (Boston: Beacon Press, 1985), 81–94. Also see Hilde Hein, "The Role of Feminist Aesthetics in Feminist Theory," *Journal of Aesthetics and Art Criticism* 48, no. 4 (1990): 281–91. Hein finds both feminist theory and feminist aesthetics to be grounded in the notion of experience (288–89).

11. Discussed by Dorothy Dinnerstein, *The Mermaid and the Minotaur: Sexual Arrangements and Human Malaise* (New York: Harper Colophon Books, 1976). Also note the feminist essentialist position of Luce Irigaray, *This Sex Which Is Not One*, trans. Catherine Porter (Ithaca: Cornell University Press, 1985), who makes a biological-sexual connection of monism to the male body (thus the term *phallogocentric*) and of pluralism to the female body. See also Judith Butler, *Gender Trouble: Feminism and the Subversion of Identity* (New York: Routledge, 1990), who warns against the use of all such binary distinctions; see especially chap. 1, "Subjects of Sex/Gender/Desire," 1–34.

that realm with dualistic definitions and judgments.[12] With Kant and the romantic aesthetic revolution, the hard boundaries took further form in the insistence on a pure, intellectual disinterestedness in the aesthetic perceiver and on autonomy for the artist and artwork. According to Marxist critic Terry Eagleton, the romantic "aesthetic ideology" amounted to a kind of denial, whereby the combined assumptions of subjectivity and universality acted as the "joker in the pack" that served to circumvent consideration of the cultural relatedness of art—including the relatedness of the critics' insistence on autonomy and universality to their own psychological and/or political agendas.[13] In other words, once culture was cleared from the field, the way was clear for the critic to fill the vacuum with projections of supposedly universal definitions and criteria for judgments and then to use them to build unconsciously self-interested canons and hierarchies of "greatness" on their basis. Because of their construction in the cultural vacuum, the resulting definitions, judgments, and hierarchies have since tended to suffer from circularity; that is, the judgments of merit serve as argument for the criteria, and the criteria serve as argument for the judgments.

The above critique of aesthetics in Western culture applies most powerfully to music, the realm of "risk-free identification" as Catherine Clément puts it; there, the greater ambiguity of aesthetic content has tended to give freer rein to masculinist denials and projections, especially since the rise of the romantic "aesthetic ideology" in the nineteenth century.[14] In 1854, Eduard Hanslick's *On the Musically Beautiful* translated the romantic aesthetic into the autonomist, or formalist, theory of music, a theory that denies the aesthetic importance of music's emotional effects and cultural functions and, instead, regards music as a purely autonomous configuration of "tonally moving forms."[15] Most influential music philosophers since Hans-

12. Susan Bordo, "The Cartesian Masculinization of Thought," *Signs* 11 (1986): 439–56, especially 448–55. Also see Arthur C. Danto, *The Philosophical Disenfranchisement of Art* (New York: Columbia University Press, 1986), for a nonfeminist perspective on the tendency of philosophy to disenfranchise art.

13. Terry Eagleton, *The Ideology of the Aesthetic* (Cambridge, Mass.: Basil Blackwell, 1990), 93.

14. Catherine Clément, *Opera, or the Undoing of Women* (Minneapolis: University of Minnesota Press, 1988), 9. Also see John Shepherd, "Music and Male Hegemony," in *Music and Society: The Politics of Composition, Performance and Reception* (Cambridge: Cambridge University Press, 1987), 151–72. Shepherd says the power and physical relatedness of musical sound "reminds men of the fragile and atrophied nature of their control over the world" (158).

15. Eduard Hanslick, *On the Musically Beautiful*, trans. Geoffrey Payzant (Indianapolis:

lick have continued his formalist views at least to some extent. Moreover, since the 1950s and the rise of analytic aesthetics, the discipline of music theory (in which musico-structural concepts are developed and applied) has separated from musicology and formed a distinct profession with its own societies, journals, and credentials. Both music theorists and analytic music philosophers tend to view music in a particularly hard-boundaried manner, excluding practical, historical information about the cultural context of music and relying instead on formalist concepts and circular argumentation.

Even a brief examination of the academic products of music theory and analytic music philosophy serves to underscore the importance of a new musico-aesthetic paradigm. For instance, theorist Leonard Meyer unwittingly provided an excellent example of the pitfalls of formalism and circular argumentation in his much-read and reprinted essay "Some Remarks on Value and Greatness in Music," when he referred to the question "What makes music great?" as the $64,000 question.[16] In the essay, Meyer gives the formalist answer that music's greatness depends wholly on "syntactical organization," and he argues for his position in a covert circular manner. "If we ask," he says, "Why is Debussy's music superior to that of Delius? the answer lies in the syntactical organization of his music, not in its superior sensuousness."[17] This is a circular argument because it starts from the assumption, based on Debussy's higher canonical status over Delius, that Debussy's music is superior, and that the reason for its superiority will provide the universal criterion for understanding musical greatness. In other words, the answer "the syntactical organization of Debussy's music" leads back in circular fashion to the formalist theory, which, in turn, leads to the

---

Hackett Publishing Co., 1986), 29 and throughout. I use the term *formalist* instead of the more frequently encountered *cognitivist* in order to avoid confusion with the sense of cognitivism found in experimental psychology, where it comprises physical, emotional, and formalistic mental functions.

16. Leonard Meyer, "Some Remarks on Value and Greatness in Music," in *Music, the Arts and Ideas: Patterns and Predictions in Twentieth-Century Culture* (Chicago: University of Chicago Press, 1967), 22–41.

17. Meyer, "Some Remarks," 36. Meyer's writings, in which he posits universal formalist criteria for musical meaning and value, remain in print and influential. His more recent work, however, shows an increased recognition of the relatedness of musical meaning and value to cultural context. See, for example, "Exploiting Limits: Creation, Archetypes, and Style Change," in *Contemplating Music: Source Readings in the Aesthetics of Music*, ed. Ruth Katz and Carl Dahlhaus, Aesthetics in Music Series, no. 5 (New York: Pendragon Press, 1987), vol. 2, 678–717.

proof of the superiority of Debussy's music (which, however, was never doubted in the first place). Here and elsewhere, circular argumentation functions so smoothly that issues of substance, such as an explanation of how Delius's or Debussy's musics are more or less sensuous or syntactical, fall by the wayside.

Those who recall the 1950s TV game show "The $64,000 Question" also may remember the scandal that broke out when it was revealed that winning contestants had been told the right answers in advance of receiving the questions. Unfortunately, the circular equation of the right answers preceding and following the questions is so common in musical aesthetics and criticism that no such scandal breaks out in the academy when the musico-aesthetic value fix is in. Again, it is the greater ambiguity and confusion about what constitutes musical content—a confusion fostered by the denial of cultural connection—that allow weak arguments like Meyer's to pass as authoritative.

A more complex example of the pitfalls of formalism and circular argumentation is found in Peter Kivy's *Osmin's Rage: Philosophical Reflections on Opera, Drama, and Text* (1988). (Kivy is the most prolific and prominent philosopher of music at present.) Following a highly questionable assertion that "all art requires theory—not just for its creation but for its appreciation,"[18] Kivy compares the judgment of Mozart's *Cosi fan tutte* under Joseph Kerman's theory of "opera as drama" with the judgment under his own theory of opera as "drama-made-music" and reaches almost comic heights of dialectic:

> On Kerman's interpretation, *Cosi* emerges as a deeply flawed though (I am sure Kerman would agree) estimable work. On my view it emerges as Mozart's most perfect opera—which may be to say the *most perfect opera*.
>
> What does this tell us about *Cosi* as a work of art? What I want to emphasize is this: it by no means follows that *Cosi* emerges as a greater work of art under my description than under Kerman's. Or, to put it another way: under my description of opera as drama-made-music, *Cosi fan tutte* is a more perfect example of that kind than *The Marriage of Figaro*; but this in no way implies that, under my description, *Cosi* is a greater work of art. Indeed, I think the opposite: that

18. Peter Kivy, *Osmin's Rage: Philosophical Reflections on Opera, Drama, and Text* (Princeton: Princeton University Press), 184.

> although *Cosi* is the more perfect opera, which is to say, the greater drama-made-music, *Figaro* is the greater work.[19]

The comedy is that amid these tortured efforts to clarify the appropriate theory on which to judge *Cosi fan tutte*, the actual experience of the music is lost to consideration. Thus, Kivy's argument here, rather typical of his musico-aesthetic work in general, demonstrates how formalist thinking tends to evade and/or control human aesthetic experience within the sharp boundaries of the theory that supposedly gives it birth "*qua* music, *qua* art, *qua* aesthetical object," as he puts it.[20] In the narrow sector of contemporary academic music, where composers' written and published theories about their music are often better known than are the compositions themselves, Kivy's view appears reasonable. It also makes sense in the somewhat wider context of the classical concert, or, to cite Primat Conehead's analytic-style definition, the "gathering of humans to absorb sound patterns."[21] In a more vital, life-connected musical culture, however, the notion that music needs theory for its existence, especially theory of the formalistic, culturally disconnected kind, is highly problematic. What music more probably needs, at least from scholars, is a greater understanding of its relatedness to life, something it may receive when the covert musico-aesthetic valuing of hard boundaries is superseded by the paradigm of soft boundaries and relatedness.

There are at least three aspects of musical experience to which the paradigm of soft boundaries and relatedness can usefully apply: (1) relatedness of musical experience to the body; (2) relatedness among the constituencies of musical experience, including the composer, performer, audience, critics, and community; and (3) relatedness of musical style to culture. In the rest of my remarks, I will explore each of these areas briefly, suggesting what the problems of traditional musico-aesthetic theory are, how the new paradigm will address them, and how it connects to intellectual and musical developments that are already in process. I will also offer some suggestions about the new types of theoretical concepts and critical

19. Kivy, *Osmin's Rage*, 261.
20. Peter Kivy, "What Was Hanslick Denying?" *Journal of Musicology* 8 (1990): 13. Kivy also denies that music can arouse what he calls the "garden variety" emotions (i.e., love, hope, fear, joy, and sorrow) "in any aesthetically significant way" (18).
21. From the "Saturday Night Live" sketch of the Coneheads with Frank Zappa, rebroadcast on *The Best of Saturday Night Live*, 28 Feb. 1991.

approaches that could be developed and used under the paradigm of soft boundaries and relatedness.

Music's Relatedness to the Body

Recognition of music's relatedness to the body appeared prominently in late eighteenth-century expression theory, but such recognition receded in the nineteenth century, when most aesthetic theorists tended to make a sharp Cartesian division of mind and body and to project sensuality away from the male-identified cultural norms onto the feminine-identified realm of the Other. (Late nineteenth-century male authors, painters, and composers frequently exhibited this projection in extreme, sadomasochistic images of female madness, hysteria, and nymphomania.)[22] Nonetheless, the connection of music to the body was maintained in Schopenhauer's tying of music to the will (the existence of which he constructs from the individual's awareness of her/his own body),[23] in Nietzsche's call for a revaluing of the Dionysian mode,[24] and in twentieth-century psycho-aesthetic writings of Julia Kristeva, Carl Jung, and Donald Winnicott, among others.[25]

In terms of actual musical experience, the denial of music's relatedness to the body has quite literally "held sway" in the context of the Western musical concert, resulting in the sharp boundaries—taboos, really—applied against otherwise common musico-physical responses of swaying,

22. See Bram Dijkstra, *Idols of Perversity: Fantasies of Feminine Evil in Fin-de-siècle Culture* (New York: Oxford University Press, 1986), 372–76; and Lawrence Kramer, "Culture and Musical Hermeneutics: The Salome Complex," *Cambridge Opera Journal* 2 (1990): 269–94.

23. Arthur Schopenhauer, *The World as Will and Representation*, vol. 1, trans. E. J. Payne (1819; reprint, New York: Dover, 1969), 255–67 and 99–103.

24. Friedrich W. Nietzsche, *The Birth of Tragedy from the Spirit of Music*, in *The Philosophy of Nietzsche*, trans. Clifton P. Fadiman (New York: Modern Library, 1984), 162–87.

25. See, for example, Julia Kristeva's characterization of music as "constructed exclusively on the basis of the semiotic" (i.e., the pre-symbolic), in *The Revolution in Poetic Language*, trans. Margaret Waller (New York: Columbia University Press), 24. Musicologist Renée Cox develops Kristeva's approach in "Recovering *Jouissance*: Feminist Musical Aesthetics," in *Women in Music: A History*, ed. Karin Pendle (Bloomington: Indiana University Press, 1991), 331–40, proposing the revaluation of flexible or cyclical musical elements and techniques which, unlike the structured, logical linear elements and techniques of masculinist music, may give us access to the "jouissance" of the pre-symbolic realm. (I wish to thank the author for allowing me to read this essay while it was still in manuscript.)

singing, and beating time. This is especially notable during classical concerts, where permitted physical response is frozen into required clapping zones between musical works (and, acting as a signifier of the unnatural repression, some occasional spasms of uncontrollable coughing during the works). These prohibitions against the body, beginning roughly with the concert performances of Kant's time, contrast sharply with the intentional bodily engagement found in the main genres and performance situations of many other musical cultures, including parts of our own popular music culture, many ancient and tribal cultures, and pre-industrial Western culture roughly up to Kant's time (i.e., before the decline of aristocratic patronage and the consequent fixing of the middle-class concert as the privileged form of musical dissemination).

Indeed, one can hardly overestimate the influence of the nineteenth-century middle-class concert and its continued hegemony as the privileged form of musical dissemination in Western art-music culture on accepted modes of musical style and experience. One notes, for instance, that the formalist theory of music arose out of the context of the concert hall. There, emotional and physical responses that had previously been welcome, accepted parts of musical experience among friends and family could now have the unwelcome effect of alerting nearby strangers to one's innermost feelings, not to mention inhibiting their ability to hear the music. Moreover, at the same time bodily response was ruled out of bounds for the concert audience, it began to be expected in the creator and performer as one of the signs of genius (a condition Kant had defined as out-of-normal bounds), and so images of the intensely sensual, physically abnormal, or even contortional performer (and composer) began to appear in published sketches and verbal accounts of Beethoven, Chopin, Berlioz, Paganini, and Liszt. Jacques Attali argues that these alienated artist-celebrities carried the denied sensual projections of their audiences and learned to feed off them in sadomasochistic demonstrations of power.[26]

26. Jacques Attali, *Noise: The Political Economy of Music*, trans. Brian Massumi, Theory and History of Literature Series, no. 16 (Minneapolis: University of Minnesota Press, 1985), 65–72. Attali gives a Marxist analysis of nineteenth-century concert culture in general, especially the orchestra and the "genealogy of the star." See Ann E. Kaplan, "Gender Address and Gaze in MTV," in *Rocking around the Clock: Music TV, Postmodernism, and Consumer Culture* (New York: Routledge, 1987), 89–142, for an analysis of the psychological relationship between star and fans in contemporary rock music. The relationship of star and audience is also relevant to the current controversy over performance practice for early or pre-romantic music, much of which was originally composed and performed

It is easy to see how, in this repressed context, the notion could take hold that one's proper approach to music as composer or listener was to attend to a set of "tonally moving forms," disembodied from motion, emotion, or extrastructural meaning. Indeed, few would fault Hanslick for failing to understand the historical relativity of the concert and the aesthetic judgments he made in its context. Today's formalists, however, are on much thinner ground, continuing to view as universal an approach to musical production and reception that modern historical research has clearly revealed to be culturally relative, an approach that has the ethnocentric effect of discounting, or discrediting, the great majority of global musical cultures throughout history.

On the other hand, when we turn from formalist critics to actual musical artists, we find more awareness and response with regard to the connection between context of dissemination and style, probably because their survival and success are at stake. So, just as composers of instrumental music responded with an increasingly formalist-oriented style as the performance context moved from church and chamber to concert hall, and later to private and academic meetings of avant-garde composers, they will also likely respond to a move of art-music back to connectedness with life. Given the threat of declining public interest and patronage, some have done so already. For example, the process and new-age idioms are a step in this direction, both in their emphasis on the "being-in-time" consciousness of the body and in their ready accessibility to the understanding and participation of a wide audience.[27]

The new, softer-boundaried performance contexts may include everyday settings, such as outdoor parks, restaurants, or other social communing places with a freer ambience and fewer physical restrictions on moving, talking, eating, drinking, or sleeping, and they may include settings

---

in a very different context from that of the concert hall. In my opinion, the unacknowledged subtext of the controversy is that some modern concert performers have found experiences of the more historically authentic instruments and techniques introduced by performance practice specialists to be less dazzling to audiences than those creatable with modern instruments and techniques, and they have therefore concluded, in ahistorical fashion, that authentic instruments and performances are not as good as modern performances. See also Nicholas Kenyon, ed., *Authenticity and Early Music* (New York: Oxford University Press, 1988), for a variety of essays on the controversy.

27. Steve Reich's music and writings demonstrate this; see *Writings about Music* (Halifax: Press of Nova Scotia College of Art and Design; New York: New York University Press, 1974), especially 9–11.

not yet imagined for genres that cross the boundaries of current convention. To our romantically acculturated minds, some of these settings may suggest an unacceptably humble, utilitarian status for music; but paradoxically, it is probably the proud insistence on *l'art pour l'art* autonomy that has resulted in its humbling ghettoization and neglect in our public life, whereby utilitarian purposes, such as entertainment at athletic events, are the musical activities that receive the most regular support in the civic sector. On the contrary, music appears to occupy a higher status culturally when it is integrated with other forms of life experience, as, for example, in its evident integration with poetry, dance, eating, weaving, and religious ceremonies of the ancient Phrygians[28] and in various hunter-gatherer societies, wherein music plays a prominent role in communal ritual and life.[29]

Relatedness of Musical Experience among Composer, Performer, Audience, Critics, and Community

Ideas borrowed from poststructural theory strongly suggest the value of softer, less hierarchical boundaries among the constituencies of artistic experience—in the case of music, the composer, performer, audience, critics, and community. For instance, the deconstructionist view of the literary work as "text," of writing as "textuality," and of reading as involving a co-creative "intertextuality" is a model that, in effect, softens the boundaries among writer, reader, and community, and emphasizes not the fixing of absolute or hierarchical value but the play of meanings among fluid constituencies.[30]

In the case of the experience-oriented performance art of music, the deconstructionist view is particularly applicable, not only because of the likelihood of widely variant performances of any given work but also

28. Renée Cox, "A History of Music," *Journal of Aesthetics and Art Criticism* 48 (1990): 395–409, especially 395–96.

29. See essays in Ellen Koskoff, ed., *Women and Music in Cross-Cultural Perspective*, Contributions in Women's Studies, no. 79 (New York, Westport, Conn., and London: Greenwood Press, 1987); and Marcia Herndon and Suzanne Ziegler, eds., *Music, Gender and Culture*, Intercultural Music Studies, no. 1 (Wilhelmshaven: Florian Noetzel Verlag, 1990).

30. For a clear and concise discussion of these issues, including their particular application to music, see Roland Barthes, "From Work to Text," in *Philosophy Looks at the Arts: Contemporary Readings in Aesthetics*, ed. Joseph Margolis, 3d ed. (Philadelphia: Temple University Press, 1987), 518–24.

because of the limitations and variations in the specificity of notational practices over the history of Western art-music, not to mention popular music, and music of other cultures. For example, in contrast to the relatively stable historical practices of "notation" for, say, novels, or even dramatic plays—which arguably preserve many of the author's intentions in the written words, music-notational practices have been neither culturally universal nor historically stable. Those practices range from an absence of notation (a vast quantity of music in the area of song and improvisatory instrumental genres and passages); to the merely mnemonic indications of phrase direction in ninth-century chant notation; to later Medieval, Renaissance, and Baroque practices (where notation of pitches and rhythms is often incomplete, misleading, or ambiguous, and where little or no information is provided on timbre, dynamics, tempo, and articulation). These crucial musical elements were all left to the co-creation of musical performers, assuming they were not occupied in performing music of their own. Even in the case of our "common practice period" (ca. 1750–present), notation of the main musical elements is still usually incomplete without the interpretation of a skilled, musical performer who is knowledgeable in the terms and techniques of the performance practice for the period and genre involved.[31]

Thus, not only is the score a bad gauge of a composer's intentions, its very inadequacy to that purpose suggests the need to reevaluate the Western art-musical view of the composer as isolated genius-creator at the top of a hierarchy—whose intentions alone determine the musical work—and to consider a demotion, if not a death, of the composer's authority.[32] The reigning notion too closely resembles Reagan's "trickle-down" theory of economics and has parallel results in terms of the musical disenfranchisement and impoverishment of the majority of the public. We should note that many of the most vituperative proponents of this compositorial domination were composers themselves (e.g., Berlioz, Wagner, Schumann, Brahms,

31. The article on "notation" is one of the longest in the standard reference work for music, *The New Grove Dictionary of Music and Musicians*, ed. Stanley Sadie (London: Macmillan, 1980), with eighty-seven pages and four authors (Ian D. Bent, David Hiley, Margaret Bent, and Geoffrey Chew). Given the complexity of the issues around musical notation and the score, the effort among analytic aestheticians, such as Nelson Goodman, to define the composer's intentions, and the musical work by reference to it, would seem to be an example of the wrong, hard-boundaried paradigm at work.

32. Roland Barthes seems to have originated the postmodern trope "death of the author"; see Barthes, "The Death of the Author," in *Image-Music-Text*, trans. Stephen Heath (New York: Hill and Wang, 1977), 142–48.

Mahler, Schoenberg, and Stravinsky). Indeed, starting in the nineteenth century, the tendency of composers less toward performance and more toward theory and criticism as a method of supporting themselves and/or disseminating their music is itself a sign of the triumph of hard-boundaried theory over musical experience in the Western art-music tradition.

Sadly, the composers are only apparently the victors in this evolution, since the disenfranchisement of music's other constituencies has the effect of alienating everyone from a healthy cultural connection to music and consequently of leaving us passive receivers, not so much for *l'art pour l'art* culture, or even for the culture of popular music, but for the multibillion-dollar industries of civic and corporate *Gebrauchsmuzak*, if I may coin a term. By *Gebrauchsmuzak*, I mean the football fight songs, supermarket music, advertising jingles, movie and television soundtracks, and other artificially produced sound environments, not to mention the mass-produced music videos and sound recordings that feed the chain of demand in the popular music world. The problem is not the supposed gap in value between high and low culture but, rather, the largely unnoticed disenfranchisement and disengagement of people from active engagement in a musical culture of their own. Where popular music as a whole fits in this picture is difficult to say, since it is comprised of so many highly variant subcultures. Chances are, though, that insofar as popular music plays on us like elevator tapes (i.e., without our awareness and involvement), it is part of the *Gebrauchsmuzak* problem as well. On the other hand, with the paradigm of softer boundaries and relatedness among musical constituencies, the process of hierarchization, disenfranchisement, and disengagement might be turned around, and a more equitable relationship might be reestablished between music and its constituencies.

Some composers from the art-music community have blazed a trail for this kind of turnaround. (Ironically, they may be freer to do so than more commercially tied popular musicians.) For example, in writings going back to the 1930s, proto-deconstructionist John Cage challenged every assumption of Western art-musical culture, and, in particular, he emphasized greater engagement of the performer and the audience in the experience of music.[33] More recently, Pauline Oliveros frequently crosses the boundaries of genre and constituency in her music, as in her explicitly feminist

33. See John Cage, *Silence: Lectures and Writings* (Middletown: Wesleyan University Press, 1939); and *John Cage at Seventy-Five*, a special issue of *Bucknell Review* 32, no. 2 (1989), ed. Richard Fleming and William Duckworth.

performance piece *Sonic Meditations* (1971), which she dedicates to "the elevation and equalization of the feminine principle along with the masculine principle." In the first of these musical meditations, entitled "Teach Yourself To Fly," Oliveros gives performing instructions that are accessible to anyone (not just professional musicians) and that emphasize the performers' engagement in the experience instead of requiring them passively to transfer the composer's intentions down the chain to the even more passive listeners. The instructions are:

> Any number of persons sit in a circle facing the center. Illuminate the space with dim blue light. Begin by simply observing your own breathing. Always be an observer. Gradually observe your breathing become audible. Then gradually introduce your voice. Color your breathing very softly at first with sound. Let the intensity increase very slowly as you observe it. Continue as long as possible until others are quiet.[34]

"Teach Yourself To Fly" may be too radical for some, but, at the very least Oliveros's instructions remind us that music is, first and foremost, experienced. Her view that valuing the feminine must mean a more egalitarian sharing of that experience, and thus a de-professionalization and de-hierarchization of it, is one that is shared by many feminists outside music, as well. Do we risk "greatness" by de-emphasizing professionalism? Perhaps, but if that means the reenfranchisement of people into active participation in a musical culture of their own, it could be worth the risk and might lead to a more generally shared cultural value down the road.

The possibility of softer boundaries and relatedness among the constituencies of a musical culture has also been raised through the explorations by twentieth-century anthropologists and ethnomusicologists of pre-industrial societies whose boundaries between the main constituencies of musical experience are frequently softer and differently focused than those of Western industrial society. For example, ethnomusicologist Elizabeth Tolbert tells of the spiritual, communal function of the lament among the Finnish Karelians and analyzes the music in context with that function.[35] Anthropologist Carol Robertson finds that music, in the form of communally performed

34. Quoted and discussed further in Robert P. Morgan, *Twentieth-Century Music: History of Musical Style in Modern Europe and America* (New York and London: Norton, 1991), 454.

35. Elizabeth Tolbert, "Magico-Religious Power and Gender in the Karelian Lament," in *Music, Gender and Culture*, 41–53.

ritual, offers the individual in the African Kassen-Nankani and South American Mapuche tribes "a web of relationships within which his/her individuality can be defined," including the web of gender relationships.[36] Communal dance, song, and religious-dramatic ritual generally figure prominently in pre-industrial music cultures, casting into considerable question the Western art-musical view of these experiences as secondary to the "pure" experience of untexted, instrumental music. The long-standing tendency of musicologists to ignore such discoveries and thus to evade the relativization of the practices and values of Western art-music, is finally giving way, thanks in great part to the influence of postmodernism—including the current movement toward making room for multicultural and popular culture studies in Western academic institutions.[37]

Relatedness of Musical Style to Culture

The mention of multicultural studies leads very naturally to consideration of the third area of musical relatedness under discussion in this essay, that of the relatedness between musical style and culture. This area of relatedness has already received considerable attention from feminist and Marxist critics, and some profound insights on the relatedness of style to culture have already been reached, making the traditional aesthetic claims of autonomy for the musical work and composer much more difficult to maintain. Nonetheless, something more than insightful criticism on the margins of musicology is needed if the conservative practices of our institutions of musical education are to be affected. For example, despite multiculturalist success in introducing jazz, popular music, and world music into the academic curriculum, the teaching methods for music history continue to ignore connections of musical style to culture, in favor of the otherwise long discredited "Great Man [*sic*]" approach, where most of what is empha-

36. Carol Robertson, "Singing Social Boundaries into Place: The Dynamics of Gender and Performance in Two Cultures," *Sonus* 10, no. 1 (Fall 1989): 59–71, and 10, no. 2 (Spring 1990): 1–13.

37. The Western ethnocentricity of musicologists is also reflected in the use of the general term *musicology* for the more culturally limited enterprise of Western musical study, and its isolation from the broader (though more narrowly titled), field of ethnomusicology, which has its own separate society and journals. The isolation, and the assumption of Western cultural superiority, is only now beginning to be challenged in musicology circles. See, for example, Judith Becker, "Is Western Art Music Superior?" *Musical Quarterly* 72 (1986): 341–59.

sized, tested, and recalled is data about composers, almost entirely male, in the traditional canon of Western art-music. Indeed, there seems to be no time for anything else, since according to standard curricular practices the whole of music history must be squeezed into at best only a few semesters out of sixteen years of public-supported education and at worst a single semester (or even no time at all). As a result of the curricular squeeze, the complex cultural evolution and relationship among musical genres, styles, media, and technology, which really comprises the history of music, remains largely unexamined, and students instead memorize simplistic, linked successions of style periods and composers—said to have influenced each other—in what essentially becomes an extension of "who's best" into the historical mode.[38]

The academic evasion of music's cultural relatedness is coupled, as is usually the case, with a diminution of women's musical activities. Indeed, a masculinist slant continues in musicology and music history teaching to a degree that would amaze cultural critics of other fields. Take, for example, *The Music of Man*, an expensively produced series of videos that accompanies a current high-selling music history textbook. *The Music of Man* clearly marginalizes women in the title and in the accounts of the music-historical periods.[39] Of the myriad of active, influential musical women of the twentieth century, this series shows only Martha Graham, Judy Collins, and Joan Baez, the last of whom is presented as a woman notable for having had a love affair with Bob Dylan and for performing his music. (In fact, Joan Baez's fame and influence as a performer and composer preceded Dylan's, and his career profited from the personal relationship with her rather than the other way around.) Clearly, a new paradigm is needed in the teaching of music history in order to challenge the masculinist slant, the preoccupation with greatness, and the denial of cultural connectedness.

With respect to the teaching and analytical practices of music theory, the paradigm of soft boundaries and relatedness is intended to lead to analytical approaches that de-reify the hard boundaries illustrated in the very terms with which we think about and analyze music (i.e., as in pitches,

38. The academic evasion of music's cultural relatedness is further discussed in Susan McClary, "Terminal Prestige: The Case of Avant-Garde Music Composition," *Cultural Critique* 12 (1989): 57–81.

39. *The Music of Man* videos accompany K. Marie Stolba's *The Development of Western Music: A History* (Dubuque, Iowa: Brown, 1990), ironically the first major history textbook to prominently include material on women in music.

chords, rhythmic motives, phrases, sections, movements, and works).[40] Under the new paradigm, application of supposedly universal, theoretical concepts would be restricted to music for which evidence of their applicability could be found in the music's own cultural practices, including the performance practices, notation, and contemporary theoretical discussion. Thus, for example, chords, sections, and periods would be applicable to a lot of eighteenth-century music, since composers notated them and theorists discussed them, but not to music across historical periods and cultures. Rather, music theorists and philosophers would be forced to deal with the cultural practices of the music they are judging, in order to develop and apply the new, softer-boundaried theoretical concepts, in a culturally related manner.

The new culturally related boundary concepts would come from the actual experience of the music, including the way it is performed, heard, taught, danced or moved to, and from any dramatic or poetic texts with which it is associated. The concepts could include terms (preferably in the language of the period) for sequences of bodily gestures that are associated with dancing or playing the music in question, or for the organization of accompanying texts or dramatic representations. Something very like phrases would probably remain valid for lots of music, given the analogous structure of accompanying poetic lines and dance motions in each case. Many other supposedly universal boundary concepts would have to be rethought and replaced, however, if we are to take the relatedness of music to culture more seriously.

Once the development of culturally related boundary concepts takes place, the way would be clear for music criticism to develop in a more legitimate and profound manner, similar to the operation of criticism in the literary and visual arts. The types of boundaries present in a musical repertory, and the way they function, would likely become a regular focus of musical study and could lead to stronger connections with general cultural criticism, such as is already found in criticism of the literary and visual arts. For example,

40. It should be noted that some aesthetic views and analytic procedures borne out of the romantic tradition emphasized relatedness, but to the extent that they operated under the assumption of universality, they were just as problematic. See, for example, Heinrich Schenker, *Free Composition*, trans. Ernst Oster (New York: Longman, 1979), in which analytical diagrams overlook prominent intended phrase and sectional endings in order to emphasize organic continuity, his universal value. Schenkerian method is a foundation of the current music theory profession, and it is often applied to repertories across cultural periods, regardless of relevance.

extrapolations from Marxist literary and art criticism suggest that in cultures of aristocratic patronage, where art and artists have been owned as property, the artistic styles reflect the hard boundaries of ownership, as can be seen in the distinct, often symmetrical, phrases, sections, and movements articulated by clear meters and mainly masculine cadences of eighteenth-century musical style.[41] The tendency of romantic and modernist music criticism has been to associate the breaking of these boundaries with "genius," which is very much in accordance with Kant's view of the concept,[42] and to base canonical hierarchizations of greater and lesser geniuses on their tendency to break the boundaries. Wolfgang Amadeus Mozart (our archetypal musical genius), for example, is a great composer because of his constant resistance to these boundaries, which takes the form of frequent feminine cadences, assymetrical phrases, metrical displacements, and surprises of chromaticism, tonality, and melodic contour.

Putting the mythology of artistic genius aside, however, Mozart's boundary breaking might be understood better in relationship to his resistance to playing his expected role within the patronage system and against conventions and authority, in general.[43] By comparison within Mozart's close circle of contacts, this was a resistance that did not appeal to Antonio Salieri, on whom Pushkin, Schaffer, and their audiences have projected such heavy doses of romantic ideology. Moreover, such resistance was probably psychologically impossible for Wolfgang's older sister Maria Anna Mozart: also a child prodigy but barred by family and culture from public musical activity as an adult woman.[44] These observations move the criti-

41. See John Berger's influential analysis of seventeenth- through nineteenth-century European oil painting, *Ways of Seeing* (New York: Penguin Books, 1977), 83–112.
42. Immanuel Kant, *Critique of Judgment*, trans. Werner S. Pluhar (1790; reprint, Indianapolis: Hackett Publishing, 1987), 176–78.
43. There is not time to develop this point adequately here, but resistance to authority is apparent in the composer's relationship to his father and in the attitudes to musical and social conventions expressed in his letters, as, for instance, when he makes fun of the French "First Stroke of the Bow" in a letter of 12 June 1778. W. A. Bauer and O. E. Deutsch, eds., *Mozart: Briefe und Aufzeichnungen, II* (Kassel: Barenreiter, 1962), 378–79.
44. See Rudolphe Angemuller, *New Grove Dictionary of Music and Musicians*, s.vv. *Maria Anna Mozart*, on her retirement from public musical achievement. Also see Eva Rieger, "Dolce Semplice? On the Changing Role of Women in Music," in *Feminist Aesthetics*, 135–49, for a discussion of the psychological effect of the "cultural muting" of musical women such as Maria Anna Mozart, Clara Wieck Schumann, Cosima Liszt Wagner, and Alma Schindler Mahler on their creativity (147–48).

cal focus from hierarchization of greatness to cultural relatedness, but they do not in any way devalue Mozart's music. Rather, they present another, more culturally related basis for appreciating that music, without requiring the devaluation and dismissal of musical repertories in which boundary breaking is a lesser factor.

In terms of current musical practice, application of the new paradigm of soft boundaries and relatedness between musical style and culture means questioning and playing with the hard boundaries of traditional and modernist styles, as in the deconstructive play of Cage, Peter Schickele (masquerading as P.D.Q. Bach),[45] and performance artist Laurie Anderson, whose characteristic electronic distortions of her own voice seem to mirror the electronic distortion and transformation of the subject in postmodern culture in general.[46]

Although the new paradigm does not aim to privilege female musical voices over male, there is still a prominent role for women to play in its application, because they are best positioned to use the paradigm to deconstruct the traditional bases of masculinist musical privilege and to explore expressions of feminine cultural identity that have been overlooked under the old paradigm. In *Feminine Endings*, Susan McClary discusses the possibilities of new discursive strategies for women composers at length, including a description of Janika Vanderwelde's *Genesis II*, in which the composer consciously decided to turn from the masculinist "beanstalk gestures" of traditional musical narrative to an exploration of birth imagery in sound.[47]

It is impossible to predict exactly what effect an untried paradigm might have on the discourse and practice of music should it become accepted and current. Based on the effect of new feminist concepts in the other arts, it does appear that a new paradigm can help lead to increased theoretical and critical activity, which, in turn, may have considerable effect on how music is taught and practiced in our society. On the pessimistic side, however, the positivistic fragmentation and isolation of music professionals into composition, theory, history, education, and performance, and the equally stark fragmentation of our musical subcultures, mean that any

45. See, for example, Peter Schickele's combination of Baroque and country western idioms in *Oedipus Tex and Other Choral Calamities* (Telarc CD-80239, 1990).
46. See McClary, *Feminine Endings*, 132–66, for further discussion of Laurie Anderson and of the popular musician Madonna as examples of women finding their creative musical voices through new feminist-minded discursive strategies.
47. McClary, *Feminine Endings*, 112–31.

new paradigm faces an uphill battle in receiving wide currency in all the relevant musical institutions, journals, and associations.[48] Institutional change is necessary in order to address the professional fragmentation and, more generally, in order to reverse the ghettoization of music in the academy as an arcane study of the Western canon relevant only to music majors pursuing careers in performance or in the teaching of more of the same.

Actually, this may be the most crucial task for which the paradigm of soft boundaries and relatedness is needed in our musical culture: to bring music out of the fragmented professional ghetto and back into relationship with people of all walks of life. At the moment, it appears as though only very extensive, interdisciplinary curricular reform from grade school to university would be able to produce such a change. That view, however, of the situation may underestimate the readiness with which teachers and students of many subjects, and people in general, would reintegrate music into their cultural awareness and activities if critical discourse in music were accessible and culturally relevant, as it would be under the new paradigm.

48. See Marcia J. Citron, "Gender, Professionalism, and the Musical Canon," *Journal of Musicology* 8 (1990): 102–17; and Bruce Wilshire, *The Moral Collapse of the University; Professionalism, Purity, and Alienation* (Albany: State University of New York Press, 1990), 255–76, for a wider, more philosophical view of the sickness of academic reification, in general, and the need for the feminist challenge to it.

Wet, Dark, and Low, Eco-Man Evolves from Eco-Woman

Andrew Ross

There is a terrible confusion about our place in nature.
—Ynestra King, *Healing the Wounds*

Does anyone really want to listen to stories about the victimization of men? This was one of the questions coursing through the culture at large in 1991. The ostensible topic may well have been the mid-life "crisis" of the white male yuppie, whose generational experience seems to have become the dominant narrative of our culture; but the underlying conditions may have just as much to do with the mid-life crises of the women's movement and the ecology movement, all too apparent in the emergence of fundamentalist strains of ecofeminism, whose Earth Goddess is now being courted by its male cognate, the Green Man, or the Wild Man of the media-struck "men's movement." The essay that follows speculates about some of the circumstances that identify this moment. As is often the case, the most symptomatic place to begin is with the summer movies.

Lincoln Green

Perhaps it was too much to expect a truly "green" Robin Hood, his Merrie Men in bioregional sync with Sherwood Forest. But Kevin Costner had been well groomed as Hollywood's ambassador of nationalist myths of environmental romanticism. Hamming his way from one pastoral field of dream to another, he had survived Madonna's most public put-down in *Truth or Dare* and had graduated to the big league of ecological hype with his production of *Dances with Wolves*. His film rhapsodized the subsistence contract between tribe and herd on a buffalo-busy prairie, while its friendliness to the Lakota Sioux stroked Hollywood's conscience about its appalling record on Native American docudrama. Most of all, Costner's persona was well tailored to the cut of modern liberal masculinity, harmlessly heroic in spite of its best testosterone-induced intentions, and thus was targeted for honor by default rather than by official history's elective aim. With a little heat, however, this new breed reduces to old school stock. The white man, now, with clean hands and dirty laundry, and the red man, with humor this time, not to mention native authenticity, mouthing, "We, who are about to die, salute you."

Environmental kitsch plays a co-starring role in all of this, for the film proved that the uncultivated prairie remains a pivotal scene for illustrating stories about the national identity of North America's postcolonial societies. The appearance of the pristine prairie always records the last moment of the native hunter-gatherer economy before the new ecological revolution gives way to myths centered around the white settler's family farm. The transformation of the "wilderness," which was once so crucial to North American expansionist destiny, has, in this century, become the very antithesis of white national identity, now so ideologically dependent upon the conservation of that same wilderness, whether on celluloid, on the Native American reservation, or in the strictly policed territories of the national parks "system" (systematizing what?).

When Costner donned the Lincoln green and set up shop in Sherwood Forest, his transnational celebrity value crossed over onto another country's ecological terrain, similarly charged with historical symbolism. The loss, and subsequently, the desperate preservation, of England's forests occupies a comparable place in the national ecological romances, not least because the forest is the leafy location of all that has been resistant to the laws and decrees of the official political and religious powers: the outlawed home, respectively, of the pagan spirit traditions feared by the church's legislators, of masterless men feared by their would-be landed masters, of lost arcadian sentiment feared by Victorian industrialists, and, most recently, of nondeveloped nature feared by would-be developers. Not that these two locations—the ecological and the ideological—are easily separable. The profitable clearing of forests, for example, had long been sanctioned by Christian theology in the name of its holy war against the "sacred groves" of pagan worship. So, too, in the twelfth- and thirteenth-century England of Robin Hood, early capitalist modes of production in the metal industry had combined with rapid increases in population to drastically reduce the extensive woodland ecosystem, hitherto the preserve of the king and the nobility, now given over to arable land reclamation.[1] The result was a terrain busily crossed by economic and cultural forces in conflict with each other: the domain of the king's laws of the vert and the monasteries' privileges, each suppressing the peasantry's demand to supplement its subsistence farming with hunting; the site of industrial exploitation of natural resources, contested by the old organic religion's interdiction against such practices as profane; and the location of the gentry's nightmares about social bandits in an unregulated territory, matched by the countercultural fantasy of a sylvan homeland for freed serfs. No wonder that the medieval tales about Sherwood Forest came to provide such an enduring myth for the national culture, or that the Robin Hood ethic of redistributing wealth would come to hold such international significance as a political allegory (the high point was the banning of Robin Hood stories from U.S. public libraries during the McCarthyist heyday).

Such historical questions may seem remote from a modern audience's response to the Costner vehicle of 1991, but they are hardly irrelevant to the accumulated associations of the Robin Hood figure as it has survived through centuries of different media: the medieval ballads, the saturnalian rituals of the May Games, mummers plays, Renaissance printed broadsides and garlands, the historical romance, the Victorian penny weekly,

1. Carolyn Merchant notes the effects of diminished forestland in *The Death of Nature: Women, Ecology and the Scientific Revolution* (San Francisco: Harper & Row, 1980): "By the late thirteenth century in London, it was becoming necessary to import sea coal from Newcastle, a soft coal with a high sulfur content which when burned polluted the air with black soot and irritating, choking smoke" (62). In Merchant's account, the demographic collapse of the fourteenth century helped the forests recover until the sixteenth century, when a more advanced ecological crisis, caused by the destruction of forests for naval construction, helped generate the first movement for conservation and a new managerial approach to nature, exemplified by John Evelyn's *Discourse on Forest Trees* (1662).

and the Hollywood blockbuster. Never a static legend, not even in medieval minstrelsy, it is only in the most recent Hollywood phase that the picture of Robin as a self-outlawed aristocrat has become an established convention, although this suggestion, which runs against the grain of the plebeian legend, goes back to the Scottish chroniclers of the mid-fifteenth century and was influentially revived by the most Jacobin of the tale's editors, Joseph Ritson, in the wake of the French Revolution. That suggestion was at last fully incorporated into popular consciousness in Michael Curtiz's lavish 1938 film, where Errol Flynn's noble Robin is posed as a self-outlawed Saxon freedom fighter resisting the Norman yoke. The 1991 version preserved the aristocratic convention and added an actual Middle Eastern location to the Crusader story, which may say just as much about U.S. foreign policy in the nineties as the Curtiz film's Saxon patriotism said about antifascist sympathies in Hollywood's Popular Front years.

Kevin Reynolds's film may have missed a golden opportunity to "green" Costner further; it barely dwells on the eco-communal yeoman order of the Merrie Men, and it deals the pagan hand to the townsman villain, Alan Rickman's deliciously sadistic Sheriff of Nottingham, whose actions are enthusiastically guided by a haggish prophetess. Instead, the film explains Robin's motives with a plot involving baronial treachery against his patriot father and the subsequent dispossession of the son's patrimonial inheritance. Robin fights, then, in the name of an absent father, as part of an initiation rite to reclaim his noble title rather than to liberate the Saxon masses. The rottenness of the State produces his "dysfunctional" family, and Robin takes to male company (including a Moor substitute father) in the wilderness to regain his legitimate place in society.

In this respect, the film's filial adventure story can be set alongside a different kind of summer movie, John Singleton's *Boyz N the Hood*, a black, urban version of filial initiation. Where dominant white Hollywood renditions of this narrative rework mythical figures—the urban Batman or the rural Robin Hood—marginal African American versions choose a contemporary realist setting.[2] Only in 1991 would a mythical Anglo-Saxon outlaw be a match for the young black gangstas who were the focus of the year's spate of black-directed films, from *New Jack City* to *Boyz N the Hood*. In fact, Singleton's film was an earnest attempt to address the issue of paternal responsibility, which dogs so much of the discourse about the "problem" of

2. See my discussion of *Batman* and *Do the Right Thing* in "Ballots, Bullets and Batmen: Can Cultural Studies Do the Right Thing?" *Screen* 31, no. 1 (Spring 1990).

young black masculinity. The " 'hood" is a south-central Los Angeles neighborhood, which is booby-trapped everywhere by the corporate police state for the "self-destruction" of its inhabitants—gun shops and liquor stores on every street corner, the omnipresence of searchlights from LAPD helicopters constantly circling overhead, army recruiters soaking up young surplus labor, and housing developers forcing rents up through the downward spiral of neighborhood impoverishment. The film presents an experiment in the social ecology of this kind of late twentieth-century urban environment. The son in question, Tre Styles, is delivered by his buppie mother into the care of her estranged, but politically savvy, husband to do a proper father's job of saving him from the gangsta life. To set up this experiment, which meets with mixed results, the film accepts the standard bromide that responsibility for the dysfunctional black family lies with its flawed matriarchal structure. Consequently, a strong, nurturing father-son relationship is posed as the only shield against a wayward life; the mother is demonized, and the environment is presented as naturally Hobbesian.

In both films—*Robin Hood* and *Boyz N the Hood*—the sons survive their initiation adventures through the respective mediation of an absent father and a present father. What the films share is an excision of mothers, mythically vacated in *Robin Hood*, sociologically expunged in *Boyz N the Hood*. As such, these films are welcome fuel for Hollywood's obsessive endeavor to find workable narratives of patriarchy for its filial protagonists.[3] After all, the summer's biggest film, *Terminator 2*, whose hardbody Sarah Connor (played by Linda Hamilton) finally signaled a response to the long-standing feminist demand for nongendered dramatic roles, would also showcase Arnold Schwarzenegger's transformation from mean cyborg motherfucker to ideal father/just warrior. The erstwhile Terminator shared his metamorphosis with the leading men of the summer's cluster of male conversion movies, *Regarding Henry*, *The Doctor*, and *City Slickers*, all focusing on the traumas of male mid-life crisis.

Hairy Green

The loudest proclamations of male mid-life crisis and anxieties about filial initiation in 1991 were to be found untrammeled in the media-hyped "men's movement," associated with the best-seller middlebrow psychology

3. See Vivien Sobchak, "Child/Alien/Father: Patriarchal Crisis and Generic Exchange," *Camera Obscura* 15 (1986): 7–34.

and self-help literature of Robert Bly (*Iron John*), Sam Keen (*Fire in the Belly*), John Lee (*The Flying Boy*), Robert Moore and Douglas Gillette (*King Warrior Magician Lover*), the writing of psychologist James Hillman, and with the men's seminars and rural Wild Man gatherings—replete with drum rituals and sweat lodges—which have become the experiential workshops of the movement. Rooted in the belief that all men share a deep atavistic masculinity that must be plumbed in order to overcome the wounds of an upbringing at the hands of overwhelming mothers and distant or absent fathers, advocates of this new male emotion therapy present it as a response to a social crisis of masculinity evolving in the West since the Industrial Revolution. Dismissive of the ruthless, exploitative codes of dominant masculinity, these men—straight, white, middle-class professionals, for the most part—are also seeking an assertive alternative to the softer or "feminine" personality types favored by sensitive men over the last two decades. A number of common themes sound throughout the literature: the pathology of the modern family has produced a "father-hunger" in men; the lessons of the women's movement have all been absorbed and need to be transcended, rather than answered, in the pursuit of authentic masculinity; the alienating pattern of modern corporate life is only the latest industrial organization of labor that has increasingly distanced fathers from their sons; the work of healing involves initiatory relationships with older father figures and a studied immersion in men's perennial philosophy of fairy tales, myths, and pre-Christian rituals.

If this is a social movement, on the parts of men-in-crisis, then it is not exactly a movement with a radical lineage or with ends that resonate with anything like familiar radical aims. Fifteen years ago, pro-feminist men's groups sprang up in most cities in North America and Britain in response to the ideas and practices of the women's movement. Groups like Men Against Sexism and Men's Liberation flourished in an uneasy alliance with feminists and with gay and lesbian liberationists (the response from women and gays ranged from damning with faint praise, to fearing cooption, to outrightly condemning homophobia) and generated a steady flow of critical literature that constitutes a significant addition to the body of work produced in women's studies and gay and lesbian studies.[4] Nowhere in the literature

4. Some of the more prominent titles in this basically heterosexual literature include Jon Snodgrass, ed., *For Men Against Sexism: A Book of Readings* (Albion, Calif.: Times Change Press, 1977); Harry Brod, ed., *The Making of Masculinities: The New Men's Studies* (Boston: Allen & Unwin, 1987); Jeff Hearn, *The Gender of Oppression: Men,*

of or about the new "men's movement" is there any mention of these activities or texts. One reason for this omission is that Bly and his fellow travelers are not engaged in a primarily pro-feminist project, and their concerns harbor even less of an appeal to sexual minorities. The broader reason for the lack of dialogue, however, lies in the difference of community. Popular or middlebrow psychology literature, like Bly's *Iron John*, is addressed to a general audience. Its market is composed primarily of heterosexual men in trouble, men who are alienated from work, romance, family, mainstream politics, and in search of some "truth" about themselves. These anxieties and desires are treated as a commodity by the author-therapists who write the books and conduct the workshops. This audience, or community, is not concerned with responding to the shortcomings of masculinist Left thought or to the universalist critiques of radical feminism; this audience may have had little direct contact with the arguments and debates about masculinity that have engaged these other communities of intellectuals and activists. This is not to say, however, that the discussion about masculinity found in the pages of these new books is untouched by such arguments, or that the desire for a movement of this sort does not have something fundamentally

---

Masculinity and the Critique of Marxism (Brighton: Harvester, 1987); Arthur Brittan, *Masculinity and Power* (Oxford: Basil Blackwell, 1989); J. Nichols, *Men's Liberation* (New York: Penguin, 1975); Robert Connell, *Gender and Power: Society, the Person, and Sexual Politics* (Cambridge: Polity Press, 1987); Michael Kaufman, ed., *Beyond Patriarchy: Essays by Men on Pleasure, Power, and Change* (London: Oxford University Press, 1987); Paul Hoch, *White Hero, Black Beast: Racism, Sexism, and the Mask of Masculinity* (London: Pluto, 1979); Joseph Pleck, *The Myth of Masculinity* (Cambridge: MIT Press, 1981); Andrew Tolson, *The Limits of Masculinity* (London: Tavistock, 1977); Emmanuel Reynaud, *Holy Virility: The Social Construction of Masculinity* (London: Pluto, 1983); Andy Metcalfe and Martin Humphries, eds., *The Sexuality of Men* (London: Pluto, 1985); Brian Eslea, *Science and Sexual Oppression: Patriarchy's Confrontation with Women and Nature* (London: Weidenfeld and Nicholson, 1981), and *Fathering the Unthinkable* (London: Pluto, 1983); Anthony Easthope, *What a Man's Gotta Do: The Masculine Myth in Popular Culture* (London: Paladin, 1986); Alice Jardine and Paul Smith, eds., *Men in Feminism* (New York: Methuen, 1987); Joseph Boone and Michael Cadden, *Engendering Men: The Question of Male Feminist Criticism* (New York: Routledge, 1990); Vic Seidler, *Rediscovering Masculinity: Reason, Language, and Sexuality* (New York: Routledge, 1989), and *Recreating Sexual Politics* (New York: Routledge, 1991).

The leading journals include *Changing Men* (United States) and *Achilles Heel* (United Kingdom). In addition, Vic Seidler has edited a selection of essays from *Achilles Heel*, entitled *The Achilles Heel Reader: Men, Sexual Politics, and Socialism* (London: Routledge, 1991).

to do with the more radical social, economic, and cultural criticism of the last twenty years.

Bly the showman has always been regarded as something of a snake oil salesman within the poetry community, or at best—with his cheesy, performative blend of Eastern mysticism, Jungian philosophy, and folk storytelling soaked in perennial wisdom—as an ersatz version of the truly holy Ginsberg. Nonetheless, his career as a poet lends philosophical authority to his position today as the paterfamilias of the emergent tribe of newly mature men. *Iron John*'s middlebrow cultural homeland lies beyond the realm of commercial popular culture, which, Bly believes, ritually degrades men and excludes any representations of men who are prepared to accept the legitimate authority of what he calls "positive leadership energy" for the sake of the community. Politically, *Iron John* positions itself beyond the twenty-year-old critiques offered by the women's movement, the separatist wing of which, "in a justified fear of brutality, has labored to breed fierceness out of men."[5] *Iron John* rejects the model of masculinity that evolved in response to feminism—that of the nondomineering, receptive, cooperative, supportive, and nonaggressive man—just as it rejects the polarizing, red meat alternative represented by John Wayne. In addition, the book attacks the whole premise of a "youth culture" that serves to defer boys' initiatory entry into adulthood. If *Iron John* is not, at least on the face of it, the revenge of patriarchy, it is quite open about the revenge of the elders, whose gerontocratic power over the young was challenged by the generational disrespect of the sixties ("never trust anyone over thirty"), and whose authority Bly seems most interested in reaffirming. *Iron John* may be yet another book originating in some authorial trauma experienced in the course of that turbulent decade. Youths, Bly concludes, need to go to finishing school with older male initiators, not with their own peers. And grown men must give up trying to hold onto their youth.

In place of the bland, domesticated men of today—"the sanitized, hairless, shallow man" of the Judeo-Christian corporate world—Bly invokes the pre-Greek myths of the Wild Man as the source of "deep masculinity" available to men who want to reclaim an energy that has been sapped by popular culture, feminism, and youth culture:

> When a contemporary man looks down into his psyche, he may, if conditions are right, find under the water of his soul, lying in an area

5. Robert Bly, *Iron John: A Book About Men* (Reading, Mass.: Addison-Wesley, 1990), 46; hereafter cited as *IJ*.

> no one has visited for a long time, an ancient hairy man. . . . Welcoming the Hairy Man *is* scary and risky, and it requires a different sort of courage. Contact with Iron John requires a willingness to descend into the male psyche and accept what's dark down there, including the *nourishing* dark. (*IJ*, 6)

Who knows where this auto(homo)-erotic look downward and this "different sort of courage" will lead? While Bly is persuaded that the engagement with this repressed Hairy Man is a highly sexualized encounter, and while the fairy tale he relates about Iron John has a heterosexual-marital denouement, the outcome of this libidinal rendezvous is difficult to place in the actual world of sexual relations. My assumption is that the meeting with the Wild Man capitalizes on the fantasy of a same-sex encounter that dare not speak its name. Too much of this stuff mimics standard exotic gay male narratives and fantasy sexual types to pass itself off as hetero male bonding, no matter how deep or courageous.

If Bly is symptomatically diffident about the question of sexuality, he is slightly more open about the racial lineage of this deep male atavism: The Iron John fairy tale that structures his book "retains memories of initiation ceremonies for men that go back ten or twenty thousand years in northern Europe" (*IJ*, 55). This, however, has nothing to do with simple Aryan race worship. Bly is an effortless name-dropper in the realm of comparative religion and world mythology. His Wild Man, as it turns out, is universally present in Mediterranean, African, Indian, Greek, Celtic, Siberian, Sumerian, Chinese, and Native American myths. If the same atavistic male sexual energy is represented in each culture, then why bother at all with cultural difference? By choosing to celebrate the suppressed Wild Men of only one (Western) culture—Pan, Dionysus, Hermes—Bly may be stealing a march on the PC-bashers. The barbarians do not lie outside the Eurocentric tradition; they are *within* it, and, what's more, they are life-affirming. With friends like Iron John, who needs multiculturalist enemies?

In the months leading up to the year of the Columbian quincentenary, it seems necessary to recall that the Wild Man of European myth has already had at least one bloody career in the New World. The accounts of Native American life written by explorers and historians from the Columbian period and from the century of exploitation that followed are heavily populated by types that divide the "good" Indian, who resembled the Noble Savage, from the "bad" Indian, who resembled the Wild Man of European medieval life (for Columbus, the operative distinction was between the "gentle" Tainos and the "warlike" Caribs). Portable features of the nature-fearing Wild Man legend provided much of the justification for the violent subjugation and near extermination of the native peoples of Mesoamerica and North America. In the light of this history, any white man acting out the Wild Man role in 1992 is playing in full redface, complete with the offensive minstrelsy of loincloths, drums, war paint, sweat lodges, tribal masks, and hoarse-making New Warriors chants.

While Bly has publicly distanced himself from some of the more theatrical excesses of the movement, he is recognized everywhere as the master-thinker behind such activities. Two other best-selling books in the movement attest to his influence in different ways. In contrast to the analytical temper of *Iron John*, Austin therapist John Lee's book *The Flying Boy* is written as a confessional narrative, describing the progress of the author's exercise in self-healing by following Bly's teachings.[6] It outlines the various stages of grieving and releasing anger through which an initial refugee from the world of men, who is unable to make commitments in his life, comes into his true, mature, masculine inheritance. Lee's story is especially revealing in its awestruck veneration of Bly himself, whose poetry he studies as a doctoral candidate for many years, and whose role as a father figure Lee uses to resolve problems with his own father. In the final analysis, this treatment of Bly may say more about the personality cult of the guru-teacher than it does about the general role of male initiators in the art of grieving.

While Sam Keen's *Fire in the Belly* does not owe quite the same debt to a guru-master, it does share the tone of Bly's own middlebrow reverence for great artists, writers, "deep" thinkers, and "meaning" junkies, especially radical theologians, who eat away at the paradoxical heart of religious experience. Anyone, moreover, who enthusiastically cites Norman O. Brown's opinion that "the loins are the place of judgment" in 1991 needs to be hit upside his head. In general, Keen is more attentive to the social and the economic contexts of the masculinity crisis than Bly is. His attacks on the theology of work, on the corporate killing fields, and on the military's claim on young male lives are sound enough, except, perhaps, when he reaches for the transhistorical metaphor: "The credit card is for the modern male what killing prey was to the hunter," or "Most men are shackled to the mercantile society in much the same way medieval serfs were imprisoned in the feudal system."[7] It isn't long before men *as a gender* are cast as victims,

6. John Lee, *The Flying Boy: Healing the Wounded Man* (Deerfield Beach, Fla.: Health Communications, Inc., 1989).

7. Sam Keen, *Fire in the Belly: On Being a Man* (New York: Bantam, 1991), 52, 55.

victims of corporate state violence, and hence as victimizers themselves. For the most part, Keen does not pursue this shaky thesis about the origins of domination and focuses instead on the emotional injuries incurred by men who cannot live up to the expectations set by dominant models of masculinity in our culture. Keen's solutions, however, do not involve contesting or reshaping these expectations; rather, they lie in withdrawal (especially from the world of women), in the discovery of wildness, and in reestablishing a spiritual reconnection to fatherhood. It is from the vantage point of the good father, for example, that Keen cites the gay male community, where arguably the strongest and most admirable forms of emotional solidarity among men exist today, as a *bad* example of unsocialized masculinity:

> It strikes me that the lack of substantial manliness one finds in some gay communities is a result not of a homoerotic expression of sexuality, but the lack of a relationship of nurturance to the young. To be involved in creating a wholesome future, men, gay or straight, need an active, caring relationship to children. A man who takes no care of and is not involved in the process of caring for and initiating the young remains a boy no matter what his achievements. This generation of men knows by its longing for fathers who were absent that nothing fills the void that is created when men abandon their families out of selfishness, dedication to work, or devotion to "important" causes.[8]

This is not quite the way that Jesse Helms would put it, but the sentiments are nonetheless in basic alignment with the official family values sanctioned by the corporate Judeo-Christian state. Indeed, the significance of the stories told by Keen, Bly, and others may lie, ultimately, in their contribution to a cultural consciousness that redefines and reaffirms the eroded authority of patriarchal familialism. The worked-up sincerity of a Keen or a Bly is not likely to be publicly received with the ritual cynicism that greets the pronouncements of morality hacks like Helms. It is no coincidence, moreover, that the "dysfunctional" family model—an overattentive mother and an indifferent father—that Bly and Keen use to describe the plight of the modern male is precisely the one traditionally used by homophobic pathologists to *explain* the "plight" of the homosexual.

It is with a good dose of irony that the fundamental question of this men's movement (*Newsweek* described it as a "postmodern social movement," because its founding moment was a media event—the 1990 airing

8. Keen, *Fire in the Belly*, 227.

of the Bill Moyers PBS special on Bly, "A Gathering of Men") is increasingly posed as: What Do Men Want? This question means something quite different from What Do Women Want? or What Do Chicanos Want? In fact, it can be asked only after questions like these others have already been addressed. Masculinity, in other words, became a salient concept only after the critiques of feminism hit home; the ethnicity of whiteness becomes a nonnormative concept only after the critiques of ethnic minorities have been established in public consciousness. Likewise for heterosexuality and the visibility of gay and lesbian rights. If masculinity today is seen as a "problem," it is largely because feminism has focused some of its attention on men in the last decade or so. After devoting themselves to the task of claiming control over their lives, women have turned to the "problem" of masculinity in areas that cover a broad spectrum, from domestic violence, to the appropriation by men of spheres and practices in the home that had traditionally been considered female domain, to rape, and to militarism, wherein men have played a unilateral role as architects of nuclear terror.[9] If straight men today are almost as wary about conventional codes of "masculinity" as women are about standards of "femininity," then it is a direct result of the social pressure exacted by the women's movement and by the alternative models of sexuality, lifestyle, and emotional solidarity offered by gay men.

How many men, however, actually share this uneasiness? How broadly, across the class spectrum, say, are these anxieties felt? And how can we differentiate these worries from the way men used to feel about their masculinity? For sure, it is important to consider differences of class, education, race, and sexual preference, but these differences may determine only the degree to which male anxiety is experienced from the position of oppressor rather than victim. So, too, the inadequacy of historical perspec-

9. Lynne Segal, *Slow Motion: Changing Masculinities, Changing Men* (New Brunswick: Rutgers University Press, 1990), 294–97. Segal also addresses the concomitant shift of focus within the women's movement, from the concept of *equality* to that of *difference*. By the late seventies, it was clear that only a minority of well-educated, professional, white women were benefiting directly from two decades of feminist thought and action. Overall, the situation for women had worsened in the course of the seventies and was still stymied by the basic contradiction that compelled capitalism to exploit for cheap labor those whose primary work for capitalism was still in the realm of reproduction and childcare. Equality was considered unachievable in the current conditions (i.e., with capitalism as it was, and with men as they were, unwilling to eradicate their own relative power). At that point, difference became the favored concept of analysis across the whole spectrum of feminism, from cultural criticism to legal inquiry. Men's difference became a "problem" subject to examination.

tive poses a real problem. In discussing the fraught question of the historical relationship between patriarchy and capitalism, Arthur Brittan notes:

> One of the problems here is that it is difficult to reconstruct masculinity before the modern era. We can talk about the role of the father in peasant communities in Medieval Europe, but we find it difficult to dig out the subjective dimension of this role. . . . Because some of us are fathers, we may remember our own fathers and grandfathers; we have biographies which intersect with the biographies of parents and children. As men, we also may believe that there is some continuity between our experiences and those who lived before us. Although the large majority of men in industrial society do not hunt and do not fight wars, they still find it conceivable that this is what they did in the past. . . . In other words, we see the past as some kind of validation of who and what we are now. The image of economic man, the rational calculator who takes a risk in order to maximize his profits and advantages, is so much taken for granted that it is not surprising that we read all history in these terms.[10]

It is precisely because this illusion of continuity persists that the sense of a crisis can be generated in the present, and it is in this context that I believe we ought to view the current crisis of masculinity with the kind of skepticism that all manufactured crises merit. As Brittan himself points out, the persuasive appeal of any crisis that relates to masculinity depends upon the assumption that men, in the past, knew who and what they were and that the secure sense of identity they once enjoyed has been very recently undermined. We used to live our masculinity as naturally as breathing air; now we are alienated from our true sexuality, from what we once knew about ourselves. Time to come home.

It is this postromantic thesis about the estrangement of men from their true selves that is now maximized and exploited through the pithy wisdoms offered by Bly and his circle. It has to be assumed that men who actually do write about heterosexual masculinity are, in some sense, always involved in a process of reasserting their own authority. The larger, more conspiratorial version of this process is one in which patriarchy modernizes and reconstitutes itself through the resolution of a manufactured crisis. All ruling groups use the rhetoric of crisis to reconsolidate their power, but this is not to say that the conditions of such crises are themselves illusory.

10. Brittan, *Masculinity and Power*, 99–100.

The latest crisis of masculinity is a case in point. In many instances, the state's increasingly repressive regulation of the body, linked to changes in the economy, labor market, and social policy, and fomented by a conservative fear of sexuality, poses clear physical obstacles to the rights and freedoms of certain groups of men—gay men and young black males—specifically on account of demonized qualities and practices associated with their masculinity. Such groups are used to living with crisis-like conditions of persecution; it is a normative part of the history that has shaped their identity politics. So, too, deindustrialization and class polarization over the last two decades has brought about a precipitous decline in job earnings for almost all men (African Americans and Latinos, in particular), who now belong to the secondary layer of today's two-tier economy. Despite the crippling effects of this economic landslide, these crisis conditions are, again, part of a familiar class logic. Increasingly, however, in and around the men's movement, we hear speculation about a crisis of the gender itself, a set of debilitating circumstances that affect men as a class.

When a crisis is presented as a general condition for all men, this is a sure sign that the process of redefining hegemonic masculinity has gone onto its overtime work schedule, distilling the old truths, compensating for the discards, incorporating this and that trace of hipness from the various countercultures, and generally shifting its contours to disguise the jagged edges. This is the often hectic labor of refashioning and repositioning dominant masculine codes, leaning heavily on the narrative of evolutionary adaptation to justify the rejection or the revival of older traits in the name of survival. And this is where Bly's Wild Man begins to merge with the grunt in jungle camouflage. After all, healing the psychically wounded foot soldiers in the gender wars might just produce a stronger, more dominant breed of man. What rough beast then, in the guise of Iron John, slouches toward the Pentagon?

There is no more reason to trust the narrative of evolution than the rhetoric of crisis. One of the historical tales told about masculine survivalism in an embattled environment is that the advent of Darwinism attached the seal of scientific objectivity to the Victorian masculine ideal of stoical discipline, reinforcing older, Hobbesian themes of brute competitiveness that hark back to a primal image of man the hunter-warrior, of men struggling as they always have for survival in a hostile environment of rivals. You do not have to subscribe to alternative romantic narratives about the cooperative tribal ethic of prelapsarian times to see how this story relates, above all, to the life of competition in a market economy, and how it therefore elevates local capitalist principles to the level of general, transhistorical laws about masculine nature.

Men are no more innately competitive or domineering than women are innately cooperative or compliant. Masculinity, defined from context to context as a set of cultural standards to be observed and emulated, is shaped by social institutions, each with a long history and a potentially changeable future, predominantly shaped by the interests and desires of elite groups. All men find it difficult to match up to those standards. Some men can afford not to. Most, however, actually do suffer from the consequences to varying degrees and fall back upon compensatory fantasies (which are often mistaken for reality by radical feminists). This does not make them losers, nor does it make them victims, both terms drawn from the noxious rhetoric of competition and domination. It does, however, place the studied mark of difference upon their masculinities and their psychosexual lives, differences that are often, but not always, related to race, class, and sexual preference. To disregard these differences and to view masculinity as a single collective property is just bad social theory. To see men as a universally exploitative class, to see male sexuality as a uniformly violent force, is to accept at face value only our (as men) most reactionary fantasies of power and to reduce the prospects of change to the occasional glimpse of chinks in a vast and formidable male armor.

Neolithic Green

Whatever its current function and eventual fate, the ideas of the "men's movement" I have been discussing are primarily a response to arguments that have linked male power to a history of systematic, hierarchical domination. The most full-blown critique of this sort has materialized within the emergent ecofeminist movement, with its description of the wholesale masculine domination of the natural world. It is no surprise, then, that the philosophy of the Wild Man takes its cue from, and presents itself as, a cognate of the ecofeminist poetics of nature. Just as women have been exploring the Great Goddess, so men can now find a spiritual personification of nature that would correspond to what Bly calls our "psychic twin" (*IJ*, 53), or what William Anderson designates as the Green Man in his recent study of this vegetative figure, long suppressed in the Christian West but consistently surfacing in Europe's art and architecture, folktales, and vestigial pagan rituals.[11] Indeed, it is this Green Man who is likely to become the neo-Jungian complement to the Earth Mother in coming years, as the search for an appropriate deity rooted in the soil displaces the much maligned tradition of worshiping patriarchal sky-gods, like Zeus, Allah, and Yahweh.

Of the so-called new social movements, the ecology movement has been exceptional in ceding a leading role, in theory and in practical activism, to heterosexual white men. It has been one of the few spaces in post–New Left politics where such men have felt they can breathe freely and easily, while indulging, to various degrees, in the wilderness cults traditionally associated with the making of heroic white male identities: the frontiersman, the cowboy, the Romantic poet, the explorer, the engineer, the colonizer, the anthropologist, the pioneer settler, and so on. In this tradition, the mark of a real man is to have direct and untrammeled contact with the wilderness. At times, the consequences of this legacy to the ecology movement have been recidivist, not only in the deep ecology wing, where a form of macho, redneck bonhomie came to inform Earth First!'s activist ethic, but also in the social ecology wing, which carried some of the weaponry of Old Left sectarianism into its battles with the deep ecologists.[12] For the most part, however, the commitment to the movement by straight white men has been charged with the kind of spiritually charged passion that they have been unable to lend so easily and righteously to movements for women's liberation, sexual minority liberation, and civil rights for people of color.

Male predominance notwithstanding, women have always played a prominent role in the movement, whether as intellectuals, as in the case of Rachel Carson, Helen Caldicott, Petra Kelly, Vandana Shiva, Carolyn Merchant, and Susan Griffin, or as activists in community and national struggles. Increasingly, however, the proponents of ecofeminism claim more than an equal share of the action. In fact, many of the arguments of ecofeminism rest upon the claim that women are the rightful leaders of the ecology movement because of their historical role as protectors and intimates of the natural world. This claim does not arise out of the unprivileged locations that

11. William Anderson, *Green Man: The Archetype of Our Oneness with the Earth* (New York: HarperCollins, 1990).

12. See the dialogues between Murray Bookchin and Dave Foreman representing the positions of social ecology and deep ecology, respectively, in Steve Chase, ed., *Defending the Earth* (Boston: South End Press, 1991). From the perspective of sexual politics, some of the insults traded between the antagonists speak for themselves: Foreman is branded by Bookchin as a "macho mountain man," Bookchin is dismissed by Ed Abbey as a "fat old lady" (11).

women share in relation to environmental threats, although it is certainly reinforced by the extremity of those threats. Women, for example, are often the frontline victims of ecological illness, especially in matters of reproductive health, where contamination by biohazards is responsible for a whole range of birth defects. So, too, women's situation in the Third World has steadily deteriorated as a result of the commercial logic of "development," especially the theoretically benign development policies shaped by former colonial powers and administratively exploited by national elites to further their own interests.[13]

Women are not the only frontline victims in these cases; they share such threats with people of color or lower class who live in First World areas where hazardous activities are located, or with peasants and tribal peoples whose subsistence living is imperiled by monocultural production. Consequently, women have no overriding stake to claim in the politics of combating these practices, although they are often the most activist among the threatened groups.

On the contrary, the special claim of ecofeminism for women's proprietary rights within the ecology movement lies with the long historical association, however warranted, of women with nature. Second-wave feminism sought to demystify this association and to disconnect the link, insistently placing women on the culture, or social-constructionist, side of the nature/culture divide. The cogency of ecological critiques, however, gave rise to concerns that the feminist repudiation of nature was itself potentially complicit with the degradation of nature. In particular, the scholarly and inspirational work of Carolyn Merchant, Mary Daly, and Susan Griffin underlined the commonality, within the modern mechanistic culture of the capitalist West, of women's oppression and ecological degradation. Consequently, some feminists sought to rethink the women-nature connection, embracing and strengthening the link to support the claim that women are the instinctive caretakers and custodians of nature. One of the results of this realignment was the transformation of the ecological critique of anthropocentrism into a critique of androcentrism. Invariably, there was a spiritual

13. Vandana Shiva, *Staying Alive: Women, Ecology and Development* (London: Zed Press, 1988); Esther Boserup, *Women's Role in Economic Development* (London: Allen & Unwin, 1970). A survey of "women in development" literature can be found in Brinda Rao's useful *Capitalism, Nature, Socialism* pamphlet "Dominant Constructions of Women and Nature in Social Science Literature" (published by the Center for Ecological Socialism, Santa Cruz).

dimension to this critique, for this was not only a philosophy but also a religion of nature. While the male land ethic, in the tradition of Henry David Thoreau, John Muir, and Aldo Leopold, had always been infused with a deep naturalist religiosity, and while ecological activism was ever distinguished by its evangelical zeal, ecofeminism brought a supernatural element to this spirituality in the form of the earth-based Goddess religions. The inspirational basis for what is essentially a liberation theology lay in the myths, symbols, and ritual practices of pagan traditions of nature-worship, Wiccan, pre-Christian creation-centered cults, or in Native American religions, all of which rest upon the principle of immanent spirituality and subscribe to a holistic worldview of the interconnectedness of human and nonhuman nature. In this respect, ecofeminist spirituality shares in the broad New Age response, over the last two decades, of holistic alternative cultures to the materialist civil religion of scientific and technological rationality.

One result of this strong infusion of neomysticism has been the born-again, Great Revivalist feel of much of ecofeminist thought and literature. The heady combination of poetry, political analysis, experiential confession, inspirational philosophy, and chutzpah magic to be found in the work of Starhawk, for example, has become one of the more influential house styles of the movement, a distinctive strategy of personal empowerment that she describes as "power-from-within," as opposed to the destructive patriarchal tradition of "power-over."[14] A modern urban witch's invocation of the power of Great Goddess can be a useful, humorous political strategy for "bending and shaping reality," as she puts it,[15] and thus for defamiliarizing the given daily truths of a culture ideologically saturated with militaristic values.

Interest in the Great Goddess has been more than inspirational, however, for it has given rise to a full-blown ecofeminist philosophy of history that often threatens to mire debates about the social origins of ecological domination. It is often unclear how seriously the imperative of reclaiming the values of prepatriarchal, earth-worshiping tribal cultures are to be taken. Andreé Collard's sentiments are quite typical. In the introduction to her well-known book *Rape of the Wild* (1988), she asserts that she does not "believe in trying to reverse time, and 'go primitive,' but it is important to broaden our

14. Starhawk, *Dreaming the Dark: Magic, Sex and Politics* (Boston: Beacon Press, 1982); *Truth or Dare: Encounters of Power, Authority and Mystery* (San Francisco: Harper & Row, 1988).

15. Starhawk, "Feminist, Earth-Based Spirituality, and Ecofeminism," in *Healing the Wounds: The Promise of Ecofeminism*, ed. Judith Plant (Philadelphia: New Society, 1989), 175.

understanding of the past and learn from other cultures and other times the way of universal kinship."[16] Despite this concession, the spirit of the book's polemic is more in line with Anne Cameron's atavistic suggestion, cited with approval by Collard, that "there is a better way of doing things. Some of us remember that way."[17] By the end of the book, she has prepared the way for a grand historical sweep:

> Historically our destiny as women and the destiny of nature are inseparable. It began within earth/goddess worshiping societies which celebrated the life-giving and life-sustaining powers of women and nature, and it remains despite our brutal negation and violation in the present. Women must re-member and re-claim our biophilic power. Drawing upon it we must make the choices that will affirm and foster life, directing the future away from the nowhere of the fathers to the somewhere that is ours—on this planet—now.[18]

There are a number of leaps condensed in this move, from an initial waiver, to an assertion of female privilege, to the final declaration of historical truths. It goes like this: We do not want to return to the past, but we ought to seek to reclaim what we have lost even though we have always had it and always will.

To understand what lies behind these rhetorical moves is to consider a philosophy of history that draws heavily upon the work of archaeologists and scholars of religion in the Neolithic period of "Old Europe," from 7000 to 3000 B.C., when egalitarian, peace-loving, nature-worshiping societies are held to have flourished in advance of the patriarchal, warrior tribes from Eurasia that destroyed the old matricentric way of life and introduced the ways of male domination to Western culture.[19] While the Great Goddess religions subsisted, in some part, elsewhere—Isis in Egypt, Ishtar in Canaan, Demeter in Greece, Magna Mater in Rome, and Virgin Mary in global Catholicism—the authentic, prelapsarian culture survived only in Minoan Crete, and thereafter in scattered, suppressed folk rituals

16. Andreé Collard, *Rape of the Wild: Man's Violence against Animals and the Earth* (London: Women's Press, 1988), 2.
17. Collard, *Rape of the Wild*, 8.
18. Collard, *Rape of the Wild*, 168.
19. See, in particular, the works of the archaeological historian Marija Gimbutas, including *The Goddesses and Gods of Old Europe, 6500–3500 B.C.: Myths and Cult Images*, rev. ed. (Berkeley: University of California Press, 1982). See also Merlin Stone, *When God Was a Woman* (New York: Harcourt Brace Jovanovich, 1976).

and heretic pagan traditions. In search of vestiges of continuity with Old Europe, Charlene Spretnak, for example, notes "the peasant rituals that persisted in parts of Europe even up to World War I, where women would encircle the fields by torchlight and symbolically transfer their fertility to the land they touched."[20]

That Neolithic society really did flourish in the form of a matricentric paradise has been disputed long and hard, and it has often been pointed out that there exists no correlation between societies wherein God was a woman, honored by female priestesses, and the social status of women or the political freedoms of the citizenry; slavery and forced labor were the order of the day in Egypt, and human sacrifices were practiced in Minoan Crete. So, too, there is no clear evidence to suggest that the fabled Neolithic egalitarianism immediately dissolved with the introduction of animal husbandry in the transition from hunter-gatherer to agricultural societies. Most social theorists trace the origin of status hierarchy in tribal societies to internal tensions resulting from the ascendancy of elders; in other words, men and women dominated other men and women through gerontocratic privilege before men dominated women through the sexual division of labor. What does seem clear, however, is the structural, or mythical, need for a golden age of organic cooperative harmony between equal peoples that no longer exists. For ecofeminism, this Edenic society flourished in the peaceful, unfortified settlements that fell to an invader culture and was dominated by a spiritually inferior gender, just as, for classical Marxism, say, the lapsarian break occurred with the rise of class society and the emergence of private property.

In *The Death of Nature*, Carolyn Merchant's more socially oriented version of ecofeminist history, the break is located much later, during the scientific revolution, between 1500 and 1700, when a mechanistic rationalism, with its worldview of nature as passive and dead, replaced an organicist cosmology with a living female earth at its center. The dominant metaphor of social consciousness of the natural world changed from organism to machine.[21] In her more recent book, *Ecological Revolutions*, Merchant describes the transformations wrought on indigenous ecologies in New England by, first, the colonial revolution—with its transplantation of

20. Charlene Spretnak, "Ecofeminism: Our Roots and Flowering," in *Reweaving the World: The Emergence of Ecofeminism*, ed. Irene Diamond and Gloria Orenstein (San Francisco: Sierra Books, 1990), 9.
21. Merchant, *Death of Nature*.

European animals, plants, pathogens, and peoples—and then by the capitalist revolution, beholden to a dynamic market economy that extinguished the subsistence farming of the colonial farmer and the indigenous trader alike. In quick succession, then, indigenous hunting and trading economies were displaced by rival settler agricultures and then drawn into a system of worldwide mercantile exchange that soon came to exploit profitably the link between enslaved African labor, American natural resources, and European capital.[22] The ethic of market production for long-term profit displaced production for short-term subsistence. Males replaced females in the fields, plows replaced hoes, maps replaced an animistic sense of space and place. What was lost was quite clear-cut in Merchant's account: the mimetic consciousness of a hunter-gatherer economy, in which humans, animals, and plants coexist as reciprocal face-to-face subjects—"an active spiritual world of maternal ancestry regulated through participatory consciousness," where "the natural and spiritual were not distinct nor were people denigrated by association with the wild."[23] And what was won? A nature-culture dichotomy, a transcendental god, and the fetishism of commodities. Merchant does not give us much of a choice here. The good organic life, of course, is irretrievably lost, as it must be for all origin stories, especially ecological ones that separate us from paradise at the same time as they blissfully deliver us from the messiness of history.

The lapsarian myth notwithstanding, Merchant's concept of "ecological revolutions" is a useful one. Such revolutions, she writes, "arise from changes, tensions, and contradictions that develop between a society's mode of production and its ecology, and between its modes of production and reproduction. These dynamics in turn support the acceptance of new forms of consciousness, ideas, images, and worldviews."[24] The point is to underline the historical agency of the natural world (as opposed to underlining the mechanism's inert nature) and to reintroduce nonhuman nature as an actor that either acquiesces to human interventions or resists them by evolving. The ecological, then, becomes a determining factor in historical analysis, alongside the economic, the political, the cultural, the demographic, and so on. While Merchant is careful to insist on the socially constructed character of the conceptions of nature that she dis-

22. Carolyn Merchant, *Ecological Revolutions: Nature, Gender, and Science in New England* (Chapel Hill: University of North Carolina Press, 1989), 55.
23. Merchant, *Death of Nature*, 50.
24. Merchant, *Death of Nature*, 3.

cusses, the binary value system used to divide her organic paradise from our fallen, rationalist world feeds into the nature-culture dualism affirmed by more essentialist ecofeminists, for whom biological reproduction, and not social reproduction, is the ground of all political value. Merchant has little, if anything, to say about the social ecology of the rationalist culture that succeeded her golden age: the contradictions of patriarchal capitalism, both libertarian and repressive; the radical democratic legacies of individual rights and freedoms; the Enlightenment idea of the public sphere; the formation of the centralized nation-state; the emancipatory potential of science; and so on. However mechanistic, instrumental, and utilitarian, it also has to be said that rationalism has thrown up evolved institutions that are not necessarily linked to capitalism's grow-or-die ethic and that are the immediate social context and imaginative horizon of most people's lives in an advanced technological society. This complex of circumstances and traditions cannot be dismissed as male property, whether in the modern or in the post-Neolithic period, without shutting out from history altogether the experience of too many people, especially women, and without forgetting all of the long struggles against hierarchical domination and injustice, which must be maintained and developed in some form if the domination of nature is now to be opposed.

Social ecologists, like Murray Bookchin, have long insisted that the roots of today's global ecological crisis are intrinsically social and not "natural." If the domination of nature evolved out of forms of social domination related to gender, race, class, and age, then it cannot be addressed as a separate issue. Among the prominent ecofeminists sympathetic to Bookchin's position, Ynestra King has suggested that the domination of man over woman is nonetheless the *prototype* of these different kinds of social domination and thus worthy of particular attention.[25] Janet Biehl, author of *Rethinking Ecofeminist Politics*, the most exhaustive critique to date of atavistic nature-worship within the movement, is more skeptical of any such claim that the position of women, whether as victim or as heiress of spiritual intuition, marks them as uniquely ecological beings. To reason that women's relationship with nature is intrinsically bound up with the ecological crisis, or that women are privileged hierophants of nature's mysteries, is to accept the patriarchal conception of what women ought to be. Biehl finds the irrationalism of ecofeminism to be an "embarrassing" and "regres-

25. Ynestra King, "The Ecology of Feminism and the Feminism of Ecology," in *Healing the Wounds: The Promise of Ecofeminism*, 19.

sive" tendency that has muddied the once clear waters of radical feminism's commitment to claiming for women the benefits of Enlightenment thought in matters of equality:

> As a woman and a feminist, I deeply value my power of rationality and seek to expand the full range of women's faculties. I do not want to reject the valuable achievements of Western culture on the claim that they have been produced primarily by men. . . . We cannot dispense with millennia of that culture's complex social, philosophical, and political developments—including democracy and reason—because of the many abuses intertwined with that culture.[26]

Biehl's commitment to the rational humanist ideals and eco-anarchist politics of social ecology is steadfast throughout her book-long search for rationalist heresies. Accordingly, this veritable "witch-huntress" holds to a rather ascetic position against the gynocentric cosmologies, is scandalized by their playful supernaturalism, and is sleuth-like in tracking down inconsistencies of argument around the women-nature question. For example, she seizes on Ynestra King's suggestion that ecofeminists can "*consciously choose* not to sever the women-nature connection by joining male society. Rather, we can use it as a vantage point for creating a different kind of culture and politics that would integrate intuitive, spiritual, and rational forms of knowledge, embracing both science and magic insofar as they enable us to transform the nature-culture distinction and to envision and create a free, ecological society."[27] Interpreting this as a betrayal of King's own commitment to socialist feminism, Biehl is outraged at the pragmatic use of a "connection" that King has elsewhere asserted is "not true": "How can this ecofeminist, who has long criticized instrumental reason, justify an instrumental 'use' of something she believes is not true? . . . An ethics cannot be based on something that is factually wrong."[28] Biehl's riposte seems to reflect perfectly the position of the rational humanist in response to what is basically the doctrine of strategic essentialism, here invoked in the context of ecofeminism. King, after all, is advocating the strategic use of the essentialist women-nature connection as one of the options open to women, who need to use all the options available to them. If this "strategy" helps to confound male adversaries who also have to deal with women's rationalist side,

26. Janet Biehl, *Rethinking Ecofeminist Politics* (Boston: South End Press, 1991), 7.
27. King, "The Ecology of Feminism," 23; King's emphasis.
28. Biehl, *Rethinking Ecofeminist Politics*, 95.

then all the better. In Biehl's political world of fixed identities and crystal clear reasoning, such strategies are dishonest: Committed politics depends on cleaving to truths and should not stoop to the pragmatic exploitation of myths or beliefs; you cannot have your cake and eat it, too. For Biehl, the admission of a different logic is clearly an "error" and has "tainted" the once "promising project" of ecofeminism.[29]

To many ecofeminists, Biehl's critique will seem dogmatic, puritanical, and, yes, politically correct, redolent of all of the bad attitudes of the sectarian Left. Bookchin's swinging attack on deep ecology of a few years ago met with a similar response. The new social movements, after all, are supposed to be the home of diversity, where politics is infused with more experimental forms of pleasure and personality than the older, more austere Left was wont to recognize. For an Emma Goldman, it was all about being allowed to dance. For a Starhawk, it may be about being allowed to cast a spell or two. Some see this as innocuous enough, others see it as the beginning of the end. Still others see it as a way of transforming the style of politics itself.

Biehl is more literal-minded than most. In her view, magic "*never* works—unless sheer coincidences come into play."[30] One wonders, then, about her attitude toward ideology, which presents itself as orthodox, up-to-date knowledge about eternal wisdoms and yet hovers somewhere between those categories of knowledge that we designate as belief, mythology, truth, disinformation, propaganda, and common sense. Magic surely presents itself as the converse: unorthodox, ancient knowledge about the latest truths. As proscribed knowledge, its symbolic power appeals to those in needy pursuit of autonomy. Look, for example, at the strategic use of black magic and satanism by teenage metalheads in the wilds of suburbia. The point of this is surely to confirm parents' worst fears about their own loss of authority and influence over their children. As a strategy, it leads more often to parental hysteria than to understanding or self-criticism, but it is one of the few modes of empowerment available to kids whose lives are highly regulated by authorities and institutions. Feminists practicing witchcraft play a similar sort of game with patriarchy. Indeed, it has become a conventional strategy of identity politics for all sorts of groups to reclaim stereotypes of themselves, including derogatory labels ("queer," "nigger," "bitch") from the dominant culture in a bid to establish control over their

29. Biehl, *Rethinking Ecofeminist Politics*, 5.

30. Biehl, *Rethinking Ecofeminist Politics*, 91; Biehl's emphasis.

own social and cultural identities. Since they feed into long-standing sexist characterizations of "feminine irrationality," the goddess mythologies espoused by ecofeminism are part of the same response. At best, they are embraced with a sense of humor and in the name of utopian creativity. At worst, they are enforced with a fundamentalist's fervor, whose utopias lie in prehistory, in a world now lost, with little persuasive hold upon a modern social environment.

The progressive ideologies of the post-Enlightenment period have promised us that our utopias lie inevitably in the future, not in the past. With the techno-scientific narrative of progress everywhere impeded by the toxic clouds of the ecological crisis, other nondystopian mythologies are clearly needed. If they are to be elements of a survivalist philosophy, then they must make sense of the lived, daily experience of people in advanced technological societies. If they are to move people beyond their short-term interests, then they must appeal to our social memory of past communal desires and to the creative imagination of diverse futures, without collapsing back into either millennial or year-one mythologies.

Cyborg Green

The most audacious effort at drafting such a mythology remains Donna Haraway's "Cyborg Manifesto," which is, perhaps, best read in the context of ecofeminist supernaturalism, for it is presented as a blasphemous, heretical tract that regards the cyborg myths it propagates with deep, irreverent irony.[31] In every respect, Haraway's mythology is disloyal to the principles of ecofeminist spirituality. In contrast to the atavism of the goddess myths, the cyborg, the "illegitimate offspring of militarism and patriarchal capitalism," is so unfaithful to origins that it "would not recognize the Garden of Eden."[32] For the cyborg, there are no ancestral homes to dream about, no egalitarian matriarchies or phallic mothers, no prelapsarian havens of unalienated labor or pre-oedipal sexuality; the cyborg is "completely without innocence"[33] and is a stranger to institutional promises of redemption and salvation. Cyborgism is hardly immanent in the earth, but its

31. Donna Haraway, "A Cyborg Manifesto: Science, Technology, and Socialist-Feminism in the Late Twentieth-Century," in *Simians, Cyborgs, and Women: The Reinvention of Nature* (New York: Routledge, 1991).
32. Haraway, "A Cyborg Manifesto," 151.
33. Haraway, "A Cyborg Manifesto," 151.

hybrid spirit is manifest everywhere in today's postindustrialist economies, where the boundaries between human and machine, human and animal, are daily breached. As such, it is a myth for workers within the new information and surveillance networks, a myth for bodies in the grip of medical technologies, and a myth for all those in late capitalist militarism's "belly of the beast."

Haraway's infidel mythology extends to the quixotic personification of nature itself as a "coding trickster."[34] On the face of it, this sounds like profane ecology. Radical ecologists traditionally stand against an anthropocentric worldview that attributes human characteristics and quirks to the physical properties and nonhuman inhabitants of the natural world. Ecofeminism stands against androcentrism and endows the natural world with a logic, most often spiritual, that transcends the rapacious interests of its male dominators. In this respect, it shares, with deep ecology, the impulse to put the interests of the "earth first," reasoning that the human species/male gender is the main threat to the welfare of the wilderness.

Andreé Collard's parti pris is representative: "I am first of all always on the side of nature. Her innocence (in the etymological sense of 'not noxious') may derive from the fact that she acts not from choice but from inherent need. Whatever nature does that seems cruel and evil to anthropomorphizing eyes is done without intent to harm."[35] Collard's position here is decidedly antihumanist. Survivalist "needs" of the planet are strictly opposed to the "choices" of humans. This position, often colloquially referred to as "eco-fascist," ultimately views humans as a threatening species, whose extinction, or draconian regulation, would remove a blight from the planet. Moreover, it perceives the species as undifferentiated and pays little heed to the social and cultural complexities that characterize human societies and their interactions with the natural world. The corollary of this biocentric position is the disembodied (male) point of view of science, unclouded by essentially human concerns, which alone can understand the rationality of planetary "needs." For most ecofeminists, there is another perspective—women's—whose special relationship with nature affords them an intuitive understanding of nature's otherwise "cruel" ways.

If we are to have a more socialized conception of our relation to the natural world, then we need not only a new attitude but also a new language

34. Donna Haraway, "Situated Knowledges: The Science Question in Feminism and the Privilege of Partial Perspective," in *Simians, Cyborgs, and Women*, 201.
35. Collard, *Rape of the Wild*, 2.

that attributes autonomous agency to nonhuman nature, but one that does not exclude a sense of dialogue with human nature. The relationship, in other words, has to be a semiotic one in order to make sense as a lived relationship. Haraway offers such a vision of the natural world when she describes it as a "witty agent," with an "independent sense of humor."[36] She chooses, as a figure for this, not the primal mother but the trickster figure of the coyote from Southwest Native American myth. Dealing with the coyote is a way of acknowledging that "we are not in charge of the world" but that we are still "searching for fidelity, knowing all the while we will be hoodwinked."[37] The resulting dialogue is respectful but not innocently reverent. It acknowledges our maturity, as an evolved species, and also the necessity of our connections with an equally evolved nonhuman nature, which is capable of getting the better of us. The coyote personification itself is highly ambiguous: "'Our' relations with 'nature' might be imagined as a social engagement with a being who is neither 'it,' 'you,' 'he,' 'she,' nor 'they' in relation to 'us.'"[38] From a humanist point of view, such a relationship is entirely corrupt and incomplete, since it promises no end in self-discovery. It *is*, however, a socially intelligible relationship, and it seems to me that such an affinity ought to make sense to anyone who has felt the incompleteness of their connection to the world and yet who refuses to explain this feeling by recourse to some expression of defeat before the "mysteries" of nature.

While Haraway's cyborg myth contains the utopian vision of a "monstrous world without gender,"[39] its current manifestations continue to be coded as male and female. Who could forget the motel room scene in *The Terminator*, which gave Arnold Schwarzenegger his most famous line?—the cyborg-eye point of view shot that produced the screen readout "Fuck you, asshole." Here, surely, was the homophobic embodiment of masculine cyborg vision, guided and programmed by a military-industrial logic that needed no translation into the Hobbesian language of competitive human relations. One might think that seeing the world in this way is as natural in an advanced technological patriarchy as seeing the world from the point of view of a plant or a beaver had been in predominantly agricultural or hunter-gatherer societies. Audiences instantly appreciated this perspective as cyborgism-with-attitude, the dominant bad boy cyborg's worldview, but they also recognized its counterpoint in Sarah Connor's parting line to the

36. Haraway, "Situated Knowledges," 199.
37. Haraway, "Situated Knowledges," 199.
38. Haraway, "Introduction," *Simians, Cyborgs, and Women*, 3.
39. Haraway, "A Cyborg Manifesto," 181.

Terminator: "You're terminated, fucker." The sequel, as I noted earlier, contains Connor's remarkable fantasy about the Schwarzenegger cyborg as "a perfect father," who has no role in or control over the reproductive process but who is programmed nonetheless to protect her son, come hell or high water. One could say that this fantasy contains prepatriarchal elements (i.e., before men's consciousness of paternity set in, before they discovered their role in biological reproduction and moved to appropriate and control the process). Its debt to technological dependence makes it finally postpatriarchal, a fantasy about the "good" welfare state of the future, which sends an agent into the present as protector. This time around, the Terminator is no warrior invader, programmed to erase any human threat to the machine-dominated future. Is he an evolved, reformed species of ecoman, programmed to learn from a son who adopts him in the name of saving the planet, or is he the latest ruse of patriarchy, who looks good only because the new terminator—the real, protean cop machine—makes Freddie Krueger look like child's play? For the same reason that movie sequels do not instill our trust in reformed characters, especially in figures so terrifying in the original, Schwarzenegger's Terminator barely persuades us of his capacity for coevolution. Whatever fantasies are woven around them, terminators are a techno-fix, attitudinally related, by kinship, to the dysfunctional nerd sensibility of their creators that is so prevalent in the AI and robotics communities.

Male cyborgs are still very much sexually different. For the men who can afford it, the cyborg myth is a narrative of domination in a world where they are fully empowered to inhabit the firmest ground of masculinity. For those who cannot afford it, cyborgism is a familiar tale of survivalism in a world where forms of social ecology that would promote coevolution in the name of sexual politics are still very much a luxury. With these kinds of historical lineage, the humanist fantasy of self-discovery cannot help but be destructive. Male cyborgs, whatever their constitution, won't recognize Bly's Wild Man and are more likely to "find" themselves in the cyberspace of virtual reality than in the wilderness or on a dude ranch. What is more important for men right now? Withdrawal from the social fray in search of some late-breaking rite of passage? Or the self-conscious reinhabitation of the world of social reproduction—a world different from, but not unrelated to, the world of the food chain and the water cycle—in order to champion change, with humor, with passion, and with politics?

"Greatness": Philology and the Politics of Mimesis

Marjorie Garber

It is natural to believe in great men.

—Emerson, "Uses of Great Men"

"Some are born great, some achieve greatness, and some have greatness thrust upon them." This essay addresses the cultural fantasy of heroes and greatness—the fantasy of "greatness" as something recognizable and objectified—and the ways in which that designation, that epithet, informs and structures our culture. *Greatness*, as a term, is today both an inflated and a deflated currency, shading over into categories of notoriety, transcendence, and some version of the postmodern fifteen minutes of fame.[1]

Today, "greatness" sometimes functions rhetorically as pure boilerplate. For example, at the conclusion of the recent American trade embassy to Japan, the Japanese prime minister, Kiichi Miyazawara, having bluntly

1. This essay was originally conceived, in a shorter form, for a panel on "Philology and the Politics of Mimesis" at the 1991 meeting of the Modern Language Association in San Francisco.

accounted for America's decline as a world power because of problems like AIDS, homelessness, and declining educational standards, politely predicted that Americans will overcome these problems "because America is a great country."[2] At other times, "greatness"—so often linked, in our national rhetoric, with "America"—seems to be its own, tautologous ground of self-evident truth. For example, the announcement of the U.S. Postal Service's plan to issue an Elvis Presley commemorative stamp—thus officially declaring Elvis dead, as well as transcendent—was greeted with pleasure by a 72-year-old Vermont woman who had written the Postmaster General almost every week since the King's death, pushing for an Elvis commemorative: "I can't imagine anybody more deserving to be put on a stamp than my Elvis," she told the *New York Times*. "I'm not one of those who believes he's not dead. He's dead, unfortunately. He was a great man, a great American. I knew that the first time I laid eyes on him in that black leather suit."[3]

I am interested not only in literary representations of greatness but also in the cultural stature of contemporary heroic figures as diverse as JFK, Martin Luther King, Paul de Man, and Bess Myerson; in politicians and entertainment figures; and in sports heroes like Muhammad Ali, who had the spectacular boldness to claim the title of greatness for himself—"I am the greatest"—in a gesture of self-nomination that is the rhetorical equivalent of Napoleon's self-crowning.

In what follows, I will be analyzing the mechanisms for producing greatness in a number of different contexts, from the politics of our so-called national pastime to the politics of the so-called Great Books, from a children's story to a presidential campaign. This is a big topic, and I will touch on a number of related issues in order to sketch out its parameters. Let me begin by establishing a couple of quick benchmarks, fairly straightforward instances in which greatness is produced as an effect of mimesis, with consequences that are political, ideological, and cultural, while appearing, to some eyes at least, to be none of these.

My investigations have taken me from Aristotle's *Poetics* to L. Frank Baum's *The Wonderful Wizard of Oz*, in which the wonderful Wizard, appearing severally to Dorothy and her friends as an enormous head without a body, a lovely lady, a terrible beast, and a ball of fire, introduces himself: "I

2. Colin Nickerson, "Assessing the Summit: Lost Face, Lost Opportunity," *Boston Globe*, 11 Jan. 1992, 8.

3. B. Drummond Ayres, Jr., "Millions of Elvis Sightings Certain in '93," *New York Times*, 11 Jan. 1992, 6.

am Oz the Great and Terrible."[4] Oz is a nice instance of Lacan's "sujet supposé savoir," the one who is supposed to know—and, of course, he turns out (perhaps like Lacan's all-knowing psychoanalyst) to be a humbug and a ventriloquist: "Pay no attention to that man behind the curtain," blusters the voice of Oz in the MGM film, when Dorothy's familiar, the little dog Toto, tugs away the hangings to disclose a frightened little man pulling levers behind the scenes. (Here, we could footnote, were we so inclined, another dictum from Lacan: "[The phallus] can play its role only when veiled.")[5] The film is more cynical than the book on the question of "greatness"; the Wizard's main speech, written for W. C. Fields, who declined the part, has him handing out a diploma in place of the Scarecrow's wished-for brains, a plaque in place of the Tin Woodman's heart, and a medal in place of the Lion's courage. Significantly, what are today in politics called "character issues" (brains, courage, heart) are thus here explicitly fetishized and commodified, displayed as assumable attributes of the surface.

Baum's *Wizard of Oz*, as it happens, was published in 1900, the same year as another seminal text on wish fulfillment—Freud's *Interpretation of Dreams*. Lacan's essay "The Signification of the Phallus," by what may or may not be coincidence, was first delivered as a lecture in 1958, the same year as Jean Genet's play *The Balcony*, which likewise turns on the consequences of the unveiling of the phallus. *The Balcony* is a wonderfully rich text for the discussion of greatness, heroes, and the politics of mimesis, since it takes place in a brothel where clients pay to enact their erotic fantasies while dressed as pillars of society's institutions: the Judge, the Bishop, and the General.

The Chief of Police, also known as the Hero, is disconsolate because no one has yet asked to impersonate him, to play his part—the Chief of Police—in a sexual studio of fantasy. To enhance his appeal, he is advised to appear in the form of "a gigantic phallus, a prick of great stature."[6] This will enable him, he thinks, to "symbolize the nation." Let this fantasmatic giant phallus, like the giant disembodied head of the Great Oz, stand as a clear example of the politics of mimesis. The Police Chief's companions, the Judge and the Bishop, are dumbfounded:

4. L. Frank Baum, *The Wonderful Wizard of Oz* (New York: Dover Publications, 1960), 127. All subsequent references to this text will be abbreviated *WWO*.
5. Jacques Lacan, "Signification of the Phallus," in *Écrits: A Selection*, trans. Alan Sheridan (New York: W. W. Norton, 1977), 288.
6. Jean Genet, *The Balcony*, trans. Bernard Frechtman (New York: Grove Press, 1958), 78. All subsequent references to this text will be cited as *Balcony*.

> *The Judge*: A phallus? Of great stature? You mean—enormous?
> *The Chief of Police*: Of my stature.
> *The Judge*: But that'll be very difficult to bring off.
> *The Chief of Police*: Not so very. What with new techniques in the rubber industry, remarkable things can be worked out.
> *The Bishop (after reflection)*: . . . To be sure, the idea is a bold one . . . it would be a formidable figure-head, and if you were to transmit yourself in that guise to posterity . . . .
> *The Chief of Police (gently)*: Would you like to see the model? (*Balcony*, 78)

This scheme, in fact, never does quite come off. The fantasy of the Hero unveiled as a phallic figurehead is revised in practice, as the character of the revolutionary Roger does choose to impersonate the Hero, but mimetically, as Chief of Police, dressing in his clothes, even wearing his toupee. Like the other pretenders in the brothel, Roger wears the traditional footwear of ancient tragedy, cothurni about twenty inches high, so that he towers over the "real" Hero and the others onstage. The Police Chief is ecstatic: "So I've made it?" he asks, and declares, "Gentlemen, I belong to the Nomenclature" (*Balcony*, 92).

Roger, in turn, mistakes the role for the real: "I've a right to lead the character I've chosen to the very limit of his destiny . . . of merging his destiny with mine" (*Balcony*, 93). Dramatically, he takes out a knife and, according to Genet's stage direction, "makes the gesture of castrating himself" (*Balcony*, 93). After this, the Chief of Police, ostentatiously feeling his own balls, heaves a sigh of relief:

> *The Chief of Police*: Mine are here. So which of us is washed up? He or I? Though my image be castrated in every brothel in the world, I remain intact. . . . An image of me will be perpetuated in secret. Mutilated? (*He shrugs his shoulders*.) Yet a low Mass will be said to my glory. . . . Did you see? Did you see me? There, just before, larger than large, stronger than strong, deader than dead? (*Balcony*, 94)

This is the apotheosis of the Hero, performed in a place called the Mausoleum Studio, since the dissemination of the Hero's image—as we have already seen with Elvis—is coterminous with his death: "The truth [is] that you're dead, or rather that you don't stop dying and that your image, like your name, reverberates to infinity" (*Balcony*, 92). Such is the reality of the brothel, the place of greatness as mimesis. "Judges, generals, bishops, chamberlains, rebels," says the Madam of the House to her customers in the play's closing lines, "I'm going to prepare my costumes and studios for tomorrow. . . . You must now go home, where everything—you can be quite sure—will be falser than here" (*Balcony*, 96).

"You must now go *home*, where everything—you can be quite sure—will be falser than here." The instruction, the desire, or the necessity to go home again, to quit the fantasy world of greatness, is another move that links Dorothy's adventures in Oz, and her longing for Kansas, with the world inside—and outside—Genet's theatrical brothel. *Make-believe* is a term that unites these fantasy worlds. "It's make-believe that these gentlemen want," says the brothel madam (*Balcony*, 61), and Oz meekly confesses that he has been only "making believe":

> "Making believe!" cried Dorothy. "Are you not a great Wizard?"
> "Hush, my dear," he said, "don't speak so loud, or you will be overheard—and I should be ruined. I'm supposed to be a Great Wizard."
> "And aren't you?" she asked.
> "Not a bit of it, my dear; I'm just a common man."
> (*WWO*, 184)

Or, as the Scarecrow points out, to Oz's evident pleasure, a "humbug" (*WWO*, 184). That this is what greatness *is*—that greatness is not only indistinguishable from make believe and from humbug but is, in fact, necessarily dependent upon them—is the somewhat tendentious starting point of this essay.

Dorothy wants—or thinks she wants—to go home to Aunty Em, to return from the technicolor splendors of Oz to the sepia "reality" of Kansas. The customers in Genet's brothel are sent home to a "real" world that is a pale copy of their fantasies. I want now to point out that the uncanniness of the return home, the simultaneity, in Freud's now-familiar argument, of the *Heimlich* and the *Unheimlich*, the home-like and the uncanny, something "familiar and old-established . . . which has been estranged by the process of repression,"[7] is persistently literalized in contemporary American culture through the figure of baseball, another fantasy world, or "field of dreams," in which greatness is figured as the capacity to control the return home, through the agency of the "home run."

7. Sigmund Freud, "The Uncanny," in *The Standard Edition of the Works of Sigmund Freud*, ed. James Strachey (London: The Hogarth Press and the Institute of Psycho-Analysis, 1955), 17:241.

A clear example of this tendency appears in the recent film *Hook*, made by America's own Oz figure, Steven Spielberg, as a rewriting of *Peter Pan* for the 1990s. For me, Spielberg's film loses all the magic of the original, not incidentally because of the "normalization" of Pan in the figure of a childish middle-aged male actor, Robin Williams, rather than a woman cross-dressed as the eternal boy. But in a crucial moment in *Hook*, when Peter's son Jack has been captured, Hook attempts to seduce his affections by replaying a scene in which the "real" father, Peter Banning/Robin Williams, failed his son by not showing up at a baseball game. The son struck out; the team lost. Captain Hook restages the baseball game in Neverland, with Jack as the hero, and posts his pirate minions in the crowd with placards. Each pirate holds a card with a letter, and the sequence is intended to spell out the slogan "Home Run, Jack." The pirates, however, being British rather than American, are unfamiliar with the terminology of the game and get their terms confused. Instead of "Home Run, Jack," the hortatory message that greets the batter at the plate is the subliminal one that surfaces: "Run Home, Jack." A great deal of the film turns on the question of which place *is* home: "I *am* home," the son, flushed with the pleasure of the ball game and the home run, defiantly tells his father in Neverland.

In the movie *Field of Dreams*, the protagonist's unconscious desire to recuperate his relationship with his dead father is accomplished through the mediation of the father's own baseball hero, Shoeless Joe Jackson, the star player unfairly disgraced, debarred from heroism, greatness, and professional baseball itself by the Black Sox scandal of 1919. Building his baseball field in the middle of an Iowa cornfield ("Toto, I think we're not in Kansas anymore"), he, too, restages an American drama of greatness: Shoeless Joe and the Black Sox get to play baseball again, reversing the ban placed on them by the baseball commissioner, and the dead father returns as a young man in baseball uniform to play catch with his now grown son. (It is of some small interest that the ghostly baseball players, returning to the boundary of the cornfield into which they disappear each evening after the game, jokingly call out to the living spectators a famous phrase from *The Wizard of Oz*, "I'm melting, I'm melting"—the last words of the Wicked Witch.)

Furthermore, this configuration of baseball commissioner, banned and disgraced hero, and the fantasy of return ("Run Home, Jack") is not, of course, a story only of the distant past, for the story itself subsequently returned, in the controversy between Cincinnati Reds baseball star Pete

Rose, banned from professional baseball for allegedly betting on games, and the commissioner who banned him, the late A. Bartlett Giamatti. The confrontation between the two men was dramatic, based and grounded (so to speak) in notions of greatness and of mimesis. Could a man be a sports hero, especially for children, when he violated baseball's cardinal rules? "Authenticity," "idealism," and "integrity" were at stake, said Giamatti, so that it was necessary for Rose to be "banished" from baseball forever.[8] The tough, eloquent stance Giamatti took on the Rose case "elevated" him, wrote James Reston, Jr., "to heroic stature in America. By banishing a sports hero, he became a moral hero to the nation."[9]

Seven days after his dramatic announcement banning Rose from baseball, Giamatti himself was dead of a heart attack. When the news of his death, flashed over the television screen, reached the denizens of a Cincinnati sports bar, Rose fans broke out in a chorus from *The Wizard of Oz*: "Ding, dong, the witch is dead, the wicked, wicked, witch is dead."[10] Quite recently, however, the issue of Rose's banishment from baseball has been revived, specifically with regard to the question of greatness. Should Pete Rose be forever banned, not only from baseball but also from its Hall of Fame? *New York Times* sports columnist Dave Anderson, among others, thought not: The "best interests of baseball," he wrote, citing Giamatti's own phrase, would be served by Rose's election to the Hall of Fame.[11]

Bart Giamatti is described on the jacket blurb of his baseball book *Take Time for Paradise* as "a Renaissance scholar and former President of Yale University and of the National League."[12] (That this can be offered not as a zeugma but as a simple compound tells its own, fascinatingly American, story.) "When A. Bartlett Giamatti died," wrote *U.S. News and World Report* in a quotation given prominent place on the front cover of the paperback edition, "baseball lost more than a commissioner. It lost an expositor. A philosopher. A poet. A high priest. Giamatti plays all of those positions with distinction in *Take Time for Paradise*." Notice, if you will, the nice cross-

8. James Reston, Jr., *Collision at Home Plate: The Lives of Pete Rose and Bart Giamatti* (New York: HarperCollins, 1991), 306.

9. Reston, *Collision at Home Plate*, 308.

10. Reston, *Collision at Home Plate*, 312.

11. Dave Anderson, "Pardon Rose, and Put Him in Hall," reprinted in the *Miami Herald*, 5 Jan. 1992, sec. 3C.

12. A. Bartlett Giamatti, *Take Time for Paradise: Americans and Their Games* (New York: Summit Books, 1989). All subsequent references to this text will be abbreviated *TTP*.

over phrase, "plays all of those positions." Giamatti is both philosopher and utility infielder. And, since his book is published posthumously, he is also, and very effectively, its immanent and ghostly figure of pathos.

Take Time for Paradise begins with a quote from Shakespeare's Prince Hal ("If all the world were playing holidays, to sport would be as tedious as to work"), which is all the more striking for its relevance to the concept of banishment in the *Henry IV* plays (and in *Richard II*). Giamatti's book ends with Aristotle on mimesis, cited, purposefully, in the chatty style of present-tense baseball talk, "the tone and style of our national narrative" (*TTP*, 101), a style, says Giamatti, "almost biblical in its continuity and its instinct for typology" (*TTP*, 99):

> So, now, I'm standing in the lobby of the Marriott in St. Louis in October of '87 and I see this crowd, so happy with itself, all talking baseball . . . working at the fine points the way players in the big leagues do, and it comes to me slowly, around noon, that this, *this*, is what Aristotle must have meant by the imitation of an action. (*TTP*, 101)

This (*this*) is the end of Giamatti's book. *Politics* for him—glossed both from Aristotle's *Politics* and etymologically from the word's roots in *polis*—"is the art of making choices and finding agreements in public" (*TTP*, 51), and baseball "mirrors the *condition of freedom* for Americans that Americans ever guard and aspire to," so that "to know baseball is to aspire to the condition of freedom, individually, and as a people" (*TTP*, 83; Giamatti's emphasis). In Giamatti's reading of baseball, Western culture is itself confirmed in its centrality: "Before American games are American, they are Western" (*TTP*, 30). It is, I think, highly significant that Giamatti should choose to frame this humanist argument in the context of *philology*, in a selective reading of the concept of *home*.

The crux of Giamatti's philological argument centers around nostalgia, around the *nostos*, the classical figure of return, and its relationship to "home plate, the center of all the universes, the *omphalos*, the navel of the world" (*TTP*, 86). "In baseball," he writes, citing the description of this "curious pentagram" from *The Official Baseball Rules*, "everyone wants to arrive at the same place, which is where they start" (*TTP*, 87). And "everyone" is a version of the classical hero:

> Home is the goal—rarely glimpsed, never attained—of all the heroes descended from Odysseus. . . . As the heroes of romance beginning

> with Odysseus know, . . . to attempt to go home is to go the long way around, to stray and separate in the hope of finding completeness in reunion. (*TTP*, 92–93)

Giamatti dramatizes his analogy with the empathic energy of identification:

> Often the effort fails, the hunger is unsatisfied as the catcher bars fulfillment, as the umpire-father is too strong in his denial, as the impossibility of going home again is reenacted. . . . Or if the attempt . . . works, then the reunion and all it means is total—the runner is a returned hero. . . . Baseball is . . . the Romance Epic of homecoming America sings to itself. (*TTP*, 95)

And what is *home*? Giamatti offers the following gloss:

> *Home* is an English word virtually impossible to translate into other tongues. No translation catches the associations, the mixture of memory and longing, the sense of security and autonomy and accessibility, the aroma of inclusiveness, of freedom from wariness, that cling to the word *home*. . . . *Home* is a concept, not a place; it is a state of mind where self-definition starts; it is origins—the mix of time and place and smell and weather wherein one first realizes one is an original, perhaps *like* others, especially those one loves, but discrete, distinct, not to be copied. Home is where one first learned to be separate and it remains in the mind as the place where reunion, if it were ever to occur, would happen. (*TTP*, 92)

Discrete, distinct, not to be copied. This serene nostalgia of origins is not the *home* of Freud's uncanny, the simultaneous contradictory presence of *das Heimlich* and *das Unheimlich*, "something that is secretly familiar," the return of the repressed, associated with the living dead, the unconscious, the female genitals, and the compulsion to repeat. Giamatti is untroubled by the *mise en abîme* of literary theory from Benjamin to Baudrillard, the space of infinite replication, of representation and simulacra, the postmodern condition of copies instead of originals. For Giamatti, home is the space of baseball, of middle America—the Marriott in St. Louis—and of "the Greeks." "Ancient," he says, "means Greek, for us" (*TTP*, 27).

Home, in short, is *Homer*—a name that has become in baseball parlance both a noun and a verb, signifying the ultimate achievement, the fulfillment of desire. To homer—to hit a homer—is to be a hero, to go home again.

Bart Giamatti was the founder of Yale's Great Books course on the Western tradition from Homer to Brecht and the author of a study of the earthly paradise in the Renaissance epic. He was a premier and eloquent defender of the concept of humanism in literary studies, and an explicit champion of both the traditional literary canon and—as these quotations will have demonstrated—the capacity of "great literature" to inform and shape human life. What I want to emphasize in citing these passages is both the conservatizing use of the canon to enforce a politics of mimesis, inclusion and exclusion, and the crucial role of *philology* in apparently establishing a ground for such a claim.

Philology and the politics of mimesis. The ideology of greatness—an ideology that claims, precisely, to transcend ideological concerns and to locate the timeless and enduring, the fit candidates though few for a Hall of Fame, whether in sports or in arts and letters—is, in fact, frequently secured with reference to a philology of origins. Yet, a specific examination of the relationship of philology to the politics of mimesis yields, as well, some interesting complications.

Consider the case of Erich Auerbach's landmark study *Mimesis: The Representation of Reality in Western Literature*, a study that takes as its starting point a sustained meditation on the concept of Homer and "home." "Readers of the *Odyssey*," the book begins without preamble, "will remember the . . . touching scene in book 19, when Odysseus has at last come home."[13] But where is "home" for Erich Auerbach?

A distinguished professor of romance philology who concluded his career as Sterling Professor at Yale, Auerbach was a Jewish refugee from Nazi persecution who was born in Berlin. Discharged from his position at Marburg University by the Nazi government, he emigrated to Turkey, where he taught at the Turkish State University, until his move to the United States in 1947. His celebrated book *Mimesis* was written in Istanbul between May 1942 and April 1945. It was published in Berne, Switzerland, in 1946, and translated into English for the Bollingen Series, published by Princeton University Press, in 1953. The politics of *Mimesis* were thus, at least in part, a politics of exile—and a politics of *nostos* and nostalgia. "Home" was the Western tradition, and the *translatio studii*.

In his epilogue to *Mimesis*, Auerbach is at pains to point out that

13. Erich Auerbach, *Mimesis: The Representation of Reality in Western Literature*, trans. Willard Trask (Garden City, N.Y.: Doubleday Anchor, 1957), 1. All subsequent references to this text will be cited as *Mimesis*.

"the book was written during the war and at Istanbul, where the libraries are not well equipped for European studies." Thus, he explains, his book necessarily lacks footnotes and may also assert something that "modern research has disproved or modified." Yet, he remarks, "it is quite possible that the book owes its existence to just this lack of a rich and specialized library. If it had been possible for me to acquaint myself with all the work that has been done on so many subjects, I might never have reached the point of writing" (*Mimesis*, 492).

This last sentiment—that reading criticism and scholarship may sometimes impede the creative process—will doubtless be familiar to all graduate students embarking on the writing of a Ph.D. thesis. Yet, it is also strikingly similar to a certain tactical enhancement of "great literature" and "greatness" in general through the evacuation of historical context. I want to suggest that the absence of a critical apparatus in a book on the evolution of the great tradition in Western letters is something more, or less, than an accident of historical contingency. Auerbach's research opportunities were limited by his circumstances; his choice of topic was not. The scholar who would later write that "our philological home is the earth; it can no longer be the nation"[14] sustained his argument through a selection of texts that he alleges were "chosen at random, on the basis of accidental acquaintance and personal preference" (*Mimesis*, 491). Out of this came a book that claimed in its subtitle, and has been taken, to set forth "the representation of reality in Western literature."

Edward Said has noted that Auerbach's alienation and "displacement" in Istanbul offers a good example of the way in which *not* being "*at home*," or "*in place*," with respect to a culture and its policing authority, can enable, as well as impede, literary and cultural analysis.[15] But what for Erich Auerbach was a wartime necessity became, for a group of U.S.-based scholars in the same period, a democratic principle of pedagogy.

I want, therefore, to move now, profiting from Giamatti's and Auerbach's speculations on home and Homer, to a consideration of the specific

14. Auerbach, "Philology and *Weltliteratur*," trans. N. and E. W. Said, *Centennial Review* 13 (Winter 1969): 17. Auerbach says, "Culture often has to do with an aggressive sense of nation, *home*, community, and *belonging*" (12; my emphasis). What Edward W. Said calls the "executive value of exile" demystifies the notions of cultural standards as "natural," "objective," and "real" (see Said, *The World, the Text, and the Critic* [Cambridge: Harvard University Press, 1983], 8–9). Notice here the difference between *real* and *realism*, the second term precisely differing from, not coincident with, the first.
15. Said, *The World, the Text, and the Critic*, 8.

kind of "greatness" embodied in the concept of the Great Books, the cultural heroes of our time for pundits from Allan Bloom to Harold Bloom. To study the "Greats" at Oxford and Cambridge is to read the ancient classics; for this generation of Americans, however, the Greats have been updated—slightly.

In search of some wisdom on this topic—of what makes the Great Books great—I decided to consult the experts: specifically, the editors of the Encyclopaedia Britannica Great Books Series, more accurately described as the *Great Books of the Western World*, first collected and published in 1952 in a Founders' Edition under the editorship of Robert Maynard Hutchins and Mortimer J. Adler.[16]

Hutchins's prefatory volume to the series, entitled *The Great Conversation: The Substance of a Liberal Education*, makes it clear that, at least in 1952, "there [was] not much doubt about which [were] the most important voices in the Great Conversation" (*GB*, xvii). "The discussions of the Board revealed few differences of opinion about the overwhelming majority of the books in the list," which included authors from Homer to Freud. "The set" continued Hutchins, "is almost self-selected, in the sense that one book leads to another, amplifying, modifying, or contradicting it" (*GB*, xvi). The Great Conversation, as Adler and his board conceived it, at the time of the election of President Eisenhower, was, it is not surprising to note, exclusively considered as taking place between European and American men, men who were no longer living at the time they were enshrined in the hard covers of "greatness." The explicit politics of the edition was, nonetheless, aggressively democratic: No "scholarly apparatus" was included in the set, since the editors believed that "great books contain their own aids to reading; that is one reason why they are great. Since we hold that these works are intelligible to the ordinary man, we see no reason to interpose ourselves or anybody else between the author and the reader" (*GB*, xxv).

The assumption here was one of enlightened "objectivity." Given a handsomely produced, uniformly bound set of volumes vetted for "greatness," the editors thought that the reader—unreflectively gendered male, an inevitable commonplace of the times—would be able to "find what great men have had to say about the greatest issues and what is being said about these issues today" (*GB*, xxv–xxvi). To aid in the process, the editors pro-

16. *Great Books of the Western World*, ed. Robert Maynard Hutchins and Mortimer J. Adler, 54 volumes (Chicago: Encyclopaedia Britannica, 1952). All subsequent references to this text will be abbreviated *GB*.

duced a curious kind of two-volume outline called the *Syntopicon*, "which began as an index and then turned into a means of helping the reader find paths through the books" (*GB*, xxv).

A chief obstacle to this process, apparently, was what Hutchins called, in a phrase later to be echoed by the likes of Bill Bennett and Lynne Cheney, "the vicious specialization of scholarship." With the help of this completely objective and apolitical edition, "the ordinary reader," we are assured, will be able to break through the obfuscating barrier of "philology, metaphysics, and history," the "cult of scholarship" that forms a barrier between him and the great authors. For example, despite the huge "apparatus" of commentary surrounding *The Divine Comedy* (an apparatus the "ordinary reader" has "heard of" but "never used"), the purchaser and reader of the Great Books will be "surprised to find that he understands Dante without it" (*GB*, xxiv).

The endpapers of *The Great Books of the Western World*, uniform throughout the fifty-four volumes, are themselves a treasure trove of information. Following Stephen G. Nichols's invitation, in his essay on "the new Philology,"[17] to inquire into the material nature of the text and its physical and cultural margins, I offer one or two brief observations about them.

The first pair of endpapers, in the front of each volume, lists the product being sold (and bought): *The Great Books of the Western World*, and the three introductory volumes that frame them, *The Great Conversation*, *The Great Ideas I*, and *The Great Ideas II* (see Figure 1). But what *are* the Great Ideas? In case we have any doubt, the editors conveniently list them for us in the second set of endpapers, the set that closes the book (see Figure 2). Remember that this is an objective, nonpolitical list, assembled by editors who "believe that the reduction of the citizen to an object of propaganda, private and public, is one of the greatest dangers to democracy" (*GB*, xiii), and that "until lately [again, 1952] there never was very much doubt in anybody's mind about which the masterpieces were. They were the books that had endured and that the common voice of mankind called the finest creations, in writing, of the Western mind" (*GB*, xi).

The Great Ideas, the preoccupations of the great authors who wrote the Great Books and who participated in the ongoing Great Conversation, in which the ordinary citizen is encouraged to think he should also take part, are listed in the second set of endpapers in alphabetical order, from Angel

17. Stephen G. Nichols, "Introduction: Philology in a Manuscript Culture," *Speculum* 65, no. 1 (January 1990): 1–10.

GREAT BOOKS OF THE WESTERN WORLD

Introductory Volumes:

1. A Liberal Education
2. The Great Ideas I
3. The Great Ideas II

---

4. HOMER
5. AESCHYLUS, SOPHOCLES, EURIPIDES, ARISTOPHANES
6. HERODOTUS, THUCYDIDES
7. PLATO
8. ARISTOTLE I
9. ARISTOTLE II
10. HIPPOCRATES, GALEN
11. EUCLID, ARCHIMEDES, APOLLONIUS, NICOMACHUS
12. LUCRETIUS, EPICTETUS, MARCUS AURELIUS
13. VIRGIL
14. PLUTARCH
15. TACITUS
16. PTOLEMY, COPERNICUS, KEPLER
17. PLOTINUS
18. AUGUSTINE
19. THOMAS AQUINAS I
20. THOMAS AQUINAS II
21. DANTE
22. CHAUCER
23. MACHIAVELLI, HOBBES
24. RABELAIS
25. MONTAIGNE
26. SHAKESPEARE I
27. SHAKESPEARE II

GREAT BOOKS OF THE WESTERN WORLD

28. GILBERT, GALILEO, HARVEY
29. CERVANTES
30. FRANCIS BACON
31. DESCARTES, SPINOZA
32. MILTON
33. PASCAL
34. NEWTON, HUYGENS
35. LOCKE, BERKELEY, HUME
36. SWIFT, STERNE
37. FIELDING
38. MONTESQUIEU, ROUSSEAU
39. ADAM SMITH
40. GIBBON I
41. GIBBON II
42. KANT
43. AMERICAN STATE PAPERS, THE FEDERALIST, J. S. MILL
44. BOSWELL
45. LAVOISIER, FOURIER, FARADAY
46. HEGEL
47. GOETHE
48. MELVILLE
49. DARWIN
50. MARX, ENGELS
51. TOLSTOY
52. DOSTOEVSKY
53. WILLIAM JAMES
54. FREUD

Figure 1. Opening endpapers to *The Great Books of the Western World* listing the product being sold therein

THE GREAT IDEAS, Volumes 2 and 3

....
ANGEL
ANIMAL
ARISTOCRACY
ART
ASTRONOMY
BEAUTY
BEING
CAUSE
CHANCE
CHANGE
CITIZEN
CONSTITUTION
COURAGE
CUSTOM AND
CONVENTION
DEFINITION
DEMOCRACY
DESIRE
DIALECTIC
DUTY
EDUCATION
ELEMENT
EMOTION
ETERNITY
EVOLUTION
EXPERIENCE

FAMILY
FATE
FORM
GOD
GOOD AND EVIL
GOVERNMENT
HABIT
HAPPINESS
HISTORY
HONOR
HYPOTHESIS
IDEA
IMMORTALITY
INDUCTION
INFINITY
JUDGMENT
JUSTICE
KNOWLEDGE
LABOR
LANGUAGE
LAW
LIBERTY
LIFE AND DEATH
LOGIC
LOVE
MAN
MATHEMATICS

THE GREAT IDEAS, Volumes 2 and 3

MATTER
MECHANICS
MEDICINE
MEMORY AND
IMAGINATION
METAPHYSICS
MIND
MONARCHY
NATURE
NECESSITY AND
CONTINGENCY
OLIGARCHY
ONE AND MANY
OPINION
OPPOSITION
PHILOSOPHY
PHYSICS
PLEASURE AND PAIN
POETRY
PRINCIPLE
PROGRESS
PROPHECY
PRUDENCE
PUNISHMENT
QUALITY
QUANTITY
REASONING

RELATION
RELIGION
REVOLUTION
RHETORIC
SAME AND OTHER
SCIENCE
SENSE
SIGN AND SYMBOL
SIN
SLAVERY
SOUL
SPACE
STATE
TEMPERANCE
THEOLOGY
TIME
TRUTH
TYRANNY
UNIVERSAL AND
PARTICULAR
VIRTUE AND VICE
WAR AND PEACE
WEALTH
WILL
WISDOM
WORLD
....

Figure 2. Closing endpapers to *The Great Books of the Western World* listing the Great Ideas

to World. Notice that this list, which includes ideas like Citizen, Constitution, Courage, Democracy, and Education, also includes entries with a more disquieting ring: Evil, Pain, Contingency, Other, and the great cornerstone of individualism, and therefore of humanist hero-making, Death.

All of these words are tamed and contained—and here we should indeed think of the Cold War containment theory—by being presented as part of a dyad. Angel, Animal, and Aristocracy stand alone; but Good and Evil, Life and Death, Necessity and Contingency, One and Many, Pleasure and Pain, Same and Other, Virtue and Vice, Universal and Particular are tethered together like the horses of the charioteer. It is perhaps too much to say that cutting free each of the dark twins in this dyad would produce an entirely different profile of great ideas and great books; but it is *not* too much to say that the last forty years of literary and cultural theory have explored, precisely, the dangerous complacencies of these binarisms, the politics of their masquerade as opposites rather than figures for one another, and the master-slave relation that informs them.

My other observation about "The Great Ideas" is one that addresses the question of packaging. On one page of this list, the ideas run alphabetically from Angel to Mathematics; on the other page, they run from Matter to World. In each case, the list fills up the entire page, with one decorative squiggle at the beginning, and one at the end. Angel to Mathematics, Matter to World. It is of some small interest, however, that the two volumes that contain the Great Ideas, the *Syntopicon*, volumes 1 and 2, choose slightly different moments to begin and end. Volume 1 ends not with Mathematics but with Love; Volume 2 thus starts with Man.

Volume 1: Angel to Love; volume 2: Man to World. You have to admit that this puts a somewhat different spin on the alphabetical iconography of greatness. Matter and Mathematics are worthy enough categories in themselves, but they seem somehow so material, lacking the humanist grandeur of Love and Man. Nor is this an accident of division based on the length of the individual articles. Angel to Love, chapters 1 to 50, the contents of the first volume, covers 750 pages; chapters 51 to 102, Man to World, the contents of the second volume, covers 809 pages. It is reasonable to think that an editorial decision has been made—and a perfectly appropriate one, given the presumptions of the Great Books project. The titles of the prefatory volumes will be an icon of the whole.

The very trope usually ascribed to deconstructionists, and to a deconstructive playfulness, the trope of chiasmus ("the politics of mimesis and the mimesis of politics"), is here quietly employed to anchor the ideology of the series; the relationship of Man to Love (*not* the relationship of Matter to Mathematics) will serve as a fulcrum, a microrelation mediating the macrorelation of Angel to World. Readers of Tillyard's *Elizabethan World Picture* and Lovejoy's *Great Chain of Being* will here recognize a familiar structure. What I find so scandalous about this whole enterprise, however, is its blithe claim that the absence of a scholarly apparatus is *preferable* because it is, apparently, *nonideological*.

I quote again from Hutchins's preface:

> We believe that the reduction of the citizen to an object of propaganda, private and public, is one of the greatest dangers to democracy. . . . The reiteration of slogans, the distortion of the news, the great storm of propaganda that beats upon the citizen twenty-four hours a day all his life long mean either that democracy must fall a prey to the loudest and most persistent propagandists or that the people must save themselves by strengthening their minds so that they can appraise the issues for themselves (*GB*, xiii). . . . [Thus,] the Advisory Board recommended that no scholarly apparatus should be included in the set. No "introductions" giving the Editors' views of the authors should appear. The books should speak for themselves, and the reader should decide for himself. (*GB*, xxv)

Angel to Love; Man to World.

I want now to turn to another crucial text of the same year, 1952, a work not included in Hutchins and Adler's Great Books Series, but one that I myself consider a foundational midcentury American text for the making of the hero—and for the theorization of fame and greatness—through an effectively placed sound bite: E. B. White's *Charlotte's Web*.[18]

You will recall that in White's tale, Wilbur, the innocent, unworldly pig, is threatened by a "plot" to turn him into smoked bacon and ham. " 'There's a regular conspiracy around here to kill you at Christmastime,' " an old sheep tells him, complacently. "Everybody is in on the plot"—the farmer, the hired hand, and, unkindest cut of all, the allegorically named John Arable, whose daughter Fern was Wilbur's first foster mother, and who is himself now—according to the old sheep—about to arrive, shotgun in hand, to slaughter Wilbur the pig in time for the holidays (*CW*, 49).

Wilbur's story is a classic fable of nature and culture, or of the transi-

18. E. B. White, *Charlotte's Web* (New York: HarperCollins, 1952). All subsequent references to this text will be abbreviated *CW*.

tion from the Imaginary to the Symbolic. The dyadic, prefallen, and preoedipal world inhabited by Wilbur and Fern Arable, in which the infant Wilbur is fed with a bottle like a human baby and wheeled about in a baby carriage, is disrupted by farmer Arable's decision that " 'Wilbur is not a baby any longer and he has got to be sold' " (*CW*, 12). The purchaser, a near neighbor and relation, is John Arable's brother-in-law, Homer Zuckerman.

Nature and Homer were, he found, the same, says Pope of the poet of the *Georgics*, but for Wilbur, the move down the road from *Arable*'s farm to that of his brother-in-law *Homer* is precisely a move from nature to culture. With the threat of impending death, Wilbur is translated into a far more dangerous—but also potentially more heroic—world of language, a world, in fact, in which philology does produce a politics of mimesis. It is in Uncle Homer's barn that Wilbur meets Charlotte the spider, whose instincts for publicity—and for understanding the way signification follows the sign—will be his salvation. Charlotte has a plan.

"Some Pig!" she writes neatly, in block letters, in the middle of her web, to be discovered in the morning by the hired hand. "Some Pig!" The word spreads quickly. " 'Edith, something has happened,' " farmer Zuckerman reports to his wife "in a weak voice." " 'I think you had best be told that we have a very unusual pig' " (*CW*, 79).

> A look of complete bewilderment came over Mrs. Zuckerman's face. "Homer Zuckerman, what in the world are you talking about?"
>
> "This is a very serious thing, Edith," he replied. "Our pig is completely out of the ordinary."
>
> "What's unusual about the pig?" asked Mrs. Zuckerman. . . .
>
> "Well, I don't really know yet. . . . But we have received a sign. . . . [R]ight spang in the middle of the web there were the words "Some Pig." . . . A miracle has happened and a sign has occurred here on earth, right on our farm, and we have no ordinary pig."
>
> "Well," said Mrs. Zuckerman, "it seems to me you're a little off. It seems to me we have no ordinary *spider*."
>
> "Oh, no," said Zuckerman. "It's the pig that's unusual. It says so, right there in the middle of the web." (*CW*, 79–81)

Such is the power of publicity. "Some Pig" is, of course superbly chosen as an epithet of praise, since it could mean anything, and shortly does. " 'You know,' " muses Mr. Zuckerman, this time in "an important voice," " 'I've thought all along that that pig of ours was an extra good one. He's a solid pig. That pig is as solid as they come' " (*CW*, 81). " 'He's quite a pig,' " says Lurvy the hired hand. " 'I've always noticed that pig. . . . He's as smooth as they come. He's some pig.' " In days, the rumor has spread through the county, and "everybody knew that the Zuckermans had a wondrous pig" (*CW*, 82–83).

Philology enters the story explicitly through the quest for new signs and new slogans, since "Some Pig," though a good, all-purpose characterization, soon begins to seem stale, and other suggestions are sought from the barnyard animals. What should be written next in the web? "Pig Supreme" is rejected as too culinary in association—" 'It sounds like a rich dessert,' " says Charlotte—but "Terrific" will do, even though Wilbur protests that he's *not* terrific. " 'That doesn't make a particle of difference,' " replies Charlotte, " 'Not a particle. People believe almost anything they see in print. Does anybody here know how to spell "terrific"?' " (*CW*, 89).

The chief agent of philological instrumentality, however, is the barn's resident research assistant, Templeton the Rat, whose nocturnal foraging in the local dump produces scraps of paper—advertisements torn from old magazines—that will provide Charlotte with something to copy. Not every piece of research pays off. "Crunchy" (from a magazine ad) and "Pre-Shrunk" (from a shirt label) are both discarded as inappropriate to a discourse of fame and transcendence. *Crunchy*, says Charlotte, is " 'just the wrong idea. Couldn't be worse. . . . We must advertise Wilbur's noble qualities, not his tastiness' " (*CW*, 98). A package of soap flakes in the woodshed, however, produces a winner: "With New Radiant Action" (*CW*, 99):

> "What does it mean?" asked Charlotte, who had never used any soap flakes in her life.
>
> "How should I know?" said Templeton. "You asked for words and I brought them. I suppose the next thing you'll want me to fetch is a dictionary." (*CW*, 99)

Together, they contemplate the soap ad, and then they send for Wilbur and put him through his paces. This is the mimesis test. " 'Run around!' commanded Charlotte, 'I want to see you in action, to see if you are radiant' " (*CW*, 100). After a series of gallops, jumps, and back-flips, the brain trust of the spider and the rat decides that, if Wilbur is not exactly radiant, he's close enough.

> "Actually," said Wilbur, "I feel radiant."
>
> "Do you?" said Charlotte, looking at him with affection. "Well, you're a good little pig, and radiant you shall be. I'm in this thing pretty deep now—I might as well go the limit." (*CW*, 101)

In sequence, then, the web declares Wilbur to be "Some Pig," "Terrific," "Radiant," and, finally, "Humble," a word Templeton finds on a scrap of folded newspaper, and one Charlotte glosses for him:

> "Humble?" said Charlotte. " 'Humble' has two meanings. It means 'not proud' and it means 'near the ground.' That's Wilbur all over. He's not proud and he's near the ground." (*CW*, 140)

Indeed, Charlotte the spider is the book's learned philologist, the erudite definer of terms like *gullible, sedentary, untenable*, and *versatile*, a scholar whose Latin is as good as her English. She describes her egg sac as her "*magnum opus*" (*CW*, 144), explaining to Wilbur, whose Latin is weak, that a magnum opus is a great work (*CW*, 145). (Neither Wilbur nor Charlotte seem to speak pig latin, the obvious lingua franca for the great conversation in the barnyard.) As this concept of a great work implies, Charlotte is also, ultimately, the book's figure of humanist aesthetic pathos, a self-described writer who foretells her own demise: " '[Humble] is the last word I shall ever write' " (*CW*, 140). Her death displaces Wilbur's and preserves him as a hero, as "Zuckerman's Famous Pig" (*CW*, 133).

The name of Wilbur's new owner, Homer Zuckerman, introduces into this little fable a tonic note of culture and, indeed, of both the Great Books and the paternal Law. That this Homeric nomination is not entirely trivial may be discerned by considering again the identity of the media agent in Wilbur's story, the resourceful Charlotte, a spider with a magic web. Charlotte, this uncanny precursor of the modern "spin-doctor," the media manipulator for political figures, is also, classically, a Penelope, weaving and unweaving her web, creating headlines that guarantee Wilbur not only his fifteen minutes of fame but also his life.

"The dissimulation of the woven texture can in any case take centuries to undo its web; a web that envelops a web, undoing the web for centuries." This is Derrida at the beginning of "Plato's Pharmacy," an essay that also begins with philological explorations, with the multiple meanings of *histos*, which means at once 'mast', 'loom', 'woven cloth', and 'spider's web'.[19] Both mast and loom; that is, both the story of Odysseus, bound to the mast, hearing the Sirens, and the story of Penelope, weaving and unweaving her web. (Is it an accident that this is also the design of Auerbach's *Mimesis*—from "Odysseus' Scar" to Mrs. Ramsay's "Brown Stocking"? A coincidence, certainly, but perhaps not altogether an accident.)

19. Jacques Derrida, "Plato's Pharmacy," in *Dissemination*, trans. Barbara Johnson (Chicago: University of Chicago Press, 1981), 63.

Recall the completely disregarded observation of Mrs. Zuckerman, on hearing the news of the miraculous web, that what they have is "no ordinary *spider*," and not, as her husband claims, "no ordinary pig." Oh, no, he assures her; the spider is quite ordinary—a common gray spider. It is the pig who is remarkable, terrific, and radiant; it says so quite clearly in the web. The text is, indeed, dissimulated behind the self-evidence of its message:

> Ever since the spider had befriended him, [Wilbur] had done his best to live up to his reputation. When Charlotte's web said SOME PIG, Wilbur had tried hard to look like some pig. When Charlotte's web said TERRIFIC, Wilbur had tried to look terrific. And now that the web said RADIANT, he did everything possible to make himself glow.
>
> It is not easy to look radiant, but Wilbur threw himself into it with a will. (*CW*, 114)

What are the politics of this mimesis?

" 'Ladeez and gentlemen,' " blared the loud speaker at the County Fair, " 'we now present Mr. Homer L. Zuckerman's distinguished pig. The fame of this unique animal has spread to the far corners of the earth' " (*CW*, 157).

> "In the words of the spider's web, ladies and gentlemen, this is some pig. . . . This magnificent animal," continued the loudspeaker, "is truly terrific. . . . Note the general radiance of this animal! Then remember the day when the word 'radiant' appeared clearly on the web. Whence came this mysterious writing? Not from the spider, we can rest assured of that. Spiders are very clever at weaving their webs, but needless to say spiders cannot write." (*CW*, 157–58)

Now, if Charlotte is a humanist, she is also a feminist. Wilbur naïvely, but unerringly, recognizes the physical stigmata of feminism, as described in the popular magazines of today. " 'You have awfully hairy legs,' " he says to her soon after they meet (*CW*, 55). Feminist theologian Mary Daly has claimed Charlotte as a fellow Spinster, tracing her ancestry from Arachne and the Spider Woman of Navajo myth, and lamenting the apparent role of the mythic female spider, however powerful, as merely the accomplice and the public relations agent of the male hero's fame.[20]

Daly's chief target here, and one worth attacking, is Joseph Camp-

20. Mary Daly, *Gyn/Ecology: The Metaethics of Radical Feminism* (Boston: Beacon Press, 1978), 396–99. Subsequent references to this text will be cited as Daly.

bell, the arch-archetypalist who is also the source for her account of the Spider Woman myth. Campbell writes, "Spider Woman with her web can control the movements of the Sun. The hero who has come under the protection of the Cosmic Mother cannot be harmed."[21] Mary Daly would prefer a more female-affirmative fable. "Is Wilbur worth it? What if the aided pig had been Wilma or Wilhelmina?" (Daly, 399). For her, Spinsters, taking their cue from "the complex and fascinating web of the spider," can spin ideas about such interconnected symbols as "the maze, the labyrinth, the spiral, the hole as mystic center . . . to weave and unweave, dis-covering hidden threads of connectedness" (Daly, 400).

There are uncanny connections between the figure of the female spider (who weaves and unweaves, who mates and kills) and the story of the hero, from Freud's essay on "Femininity" to *The Wizard of Oz* to Darwin to *Goodbye, Mr. Chips*. Despite Joseph Campbell, it is clear that the spider's transgressive and sexualized power, and, indeed, her relationship to the psychoanalytic figure of the phallic woman, renders her potentially threatening, as well as nurturant. Shakespeareans will recognize the uncanny and ambivalent power of magic in the web and of the spider in the cup. In Genet's *Balcony*, the powerful fantasmatic Queen, who never appears, is described as "embroidering and not embroidering," "embroidering an invisible (and an 'interminable') handkerchief" (*Balcony*, 62, 69). In the film *The Kiss of the Spider Woman*, the "spider woman" is a powerful, transgendered storyteller, a gay man who sometimes calls himself a woman and who "embroiders" (the word is literally used) the plots that are his own version of Penelope's web.

My point is that Charlotte's web, like the prisoner Molina's web, frames the sign. It produces an object of desire—Wilbur—who seems to stand free of the apparatus that produces him—like the Wizard of Oz, like the apparently freestanding Great Books that are, similarly, showcased as self-evidently great, decontextualized, and made into icons. Wilbur—TERRIFIC, RADIANT, and HUMBLE—emerges as something like the ideal political candidate, with only invisible strings attached.

Wilbur himself makes one vain attempt to spin a web, to become the

21. Joseph Campbell, *The Hero with a Thousand Faces* (1949; reprint, Princeton: Bollingen, 1968), 71. Campbell's reading of the place of "woman" in the heroic scheme of things can be deduced from the listing under that heading in the index: "symbolism in hero's adventures; as goddess; as temptress; Cosmic Woman; as hero's prize; *see also* mother."

self-sufficient spider-artist (albeit with string attached). Under Charlotte's indulgent direction, he climbs to the top of a manure pile with a string tied to his tail. " 'You can't spin a web, Wilbur,' " counsels Charlotte after this sorry adventure, " 'and I advise you to put the idea out of your mind. You lack two things needed for spinning a web. . . . You lack a set of spinnerets, and you lack knowhow' " (*CW*, 59). Here, again, nature and culture, or biology and destiny, are linked together. Pigs, it seems, can't fly. Or can they?

For a generation brought up on *Charlotte's Web*—for my generation—the intuition that Wilbur resembled a political candidate, and, in a way, the ideal political candidate, was literalized in one glorious gesture by Jerry Rubin and the Yippies—the Youth International Party. At the 1968 Democratic National Convention in Chicago, the Yippies nominated a pig for president, with the campaign pledge, "They nominate a president and he eats the people; We nominate a president and the people eat him."[22] Perhaps significantly, in the context of the rhetoric of nostalgia and the politics of mimesis, this pig had a classical name: "Pigasus." Who says that pigs can't fly?[23]

The tangled web of philology and the politics of mimesis—or rather, at this juncture, of politics as a version of mimesis—was actualized in the media-conscious sixties through a metonymic figure, that of the *network*, an electronic web. As in all of those old movies and newsreels, in which the concentric circles of radio signals were seen to spread out across the country in a widening ripple effect, the spin-doctors of media culture dissimulated their messages.

"*We have to be very clear on this point*," wrote Richard Nixon's speech writer, Raymond Price, "*that the response is to the image, not the man*. It's not what's there that counts; it's what's projected—and carrying it one step further," Price continued, "it's not what *he* projects but rather what the voter receives. It's not the man we have to change, but rather the *received impression*. And this impression often depends more on the medium and its use than it does on the candidate himself" (Price's emphasis).[24] As we have just seen in the case of Wilbur.

22. Abbie Hoffman, *Soon To Be a Major Motion Picture* (New York: Perigee Books, 1980), 144.
23. "The time has come, the Walrus said, / To talk of many things: / Of shoes—and ships—and sealingwax— / Of cabbages—and kings— / And why the sea is boiling hot— / And whether pigs have wings." Lewis Carroll, *Through the Looking-Glass, and What Alice Found There*, chap. 4, stanza 11.
24. Joe McGinniss, *The Selling of the President* (1969; reprint, New York: Penguin Books,

To us this is no longer a surprise. The use of advertising in political campaigns is, by now, commonplace; the *Boston Globe*, for example, currently features "Advertising Watch," a regular column in which campaign commercials are described, named (each has a title, like that of a short subject or a feature film), and analyzed for truth and political effectiveness. The work of Michael Rogin, among others, has described "Ronald Reagan, the Movie" as a commodified, empty fiction.[25] There was a time, however, when political advertising, and the involvement of ad men in political campaigns, was not only surprising but transgressive—and, if you were an ad man, both exciting and lucrative.

Journalist Joe McGinniss himself became a "nonfiction star of the first rank"—according to the bio-blurb on his book—when he wrote *The Selling of the President*, the book that exposed to the general reading public "the marketing of political candidates as if they were consumer products, . . . selling Hubert Humphrey (or Richard Nixon) to America like so much toothpaste or detergent" (*SP*, xiv). Or, as in the case of Wilbur, soap flakes. McGinniss chronicled in fascinated—and fascinating—detail the machinations of men like Raymond Price, Roger Ailes, Leonard Garment, and Frank Shakespeare in the packaging of Richard Nixon. For me, there is a certain pleasure even in the accident of these names: Price, Garment, Shakespeare, the very allegorical structure of hero-making.

The element of "Some Pig" in the Nixon success story is considerable; the back room boys work on Nixon's "personality problems," on his "lack of humor," on his need to concoct some "memorable phrases to use in wrapping up certain points," and so on (*SP*, 73–75). Sound bites are very much at issue, as are their visual counterparts, photo opportunities. At the end of a staged television panel discussion—one of a number scheduled coast-to-coast throughout the campaign—"the audience charged from the bleachers, as instructed. They swarmed around Richard Nixon so that the last thing the viewer at home saw was Nixon in the middle of this big crowd of people, who all thought he was great" (*SP*, 72).

Once again, as with the words in Charlotte's web, as with Angel to Love and Man to World, let us focus on the framing of the sign. J. Walter Thompson advertising executive Harry Treleaven, a mastermind of Nixon's

---

1988), 37; emphasis in original. All subsequent references to this text will be abbreviated *SP*.

25. Michael Rogin, *Ronald Reagan, the Movie, and Other Episodes in Political Demonology* (Berkeley: University of California Press, 1987).

first successful campaign, submitted a passionate memo explaining "Why Richard Nixon Should Utilize Magazine Advertising in the State of New Hampshire Primary":

> This writer believes firmly that the chances of overcoming Richard Nixon's cold image and the chances of *making* him loved and *making* him glamourous via commercial exposure on television (where admittedly he has not been at his best) are far less than the chances of *making* him loved and *making* him glamourous via saturation exposure of artfully conceived and produced four-color, full-page (or double spread) magazine advertisements. . . . Are women going to vote for a Richard Nixon they currently believe to be cold, unloving, unglamourous? No. . . . But rich, warm advertising in a woman's own medium, the service magazine, next to her cake mixes and her lipstick advertisement will go a long way, I believe, toward making Mr. Nixon acceptable to female viewers. . . . Warm, human, four-color magazine illustrations depicting Dick Nixon the family man, perhaps even surrounded by his beautiful family, will allow the women of America, and, initially, the women of New Hampshire, to identify with him, and his home life. . . . This warm visual image . . . will sell his qualifications to voters who can study the advertisement leisurely in their home. (*SP*, 218–19; Treleaven's emphasis)

Here is that American "home" again, full of "warm, human, four-color . . . illustrations." Run home, Dick. (Even real estate agents now sell "homes" rather than "houses"—at least in ads targeted to the middle-class "homeowner." This, too, I think, is part of the contemporary rhetoric of nostalgia.)

"It's not what's there that counts, it's what's projected," wrote Raymond Price about candidate Nixon. This pronouncement is strikingly similar to a recent remark made by rock star George Michael: "It's not something extra that makes a superstar, it's something missing."[26]

For me, the question is really not one of elegiac loss but of the political uses of nostalgia. Are great books most in need of being called "great" when their link with the culture is most tenuous? Has political life, as we commonly understand it—from Wilbur, to Nixon, to Reagan, to Bush—become an arena in which what is *imitated* is mimesis? (Recall, for example, George Bush, pretending that he buys his socks at JC Penney in an attempt

26. Interview with George Michael entitled *Music, Money, Love, Faith* (MTV Networks, 1988).

to stimulate the economy; Reagan, "remembering" wartime events that he saw, or acted, in Hollywood B-pictures; David Duke, transforming himself, by plastic surgery, into the boy next door, a matinee idol for voters who have been trained by recent history to think actors are politicians, that there is such a thing as "looking presidential.") Is "greatness" largely or entirely an effect—and if so, what kind of effect? A stage effect, a psychoanalytic effect, or an effect of nostalgia? It's not something extra, but something missing.

What is at issue is overcompensation and an anxious fantasy of wholeness, as with Oz the Great and Terrible, and with Genet's Chief of Police and his fantasy of the giant phallus. Mortimer Adler, updating his list of "Great Books, Past and Present" in 1988, lists thirty-six new white male authors who published between 1900 and 1945, and an additional eighteen authors—also all male and all white—who published between 1945 and the present. He is worried, however, about his capacity to see clearly: "Could it be that my nineteenth-century mentality . . . blind[s] me to the merit of work that represents the artistic and intellectual culture of the last forty or so years?"[27] Adler's concern is that he may fail to identify some of the great works, but he is entirely convinced not only that they are there to be found but that greatness can be pinpointed, however tautologous the test. "If we say that a good book is a book that is worth reading carefully once, and that a better book than that—a great book—is one that is worth reading carefully a second or third time, then the greatest books are those worth reading over and over again—endlessly."[28]

Wilbur, Oz, the Great Books, the Great Tradition. Greatness is an effect of decontextualization, of the decontextualizing of the sign—and of a fantasy of control, a fantasy of the *sujet supposé savoir*, of a powerful agency, divine or other. "If you build it, he will come"; "a miracle has happened and a sign has occurred here on earth, right on our farm, and we have no ordinary pig." Someone knows; someone—someone *else*—is in control. The political logic of this is as disturbing as its psychology.

"Good" books, like "competent" politicians, are, in our inflated culture, somehow not good enough. From the canon debate to the political arena, "greatness" has become an increasingly problematic standard. If we have greatness thrust upon us in either sphere, we should recognize it as

27. Mortimer J. Adler, *Reforming Education: The Opening of the American Mind*, ed. Geraldine Van Doren (New York: Collier Books, 1988), 350.
28. Adler, *Reforming Education*, 343.

an ideological category, a redundancy effect, a "recognition factor," as the pundits say. It seems clear that anxieties about greatness in literature are closely tied to anxieties about national, political, and cultural greatness, and that the more anxious the government, the more pressure is placed upon the humanities to textualize and naturalize the category of the "great." This is no reason to discard such a category entirely, even if it were possible to do so. But it is a good reason to be wary, and to pay some attention to that man behind the curtain—or, if anyone tries to sell you one, to be cautious about lionizing "some pig"—however terrific, radiant, and humble—in a poke.

"At the End of the Day": An Interview with Mairead Keane, National Head of Sinn Fein Women's Department

Laura E. Lyons

As National Head of the Women's Department, Mairead Keane has been responsible for finding out what concerns Irish women feel are important to their daily lives. Her position involves both working with other activists to advance those issues outside of Sinn Fein and formulating policies and developing educational programs that address those concerns within the party. Sinn Fein is a legally recognized political party, which operates through electoral politics in both the six counties of the North and the twenty-six counties of the Republic of Ireland to end the partition of the country resulting from British rule in the six counties since 1920. Although Sinn Fein rejects media constructions of itself as the "political wing of the Irish Republican Army," the party identifies with the goals of the IRA, while reserving the right not to endorse all IRA activities.

Electoral politics is, of course, about representation, but in all thirty-two counties of Ireland, Sinn Fein's access to representation is severely curtailed by legislation that prohibits interviews with members of Sinn Fein from being broadcast. In the six counties, the successful election to parliament of Bobby Sands through Sinn Fein during the 1981 hunger strikes led to new laws that prevent prisoners from standing as candidates and that require a five-year waiting period before ex-prisoners are allowed to campaign for office. Given the overwhelming obstacles that prevent Sinn Fein from representing their platform, it is not surprising that they hold no positions in the Republic's Dáil Éireann.

Sinn Fein works across and against the artificially imposed border of partition, and their work must necessarily take place not just in Ireland but in the international arena, as well. In addition to geopolitical borders, Mairead Keane also discusses in this interview less obvious borders, the ideological boundaries that map out both the divisions and intersections between Irish Republicanism and feminism and the roles of the church and the state, which Sinn Fein envisions for a new, secular, and democratic Ireland. These demarcations are always subject to negotiation in an ongoing process of debate that, as she points out, takes place both inside and outside the party, theoretically and on the ground.

This interview with Mairead Keane took place in Austin, Texas, on 26 March 1991, at the end of the day, her last day of a month-long trip to the United States, during which she met with students, church groups, artists, politicians, academics, activists from solidarity groups, women's organizations, and representatives from other national liberation struggles.[1] In Irish-English, "At the end of the day" suggests not just the time of this interview but a considered response, a weighing of factors that allows one to come to conclusions and say "in the final analysis," or "when all is said and done." For Sinn Fein, which means "ourselves alone" in Irish, it is the national question, the problems of partition, which must be both asked after and resolved at the end of the day.

1. Ms. Keane's visit to Austin, Texas, was funded through the generosity of Genevieve Vaughan and the Foundation for a Compassionate Society and was coordinated by the Irish Women's Studies Group. Based in New York, the Irish Women's Studies Group is composed of women in the United States who want to examine the intersection between national liberation and women's liberation in Ireland by bringing women active in the Irish Republican struggle to the United States. Sinn Fein Women's Department is located at 44 Parnell Square, Dublin 1. Telephone: 726100/726932. Fax: 733441. For more information, write to the Irish Women's Studies Group, c/o Jan Cannavan, 922 East 15th Street #1A, Brooklyn, NY 11230. I would like to thank Ann Cvetkovich, Barbara Harlow, and Lora Romero, who each read the full transcript of this interview and made valuable editorial suggestions.

• • • •

LL: I want to ask you about your background, your role as a representative of Sinn Fein, and the ways in which the two might be related. Having just read *Ten Men Dead*, by David Beresford, which is about the 1981 hunger strike, I was particularly interested in the communiqués that each man sent to Sinn Fein about himself before going on the strike. The men provided information on where they had grown up, their earliest memories of the troubles, their initial reasons for getting involved in the struggle, their arrest records, their family, and any other information they felt might be of use in mobilizing the community outside of the prison and making their case for political status. I was struck by the ways personal narrative and political history are almost inextricable in those short communiqués and by the ways these men, who were about to embark on an extraordinary protest, presented themselves as people whose stories were somewhat typical, or representative, of the history of their community. Since you are speaking as a representative of Sinn Fein Women's Department, could you say something about your own personal history and how you see that history as being important to your status as a representative?

MK: Well, you're right about the book being fascinating, and it is interesting that you should begin with the hunger strikes, because, in a way, that was how I began as an activist, as well. So, I suppose my own background had an impact in terms of where I am today, in that my involvement in Irish solidarity work began in the United States, where, at the time, I was living and going to school in southern California at Golden State College and coming to political activism—all at the same time as the hunger strikes. I had been involved just for a very short period of time with the Students for Economic Democracy, who organized on the campus at the time, and we were doing a rent control survey, canvassing in Santa Monica. Also, from literature tables, I got information on and became interested in working on the issue of El Salvador. And from that point I became politicized.

My family traditionally had been nationalists, and I was always verbally supportive of the struggle in the six counties, but at that time my support would not have gone beyond that, because in Ireland, as in other countries, we tend to live in ghettos of the mind. My family's political allegiance was Fianna Fail, which is the largest party in the twenty-six counties. My father was active in local politics as the constituency chairperson of Fianna Fail, and our family was anti-British. For example, when Michael Gaughan died on hunger strike in Britain,[2] my mother marched at the funeral. When the struggle erupted in the six counties [1969], there was massive support, but then, of course, the establishment got their act together and tried to criminalize the struggle.

And so, coming from that kind of verbalized nationalism and leaving Ireland when I did—when I was eighteen, I went to Spain to be an au pair because there was no money for college—helped to politicize me. Even at this point, I never was really interested in the war, but after I went back to school—and, again, that's how I ended up in southern California during the hunger strikes—I just started through, first, political science, because I was always interested in politics. Then, all of a sudden, I made the link, I suppose, between the reality of being verbally supportive of the struggle in Ireland and the activism I was just getting involved in on other issues. Of course, once I had that link in my head, it seemed natural to examine what was going on in my own country. Initially, the problem was: How could I get involved in Ireland while I was living in the United States? I was able to do that through Noraid [Irish Northern Aid], a solidarity group here in the United States. With Bobby Sands on hunger strike, I actively looked for a solidarity group. I finished school, worked with Noraid, and then went back to Ireland a few years after I finished school. So, in one way, I became politicized because I emigrated, and I became politicized, too, I suppose, on feminist issues through my marriage, my child, and by going back to school. There was a conscious development on my part regarding feminism. My history certainly has had an impact on my politics. And, I suppose, my role in Sinn Fein is to further interest in women's issues and in politics, and I am conscious of that.

LL: Would that be a fairly typical history of the ways women get involved in Sinn Fein? Or have more women become involved in Sinn Fein because of living in or having relatives who live in the six counties?

MK: Most people who get involved in Sinn Fein, particularly in the six counties, come from Republican families, or they see themselves, in some ways, as victims of the British occupation. People in the United States say to me, "Where are you from, Belfast or Derry?" And when I tell them I'm from Dublin, they look a bit perplexed and say, "Oh, that's in the South." People see

2. In 1976, IRA members Michael Gaughan and Frank Stagg died while on hunger strike for political status in British prisons.

the Republican struggle as a conflict exclusive to the six counties. In terms of people coming into Sinn Fein whose families aren't already involved in the party or the struggle in the six counties, it is much more difficult. For example, if I had not become involved in a solidarity group in the United States, I might not have ended up working for Sinn Fein in Ireland. The reality is that if you get involved with Sinn Fein, it means that you will be harassed by the Special Branch, that you will never have any work, and that you will live on little money. If you have a job and you belong to a union, you will never advance economically. People have to consider all those factors before they come in. On top of that, particularly with young people coming in, the Special Branch goes to their parents and says, "Oh, your son or daughter is in the IRA," to scare them off.[3] With all that, it is very difficult for people to get by it all and to join Sinn Fein. For the most part, our people are from Republican families or from working-class areas where Sinn Fein is getting involved in issues. If they are working class, they know police harassment anyway, so they are much more likely to get over that. In middle-class areas, you have to have the traditional Republican family history, because you have more to lose at the end of the day. In the six counties, the struggle is relevant to the person on the street, so our people are clear on why they should get involved. They are getting involved because they are getting beaten off the streets.

LL: In 1979, Sinn Fein established a Women's Coordinating Committee, which became, in 1980, the Sinn Fein Women's Department. Could you discuss the initial motivations for starting a separate women's division? What kinds of pressures—both within and outside the party—contributed to the formation of the Coordinating Committee?

MK: Initially, I think women came together through their involvement in the nationalist struggle, which politicized them about their own oppression, and they came together through the efforts of the women's movement, which, at the time, was campaigning in the South, largely for equality in employment and for the right to contraception. Women came together to discuss the issues that were affecting them not only as women but also as women political activists, and there was a need to have an organized political voice within

3. Actions against those who work for Sinn Fein often go beyond harassment. On 5 February 1992, an off-duty officer of the Royal Ulster Constabulary shot to death three people and wounded two others in Sinn Fein's Belfast office. The officer committed suicide after claiming responsibility for the deaths.

the party. This culminated in the discussion about departments and the need to have a separate department in which women could come together and meet as women, as women only, to discuss, to debate, and to push forward the issues important to us. There was a need for a group that would serve as a support for women within the party.

LL: What, in the early days of the department, did women see as "the issues"? Were they different from the issues that we see as women's issues today?

MK: No. I think they are still the same issues: childcare, violence against women, the occupation in the six counties, political prisoners, and the need to develop actively around the prisoners so that the campaign will get support. With the development of the department, there was a need to have a policy, and that was passed at the party conference as the Women's Policy Document, which incorporated all of those issues within a three- or four-page document and had an introduction that analyzed the fact that women were involved in the national liberation struggle and that the issue, for them, was national liberation. In that introduction, we explain that partition affects women on both sides of the border, that partition affects women's health, childcare, employment, and reproductive rights.

LL: How has the Women's Department evolved from that time until now, in terms of overall leadership in the party? Have there been any particularly difficult moments in its development?

MK: Initially, all that rush of energy in women coming together—lobbying for the department and passing policy—was exciting. In some sense, the department has been seen as an elite group of women who are concentrated in Belfast, Dublin, and, maybe, Derry. In some ways, women from rural areas, and some other Republican women, generally felt that that was what was happening. But they wouldn't have said anything, because the correct thing to do was to have the Women's Department.

While all this great policy was progressive and good, we had to move to get a position on abortion, which became a debate inside Sinn Fein. There was a lot of debate over the right-to-choose motion within the Women's Department; there was as large a variety of opinions on the issue as there were women in the department. There was, however, a right-to-choose motion put forward in 1986 or 1987 by Sinn Fein in Derry. It was passed, but it led to problems for us politically, because we are not a major party—we are not in the mainstream, and we can't advance the issue even if we pass it, because tomorrow we won't be in power. The next day, the media headlines were, "Sinn Fein is not content with murdering people, it's now going to murder babies." We are involved in an electoral strategy, so it caused problems for us. During the next year, there was certainly a move to put our policy where it is right now, which is basically that we agree with abortion under certain circumstances, like ectopic pregnancy, for example. But while that happened, the whole campaign for the right to information on abortion, which is a progressive issue, was going on, and that was the issue that should have been pushed—that was the issue that Republicans should have been involved in and subsequently are. The right-to-information position is the most progressive step one can take on that issue, rather than the actual right-to-choose position. At the end of the next year, there were motions on the right to information on abortion. Because of the paranoia of some people, the most watery motion was passed, and all the others were defeated because of the debate on the right to choose, which was a major setback for us.

Just after that, I got the job of heading the Women's Department, and my job was a healing one. First, I felt that we had to bring everybody together and to build a common view, and that's when I started a series of meetings with Gerry Adams, the president of Sinn Fein. He felt that the Women's Department was pushing the issue of abortion far ahead of our base of support without doing the groundwork, and he felt that we had to do the groundwork before we advanced the issue. That, basically, was my own position, in that I didn't feel that having a right-to-choose platform would ultimately advance the issue, even though I myself believe in the right to choose. Also, some women felt that the Ard Chomhairle, the national executive, was making the decisions and that they wouldn't promote women, wouldn't run them as candidates, or have a policy on childcare. Then we had the meeting with Gerry Adams and other executives and with women in the party. He raised, as did other women, the issue of making sure that the party does the groundwork on controversial issues, like abortion, first; otherwise, we can't advance the issue, and that will affect the group's base of support. We have to be critically acute in terms of our tactics on every issue.

A number of decisions were taken at this meeting. One decision was to discuss issues like abortion within the party, so that we would advance issues internally before we would get to an Ard Fheis, the annual party conference. Another decision was that we would actively—at the grassroots level and at the national level—promote women into leadership positions. We certainly have done that to the full extent at the national level.

Gerry Adams actively campaigns in rural and in urban areas—wherever he goes—to make sure that women are on the platform. He talks about the need to involve women in the struggle, and in Sinn Fein's Belfast office, there have been many events and efforts to recognize women's involvement in the struggle in the last twenty-some years. He was very much the push behind *Women in a War Zone*.[4] He doesn't just pay lip service—he actually learned something from the whole experience. He reads more, and he realizes that he had been guilty, as all men are, of theoretically agreeing to the new roles but not giving serious attention to them. His commitment has a spin-off effect on other people because of his leadership position. This year, for example, we have women involved at the national level in a lot of different areas—general secretary, head of trade union, head of education, director of publicity. We are well represented on the national executive, and we are working on representation at a grass-roots level. It's more difficult at the rural level. Those were the lessons we learned.

Another lesson that has yet to be learned is that the Women's Department is for all women in the party; it is for whatever issues women feel the Women's Department should be active on, whatever issues they think are important. I did a series of meetings around the country to find out what women wanted the department to do, and the major issue that came up was childcare. We have tried to provide every woman who works in a head office with childcare money, and to some degree we have been successful in this. The local offices in Belfast, Derry, and Dublin provide such money for their women employees. The issue now is that every conference organized should have a crèche. In the smaller, local areas, those who want to go to their local Sinn Fein party meeting must face two issues: who provides the childcare, and who pays for it. In families with two political activists, one of whom is a woman, is it she who stays home? Of course, it is, for the most part, and that needs to be changed. That's the point of education. So, we're in a situation now where we have a department that is well in tune with the overall party. We try to make sure that the quotas are filled on the national level, but we don't just pay lip service to having one-quarter of the positions filled by women. We actually get areas to make sure that they nominate women, so that we get a good cross section of women on

4. Published in 1989 by Sinn Fein's An Phoblacht/Republican News Print (AP/RN Print), *Women in a War Zone*, edited by Chrissie McAuley, chronicles the effect the last twenty years of the struggle have had on women's lives in the six counties and documents the important roles that Republican women have taken in resistance to occupation.

the national executive, and so that we get women from all areas. And, of course, the Republican Women's Conference is also developing an agenda to give focus, to push the issues annually and nationally.

LL: What is the Women's Conference?

MK: The Women's Conference is organized by Sinn Fein's Women's Department. It is a public conference, which is open to men and women inside and outside the party. We deal with a variety of issues and topics—women and the European Community, sexual abuse and pornography, and women political prisoners. We also have a bit of drama—theater—as part of a cultural session. 20/20 vision, a working-class theater collective from Derry, has been asked to our conferences. At the last conference, they dealt with a gay relationship through drama, which is a really good way of getting people to deal with the issue of homosexuality, because people are more likely to accept talking about it in that way. They also did a piece that dealt with a family in Derry, whose unwed daughter becomes pregnant. It was really quite brilliant. We've managed to have about 120 women at the conference, which is very good in terms of our department's development. We also give presentations to the most recently released political prisoners from Maghaberry, or other prisons. Jennifer McCann was the last one we made a presentation to. She has agreed to coordinate a women's committee in Belfast. She spent ten and one-half years in jail, and she just got out this last year. She's very enthusiastic.

LL: You write in the foreward to *Women in a War Zone* about how women's contributions have been largely written out of Irish history and that the book is important because "for the first time it is the women involved in the struggle who document their own history. They are volunteers in the IRA, political activists in Sinn Fein, campaigners, fund-raisers, political prisoners, and the relatives of prisoners. They provide the IRA with safe houses, care for volunteers on the run, and confront the British occupation forces on the streets. They are the solid bedrock of the national liberation struggle."[5] Given that women's contributions have often been excluded from history, I wonder if you could discuss some of the women's organizations that preceded the Women's Department, such as the Ladies' Land League, the suffragette movement, and Cumann na mBan. What do you think is the relationship between these early groups and your own work within Sinn

5. McAuley, *Women in a War Zone*, 5.

Fein? What organizational lessons do you think women learned from these early groups?

MK: There have always been active women in the struggle throughout Irish history, and a lot of that work has not been documented, so we don't know about it. Certainly, during the Ladies' Land League, the women were more radical than the men, but they were only allowed to fill the vacuum when the men were in jail. However, the debate between feminism and nationalism was put aside probably at the time when Cumann na mBan, a nationalist women's group, was formed in 1914. For them, it was the primacy of the national question. Cumann na mBan is always portrayed as playing a backup role to the actual volunteers in the 1916 Uprising, but this group was organized around the country and did a lot of the work. These women had an influence after the uprising in terms of becoming politicized as women through their active participation. And then, of course, there were the women who were in the Citizen's Army and who were accepted as equals in the army. That history is all there and culminated in the Proclamation of the Irish Republic. I think that the quote about equal rights for everybody is included not because the men were feeling benevolent and decided to put it there but because of the influence of the women's movement as a political force at the time, as a vision of where Ireland was going.[6] Unfortunately, when the Republicans lost the War of Independence, the leaders of the movement were executed, and the leaders of the women's movement were not really coherent. There was a bit of a gap at that time. A lot was lost, certainly in terms of the development of the movement for those years from 1926 to 1969. What women have learned today from those women's experiences of fighting in the uprising and actively participating at the turn of the century is that women must put their demands on an agenda, and they must put them on the agenda in a strong, coherent manner. There must be a strong women's movement that clearly knows what it wants in terms of national self-determination and can link women's demands to that core issue of self-determination.

We are now making sure that this message becomes part and parcel of Republican ideology through a video program, which is currently one of

6. Written by the leaders of the 1916 Uprising, the "Proclamation of the Irish Republic" states: "The Irish Republic is entitled to, and hereby claims, the allegiance of every Irishman and Irishwoman. The Republic guarantees religious and civil liberty, equal rights and equal opportunities to all its citizens" (quoted in Padraig Pearse, *The Best of Pearse*, ed. Proinsias MacAonghusa and Liam O'Reagain [Cork, Ireland: Mercier, 1967], 188).

the Education Department's top priorities. The video educational program is all about finding and building a common view among Republicans of where we are going. We want to look at strategy and then build the view with the strategy. With the videos, we look at women's history as an integral part of the whole program and not as something tagged on at the bottom or done as a separate video. We completed the first video six months ago. It looks at women's involvement, from 1798 through today, as an integral part of the Republican struggle. The next video we will do is on the ideology of Republicans, and feminism is included as part of that ideology. That will certainly be a first. What we are saying to Republicans is that feminism is part of the ideology. Feminism is not imported from America; it is here and it has always been here. It is part of our Republican history.

LL: In an interview in *Spare Rib*, you discuss how the "mobilization of the new right has put the women's movement on the defensive in the eighties. Although new women's groups have sprung up across the country and in local communities, women have not managed to assemble effective opposition."[7] You go on to say that the women's movement has failed in its inability to address the issue of partition. Could you elaborate on the specific differences between the problems women currently face in the six counties and in the twenty-six counties? For example, how does partition affect women's access to birth control, abortion, and their ability to obtain a divorce?

MK: Well, the British partition of Ireland in the 1920s took on a different face in each state—one as colony in the six counties under the direct influence of the British, the other as neo-colony in the twenty-six counties. British involvement in Ireland and partition have social, economic, political, and military dimensions. Obviously, in the area of occupied Ireland—the six counties—it's the military dimension that is prominent, in that the British are actually on the streets. We have an army of occupation and all that that entails particularly for women, which quite clearly includes harassment, political prisoners, raids on houses, plastic bullets, and a shoot-to-kill policy, among other things. But it's also about the social and economic conditions that stem from living in a colony where large numbers of people are unemployed and living on welfare. There is poverty, basic poverty, poverty and repression. On the other side of the border, in the twenty-six counties, a neo-colony has developed, which is under the indirect influence of the

7. Jo Tully, "Women and National Liberation: Reports from around the World, Ireland," interview with Mairead Keane, *Spare Rib* 204 (August 1990): 49.

British, is reliant on multinationals, and has an economy that is in the interest of big farmers and big business. There is a large percentage of people who are living on low incomes or who are unemployed; there is also an enormous percentage of people living below the poverty line, most of whom are women. In terms of the social and economic realities, it's the same for people on both sides of the border and for women, because women end up bearing the brunt of those kinds of policies. The difference, of course, is that women in the six counties live under the occupation, and they have the added threat of an army on the streets. The state that developed into the twenty-six counties faced the strong influence of the Catholic church, whose influence was enshrined in the 1937 constitution.[8] Control of other institutions, like education, stayed with the church in a way that was repressive for women, and it has been difficult to advance women's issues. On the other side of the border, you have the influence of Protestant fundamentalism and the same kinds of reactions to women's rights and women's issues. Partition stops, or certainly hinders, the development of a secular country. Partition must be on the agenda. It shouldn't be the next issue—it should be the issue that women are addressing now to bring national democracy to the country.

LL: What is the relationship between mainstream feminism and the Republican movement today? What effects have the agendas of feminism and Republicanism had on one another? I'm thinking, also, of the way in which Nell McCafferty has asserted that it has, so far, proved easier to get Republicans to take up feminism than to get feminists to engage seriously in a discussion of Republicanism.

MK: In terms of the influence of feminism on Republicanism, I think that we were actively campaigning on those issues, but also, at the same time, women were campaigning on occupation issues, which were important to women's lives in the six counties. Women in the nationalist struggle were also becoming conscious of factors that were inhibiting them in fulfilling their

8. In addition to legally forbidding divorce, Article 41 of the 1937 Irish Constitution articulates the fundamental importance of the family and of the mother to Irish society: "In particular, the State recognizes that by her life in the home, woman gives to the State a support without which the common good cannot be achieved. The State shall, therefore, endeavor to ensure that mothers shall not be obliged by economic necessity to engage in labor to the neglect of their duties in the home" (quoted in Basil Chubb, *A Source Book of Irish Government* [Dublin: Institute of Public Administration, 1964], 57).

roles, so their consciousness—a feminist consciousness, if you want to call it that—was developed from their actual political activity on the ground. They may have been influenced by the feminist movement and the work that feminists were doing, but they were influenced more by their own experiences. And that's how the Women's Department came into existence. It wasn't because feminists suddenly had influenced the movement. They had raised consciousness—there is no doubt that they had raised consciousness—but, in some ways, people would have been hostile to the way feminists were organizing. And, of course, it wouldn't be just Republican women who would be hostile; it would be working-class women, as well. The women's movement had not organized among working-class women in the twenty-six counties because they hadn't actively put a policy on the agenda for women's issues. Subsequently, that led also to a split in the feminist movement because of an emphasis on consciousness raising instead of on policy. I don't want to underestimate the work they did, because there is quite a lot of work in raising consciousness, but in terms of politicization of Republican women—that came from their own experiences as women. Feminists, who are campaigning for equality within the system, have not actively taken on the issue of partition in any great way, and that is a challenge. Feminists have to ask themselves why things have not changed for the vast majority of women in this country in the last twenty years. What do we need to do? We feel women need to be involved in the building of a strong women's movement that links women's self-determination with national determination.

LL: Since we have been talking about the various ways women get involved in the national struggle, it seems important to discuss how the imprisonment of Republican women has drawn attention to the role of women in the movement. I'd like to ask you about two specific situations: first, the "no wash" protest in Armagh in 1980 and 1981, during which women political prisoners turned their bodies against the prison authority by refusing to wash and by smearing their bodily issues on the walls; and second, the ongoing strip searches of women prisoners. Could you say something about the ways in which both the prison system and the Republican movement have had to come to terms with the presence of women? How has the treatment of women prisoners affected attitudes about women's participation in armed struggle in Northern Ireland?

MK: Well, I think, initially, in 1969 and in the seventies, when women got involved in the armed struggle, they felt accepted as equals in the armed struggle, and this is in all the interviews with women volunteers in the IRA.

So, I don't know exactly if it was a matter of the movement having to come to terms with women participating in the armed struggle. There is a history of women being involved and accepted as comrades in fighting against the Brits. Maybe you're thinking of Mairead Farrell's statement about how when women first started going into prison, the attitude was that women shouldn't be involved in doing this kind of work. But that attitude would have come more from society, because of the traditional attitudes. For example, when Mairead Farrell was shot dead on Gibraltar, people would say, "She was such a nice girl. Why did she ever get involved in all that?" It has more to do with society's image of the role of women and what women "should" do.

LL: Whereas, for Republican communities, it would seem natural for women to "get involved in all that"?

MK: Well, it would be respected and accepted that Mairead Farrell was an IRA volunteer. Women, as well as men, are IRA volunteers, and that is definitely accepted. Also, I think respect for women in the nationalist struggle developed to a greater extent through the Armagh prison protest and the whole fight for political status. That is probably what Mairead Farrell was saying initially about women being on the no wash protest. The attitude of the general public was, "How could these women go through with such a protest?" Later, the public admired and respected these women. The women in Armagh became very politicized themselves about their own oppression as women—in jail and through the education classes, which they organized for themselves. The prison system, I think, has tried to break and take the spirit out of women political prisoners, and the tool they used in Armagh was the strip search, which was designed to degrade, to humiliate, to break their spirit, and to break the resistance of the prisoners. But, you know, strip-searching is used everywhere for this purpose.

LL: It is used extensively in the United States's prison system, for example.

MK: Yes. It's used in a certain psychological way against women in Armagh, Maghaberry, and in British jails, where ten or more screws [prison guards] would be forcing women down, making them put their hair on top of their heads, making them turn around in a certain degrading fashion.[9] And the screws and the prison officials knew that this was affecting women psycho-

9. Over four thousand strip searches of Republican women have been carried out in Armagh, Maghaberry, and British prisons. While on remand in the all-male Brixton Prison in England from 1 July 1985 to 30 September 1986, Ella O'Dwyer and Martina Anderson, Republican prisoners, were each strip-searched four hundred times (see McAuley, *Women in a War Zone*, 75).

logically, even though it never broke their spirit. Prisons still use strip searches, but they don't use them as extensively as before, and that is because of a campaign both inside and outside the jails on the issue. The strip-searching campaign politicized, more than anything, a lot of women about the Republican struggle and about Republican women in the struggle. A lot of women actively got involved in the strip-search campaign in the South. Trade union people, clergy, and religious people also went on delegations to the jails. Maybe, in some ways, for the religious people, it was because "those poor girls are getting strip-searched and have to take their clothes off." But from the women's organizations' points of view, strip-searching was an attempt to degrade and to dehumanize the women prisoners. And that politicized women in the women's movement quite a bit. A lot of women got active in that campaign and subsequently read more and got interested in the Republican struggle because the campaign hierarchized not only the strip-searching question but also the struggle that these women were involved in.

LL: So, these women were being strip-searched not just because they were women but because they acted on their political beliefs, which were threatening to the state. What is the problem like in Maghaberry now?

MK: They still use strip-searching. There was a lot of pressure brought on the British government to do away with strip-searching, but they didn't take it away. They still use it as a method of control and it's still legally sanctioned, so we are trying to highlight the fact that strip-searching is still used. But there are other issues in the jails, too, like censorship and isolation, that need attention.

LL: What are the prison's other ways of dealing with women political prisoners?

MK: Well, there is the whole issue of keeping remand prisoners separate from sentenced prisoners. In Maghaberry, there are about twenty-four women political prisoners. If they are separated, small numbers are kept together. The sentenced prisoners would like to interact with the prisoners on remand. Another reason prisoners are separated is because there is plenty of prison staffing in Maghaberry, and there are fewer women political prisoners. The staff tends to read everything that comes in, and they tend to censor more heavily. In the prison at Long Kesh, in the H blocks, there are more prisoners per guard to deal with. But in Maghaberry, it is sometimes months before prisoners get letters or our newsletter. If we don't get involved, the prisoners might not receive anything, and so they may feel really isolated from the movement.

LL: I want to get back to the issue of the body. The no wash protest and strip-searching appear to be occasions for a rapprochement between women in the Republican movement and feminists. In response to both of these situations, feminists have taken up the issue of "bodily integrity," whereas for Republican women the more central issue would seem to be their political status as women engaged in armed struggle and, therefore, subject to the disciplinary institutions of British occupation.

MK: You are right. These are two times when women outside the Republican movement have become involved in campaigning to highlight what they see as an abuse of the basic human rights of women political prisoners. You could say that, but it also probably has to do with the heightened profile of women in the struggle at the time, in that women on the no wash protest got the attention of the media, as did the issue of strip-searching, so it would be seen as an attack on women's bodies, on women's rights to control their bodies.

LL: This is something that particularly interests me—that is, the issue of the body and its integrity, or wholeness, which feminists take up. I wonder if concern over bodily integrity isn't a way for some feminists *not* to come to terms with the political commitments of these women.

MK: Well, I think there are actually two factors involved here. First, we're actually talking about British and Irish feminists who took up the issues. But in one way, if it actually brings women to support the struggle, then it's good, because people come in to work on plastic bullet abuse, or shoot-to-kill policy, or whatever. They come because of human rights issues, and they get interested in the struggle; through that interest, they get politicized about women as political prisoners. So, in that sense, if their involvement happens, it is great.

LL: By way of human rights?

MK: Yes. In a way, that is okay, because I don't think we can be hard or stubborn with other people—people who come in through human rights issues. Some of the people who get involved on the basis of human rights can be a problem—for example, the ones who make analytical statements claiming, "Well, I am against what is happening to these women prisoners on the basis of human rights, but I don't support the political project they are involved in." These people artificially divide the issue. It is extremely patronizing to think that it is because of the men that women are involved, that our women prisoners are just supporting the men in Long Kesh, when what they are really doing is fighting for their own political status and using whatever weapons they have to use. Women who get involved because women's bodies have been violated, and actually take it up as a human rights issue and a women's issue, are actually advancing the cause of the struggle at the end of the day, because they are raising awareness. Some of those women may get involved just in those issues and then they may leave, like some who got involved in the strip-searching campaign.

LL: For those women whose involvement might come first through human rights, do you think it's a matter of looking at the violation of women's bodies as being related to the violation of the body politic of Ireland through partition?

MK: Yes, that's an interesting way of thinking about it, but I think that is a long jump to make. One can work around the strip-search campaign and actively get involved in stopping strip searches but never make any other advances, never link partition to that issue. To do that, one would have to be seriously open to questioning the women's movement and what progress has, in fact, been made for women. There are a lot of women who are only looking for equality within the system—they don't actually see anything wrong with it for themselves. And if they can get equality within it, they aren't going to be in favor of a radical change at the end of the day.

LL: I want to ask you about the church, but I wanted to come up with a question that wouldn't just go over constructions of the problems in the six counties as being simply sectarian, or religious politics, when, as your other answers indicate, the problems are better understood in terms of a system that has inequitable socioeconomic relationships as part of its foundation. I want to ask you about something that the Marxist critic Stuart Hall said. He asserts that in social formations, "where religion has been the ideological domain, . . . no political movement in that society can become popular without negotiating the religious terrain. You can't create a popular movement in such social formations without getting into the religious question, because it is the arena in which this community has come to a certain consciousness."[10] Would you agree with Hall's assessment on the necessity

10. Stuart Hall, "On Postmodernism and Articulation," interview with Lawrence Grossberg, *Journal of Communications Inquiry* 10, no. 2 (Summer 1986): 54.

for any movement that wants to create a popular base of support to come to terms with or to engage the religious ground on which people have come to understand their lives? How do you see Sinn Fein working to negotiate that religious terrain?

MK: Yes, I think we would first distinguish between the Catholic church, specifically, the hierarchy of the church, and the ordinary believers. I think, in a way, a lot of our supporters, who are both Republican and Catholic, don't accept the hierarchy's view of our struggle because they are actively involved in the struggle. And in the history of our struggle, the church was, at times, on the side of the people and identified with the people. But the British have managed to appease the church in order to get the hierarchy on their side. The hierarchy of the church always acts on self-interest, which is not the common interest of the people. And that, of course, is not the doctrine of the church: "Feed the hungry, help the poor," and all of that. So, I think that when it comes to the history of the church, and the history of the church involved in Irish life, Republicans, and even the general Irish population, are cynical about the hierarchy of the church, but that doesn't mean they don't believe in their religion.

LL: Or aren't affected by it, particularly during the divorce referendum?

MK: Oh, absolutely. People filter what the church says, and they take what they agree with and throw out the rest. Now, in some areas, it is quite clear that the church is entrenched and still manages to influence the culture of the people through the educational system, especially in the areas of sexuality and divorce, where the images of women, men, and relationships are formed according to Catholic doctrine. The church hierarchy has managed to have socialization on these issues as an integral part of education. In areas like Dublin, people tend to be very much in favor of divorce, but in rural areas, the church could play off fears that women were going to be left and that men were going to move in with other women. The church still has footholds in certain areas of the country, less so in the urban areas, more so in the rural areas, obviously. In terms of dealing with the church, we don't, really—we deal with it on our terms. We deal with the justice of our struggle and what we are doing. There have been priests who have become involved, like Des Wilson and Father Raymond Murray, both of whom have actually exposed British injustice in the six counties and, in doing so, have gone against the hierarchy of the church.

Sometimes the clergy is so blatantly pro-British that it is obvious to everyone, not just to Republicans, what their agenda is. Cathal Daly is an example of someone who is constantly working from the pulpit for the British agenda. He is a bishop and Cardinal of All Ireland, and he spends most of his time criticizing the IRA. Daly was recently interviewed on "60 Minutes" regarding the Birmingham Six. In his office, he had a poster with UDA [the pro-British Ulster Defense Association] and IRA in bold letters, with blood dripping down from the letters. This is an example of concentrating on the symptoms of the problem without tackling the real causes of the conflict. It is interesting to me what Stuart Hall says: It is true that where the church has control, you have to get in there not just by working with people but by actually trying to work with the religious people, as well—you have to politicize them about what is going on. Republicans need to do more work in that area—we need to get religious people to take up liberation theology and support those radical nuns and priests. Whether such members of the clergy could influence the hierarchy is hard to say, because the church is also controlled from Rome, but they could make waves. I think we could help make them conscious of doing that kind of work, of finding ways to do that.

LL: One of the most frequent attacks on certain strands of feminism in the United States is the way in which feminism essentializes women's experiences. The place of men in women's movements is often difficult for both men and women to negotiate. I'm interested in those Republican men who include feminism in their course of study in the prisons. In issues of *The Captive Voice*, put out by Republican prisoners, I've noticed that men occasionally contribute pieces on the role of women in the national struggle. Do you think such study has changed the movement as a whole?

MK: Well, I think the fact that we have a Sinn Fein Women's Department would encourage men, particularly political prisoners in jail, who assume a different role within the movement *because* they are in jail. In the case of political prisoners, when they are in jail, they focus educationally on different issues. They have a lot of discussions on feminism and women's oppression, and they actively contribute articles on these issues for our publications. Certainly they approach feminism from a man's point of view, and their discussions circulate through other jails besides Long Kesh. These prisoners want to know about feminism because they are politically minded people in a revolution that involves feminism in parts of that movement. In terms of the influence of feminism on Republican men, I think their awareness and acceptance of this issue parallels the development of the Women's Department—initially, men were obviously feeling threatened. Progress comes through education, by actually taking up the issues in a nonconfrontational forum, by debating in a coeducational way how feminism forwards the equality of men and women, what that means, and how that actually gets translated in people's real lives. Women political prisoners, and the rights given to them, have influenced their male comrades and the movement as a whole. Now, I think there is an acceptance of feminism theoretically, at least with the majority of political activists.

LL: The desire to construct feminism as something "foreign," particularly with regard to Republicanism, is interesting because it seems another way of saying Irish women must be getting this from somewhere else, or they must be doing something that somebody else is telling them to do. They are either parroting men or, in this case, they are following the lead of women outside Ireland. In both cases, women are denied the ability to have and to act on their own political beliefs.

MK: Until people become politicized, men, and also some women, who are threatened by feminism will act in certain ways because they feel threatened. They may feel they have to say all the right things, but they don't really understand what they are saying. We need to get rid of all that, so that people can sit down in comradeship and discuss oppression and what it means in terms of black people and oppressed people in other countries, and what it means for the Irish and the history of British involvement, and what it means as women, and what James Connolly meant when he said "Women are the slaves of slaves." Did you ever read Alice Walker's book *The Third Life of Grange Copeland*? I think it is very good at showing women as an oppressed people within a larger group of oppressed people.

LL: Why don't we go on to talk about some of those connections. What relationships do you see between the border that separates the six counties of the North from the twenty-six counties in the Republic and other geopolitical borders? What kinds of resistance movements get organized around such borders?

MK: Well, that's a good question. I think in terms of our *own* struggle, we would see the border as artificially imposed on us by a foreign oppressor. The occupied territories seem the most similar situation to me. It might be a little different here with the U.S./Mexican border.

LL: Although, for example, Texas, where we are right now, was not always part of the United States.

MK: Yes, right. Living near the border, you have situations where people are separated from their natural hinterlands, families are separated, towns are split up, spy posts are erected to stop people from crossing the border, armies of occupation grow, and armies police the borders. All of these combine to harass people daily, to terrorize people who live in those areas. That is how it happens in Ireland. Now, I suppose that it might be a bit different in the United States, in that you have no army of occupation, but it certainly is the same situation in the West Bank.

In San Diego, where I just visited, I saw these big signs showing a man, a woman, and a child, with the words, "Beware! Stop! Be Careful People Crossing!" There are posts beyond San Diego where people bring illegal immigrants over the border. These immigrants are dropped off, and then they have to try to cross the highway. Many people have been killed there, run over. It is really horrible to look at those big signs showing people running. I think, in terms of the problems that come about because of our border, we would quite clearly have sympathy with any people who are suffering because of occupation, because of interactions that result from borders, like here, in the United States, where people are trapped in cars, or bribed into paying out huge amounts of money to get help crossing the border, or put into detention camps.

LL: I was thinking, too, of the sheer amount of money that goes into establishing that border and protecting it. In the United States, an enormous amount of money goes into fortifying and protecting the border with Mexico. In the West Bank, too, the cost of military personnel is enormous. How much, exactly, does the British government spend on the border between the six and twenty-six counties?

MK: It is estimated that the Dublin government alone spends $1 million a day patrolling the border. The money spent is enormous, and it prevents a lot of economic opportunities on both sides of the border. Beyond that, the border means harassment. The British use borders to spy on people in their big watchtowers with all their expensive electronic equipment. Also, they are an inconvenience to local people, people who might live five miles from a town they'd like to go to but who will have to go fifty miles out of their way to get there because they can't cross everywhere. And where they *can* cross, they must deal with border guards and all of that. This is a particularly hard financial burden on farmers whose fields are right on the border, whose fields might be broken up to build spy posts, which quite clearly is one of the major threats to people living in those areas. In the last year, there has been a major campaign to reopen some of the border roads that the British closed, and these campaigns have been very successful. People from the North have managed to open up some of the roads even under fire by plastic bullets! Now the government has brought in legislation, a typical British solution, that allows them to seize equipment and to arrest and imprison people for actually operating the equipment to open the roads.

LL: So, people have been trying to open the roads themselves—to "retake" the border and to "redefine" it.

MK: Yes. And, as I have said, it has been very successful at opening a few roads, but the Brits have gone back and broken them up. With the legislation to seize equipment, they can basically lift [arrest] you. Again, the law is being used as a tool by the Brits to defeat the border campaign.

LL: Does the government in the twenty-six counties have to share a certain amount of the cost for the border?

MK: Yes. The cost to maintain this border is high. Both North and South share equal amounts, but the British spend millions, as well, because they have to have guards out there with special tactics, and the army of the southern state police it on the southern side. There are British soldiers on both sides of the border. The Brits spend millions on their surveillance technology used at the border and in the six counties. So, in terms of the similarities between the Irish border and the U.S./Mexican border, the most obvious parallels are the financial burden to the public and, particularly, the harassment of the people living near the border. In some ways, though, I think that harassment at the border would be more of a problem for the Mexican people and for the Mexicans now living within the U.S. border than for us. So, while there are similarities, I think they more clearly, more obviously, parallel the Palestinian situation, because both situations involve occupying armies. Now, the border that has been taken down between East and West Germany is also important, and, of course, what we are saying about that is that if there can be such celebration over that border coming down, and, really, over borders coming down throughout Eastern Europe, why not over our border, too? But people don't seem to be making that connection.

LL: What effects, if any, will the EEC have on the border? Part of the EEC's mission is to do away with the problems that geographical and national borders impose. Is there a special exception in the EEC objectives for Northern Ireland in order to maintain that border? There is a move to issue EEC passports, which would seem to make it much more difficult for the British to have control over who is coming in and who is going out of the six counties.

MK: The European Community is interested in the free movement of goods and services across borders, and it is not interested in taking sovereignty away from countries. Margaret Thatcher and her successor have made it quite clear that Northern Ireland is an integral part of the United Kingdom and that nobody has the right to say anything about it. Both the EEC and the British government are interested only in big business and in making bigger profits at the end of the day; they are not interested in advancing the position of any people in any country and certainly not a country on the periphery, like Ireland, which will be a big processing plant for goods. The new EEC won't be bringing down the spy posts or giving people greater economic opportunities in Ireland. Margaret Thatcher has always been interested in the EEC for the building and development of a richer Britain, obviously richer for only a certain class of people. She was never interested in doing anything else. She is quite resistant to anything that would replace British sovereignty with some kind of European rule, as are Mr. Major and the Tory party.

LL: In your talk last night, you mentioned doing work with other solidarity groups and sharing platforms with representatives from the FMLN [the El Salvadoran Farrabundo Marti National Liberation Front] and Native American groups while you've been in the United States. It would be interesting to talk about notions of solidarity and the relationship between tourism and politics. In part, I am interested in this because of my own trip to Belfast. Can you talk about the usefulness of trips, such as the Noraid solidarity tours, in which people come into the country and take information out? How is that different from having people, like you, come here to bring information into the United States?

MK: Well, I think the important thing about being here, in the United States, is that people are asking me what they should do. The first thing they should do is get alternative sources of information about Ireland, information other than what they get from the mainstream media. When they do that, it's possible for them to learn, to go into the occupied area, and to see what British rule in Ireland is like. I don't think anything can substitute for that, and, for that reason, we need people to be personally involved. One needs to be living under occupation to see for oneself what it is like to live in an area with armed forces on the street and all the paraphernalia of an occupation—tanks, guns, fortresses, whitecoats. Informing people about what is happening in Ireland and about what British rule means for Irish people under occupation and encouraging people to visit the country are all part of building support for the Irish struggle.

Sinn Fein is trying to encourage delegations to go to Ireland with different people—with, for example, the Irish People Tour, a group of interested people that goes to Ireland every year. I think it's important for activists, as well as academics, to go, so that they can become informed about the situation in Ireland. If you're involved in education, you are supposed to present a balanced position of knowledge, and if you don't get information directly from Ireland, you have an unbalanced position. To really know about Ireland, you have to go there.

LL: This kind of work argues against the myths people here, in the United States, would have, being subject to certain kinds of media representation.

MK: Absolutely. You've been there; I'd be interested to know the ways you think your attitudes have changed. What did you learn?

LL: The thing that was most startling for me was the degree to which the Republican cause has support in its communities. I don't think I was prepared for how organized or cohesive the communities were, because in the United States, the IRA is usually figured as a random collection of people who really don't have any representative status. Seeing the public murals—murals supporting Sinn Fein and the IRA, as well as murals done in solidarity with the people of other national liberation struggles—in Republican communities throughout Belfast made me understand how important the Republican movement is to the community and how committed the people are to ending both the occupation and partition. I had to confront how powerfully the media had influenced my ideas about the six counties, even though I wanted to believe that my training, as someone who has been taught "to read carefully," would make me less subject to those media representations. But I also think that by coming from the United States, where the military isn't seen very often—there are camps and bases outside of or at the edges of cities, but one doesn't have a chance to see them, or at least not before the Gulf War—the amount of security forces on the streets in Ireland, and the deliberate tension they caused, was quite alarming, though that word doesn't seem quite adequate. The soldiers not only had guns but they were always pointing them at someone—not carrying them at their sides, but *pointing* them.

MK: Yes, I think that sometimes surprises people the most.

LL: You talk about the need for academics—and all kinds of people—to go to Ireland, and you've talked to women's groups, church groups, solidarity groups, college students, and professors. How did these different audiences affect your own presentation of the issues? Is it the same thing, for example, to talk to Irish Catholics in New York and to talk to people in Austin, or elsewhere?

MK: I think that depends on the audience. Obviously, the Irish communities here, and people doing solidarity work here, are more informed—they have been to Ireland and they know what is going on. So, I talk about the latest issues, in terms of Sinn Fein strategy, or the latest human rights abuses, highlighting them and bringing the latest news from Ireland. But, again, there's never an audience who knows everything; there are always those who have just come in. We are constantly educating people about the national struggle. On this trip, I have visited colleges, as well as activists in various struggles, women's groups, and women's centers, so, quite clearly, most of these people don't have any information about Ireland. The information people get here is that Ireland is either leprechauns and shamrocks or the terrorists, so, for us, it's a matter of explaining Ireland's history, why people are engaged in a war situation, what Sinn Fein's position is, and what we do. And, obviously, when we're talking to women, it's a matter of explaining the position of women in Irish society. I have found that most people are overwhelmed by two issues. One is censorship, the legislated restriction on information about the conflict both in the United Kingdom and in the Republic. The other issue that gets a lot of response is human rights abuses, which seems to contradict the perception of Britain as a country founded on civil rights, with common law and freedom of speech. When one talks about censorship, when one talks about human rights abuses—the removal of the right to silence and no-jury courts—people have lots of questions about those issues because they don't have any real information on Ireland.

• • • •

MK: I have enjoyed this trip to the United States very much. The people I have met genuinely want to know about Ireland. Although I get a wide variety of questions about Ireland, oftentimes people want to know Sinn Fein's position on the armed struggle. How informed do you think the people reading this interview will be?

LL: I can't say how much people who read *boundary 2* will know about Ireland, because even though this journal has a highly educated audience, it's always hard to tell what people in the United States know about any given geopolitical conflict. In part, my strategy was to limit those issues to the introduction, because it seems to me that part of the problem of discussing the thirty-two counties is that the discussion always begins and ends with IRA violence. I wanted to find other ways to begin the conversation and to look at different issues. So, it isn't that I want to overlook those questions. But you could certainly say something about them now.

MK: In terms of the relationship between Sinn Fein and the IRA, it's often said that Sinn Fein is the political wing of the IRA, but this is not true. We are part of the same movement and have the same objective—that is, the IRA fighting militarily against the British, and Sinn Fein working politically for the same objective. We believe that the struggle has to be advanced in many forms—social, cultural, political, and military—and we're fighting politically. On the question of peace in Ireland, what I've been saying in this country for the past three weeks is that we are interested in bringing peace to our country; that is what we're all about. We're fighting for peace. We're fighting for freedom, justice, and peace. And we have, in our scenario for peace, a document that actually states how we feel peace can come about in the country.[11] In that document we are saying that the British must disengage from Ireland and that they must do that within the lifetime of the British government. They must release all political hostages unconditionally, and they must disband Loyalist forces. Irish people will call a constitutional conference, in which all political forces on the island will be represented, including women, trade unionists, Loyalists, and Republicans, and they'll look to the Irish people to decide what kind of country they want. It's not for the British to decide. There was a question raised after a meeting in San Francisco, where I was sharing a platform with Native Americans. Somebody asked, "Well, who's going to mediate at this constitutional conference?"

11. *A Scenario for Peace: A Discussion Paper* was written and published by the Ard Chomhairle, Sinn Fein's National Executive, in May 1987 and was reissued in November 1989. The group issued the paper as an attempt "to answer those who claim that there is no alternative to the continuation of British withdrawal." Sinn Fein does not consider the document definitive or exclusive of other alternative proposals.

And a fellow from the Native Americans said, "We will." So, we have an offer. Wouldn't that be great—to have the Native Americans mediate at our constitutional conference? That solves that problem.

That is our scenario for peace. I think many people don't know that we have this document. Also, in the last year, the British have made a couple of interesting statements: they've said that they can't speak to the IRA; and then they've said that they would have to talk to Sinn Fein at some stage, but that Sinn Fein must give up supporting the armed struggle. What *we* are saying is that we are willing to talk to the British unconditionally—we're not asking them to withdraw their armed forces, all thirty thousand of them, more than twenty thousand in the nationalist areas. And people don't know that. In the United States, we are often portrayed as mindless terrorists, while, actually, we are saying that we will sit down and talk with people, and we are actively interested in cultivating peace with the British. We are saying, "Let's talk, let's talk unconditionally."

Index

Contributors

Salwa Bakr was born and raised in Cairo. She is the author of four collections of short stories: *Zinat in the President's Funeral* (1986), *The Shrine of 'Atiyyah* (1987), *The Gradually Eroded Soul* (1989), and *The Peasant's Dough* (1992). She is the author of a novel *The Golden Chariot Won't Ascend to the Heavens* (1991) and is completing a forthcoming novel entitled *The Description of the Bulbul* (1993).

Claire Detels is associate professor of music at the University of Arkansas, Fayetteville. Her research areas are musical aesthetics and nineteenth-century opera. Her publications include articles on Verdi and Puccini operas in *International Dictionary of Opera* (St. James Press, forthcoming) and "Puccini's Descent to the Goddess: Feminine Archetypal Motifs from Manon Lescaut to *Turandot*," in *Yearbook of Interdisciplinary Studies in the Fine Arts*.

Margaret Ferguson is professor of English and comparative literature at the University of Colorado, Boulder. She is currently finishing a book entitled *Partial Access: Female Literacy and Literary Production in Early Modern England and France* (Routledge, forthcoming). She is the author of *Trials of Desire: Renaissance Defenses of Poetry* (1983) and coeditor of *Rewriting the Renaissance* (1986) and *Re-membering Milton* (1987).

Carla Freccero is associate professor in the Literature Board and Women's Studies Program at the University of California, Santa Cruz. Her related work includes "Notes of a Post Sex-Wars Theorizer," in *Conflicts in Feminism*, edited by Marianne Hirsch and Evelyn Fox Keller (1990). She is also the author of *Father Figures: Genealogy and Narrative Structure in Rabelais* (1991).

Marjorie Garber is professor of English and director of the Center for Literary and Cultural Studies at Harvard University. She is the author of two books on Shakespeare and, most recently, *Vested Interests: Cross-Dressing and Cultural Anxiety*, a literary and cultural study of transvestism.

Barbara Harlow is associate professor of English at the University of Texas, Austin. In addition to articles on Third World literature and critical theory, she is the author of *Resistance Literature* (1987), a study of the literature produced in the context of organized resistance movements. *Barred: Women, Writing and Political Detention*, an analysis of women political prisoners and the role played by writing in new forms of political and cultural organization in and outside prison over the last three decades, is forthcoming.

Laura E. Lyons is a graduate student in English at the University of Texas, Austin. She is writing a dissertation on issues of representation in the literature and cultural politics of Irish nationalism.

Anne McClintock is assistant professor of gender and cultural studies at Columbia University and is the author of *Maids, Maps, and Mines: Gender and Empire in Victorian Britain and South Africa* (forthcoming). She has written monographs on Simone de Beauvoir and Olive Schreiner and is currently writing a book entitled *Power to Come: Women and the Sex Industry*. She is editing a book collection on sexwork and technosex entitled *Screwing the System* and is coediting, with Ella Shohat, two book collections, one on sexuality and imperialism, the other on Third World culture.

Toril Moi is professor of literature and romance studies at Duke University. She is the author of *Sexual/Textual Politics* (1985) and the editor of *The Kristeva Reader* (1986) and *French Feminist Thought* (1987). Her most recent book is *Simone de Beauvoir: The Making of an Intellectual Woman* (Basil Blackwell, 1993).

Linda Nicholson is professor of educational administration and policy studies, women's studies, and political science at the State University of New York, Albany. She is the author of *Gender and History: The Limits of Social Theory in the Age of the Family* (1986) and the editor of *Feminism/Postmodernism* (1990). She edits the book series Thinking Gender for Routledge. At present, she is at work on a book currently entitled *The Genealogy of Gender*.

Mary Poovey is professor of English at Johns Hopkins University. Her most recent book is *Uneven Development: The Ideological Work of Gender in Mid-Victorian England* (1988). She is currently working on a book-length study of statistical thinking between 1654 and 1850.

Andrew Ross is director of the American Studies Program at New York University. He is the author of *Strange Weather: Culture, Science and Technology in the Age of Limits* (1991) and *No Respect: Intellectuals and Popular Culture* (1989) and the editor of *Universal Abandon* and *Technoculture*.

David Simpson is professor of English at the University of Colorado at Boulder. His most recent books are *Romanticism, Nationalism, and the Revolt against Theory* (1993); (ed.) *Subject to History: Ideology, Class, Gender* (1991); and *Wordsworth's Historical Imagination* (1987).

Kathryn Bond Stockton is assistant professor of English at the University of Utah, Salt Lake City. Her research interests include contemporary theories, Victorian fiction, and African American literature. Her book on spiritual materialism and desire between women is forthcoming from Stanford University Press.

Jennifer Wicke is associate professor of comparative literature at New York University. She is the author of *Advertising Fictions: Literature, Advertisement, and Social Reading* (1988) and writes on film, Freud, postmodernity, and modern literature and culture. Her book on the politics of feminist theory is forthcoming from Basil Blackwell; her current project is a study of consumption and gender.

A000016264878